Can't I Love
What I Criticize?

Can't I Love What I Criticize?

The Masculine and Morrison

SUSAN NEAL MAYBERRY

The University of Georgia Press Athens and London

Publication of this book was made possible in part by a gift from Alfred University.

Paperback edition, 2026

Set in Sabon by BookComp, Inc.

EU Authorized Representative Easy Access System Europe—Mustamäe tee 50, 10621 Tallinn, Estonia,gpsr.requests@easproject.com

Printed digitally

The Library of Congress cataloged the hardcover edition of this book as follows:
Mayberry, Susan Neal, 1951–
Can't I love what I criticize? : the masculine and Morrison / Susan Neal Mayberry.
p. cm.
Includes bibliographical references and index.
ISBN-13: 978-0-8203-2945-1 (hardcover)
ISBN-10: 0-8203-2945-2 (hardcover)
1. Morrison, Toni—Criticism and interpretation.
2. African American men in literature.
3. Masculinity in literature. I. Title.
PS3563.O8749Z76 2007
813'.54—dc22 2007015076

Paperback ISBN-13: 978-0-8203-8130-5

To the two who gave me life

and the three who made me free

Contents

Acknowledgments

Writing represents a journey in liberating, companionably solitary confinement. Nobody, however, can do the time alone. Writing is, as Toni Morrison describes it, a "craft that appears solitary but needs another for its completion." My four-year stint in solitary was eased considerably by the finishing touches of a number of astonishingly considerate others: Nancy Furlong and Gail Walker provided psychological guidance; Karen Porter sociological assistance; Laurie DeMott theological aid. Phyllis Gorfain, Candis LaPrade, and my colleagues in the English department at Alfred University, especially Ben Howard and Melissa Ryan, as well as the consummate professionals at the University of Georgia Press, notably Nancy Grayson, Courtney Denney, Daniel Simon, and Erin New, offered sound editorial and design advice; two anonymous readers invaluable research suggestions; Nancy Mayberry and Herbert Mayberry gracious family counseling. Undergirded by such fellowship, writing evolved for me into an adventure as well as a trip, an experience of self—segueing into other discoveries. Adopting an androgynous approach, allowing Morrison's men to lead, sent me to places where I was as free to love as to criticize. I took frequent refreshment along the way from the enthusiasm and honesty of students in my Morrison seminars, especially Kristin Bowers, Jaime Lacerte, and Jason Campbell. I owe much to the unflagging service of the staff at Herrick Memorial Library; to generous financial support from Alfred University administrators; and to university trustee Marlin Miller for the release time associated with the Fred H. Gertz Endowed Chair in English. I simply enjoyed Jake, Son of Solomon, who, despite his fierce desire to fly on off, sat loyally by my side in his un-endowed and under-stuffed chair.

I continue to appreciate the spirit of Toni Morrison, friend of my midlife (and midwife) mind, and the advocacy of the Toni Morrison Society, particularly its founder, Carolyn Denard, and president, Yvonne Atkinson. I marvel at the unfailing generosity of my children, Neal McDowell and Caroline McDowell, who tolerated my absent-minded presence even when they thought I had misplaced my sanity. Most of all, I thank my husband, Tom McDowell, who encouraged and believed in me because he wanted to. I like to consider this book my token of affection to all of you, my dedication echoing Morrison's own epigraph to *The Bluest Eye*. However, I am well aware that the real gift comes from those who shared with me the closed yet wide-open space which allowed me room to move.

Can't I Love What I Criticize?

CHAPTER 1

Something Other Than a Family Quarrel

Morrison's Review of the Masculine

Toni Morrison's delight in flouting traditional as well as fashionable bottoms and tops finds her denounced by some politically stylish scholars for not carrying their latest lines. In a 1971 article, which posits "What the Black Woman Thinks about Women's Lib," she has already begun to close down this kind of criticism with her usual comically blunt opener: "Well, she's suspicious of what she calls 'Ladies' Lib.' It's not just the question of color, but of the color of experience" (15). The essay explains that attempting to find consensus among African American women on any subject is a doomed prospect because they have consistently, and deliberately, defied classification. However, it also surmises that critiques of masculinity and support for feminist issues, viewed by many black women and men alike as a predominantly white "family quarrel," remain even more elusive because relationships between black men and black women have been historically different from the majority of their white counterparts. Accused of designing female victims, castrating women, and messed-up men, Morrison retorts that black women have borne their crosses "extremely well" and "everybody knows, deep down, that black men were emasculated by white men, period. And that black women didn't take any part in that" (Stepto 384). Thus, Morrison's review of masculinity suggests that not only have black men successfully retained their special vitality in spite of white male resistance; their connections to black women have saved their lives.

Because Morrison's mantra intones Other as integral to Self identity, her vision of masculinity must be conjoined with her idea of the feminine. Her form of feminism aligns her with a tradition that refuses to exclude the masculine. Like Zora Neale Hurston, Morrison evaluates the position of the black woman in America as having been, since her beginning, "de mule uh de world," a scapegoat for suppressed black male frustration and rage but nonetheless a stubborn workhorse liable to kick or bite upon provocation and seeming not to have become the "true slave" that white women discern in their history (14). Forced out of her "profound desolation" to invent herself, this woman has combined being a responsible person with being female. As such she has come to feel morally superior to white women, and to their men, and free to confront her world, including her man, on her terms ("What the Black Woman Thinks" 63). Morrison's is the "womanist" insight that relationships between African American men and African American women must be understood not only in terms of the intersections of gender and race but also with respect to their participation in a larger, historically racist culture.[1] In "The Race for Theory," Barbara Christian extends this skepticism to include literary critics who rely on current theoretical "isms" to read texts written by black women because such theories have been constructed in almost every case without any reference to these texts. In "Rootedness: The Ancestor as Foundation," Morrison confesses her disappointment with the vocabulary used to describe her work because she dislikes finding her books praised or condemned when the conclusions are "based on criteria from other paradigms" (342).

Nellie McKay distinguishes between black and white feminist literary traditions by the presence or absence of their creative ancestors. She observes that most white women writers claim to have invented the authority for their voices in an effort to break the silence of what Virginia Woolf called "Shakespeare's sisters." Contemporary black women writers, however, look to the examples of their grandmothers, mothers, aunts, and sisters to continue a powerful artistic heritage that is not white and not male (McKay 399). Sapphires and Geraldines instead of Philomelas and Lavinias, African American women have traditionally participated in the community "signifyin(g)." Describing the women in her own family as the "culture-bearers," Morrison, like Hurston, remembers the storytelling as a shared activity between men and women. Recollecting no imbalance or struggle for dominance within her community's gender relationships, she uses the word *comrade* to describe the marriages that she knew. While many of her foremothers could not read, they were articulate, and their talents were on display for their immediate family and extended community members along with white society (McKay 398–

99). Henry Louis Gates Jr. traces this androgynous nature of African American discourse and hermeneutics back to the Yoruba trickster figure of Esu, depicted as paired male and female statues or as one bisexual figure, which supports Morrison's claim that hers is a discursive tradition that escaped the trap of gender bias inherent in Western communication (Gates 29–30).

Morrison's approach to gender and race echoes that of bell hooks, who asserts that black women have sidestepped the feminist movement because they do not perceive in feminist theory and practice, especially in the material made available to the public, potential solutions. The Sisters, according to hooks, reject women's liberation as expressed by middle-class white women because it ignores the fact that not all men benefit equally from sexism. Many bourgeois white women, especially radical feminists envious of and angry at privileged white men for denying them an equal share in class advantage, imply that the empowerment of women must occur at the expense of men. In addition, by equating women's liberation with the female acquisition of equality to males, liberal feminists create a situation in which they, "not men," reduce the feminist movement to "women's work." Arguing that antimale sentiments have alienated numerous poor (especially nonwhite) women from the feminist movement because they believe that they have more in common with men of their race and class than with bourgeois white women, hooks, like Morrison, identifies black men as "comrades" with black women in common struggle ("Men: Comrades in Struggle" 527). Objecting to Clyde Franklin's accusation that black women "stood silently by" during the so-called Second Reconstruction of the 1960s and 1970s ("Black Male–Black Female Conflict" 363), hooks claims that black women have "shared equal responsibility in all struggles to resist racist oppression" and that before this particular liberation effort, black men recognized their contributions ("Men: Comrades in Struggle" 528). She maintains that "the reconstruction and transformation of . . . masculinity is a necessary and essential part of feminist revolution" and that, despite patriarchy and sexism, there is "potential among Black men for radical transformation with respect to their gender attitudes and behavior" (*Talking Back* 18). Frances White adds that many black nationalists, male and female, "remain openly hostile to any feminist agenda" (506). She also believes, however, that it becomes possible to articulate a feminist black nationalist ideal on the basis of the feminist revisions of the Afrocentric historical master narrative in which writers like Morrison are engaged (511). All agree that there is a "special tie binding people together who struggle collectively for liberation" (hooks, "Men: Comrades in Struggle" 528). Having known this experience of shared conflict, the tie of resistance that binds, black women who acknowledge the reality of sexism nonetheless refuse to respond to black men in kind.

Morrison's assessment of African American masculinity warrants comparison to that of another black woman writer frequently addressed as feminist. Alice Walker also challenges the definitions of gender as they are formulated by most white American feminists. Walker insists that white feminists as well as some black people define the issues in terms of blacks on the one hand and [white] women on the other and, in so doing, deny the black woman her womanhood. While she concedes that many black women hesitate to confront the reality of sexism because they feel they must protect black men, she also argues that critics of both races and genders miss the obvious fact that people of color come in both sexes.[2] In refusing to elevate gender above race or race above gender, neither Walker nor Morrison aligns herself with "prevailing white feminist groups" or with "blacks who refuse to acknowledge male dominance in the world." Because their work "does not yield to easy generalizations and nicely packaged clichés," both writers continue to "resist the trends of the times without discarding the truths upon which they are based" (Christian 91–92).

Morrison's treatment of her male characters becomes a key to her success in countering the temptations of exclusionary feminism. *Song of Solomon* can be singled out as showcasing black men. Its writer says of the book: "Men are more prominent. They interested me in a way I hadn't thought about before, almost as a species" (Watkins 50). Because of the dual-gendered emphasis of her personal and artistic background, however, and because her writing has become increasingly preoccupied with the "relationships of black men and black women and the axes on which those relationships frequently turn," all of Morrison's books explore masculinity and masculine types. They also examine ways in which the stereotypes underlie men's individuation and affect how men and women "complement each other, fulfill one another or hurt one another and are made whole or prevented from wholeness by things that they have incorporated into their psyche" (Davis 419). Identifying metaphors of the masculine in *Song of Solomon* as dominion or flight, Stephanie Demetrakopoulos maintains that Morrison's male figures exist in vacuums, are pathologically out of balance, ungrounded in nature or the feminine, and isolated from or rejected by white male culture. Assessing the values of these men as influenced by African American culture (but not characteristic of that culture only), "most men in the world have never really known a woman," Demetrakopoulos concludes (85–86).

Studies in masculinity and manhood dispel these myths as they support Morrison's as a more even-handed approach to gender. Recasting sociological confirmation that black masculinity may be more connected to women than its white counterpart, her folk wisdom claims, "won't no woman ever kill [the black man]. What's likelier is that it'll be a woman save his life" (*Song of Solomon* 140). Michael Kimmel describes the 1990s as the decade that will be remembered for eyeing men almost as a species, for offering America a "crash course on male sexuality" (540). Critics of masculinity studies argue that reading canonical literature amounts to reviewing men and that, since all men perpetuate sexism in one form or another, separate classes in men's studies merely endorses hegemony. Kimmel and Michael Messner, however, insist that the traditional approach "routinely deal[s] with men only in their public roles. . . . Rarely, if ever, are men understood through the prism of gender" (ix). In other words, supposedly "ungendered" academic courses do not deal with men qua men. These social scientists maintain that masculinity is a learned behavior, credit the pioneering work of feminist scholars with making us aware of the centrality of gender in our lives, and stress that men as well as women must understand and assume responsibility for eliminating sexism.

Clyde Franklin concurs but, inverting Sojourner Truth's 1852 plea, demands "Ain't I a Man?" His pioneering scholarship on African American masculinity, along with that of such scholars as Manning Marable and Robert Staples, questions which man is being studied and searches for the history behind and facts beyond black male stereotypes. It suggests that social science literature has been guilty of perpetuating negative stereotypes about African American men as a result of applying white American norms to black American behavior. Staples proposes that the marginality of black men more than cancels out their status as males in American society. Describing the history of black masculinity in America as being reduced to property, submissive, nonprotective, powerless, yet representative of "stud supreme," Franklin states that in early America, "Black males were not human, and thus it was impossible for them to be masculine." He adds that among "all the aforementioned sex-role dimensions, perhaps none was more important to the Black male than society's refusal to extend him 'manhood.'" Acquiring the masculinity peculiar to black men involves a "difficult and tedious social construction" anyway because of the "numerous adaptations that must be made in a racist society." In a very real sense, the ambiguity surrounding this particular sex role today may partly result from "the legacy of a nondefinition of the Black male slave sex role, and continued reluctance to perceive the Black male as a man—at least in the hegemonic sense of the word." Despite the numerous black masculinities perceived as falling outside a culturally prescribed norm endorsed by "white males who have vested interests in supporting the hegemonic model," "thousands of Black males keep trying to be men" (273–77).

Examinations of African American masculinity reveal that adult black males have, under threats of violence and often via liaisons with white women, been reluctantly acknowledged as men in America for a mere half-century. In addition, the stereotypes shrouding black sexuality indicate that these men have been concomitantly viewed as aberrant and only partially capable of assuming the masculine role. Robert Brannon identifies the four traditional rules of American manhood as Avoid Sissy Stuff, Be a Big Wheel, Be a Sturdy Oak, and Give 'em Hell. Breaking the general categories into more specific characteristics (provider, protector, pillar of strength; independent, active, achievement- and risk-oriented; dominant in interpersonal relationships, level-headed and self-contained, emotionally restrained), Joseph Pleck concludes that traditional expectations of what it means to be a man within Western culture are problematic, historically specific and unattainable, and generally lead to self-depreciation. Earlier studies on maleness assume that white, heterosexual, middle-aged, and middle-class masculinity defines the sole sex role into which men struggle to fit. Other forms—like working-class men, men of color, gay men, younger and older men—deviate in significant ways from the normative. Such conventional definitions, however, replicate precisely the power relations that subordinate the men.

Current research, and Morrison's fiction, focuses on variations in masculinity. Challenges like Franklin's to the hegemonic definition refute the idea that a singular masculinity exists. Instead, scholars have come to understand that the "hegemonic model corresponds to the actual character of a small number of men" and that different men construct different versions of masculinity, each of which must be individually examined. America's awkward treatment of such black men as Booker T. Washington and W. E. B. Du Bois, who depart significantly but in an acceptable manner from social expectations, reaffirms the inadequacy of using traditional models to study black men. Moreover, an analysis of black men who challenge the institutional power structure through traditionally male means of violence and sexism has led to the establishment of androgynous, homosexual, bisexual, and traditionally heterosexual black masculinities. These constructions developed simultaneously with social conditions producing certain characteristics of African American males in the 1980s, crises which have become even more acute over the last twenty years: disproportionately high rates of young male suicide and black-on-black homicide, high incidence of drug-related disease along with heart attacks and prostate cancer, decreased life expectancy, reductions in employment rates and real earnings, and a preponderance in numbers of arrests and the prison population ("Ain't I a Man?" 276–79).

Such conflicts cause many African American males to experience anomie, a rootlessness that arises when individuals internalize socially inculcated needs and desires but face structural impediments to realizing them. Franklin maintains that black men experience more anomic situations than others in American culture. As a result, individuals or groups of black men adapt to the perceived futility of joining mainstream society by manifesting specific masculinities. These include a black masculinity that conforms to mainstream society's proscriptions for heterosexual males; a ritualistic black masculinity, which appears to conform but merely goes through the motions; an innovative black masculinity, the most publicized, feared, and reviled form, which becomes either socially distasteful or glorifies heinous means of achieving material success; and an alarming number of what might be described as an increasingly retreatist black masculinity, men who simply withdraw from the system. Despite the downside, Franklin applauds the efficacy of black masculinities as providing a means of constructing new goals for all men in American culture ("Ain't I a Man?" 280–82).

Admonishing against the use of "sterile statistics" alone to illuminate or empower black men, African American sociologists and psychologists affirm the need for a black men's studies program that would evaluate the status of black men in their everyday contexts ("Ain't I a Man?" 282–83). Richard Majors, in particular, argues the need for comprehensive, long-term policies, which "focus on social, economic, and political forces that shape the lives of Black males" and which are "designed to address causes rather than symptoms" of what has become the behavior of an entire generation of endangered black youth (*American Black Male* 315). Questioning whether these youth are victims or victimizers, Jewelle Taylor Gibbs agrees with Majors and examines their anger. She asserts that in response to discrimination and exclusion from mainstream channels of achievement, personal development, and social mobility, young black males find themselves "increasingly socially isolated in inner-city ghetto neighborhoods, confined to low-skilled, dead-end jobs, subject to constant harassment by police and prosecutors, and manipulated by the mass media and unprincipled politicians to exploit the deeply entrenched cultural paranoia over the myth of their sexuality and aggression." In short, they have been "forced into the defensive position of unwilling victims, caught between a rock and a hard place," and have responded predictably to such victimization with frustration and rage. Without "effective preventive strategies to rescue young Black males from this escalating cycle of self-destruction and violence," Gibbs concludes, America will "lose another generation of Black youth" (142–43).

Some cautionary voices include in their means of prevention Morrison's conviction that "we need to love ourselves." Although she declares in *Song of Solomon* and reiterates in a Bill Moyers interview that her people are being "devoured," Morrison likewise maintains in *Beloved* and in that same interview that their slave ancestors have already sacrificed themselves so that contemporary black males are "Stamp Paid" and free to love. Her work represents as much a tribute to the marvelous coping strategies of black men as a lament for their bouts of self-destruction. Richard Majors and Elijah Anderson support Morrison's perspective with their studies of what they call the "cool pose" and "code of the street." While these modern manifestations of alienation have certain profoundly negative outcomes, both also reveal the remarkable resilience of the African American community. The phenomenon of cool dates back in Africa to at least 2000–3000 B.C., expressed in oral culture, character building, art, linguistics, dance, initiation and mating rituals, warrior cults, and the concept of health. Quite different from the cool of their forebears, the contemporary cool pose provides black boys, denied the means to enact traditional roles of masculinity, with creative ways of managing a public persona. The code of the street reflects an institutionalized oppositional culture, which emerges "where the influence of the police ends and personal responsibility for one's safety is felt to begin, resulting in a kind of 'people's law,' " based on " 'eye for an eye' 'street justice' " (Anderson 10). Until America reestablishes a viable mainstream economy in the (neighbor)hood that nullifies the vicious inner-city cycle (anomie, which fuels violence that confirms stereotypes that legitimize an anomic cool pose and code of the street), the traditions of the Black Grandmother and the Decent Daddy remain to hold the community together. But held they have.

The cool pose provides black males with a method of symbolically demonstrating masculinity and visibility, a gambit calculated to disarm the other guy. However, cool pose "can directly or indirectly contribute to disproportionate rates of marital and female abuse, crime, alcohol and drug abuse, and violence" (Majors, *American Black Male* 258). A frontier ethic enables the code of the street to provide a practical strategy for survival in public neighborhood spaces where even abstract justice does not exist. However, the code tolerates a drug trade and common street criminals so that decent people find it "increasingly difficult to maintain a sense of community" (Anderson 325). Vera Paster submits that the "most disastrous of social indicators are disproportionately associated with the lives of African-American males. Yet even the highest casualty figures indicate that most Black men not only survive the gauntlet but also cope adequately in the world" (216). Maintaining that black males have become "the scapegoats of this society," Paster remains astonished at their ability to "withstand even severe distress if there are sufficient strengthening resources." Although these men are often physically and psychically wounded during every passage of their lives, they still stand with "minds healthy and . . . souls intact" (229).

Despite the dearth of studies about fathers in African American families, the myths implying their nonsupport, and the domination of black mothers in mainstream literature, the black father, in fact, embodies one of these strengthening resources. John and Julia McAdoo aid Stephanie Coontz in releasing America's families from the elegiac trap of nostalgia. The McAdoos outline traits crucial to any definition of African American family stability and conclude that the debate about these relationships "seems to be around the wrong issues. It should not focus on whether we will survive—we will—but rather on what can be done . . . to thrive" (295). They call for "less emphasis" placed on evaluating black fathers from a middle-class Eurocentric perspective and more on developing a multicultural perspective. Joining Coontz in stressing the resilience of African American families as they dispel the myth of the black family collapse, these researchers point out that during slavery and throughout the postenslavement experience, black fathers "have found ways to mitigate the negative consequences of occupational and educational discrimination on the positive roles they play within their family and community" (295–96). Coontz warns that in the face of an increasingly downwardly mobile society, "white working-class Americans may have to seek those sources in the next decade" (254).

Michael Hanchard goes further to debunk the so-called crisis of the black male. Agreeing with Coontz that the way we were never was, he suggests that relations between black men and women and their children are "rarely considered against the backdrop of rising divorce rates, family dysfunction, and cultural conservatism in the nation as a whole" (467). Viewed in isolation, the black family becomes simply another receptacle for dominant values that have not worked for the dominant group in the first place. Debates concerning black males are less about them than about racial discrimination inside and outside the black community. Hanchard argues that the failings of particular black men should not condemn black men in general and that, accustomed to crisis, the African American community has reacted predictably with creative though nontraditional responses to fatherhood (469–72). Franklin adds that the many studies about conflicts between contemporary black men and women overemphasize blame; researchers have censured white culture, black men, and black women in turn. Asserting that the conflicts are "individually caused and culturally nurtured," Franklin, like Morrison, advocates greater stress on empathy and androgyny (359). Marable reiterates that the "strongest ally Black men have in their battle to achieve Black freedom is the Black woman. Together, without illusions and false accusations, without racist and sexist stereotypes, they can accomplish far more than they can ever accomplish alone" (23). Applying theories honed in her study of black women's traditions to the examination of black manhood as representative of racial crisis, Hazel Carby's *Race Men* (1998) provides an example of such solidarity in action.

Contemporary efforts to understand African American masculinity, which have redoubled during the past decade, arise primarily from literary-critical and cultural studies perspectives. Mark Anthony Neal uses the term *New Black Man* to represent his intention "to create new tropes of black masculinity that challenge the most negative stereotypes associated with black masculinity, but more importantly, counter stringently sanitized images of black masculinity, largely created by blacks themselves in response to racist depictions of black men" (xx–xxi). This mode of manhood looks to the twin traditions of racial and gender equality, manifest in African American folklore and the writings of male ancestors like Frederick Douglass and W. E. B. Du Bois, as examples of resistance that "embodies the potentiality of a liberated and liberating Black masculinity." Taking his cue from the progressive politics of the black feminist movement, the New Black Man, or what Rudolph Byrd calls in *Traps* (2001) the "tradition of John [the Conqueror]," creates "radical strategies and emancipative models" to avoid the specific traps of sexism, homophobia, patriarchy, hegemony, and "other species of slavery" (Byrd and Guy-Sheftall 22).

The most extensive recent studies on black manhood as a culturally contested arena include Marlon Ross's *Manning the Race* (2004) and Maurice Wallace's *Constructing the Black Masculine* (2002). Joining such gender-progressive, antihomophobic texts as Phillip Brian Harper's *Are We Not Men?* (1996), Keith Boykin's *One More River to Cross: Black and Gay in America* (1996), and Michael Awkward's *Negotiating Difference* (1995) in making the case for distinguishing black manhood from the larger field of masculinity studies, *Manning the Race* explores how "men of African descent were marketed, embodied, socialized, and imaged for the purposes of political, professional, and cultural advancement during the early decades of the twentieth century." Ross explains how the entrenched system of Jim Crow "conspired to unman, and thus discredit, black men as influential leaders" and probes via the Jim Crow paradox the "changing meaning and enactments of race, gender, nation, and sexuality in modern America." As it insists on black men's "deficiency as men," Jim Crow "necessarily also demands that they adhere and aspire to the social codes established for the conduct of men" (1–2). Adding, like Wallace, historical edification to the cultural critique of African American manhood as a long, layered process of transformation, Ross resists categorizing black manhood either in reaction to or imitation of the hegemony of white masculinity. While the extremes contribute to the history of black masculinity, neither "satisfactorily adjudicates the complex maneuverings entailed in the ever-changing project of black manhood reform." Ross determines that not only has African American manhood been shaped by hegemony; it has, as a dialectical process, "disrupted the dominant discourse on race and masculinity" (7–8).

Wallace, who traces the construction of African American masculinity from 1775 to 1995 through visual and literary contexts, explores how America's "preoccupations with gender and sexuality infect not only the writerly record but the larger issue of the social ideal of black masculinity" (xi). He agrees with Arthur Saint-Aubin that, as late as 1994, African American men were either ignored or viewed as "a mere variance of European American, middle-class, heterosexual men" (Saint-Aubin 1056) and finds the body of scholarship on black masculinity ironically modest when compared with the West's high profile on the black male body as a "walking palimpsest of the fears and fascinations possessing our cultural imagination" (Wallace 2). Noting that 1994 witnessed a second wave in masculinity studies, following a first-wave post–men's movement deconstructionism inspired by continental poststructuralists, Wallace attempts to "elaborate a scheme of generative modes by which African American men have historically survived the self-alienating disjunction of race and manhood in American culture" (5). He identifies modern American manhood as "an affair between men," an "endless rivalry for the power and privileges of patriarchy animated by the psychic discomfiture of men's mutual fears and desires for one another," including "certain racial preoccupations." He argues that the New World American male invented himself not only by the repudiation of the female but by the "homosocial counterconstruction of black male savagery." Confirming that at no point in the history of the New World has "race not constituted a defining feature of our national manhood," *Constructing the Black Masculine* reveals how racial difference "exacerbates an already contentious homosocial rivalry over patriarchal prerogatives" (1–2). It concludes that we may not only have to "abandon all references to a singular black masculine identity for an increasingly nuanced plurality," but we may have to "face up to the problem that even the most plural conception of masculine formations . . . risks reconstitution into smaller, subtler regimes of heteronormativity and patriarchal prerogatives in black contexts" (15).

Marcellus Blount, George Cunningham, and Jeffrey Leak blend critical theory and literary analysis into the cultural studies perspective on black men. Blount and Cunningham maintain that, while African American men "rarely if ever provide a strategic site for interrogating constructions of gender and sexuality within contemporary theory," the opposite also holds true. Critical theory rarely informs social science and public policy debates that illuminate black manhood. As a result, representations of African American males have frequently become reduced to conservative cultural agendas. Characterized by a tone of "antagonistic cooperation," the essays contained in *Representing Black Men* (1996) occur in dialogue with feminism and queer theory to analyze images of black male agency, which originate in literature and cultural studies (x–xi).

Jeffrey Leak focuses on more specifically literary contexts. His 2005 book, *Racial Myths and Masculinity in African American Literature*, recognizes long-standing legends associated with black men as it establishes a call-and-response relationship between generations of canonical and noncanonical writers. Specifically, it compares ways in which nineteenth- and twentieth-century African American novelists explore black masculinity via myths of inferiority, sexual prowess, criminality, cultural depravity, and homosexual emasculation. Indebted to Robert Stepto and Northrop Frye for his theory of "pregeneric myths," Leak asserts that the tradition of African American literature remains bound historically and linguistically to a legendary quest for freedom and literacy. Including a chapter on Morrison's *Song of Solomon*, Leak calls for a systematic examination of masculinity in the fiction of African American women writers, citing Morrison's body of work as especially noteworthy. Although I began this project three years before Leak publicly acknowledged that Morrison "provides us with complex and compassionate constructions of black masculinity in tandem with her powerful and complicated explorations of black femininity" (136), I am delighted to find my ideas welcomed by the kind of critic Guy-Sheftall identifies as a "Black male feminist" (347).

If black women will not be classified, then black men refuse to be pigeonholed. Relationships between them continue imperfect: Guy-Sheftall stands by her description of Robert Staples's response in the *Black Scholar* (1979) to representations of black men in Ntozake Shange's *For Colored Girls Who Have Considered Suicide When the Rainbow Is Enuf* (1974) and to charges of black male sexism in Michelle Wallace's *Black Macho and the Myth of the Superwoman* (1978) as "hateful" (346). Neal admits that he can never fully live up to the ideal of the New Black Man (xx, 159). But creative criticism about masculinity in America and a new language spoken to, by, and about men with a "strong commitment to diversity, . . . strong support for women and feminism, and strong faith in love and the value of listening" may enable all of us to imagine a strong New Black Man who will transform American manhood (Neal 159).

Never the naïve optimist, Toni Morrison always affirms the ideals made possible by the egalitarian principle but not necessarily the imperfect people who administer it. Her expression of masculinity allies her with Robin Kelley's views:

> Black men ought to be whomever or whatever they want to be, without unwarranted criticism or societal pressures to conform to a particular definition of manhood. They could finally dress down without suspicion, talk loudly without surveillance, and love each other without sanction. . . . Not in my lifetime. Any fool can look around and see that the situation for race and gender relations in general, and for black males in particular, has taken a turn for the worse—and relief is nowhere in sight. (305)

Morrison's male characters reflect Kelley's kind of authenticity and an individuality that counters the tendency in American literature to veil their humanity behind "an abstracted identity projected onto [them] by the white author's notions of what a Black man represents, or ought to represent" (Andrews 61). Toni Morrison remains always cautionary as she asserts possibility.

Thus, even though she calls on critics to address in depth the major traits that constitute the African American literary canon, including the men who are "outside of that little community value thing," Morrison does not uphold Demetrakopoulos's assessment of black male "archetypes" as sterile. On the contrary, she applauds what she calls the "incredible amount of magic and feistiness in black men that nobody has been able to wipe out [although] everybody has tried" (Stepto 383–84). When colleague Gloria Naylor wonders whether or not she should feel compelled to reveal the goodness of her male characters, Morrison replies in no uncertain terms: "Yes, you should" (Naylor and Morrison 580). My hope for the present study is to embrace Morrison's men from all their circuitous angles. Addressing the books and their male figures chronologically, and taking an androgynous tack, I allow close readings of the men to lead me to novel conclusions about Morrison and the masculine.

The Bluest Eye acts as a masculine manifesto. If Morrison has the courage to connect Cholly and Mr. Henry and Soaphead Church with the most heinous of crimes against nature, just as she will do with Bill Cosey in *Love*, she also has the clarity to contextualize their pedophilia in terms of white Western tenets of sexual repression, competitive ownership, physical beauty, and romantic love. *Sula* commemorates as conducive to androgyny the vitality of America's beautiful black boys, even while it laments its loss. *Song of Solomon* provides a fight-or-flight manual for black male survival, grounding it inside a feminine circle. *Tar Baby* employs the "nigger in the woodpile" to pit black male fraternity against white male enterprise, to counter classical form with antiromantic feeling. Morrison's trilogy about love and its excesses (*Beloved*, *Jazz*, *Paradise*) traces African American men as they locate their blues roots in rural slavery and discover their entrancement with the concrete plantation, or elusive possibility, defined by the Jazz City. It then lauds the failure of their attempts to create their own American paradise at the expense of others. Her latest novel, *Love*, converts Lacan's limited Law of the Father into an expansive "decent daddy" possibility.

Viewed collectively, Morrison's male characters reveal that issues of gender, race, class, and age cannot be segregated; conflicts between African American men and women result not from sexual disease but from cultural dis-ease, the cure for which includes radical structural surgery. To single out her men is not to negate the preeminence of her women. It means, rather, to recognize their interconnectedness along with the balance between them. It confronts the limitations and celebrates the power of authentic, multifaceted, African American masculinity and welcomes the androgyny and the humanity that establish the griot. Guitar Bains, one of Morrison's most magical men, warns another, Milkman Dead, who becomes even more alive: "Everybody wants the life of a black man." Desiring not his "dead life" but becoming the bane of his "living life," black women, in particular, Guitar claims, resent the chances he takes unless the risk revolves around them. Adding that a man's life is no good unless he can choose what to die for, Guitar declares that he stakes his on the love of his people, especially his woman. His reply, when Milkman challenges the seeming contradictions within his friend's statements, echoes the voice of their creator and defines a focus for this book: "Can't I love what I criticize?" (*Song of Solomon* 222–23).

CHAPTER 2

Black Boys, White Gaze

A Respectful Publication of *The Bluest Eye*

Twenty-three years after it appeared in 1970, *The Bluest Eye* was still mislabeled fiction for adolescents. Morrison's afterword to the 1994 Plume edition describes the initial publication of her book to be "like Pecola's life: dismissed, trivialized, misread" (216). In fact, *The Bluest Eye* represents its creator's masculine manifesto. Morrison deliberately places her black male characters into situations where their behavior becomes virtually unredeemable, yet she simultaneously urges us to forgive them. Because we must "handle why" as we "take refuge in how" they react as they do, we learn that the earth itself resists the seeds of African American virility, that the blame for much of their self-destructiveness lies not with black boys but with American culture (5–6).

Although Morrison praises Plume's long overdue "respectful publication," the Library of Congress continues to offer two telling subject headings as part of its cataloging-in-publication data: 1. Afro-Americans—Ohio—Fiction. 2. Girls—Ohio—Fiction. Combined, the data suggest that Morrison's debut novel depicts the lives of African American girls residing in Ohio, which, narrowly defined, it does. Reading any of Morrison's fiction carefully, however, trains us to notice absence. What remains stunningly excluded from the book's cataloging information but vividly included on its pages is the story of African American boys living in Ohio. The cultural influences that shape the darkness at the heart of *The Bluest Eye* act on and are enacted by its female and male characters. An artist's androgynous rendering of a dejected child on one jacket cover captures what even the Library of Congress misses: abuse destroys the black boys living in Lorain, Ohio, as well as the girls.[1]

The novel opens by parodying canonical children's literature. Visual contrasts between versions of the Dick-and-Jane primer suggest uncontrollable speed and disjointed sound, as uncooperative groups of letters topple over into one another so that individual signs appear to battle for placement. Like real life, reading beyond page 1 leads, in the beginning, to more questions than answers; we really can't judge a book by its cover. Our initial instinct here is to blame the disorder of the black figures for our confusion when, in actuality, the distorted structures or lack of supporting structures surrounding the figures deprive them of meaning and cause our discomfort. Read by innocent, uninhibited children, the opening passages would seem an amusing picture and sound game. Read by experienced, more restrained adults in the context of the rest of the book, the increasingly chaotic text ridicules the banal and unrealistic "happiness" of the generic middle-class white family and foreshadows the inexorable disintegration of a specific lower-class black family, the Breedloves.

Much of the novel's powerful irony results from its call-and-response structure, its clash of race, gender, and class as the simplicities of the white-family primer are answered by the complexities of black-family life. The textbook editor-turned-writer inverts stereotypical details of typical 1940s textbooks, distorted excerpts from which reappear as mocking chapter headings, to take us beyond a first-page glance at her rendition of Dick and to answer the question of why the text—and African American boys—disintegrate. *The Bluest Eye* examines the destructive effects on black males of Western-imposed concepts of repressive sexuality, competitive ownership, physical beauty, and romantic love.[2] It shifts the reader's "gaze" away from the black figures to focus on the white power structures that cause those figures to battle each other for predominance. It uncovers the lack of supportive structures that would allow the figures to cooperate in the making of meaning.

The childlike, deceptively innocuous language that encourages some naïve readers to view *The Bluest Eye* as "adolescent fiction" offers a sophisticated critique of gender issues with the juxtaposition of its nouns against the ensuing black narrative. The most specific and most powerful nouns in the opening passage are two proper names: Dick and Jane. Morrison has long acknowledged an intention to rewrite Jane, to write about girls like herself whom she never encountered in the books of her childhood. Consequently, the synthetic white baby-doll of the primer pales against the vitality of Frieda, Claudia, and even Pecola. A Dick-and-Jane primer, however, ostensibly involves Jane *and* Dick. Introduced by name at the outset, Morrison's Dick is never called on to play. As the Breedlove family story unravels, the boy's presence is located most palpably in his absence. We might interpret this omission as Morrison's deliberate inversion of the traditional male-centered structure found in books written by both black and white male writers. Given the complex inclusion of male characters in the rest of the novel, however, it becomes likely that she also wishes to call attention to the dehumanization, devaluation, and withdrawal of African American boys as the black community responds to white-imposed values.

If she identifies the Breedloves with the stark, unyielding black print distorted from the white-family primer, she associates the MacTeers with supple, quill-shaped leaves and the passing of seasons. Survival for black children in either family includes learned abuse. The MacTeer manifestation, however, combines the pliancy to endure a steady diet of violence from overstressed adults with a redeeming love as "thick and dark as Alaga syrup" (12). Mama becomes a voice and hands that simultaneously hurt and soothe; Daddy is a craggy face and naked body that inspire fear yet provide security. As change-of-season rawness gives way to numbing cold, Daddy's features assume the bleak, threatening harshness that, for poor people, defines winter: "His eyes become a cliff of snow threatening to avalanche. . . . His skin takes on the pale cheerless yellow of winter sun; . . . his high forehead is the frozen sweep of the Erie, hiding currents of gelid thoughts that eddy in darkness" (61). Daddy has been principal strategist in charge of winter siege since autumn, when grownups discuss Zick's Coal prices in "tired edgy voices" and drag children along railroad tracks to scavenge for the tiny pieces that have dropped off train cars headed for steel mills. A "Vulcan guarding the flames," he drills his family in the tactics of conservative heat management, only to stare with them over the breakfast table on "dark icebox mornings at four stewed prunes, slippery lumps of oatmeal, and cocoa with a roof of skin" (9–10). Unlike the smile of the father in the white primer, Daddy's zippered mouth is that of "Wolf killer turned hawk fighter," who "worked night and day to keep one from the door and the other from under the windowsills." Fierce protector of hearth and home, laboring under economic constraints that make him cruel to be kind, he will not "unrazor his lips" until spring brings its gardens (61).

With the arrival of Maureen Peal's false spring, Daddy's naked body arouses increasingly conflicting emotions. As Mary Pipher documents, despite the proliferation in the United States of children having children, the sexual attitudes we have inherited from Puritan forefathers dominate in distorted ways so that actual knowledge about sex and sexuality among our young people remains shockingly limited (208–9). Morrison's eleven-year-old Pecola is terrified that she has killed herself when she experiences her first menstrual period; worldly Maureen Peal explains menstruation as blood not needed to supply a baby through the "like-line" connected to the belly button (70). Thirteen-year-old Cholly, however, under pressure from cool but equally ignorant older male cousins like Jake, figures out how his body works by fumbling and giggling his way into sex with an equally naïve Darlene, whose mother, stupefied from overeating and drinking at the funeral banquet of Cholly's sole caregiver, still threatens to "whup" her for getting her clothes dirty. Cholly then abandons everything with which he is familiar out of a "wildly irrational" fear that Darlene might be pregnant, identifying with his own father, who fled his unborn son (151). While the girls are left to cope with mothers, like Darlene's and Claudia's, who respond to daughters suspected of "playing nasty" by reaching for the nearest switch, the boys without fathers run off in dread of and bewilderment about girls (30). Morrison inverts white stereotypes involving unlicensed black male sexuality to suggest that the danger lies with white, not black, male sexuality. White, middle-class, puritanical attitudes toward sex have solidly infiltrated the African American community, to the detriment of its young men.

The allusion to Daddy's nakedness, symbolizing the thrill and terror of unknown, forbidden sexuality, becomes a weapon with which black boys can intimidate black girls, who have been bludgeoned by their mothers to believe that sex is nasty. Heady with the musk of their own virility, Bay Boy, Woodrow Cain, Buddy Wilson, and Junie Bug surround Pecola "like a necklace of semiprecious stones." The taunt they so gaily chant to harass their victim repeats: "Black e mo. Black e mo. Yadaddsleepsnekked. Black e mo black e mo ya dadd sleeps nekked. Black e mo" (65). Noting wryly the "wildly fitting" incoherence of two insults about things over which the victim has no control, Morrison's narrator focuses on the boys' racial and masculine self-hatred: "It was their contempt for their own blackness that gave the first insult its teeth. They seemed to have taken all of their smoothly cultivated ignorance, their exquisitely learned self-hatred, their elaborately designed hopelessness and sucked it all up into a fiery cone of scorn that had burned for ages in the hollows of their minds—cooled—and spilled over lips of outrage, consuming whatever was in its path" (65). After the boys' macabre war dance has been curtailed, however, by the physical threat of Frieda "with set lips and Mama's eyes" and the psychological intimidation veiled behind Maureen Peal's wide springtime eyes, Daddy's nakedness persists as the girls' topic of conversation and leads them to battle among themselves.

Although Maureen diverts Pecola's tears of helplessness with an offer to buy her ice cream, it quickly becomes apparent that an overprotected, "high-yellow dream child" merely indulges voyeuristic curiosity about male sexuality (62). Pecola sublimates her disgust with Cholly's sexuality by agitatedly declaring that only a "dirty" father would be naked in front of his own daughter. Her defensive response triggers the anger of the MacTeer girls, who "had seen [their] own father naked and didn't care to be reminded of it and feel the shame brought on by the absence of shame" (71). When Daddy passes by the open door of their bedroom late at night on his way from the bathroom, he looks in on his girls. Wide-eyed awake in their beds, Claudia and Frieda react to his naked presence with mixed feelings of fascination, shame, and security. They watch Daddy go back to his bedroom, "confident that his little girls would not lie open-eyed like that, staring, staring." However, the dark "took only him away, not his nakedness. That stayed in the room with [them]. Friendly like" (71–72).

While puritanical misconceptions about sexuality certainly provide weapons with which the boys and girls of Lorain can beat up on each other, Daddy's comfort with his body and Mama's practical ministrations about menstruation help the MacTeer girls hold their own. Mama responds to reported sex play by reaching immediately for a switch because she'd rather "raise pigs than some nasty girls." On the other hand, her eyes are sorry and her arms protectively encircling when she realizes her mistake and takes Pecola inside to help the "little-girl-gone-to-woman" through her first period (31). This tough love and the music of her laughter, as her daughters wait outside the bathroom door, grant Frieda the courage to defend Pecola against bullying by the likes of Woodrow Cain. Her conflictedness about Daddy's nakedness, however, causes Frieda to bully Woodrow in turn by turning against him his rigidly masculine image of himself.

Morrison intends to illustrate not only the damage that boys with sexual weapons can inflict on girls but to emphasize that repressive, Western-influenced sexual attitudes can do damage to both. When Frieda yells at Woodrow, "Leave her 'lone, or I'm gone tell everybody what you did," she essentially emasculates him. While Woodrow figuratively wields his penis to abuse Pecola sexually, again in metaphor, Frieda hits him where it hurts by threatening to reveal that "Mrs. Cain told Mama he won't quit [wetting the bed]." Enuresis occurs in four out of five cases among boys. It is frequently accompanied by feelings of insecurity and inadequacy, which can be aroused when a boy's mother is too interfering and his father not supportive enough. Frieda's derisive dismissal of an uncontrollable symptom echoes the voices of the women sitting around her mother's kitchen table in their scathing indictments of male sexual behaviors: "Old nasty" (66, 80).

Approached as "lust and simple caring for," sex is a vehicle of communication, intimacy, and physical pleasure; wielded to humiliate or control, it becomes a weapon of mass destruction (122). Recollecting no power struggles between the men and women in her family, Morrison describes them as *comrades*, a term suggesting the solid partnerships cemented on the field of battle against a common enemy (McKay 398–99). Despite the attacks on their union, primarily by white power structures, the MacTeer parents cooperate to keep their family intact. Laughter and music counter overwork and underpay. And this comradeship is generational; Big Papa and Big Mama are senior officers in the company. Claudia stops her systematic destruction of the blue-eyed Baby Dolls routinely given to little black girls for Christmas as adult pressure converts her feelings about them from "pristine sadism to fabricated hatred, to fraudulent love" (23). Contact with these same adult comrades-in-arms, however, allows her to comprehend that, had they taken her seriously enough to ask her what she wanted for Christmas, "they would have known that [she] did not want to have anything to own, or to possess any object." Children desire not to have but to be, to experience with all of their senses engaged. Claudia would have responded, "I want to sit on the low stool in Big Mama's kitchen with my lap full of lilacs and listen to Big Papa play his violin for me alone" (21–22). While the smells and warmth of Big Mama's kitchen represent essential ingredients in Claudia's ideal experience, the sounds of Big Papa's music remain equally as important.

Because children are just learning to read their primers, they have not yet broken the codes necessary for conceptualizing language or for assigning value to symbols. Thus, they rely directly on their senses to sign with the world. Concurring with Richard Wright's childlike fred-daniels, Morrison illustrates how taking children seriously asks us to question an adult culture that attaches greater value to symbols than to experience and thus values abstractions or things over human life.[3] In a parody of the way Faulkner's instinctual Benjy requires the natural scent of his sister, Claudia and Frieda are drawn to their mother's new roomer, Mr. Henry Washington, by his wonderfully eclectic smell: "Like trees and lemon vanishing cream, and Nu Nile Hair Oil and flecks of Sen-Sen" (15). Initially, all of the MacTeers react positively to Mr. Henry. However, because they continue to trust their noses, the children react less violently to the man after he molests Frieda than do the adults, including most readers.

The female MacTeers eagerly anticipate Mr. Henry's arrival; sparring women highlight his sweet maleness. The girls imagine a roomer to be pleasantly mysterious, and Mama is "all ease and satisfaction" in discussing his community standing with her friends (12). Their "gently wicked" analysis heads immediately to his sexuality. Not bothering to hide their curiosity, the women wonder why Henry leaves his current lodgings with Miss Della Jones. They learn that the "old crazy nigger [whom Della] married up with didn't help her head none" and that she is "too addled now to keep up." This leads to the revelation that her husband left her for "that trifling Peggy" because "he couldn't take no more of that violet water Della Jones used. Said he wanted a woman to smell like a woman. Said Della was just too clean for him." Responding to this information with " 'Old dog. Ain't that nasty,' " the women cheerfully skewer their sisters for slackness, ignorance, ugliness, and greed while attacking the men for running away from clean women (13).

Even a surname connecting him to the "father" of his country fails to protect Henry from skepticism about his masculinity. The women speculate as to why he never marries Della or anyone else: "How come? Somebody cut it off?" They argue over whether or not he is "picky" or the pickings merely slim (14). Persuaded chiefly by financial exigency, Mama maintains that the roomer, who will be compelled to "pick at" Frieda, is just a sensible, steady worker with quiet ways (99). Only the girls, not yet comprehending the full meanings of words but watching faces and listening for "truth in timbre," rely on their senses to critique Mr. Henry (15). The women disguise, repress, and criticize their natural selves and find the instinctual ways of the men disgusting, and the men finally reject the women's artificiality. Ultimately, everybody's sexuality becomes distorted, resulting in isolation, alienation, and pedophilia.

Mr. Henry's appetites, represented for all to read in his face, have certainly been misshapen by the black community's adaptations of white sexual mores. Claudia and Frieda are immediately attracted to his ready smile, which shows "small even teeth with a friendly gap in the middle" (915). Here Morrison obviously plays with the phrenological notion that a gap-tooth indicates a powerful libido, made famous by Chaucer's Wife of Bath. Other signs of a strong but repressed sexuality are the thick, hairless leg that Claudia and Frieda glimpse leaning out of his bathrobe and the pornographic magazines scattered close by the Bible in his room. Henry certainly knows his white pin-up girls. Breaking with the protocol that prohibits adults from acknowledging children, he introduces himself to Frieda and Claudia by teasingly referring to one as Greta Garbo and the other as Ginger Rogers. His next trick entertains them with a disappearing penny, a charming gesture that makes Daddy smile for the first time like the father in the white family primer. Mr. Henry continues to offer seemingly innocent compliments and harmless bribery to prompt affection from the MacTeer girls. Only after the fact are we horrified to comprehend the sexual gratification that he must have experienced as the little girls' hands wander over his body, searching for the hidden coin, while Daddy smiles and Mama's eyes go soft.

Henry's "girlie magazines," which Claudia proposes to Frieda and Pecola as pleasure reading for a boring Saturday afternoon, prepare us for a clandestine visit from two of the local prostitutes, China and Miss Marie, also known as the Maginot Line. In a community controlled by "good Christian colored women," Mr. Henry's sexual appetites find satisfaction with partners who despise both men and "unclean" women like themselves. Attempting to secure his privacy, this concupiscent emperor of ice cream offers Claudia and Frieda money to go out and enjoy a cone. The girls return early, however, to observe through their living room window the "fancy women" that Mama and Big Mama hate. The sight of Mr. Henry sucking and licking China's fingers reminds them of his girlie magazines, making their flesh crawl with "terror and obscure longing" (77). Their mother's heated disapproval, coupled with the church women's frightening stories about the Maginot Line's terrible exploits, contradict any signs of sweetness or lonesomeness the girls sense beneath the fat fortifications of her face. Further challenge to their instincts occurs when, asked directly by Frieda about the identity of his guests, Mr. Henry chokes on the soft drink he has substituted for China's fingers and laughs the familiar "grown-up getting-ready-to-lie laugh" (78). As Claudia looks away to keep from seeing his kindly teeth frame an untruth, he identifies the women as members of his Bible class come to pray with him. Noting that Mrs. MacTeer "don't take to" visitors and so much Bible study, he requests that the girls not tell their mother. Interpreting Mama's declarations literally by assuring themselves that Marie didn't eat off any of the family plates, Claudia and Frieda decide to keep Mr. Henry's secret primarily to avoid their mother's fussing.[4]

All the factors are now in place to render inevitable Henry's molestation of one of the children. Dependent on but repelled by the unnaturalness of the churchwomen, he leaves the house of a female already crazed by a husband who abandons her because she is too clean. Then he brings to the MacTeers on a Saturday night in autumn powerful but unsatisfied sexual urges. Sublimating, like the rest of the black community, physical drives into religious ones, he restrains these compulsions during winter hibernation with the aid of women like China and Marie, who view him and themselves as disgusting. On a Saturday afternoon in early spring, however, Claudia returns home to discover the aftermath of Mama singing, Daddy cursing, the neighbors screaming, and Frieda crying reverberating in the vacuum of an uneasy silence. Mr. Henry has violated Frieda. Prevented access to the prostitutes and relief from overwhelming appetites, he cannot prevent himself from a springtime pinch of the freshest, and most vulnerable, flesh available to him—a female child. The girls discern accurately Mr. Henry's concession to sex as "simple caring for." However, while signs of a distorted lust also appear, they do not have the experience required to read them. The parents remain oblivious because they need the rent money and because their children, out of fear and love, do not show them the signs.

Morrison obviously attacks destructive white sexual attitudes that have negatively affected the black community. She chooses in this section, however, to treat the situation comically. As relayed by one little girl to another: after Frieda tells her parents that Mr. Henry pinched her breasts, Daddy knocks Mr. Henry off the porch by throwing a tricycle at his head; Mr. Henry stands up singing "Nearer My God to Thee," upon which Mama, hitting him with a broom, tells him to keep God out of his mouth; Daddy grabs a gun out of the hands of one of the neighbors who has come running at the noise and, over Mama's protests, shoots at Mr. Henry, who jumps out of his shoes and runs off in his socks; Claudia is jealous of the attention Frieda receives and regrets missing the action; Frieda is crying only because another neighbor says she might be ruined, and she doesn't want to get fat like ruined Miss Marie. Finally, Claudia suggests that she and Frieda go to Pecola's for whiskey, which has prevented China and Poland (pronounced "Po'land"?), also ruined, from getting fat and which will "eat up" Frieda, too. In the aftermath, Mama, still in her hat, wanders aimlessly about, singing of trains and Arkansas.

Like Mama, and like Poland at the conclusion of Pecola's visit with the three madams, black women from all walks of life fortify themselves against the blues by singing about trains and traveling while black men cope by traveling aimlessly on those trains.[5] Approaching "conflict, dominion, and power differently," women "probably don't" want to change things, Morrison contends, while men transcend conflict and exercise power by moving on (Tate 122–23). In an ironic reversal of romantic poetry, which involves absent women sending white men into autoerotic flights of fancy, long-gone male figures stimulate black women into singing the blues. In *The Bluest Eye*, rovers Dewey Prince and Johnny inspire Marie's best food stories, a sky-soft brown boy makes Poland's dirt leap for joy when his feet touch the ground, and Mama sings achingly of that delicious time when "my man" leaves her. Colored by the "greens and blues" in the women's voices, misery takes the grief out of the words and leaves the children either wondering what love feels like or nursing "a conviction that pain [is] not only endurable, it [is] sweet" (26).

The self-destructive strategies manifested by the black community to endure abuse and repress self, modified from certain of the white community's approaches to religion and art, trickle down; they collect finally in a deep wellspring that poisons children, now primed to continue the cycle. However, with a modicum of luck and even less love, these community children often rebound sturdy enough and instinctual enough to prevail. Although Mama and Daddy, and some readers, remain ready to crucify Mr. Henry for actions that all, in part, are responsible for, Claudia and Frieda "loved him. Even after what came later, there was no bitterness in [their] memory of him" (16). Morrison does not defend Mr. Henry's assault on Frieda's innocence or, for that matter, the whores' indifference to Pecola's. Neither does she demonize any of them. Instead of placing the blame on the victims, she directs her verbal attack toward repressive Western systems that revere abstractions over human experience and victimize people.[6]

All the black figures in Morrison's primer fall victim to the failings of white structures; the Breedloves, however, are virtually driven off the page. Without the presence of ordering principles, letters bleed into one another. Likewise, deprived of any support, the Breedloves, male and female, absorb the community's runoff, manifest the inevitable aberrations, and are finally "put outdoors" (17). Claudia distinguishes between being put *out* and put out*doors* as the difference between metaphysical and physical states. While the black people she recalls exist already situated on the hem of life, being placed outdoors means no covering at all, an irrevocable end to something, nowhere else to go. As a result, African Americans especially crave ownership. Many have literally had bred into them a keen hunger for "some nice little old place" (18).

Their property, then, prevents the MacTeers from becoming the Breedloves. Although the MacTeer house, with its dark, aging rooms peopled by roaches and mice, in no way resembles the gleaming green-and-white framework of the white-family primer, it belongs to the black family. The Breedloves represent "renting black[s]." Even the fire in their living quarters indicates a vast difference in hearth and home from that in the MacTeer house. While Daddy, with strict discipline and great sacrifice, keeps the MacTeers' winter fires burning, the coal stove at the Breedloves possesses no such guardian of the flames. In spite of the fact that individuals attend constantly, though reluctantly, to its regimen, the fire takes on a life of its own, routinely dying in the cold of early morning. The peeling green paint on Claudia's house suggests that her family hangs on by a thread. Sammy's family, however, does not subsist in a house but "festers" in an abandoned storefront offering only a history of defeat together with others who maintain no order, form no family, provide no warmth (35).

The men associated with this storefront are victims, bullies, or gone. Originally housing a furniture business, the structure "foists itself on the eye of the passerby in a manner that is both irritating and melancholy" so that visitors to the neighborhood wonder why it has not been torn down and residents simply look away. Its population, fluid since the Breedloves' displacement, includes slow-footed, shivery teenaged boys, who huddle about its corner to "feel their groins, smoke cigarettes, and plan mild outrages" (33). Betraying themselves as novices to sex, smoking, and crime, they merely kill the time that is killing them. Since the real-estate office, Hungarian bakery, pizza parlor, and even the Gypsy family, which succeed each other as building occupants, cannot last long, these boys lack sustained positive role models or creative outlets. As such, they fail to develop any core sense of self and thus hang together in gangs, which subsume their identities and assign selves to them that either dominate or are dominated by others.

The interior of the Breedloves' storefront appears as daunting as the exterior. It looks, in fact, as "unimaginative as a first-generation Greek landlord could contrive it to be" (34). Morrison describes its furnishings as having been owned but not known, void of the associations with human experience that give meaning to things. These missing memories divulge no "happy drunk—a friend of the family, with a fat neck, unmarried, you know, but God how he eats!—[who] had sat at the piano and played 'You Are My Sunshine.'" No "HE" dreamed about by a young girl who carefully places for him a blue ball on a tiny, artificial Christmas tree (35–36).

Instead of providing comfort to men who imbue things like old pianos and dust-laden Christmas trees with cherished associations, the Breedloves' furnishings provoke in men unpleasant physical reactions: an increase of acid irritation, a flush of perspiration as they recall circumstances surrounding a piece. In a scene as absent of names or racial identifiers as the items are of memories, Morrison nonetheless unmistakably depicts Cholly emasculated by a crude, white delivery man who refuses to take responsibility for a ruined sofa:

> "Looka here, buddy. It was O.K. when I put it on the truck. The store can't do anything about it once it's on the truck. . . ." Listerine and Lucky Strike breath.

> "But I don't want no tore couch if'n it's bought new." Pleading eyes and tightened testicles.
>
> "Tough shit, buddy. *Your* tough shit." (36)

When the things surrounding people constantly remind them of humiliation, when every something eagerly anticipated disintegrates consistently into defeat, the result is a joylessness that pervades everything and prevents any action. The "stink of it" keeps men from even repairing the damage, "which became a gash, which became a gaping chasm that exposed the cheap frame and cheaper upholstery." Morrison compares the split sofa, to pay for which Cholly must still scrape together $4.80 a month, to the rotten front tooth she will associate with Pauline. The pain of both diffuses to other parts and "limits the delight of things not related to it" (36–37).

The Breedloves' storefront world looms far bleaker than the crumbing MacTeer house in large part because of this encroaching presence of white bullies. Morrison describes her work, in general, as "marginalizing" the white world. Commenting that white readers are unaccustomed to the kind of ground-shifting that renders the central focus of a book away from white people, she notes that, unlike black male writers, black female writers ignore relations with white males (Dreifus 74). While the MacTeer family has almost no contact with white men, other than as anonymous obstructions to survival, white males either assault or dismiss each Breedlove.

Cholly's treatment by the delivery man becomes one of many psychological castrations suffered at the hands of white bullies. Morrison reveals how an experience at age thirteen with some white hunters fixes forever his attitudes toward sex and women. Naïve about death and sex, he wonders how he should feel during the wake of the grandmother who has reared him, when he becomes attracted to a visiting male cousin who exhibits the dubious sophistication of a teenager a couple of years older. Cholly takes but chokes on a proffered cigarette. In return, he introduces Jake to several neighborhood girls, one of whom accepts Cholly's tentative invitation to go for a walk. Giddy from the scent of pine and muscadine and the promise of rain, giggling and wrestling his way into arousal, Cholly is just beginning to figure out how his body works when the threatened explosion of orgasm retreats before the shock on Darlene's face, along with the asthmatic snicker and unmistakable smell of white men. Two hunters race their flashlight over Cholly and Darlene's bodies, after which they force Cholly at gunpoint to "get on wid it," "coon baby," in a sadistic rape within a rape. The flashlight making "a moon on his behind," Cholly can "do no more than make-believe" and must stifle a choking violence born of complete helplessness. He redirects his rage and hatred toward the girl, whom he yearns to strangle or rape—"hard, long, and painfully"—as she covers her face with hands like "baby claws." After the hunters leave, however, he merely helps her to pat around in the dark for her panties and waits as she puts them on "with the movements of an old woman" (148–49).

Nursing resentment toward Darlene, Cholly never once considers focusing his outrage on the hunters because, as Morrison knows, "Such an emotion would have destroyed him." In addition to the overwhelming imbalance of power, his "subconscious knew what his conscious mind did not guess—that hating them would have consumed him, burned him up like a piece of soft coal, leaving only flakes of ash and a question mark of smoke. . . . For now, he hated the one who had created the situation, the one who bore witness to his failure, his impotence. The one whom he had not been able to protect, to spare, to cover from the round moon glow of the flashlight." Teenagers and rednecks initiate Cholly's elementary education in sex. He then goes straight to graduate school to a blur of black women who give him back his manhood, which he can now accept only "aimlessly" (150–51).

If Cholly remains irreparably scarred from direct attacks on his body and psyche by white men, white males damage Pauline and Pecola by misreading or overlooking them. The females' reactions become refractions through which we can view masculinity. Indulging herself by electing to have her second child in a hospital, Pauline is jammed in a large room together with a "whole mess of women." Already in labor, she endures a "little old doctor" ramming his gloved hand "up between [her] legs," followed by the humiliation of being displayed without her permission so that another old doctor could "learn some young ones about babies." Although not specifically identified as such, the doctors are obviously white. They go about their business ignoring Pauline but gently "shucking [the white women] with nice friendly talk." The physician in charge never once looks straight into the black woman's face but speaks across her to address his colleagues: "Now these here women you don't have any trouble with. They deliver right away and with no pain. Just like horses" (124–25).

Empowered by the embarrassment of one young doctor who does meet her gaze, Pauline begins to moan "something awful" just "to let them people know having a baby was more than a bowel movement," that, although she can bear the pain with "no fuss," she hurts "just like them white women." Her response incorporates a typically understated indictment of the widespread insensitivity to females by some men in the modern medical profession: "'Cause [a mare] can't say [the pain], they think it ain't there?" (124–25). While her white employer appears far more generous toward his housekeeper than her attending physicians, he, too, fails to perceive her as a complex human being. Mr. Fisher catches on only to the image of Pauline that suits his line of work. Locating in the home of a wealthy white family the beauty, order, luxury, and power that she cannot create in her storefront, Pauline increasingly neglects "her house, her children, her man." Satisfying the Fishers' need for an ideal servant meets her need for self-worth. Renaming her Polly, Mr. Fisher has nothing but praise for the black mammy figure that, like a parrot, Pauline imitates. He swears that he would "rather sell her blueberry cobblers than real estate" (127–28).

White men have no use at all for Pecola or acknowledge even a limited perception of her. During one of the most heart-wrenching scenes in the novel, Pecola, like the Maginot Line, attempts to protect herself, deflect her sense of unworthiness, and appease some part of her craving for love by treating herself with food. Morrison shifts to the present tense to capture the immediacy and significance of the moment for the child. Three pennies in the bottom of her shoe, she climbs the wooden steps of Yacobowski's Fresh Veg. Meat and Sundries Store with an eleven-year-old's anticipation of the salty-sweet taste of peanut butter and caramel Mary Janes. His gray head looming up over the candy counter, Mr. Yacobowski turns bleary blue eyes ever so slightly toward his customer but senses "somewhere between retina and object, between vision and view" that he "need not waste the effort of a glance." In a powerful voice that simultaneously accuses and excuses the white man, Morrison's narrator asks:

> How can a fifty-two-year-old white immigrant storekeeper with the taste of potatoes and beer in his mouth, his mind honed on the doe-eyed Virgin Mary, his sensibilities blunted by a permanent awareness of loss, *see* a little black girl? Nothing in his life even suggested that the feat was possible, not to say desirable or necessary. (48)

The answer is that Mr. Yacobowski does not look at Pecola because, for him, there is nothing to see.

Mr. Yacobowski's attitude illustrates the white male "gaze" that imperceptibly transforms the self-worth of black children into self-loathing. As she looks up at him, Pecola perceives not only the "vacuum where curiosity ought to lodge" but a "total absence of human recognition" (48). As she attempts to identify some glance lurking in his eyes, even the disgust and anger she has met before from grown white men, she locates the edge of distaste familiar to her from most white people. She associates with that edge the one thing static about her—her blackness. As she makes the "quietly inoffensive assertion of a black child's attempt to communicate with a white adult," pointing her small finger at his display case, Mr. Yacobowski simply cannot see from her vantage point. The "angle of his vision, the slant of her finger, makes it incomprehensible to him" (49).

Frustrated, the white candy man acts out Morrison's black-family primer. He blames Pecola's inability to communicate on her confusion instead of his inability to support her and snarls, ironically in Jesus' name: "Christ. Kantcha talk?" (49). She freezes out of fear, unable to get across to him the coins she holds; he hesitates to touch her hand. Their exchange is forced and based on self-serving instincts: his for her money, hers for his sweets. Only the brief grazing of his nails on her damp palm breaks their "glazed separateness." Outside the store, shame wells up in her to vie with anger for predominance. Though indignation offers at least a flash of essence, Mr. Yacobowski's gaze prohibits a sustained burn, and Pecola quickly turns for comfort to the blue-eyed, blonde-haired, smiling rosy-cheeked face of Mary Jane on the candy wrapper. To eat the candy is "to eat the eyes, eat Mary Jane. Love Mary Jane. Be Mary Jane" (50). "Nine lovely orgasms with Mary Jane" constitute a savage inversion of the transforming ritual of transubstantiation. Instead of finding new life through the sacrifice of a caring Other, Pecola is sacrificed by the distorting process of the white male gaze to become reborn into nonbeing.

These rites become uplifting or degrading in direct proportion to their relationship with ownership and power. Although an exchange of equal material value, candy for money, supposedly determines the encounter between Mr. Yacobowski and Pecola, their race, class, gender, and age differences prohibit reciprocal service. Alternatively, the ritual of Christian communion involves specific symbolic gestures that call for clergy to minister to their congregation and vice versa, much in the same way that Christ washed the feet of his disciples. Here, power derives from giving over possession; leader and follower exchange positions and take nourishment from mutual sacrifice. The pennies, lying flat in Pecola's extended palm, resemble communion wafers, accepted by Mr. Yacobowski and changed into the candy that Pecola eats to penetrate Mary Jane's goodness. However, in contrast to the intent of communion, during which every broken self becomes whole through the ritual of transubstantiation, Pecola must deny her black self to become one with white Mary Jane.

Christian communion enacts symbols that show the value of service to all people while Pecola's communion with Mary Jane, a symbol of the white gaze, demands that she accept Mr. Yacobowski's commoditized values and the devaluing of her own life.

The pennies, pressed between foot and shoe of the poor black child, feel "painful." It is a "sweet, endurable, even cherished irritation, full of promise and delicate security" but disturbing nevertheless (47). Pecola's primary comfort comes not from money but from the uncommodified things that buffet her path, familiar to and thus loved by her but unwanted by others. These include the dandelions at the base of the telephone pole, which most people call weeds and destroy. Thinking them pretty, Pecola wonders if others reject them because they are "so many, strong, and soon." She ponders the sidewalk crack shaped like a Y and the one that swells the concrete, thinking that, though the latter split had occasionally tripped her up, skates would glide evenly and quietly over such a smooth, old walkway. Fully experiencing these inanimate images makes them useful to her. They represent the codes of her world, "capable of translation and possession." Knowing them, she owns them. She "owned the crack that made her stumble; she owned the clumps of dandelions whose white heads, last fall, she had blown away; whose yellow heads, this fall, she peered into" (47–48).

Here Morrison outlines an alternative to the concept of ownership embraced by the European immigrant storekeeper and imitated by "propertied" African American families as best they can. While owning "some nice little old place" may unify black families living on the hem of a white male–dominated world and fortify them against being put "outdoors," the price of this possession can be costly, requiring that more energy go into things than into people. Pecola's holistic ideal of ownership involves a kind of communion with others that makes objects valuable only insofar as they are associated with the experiences of people. Owning things in this sense gives Pecola no power over others but makes her "part of the world, and the world a part of her" (47–48).[7]

In addition to ultraconservative Western attitudes toward sexuality and ownership, two other white male concepts help turn MacTeers into Breedloves and do irreparable damage to the men in black families: the ideal of physical beauty and the concept of romantic love.[8] Morrison asserts that the Breedloves do not live in the storefront simply because of their race and class; they stay there because no one could have convinced them that they are not uniquely ugly. Although close examination reveals no immediate physical reason for this ugliness, readers come to realize that its source lies in the Breedloves' own conviction:

> It was as though some mysterious all-knowing master had given each one a cloak of ugliness to wear, and they had each accepted it without question. The master had said, "You are ugly people." They had looked about themselves and saw nothing to contradict the statement; saw, in fact, support for it leaning at them from every billboard, every movie, every glance. "Yes," they had said. "You are right." And they took the ugliness in their hands, threw it as a mantle over them, and went about the world with it. Dealing with it each according to his way. (39)

Her words couched in the mesmerizing language of the biblical creation story, Morrison's narrator, unquestionably and scathingly, identifies the mysterious "master" as a white male god who looks down on black people and re-creates them according to his own image. She describes the process of the white gaze, which, when absorbed and reflected by black people, becomes de-creative. Using a term that she will refer to again in a 1994 film interview with Bill Moyers as the *master narrative*, Morrison here connects seeing with knowing.

Medieval optics provides a helpful background for the power relations troped in this scene: medieval vision theory credited both the seer and the object of sight as active contributors to the process of vision. According to the long-held theory of extramission inherited from Aristotle and Augustine, the "visual ray, the strongest concentration of the body's animating fire, is projected from the eye to touch its object. In the act of vision viewer and image are connected in a dynamic communication. . . . In the activity of seeing, the life energy of the viewer goes out to and takes the shape of the object contemplated" (Miles 45). Embedded within this process are paradoxes of power and powerlessness, activity and passivity, self and other, emotion and knowledge. Early modern optics replaced this interactive model of vision with the phenomenological aspects of vision, which emphasize objectivity: distance, detachment, spatialization, simultaneity. However, either of these alternative ways of seeing, acknowledged by Evelyn Fox Keller as shaping our assumptions about how we know, reveals that seeing has always been our most powerful metaphor for knowing. It thus influences subject-object, gender, and power relations: white males have traditionally been the seers in American culture; others, especially black males, the seen.

A "high-yellow dream child" introduces Claudia and Frieda to the "white gaze." Blissfully enjoying their senses, cultivating their dirt, and admiring their scars, they can destroy white dolls but cannot dismiss the "honey voices of parents and aunts, the obedience in the eyes of [their] peers, the slippery light in the eyes of [their] teachers when they encountered the Maureen Peals of the world." Only their support for each other allows the sisters to know that Maureen is not worthy of the hatred they feel toward her, that the "*Thing* to fear was the *Thing* that made *her* beautiful, and not [them]" (74). Alone and far more passive than Claudia or Frieda, Pauline indulges her ugliness, introduced to her by white male movie directors. After leaving her people to go up north with Cholly, she escapes the lonesome bleakness of the storefront by giving herself over to the white images flashing on the silver screen in a black theater. There she also reawakens her memory of darkened woods, lonely roads, riverbanks, and gentle knowing eyes, melancholy childhood fantasies in which burgeoning sexuality transforms into sweet yearning, the physical lover into a mysterious Presence. Church spirituals nourish these romantic dreams, joining love and death into desire for the precious male Stranger who will take Pauline's hand and lead her on; a contralto voice captures the dark sweetness Pauline cannot articulate.

Hearing black spirituals and seeing the white silver screen, then, shape Pauline's assumptions about how she knows herself. From what are actually simple pleasures, she learns "all there was to love and all there was to hate." They become her education in romantic love and physical beauty, according to Morrison probably "the most destructive ideas in the history of human thought." Both "originated in envy, thrived in insecurity, and ended in disillusion. In equating physical beauty with virtue, [Pauline] stripped her mind, bound it, and collected self-contempt by the heap. . . . She regarded love as possessive mating, and romance as the goal of the spirit. It would be for her a well-spring from which she would draw the most destructive emotions, deceiving the lover and seeking to imprison the beloved, curtailing freedom in every way" (122).

And, as mother wit would have it: "Educate a woman, and you educate a family." Pauline passes this knowledge on to her children. Into her daughter she beats a fear of growing up, of people, of life; into her son she beats a "loud desire to run away" (128). Like Dick in the black version of the white-family primer, Sammy disappears once he is named. He wields the ugliness with which his mother cloaks him like a weapon, adjusting his behavior to it, choosing companions who are fascinated or intimidated by it. Unlike Pecola, who reacts to her parents' ugly battles by "experimenting with methods of endurance," Sammy has run away to see new sights—by the time he is fourteen—no less than twenty-seven times. The only words he speaks in the novel, screamed after pummeling Cholly about the face in an attempt to beat him off Mrs. Breedlove, are "You naked fuck!" and "Kill him! Kill him!" To which his surprised mother, having knocked his father back into the stupor out of which she provokes him, responds, "Cut out that noise, boy" (43–44). Sammy does not remain long enough to be pictured, like Cholly, as adding a course in white bullies to his curriculum of despair, dissipation, and violence directed at the petty and the weak. However, Morrison allows us to see his prospective education spread out in front of him through his father's and his father's father's lives. Sammy is, no doubt, named for his grandfather-gone-missing, Samson Fuller.

Drawing the cords of restrictive Western thinking about sexuality, ownership, physical beauty, and romantic love tightly around various secondary black and white male characters in *The Bluest Eye*, Morrison sketches more fully two men of color who choke on their own thoughts. Encouraged to leave home before he can walk, Cholly begins his southern boyhood with less welcome than does his son. When he is four days old, his mother "wrapped him in two blankets and one newspaper and placed him on a junk heap by the railroad." He is rescued by his Great Aunt Jimmy who, as her name suggests, takes over the roles of both mother and father. Jimmy forbids her niece to see the baby, drives the girl away with a razor strap, rears Cholly herself, and takes occasional delight in telling him about her efforts to save him after implying that his mother "wasn't right in the head" (132). Morrison includes Aunt Jimmy among the strong black grandmothers who, having "carried a world on their heads" and re-created it in their own image, are "through with lust and lactation, beyond tears and terror"; they are "in fact, and at last, free" (138–39).

Jimmy's charge, however, pays a price for freedom gained so late in life. Grateful to eyes whose perspective contains a "puree of tragedy and humor, wickedness and serenity, truth and fantasy," young Cholly feels simultaneously repulsed by his great-aunt's aging body (139). His future physical reactions to women undoubtedly become affected by his intimacy with this old woman, who is free to eat cooked collard greens with her fingers, to suck her four gold teeth, to wear the nasty-smelling asafetida bag around her neck, and to press her wrinkled, sagging breasts against Cholly for bed warmth during winter. At times like these Cholly wonders whether or not he might just as well have died on the ash heap. Here Morrison addresses the unnaturalness of aging mothers who, instead of supporting younger ones, overpower them; she also acknowledges the complexity of the issue. Orphaned after Jimmy's death, Cholly aches for the fear of whippings and the smoked hock his aunt offers him from her own dish, clumsily holding the meat out to him with such affection in her bent fingers.

Like many black boys, Cholly comes to be reared by an old woman because of the existing support system—or lack thereof. His unmarried mother is too young to cope alone—and beaten for not coping—and his terrified father has run off. Four years of schooling give Cholly the courage to ask his aunt about his father's identity and the origin of his name. Jimmy responds to this hesitant query, however, by recollecting that she called him Charles Breedlove for her dead brother, who was a decent man. His own father, whom she vaguely remembers as "Samuel. No. . . . Samson Fuller," abandoned him before birth; his mother hadn't named him anything before she threw him away, and, besides, "ain't no Samson never come to no good end" (133). So much for psychologist Michael Gurian's insistence on the importance of lineal integrity, the respected voices of a boy's ancestors helping to guide him into manhood (257).

After giving up on school two years later to take a job at a feed and seed store, Cholly finds a substitute father in the person of a friendly old drunk named Blue Jack, who works in this preponderantly male place as a drayman. Cholly loves the old man, loves his "old-timey" stories about black people hollering when the Emancipation Proclamation is signed and his ghost stories about decapitated white women coming up from the swamp to cry for a comb. Similar to Marie's motivation for befriending Pecola, Blue entertains himself by bragging to Cholly. His personal stories are rough like Marie's, celebrating the women he's had, the fights he's been in, and the lynching he avoids that others don't. As a result, when Cholly attempts to cope with what he believes to be his own personal crisis involving a possibly pregnant Darlene, he cannot talk to Blue. The old man stays "drunk too often these days to make sense," and, besides, he can't reveal his shame to "Blue the woman-killer." In his very normal boy's need for adult male company, Cholly finds lonely "much better than alone" (134–51). Ultimately he will model the two male figures who dominate his adolescent life, one absent and one present: he deals with conflict either by running away like his father or, like Blue, by drinking and fighting.

However, Morrison refuses to dismiss the African American male as merely "isolated" and "pathological" (Holloway 86). Her review focuses steadily on the forces causing these distortions and confirms the vitality and viability of black men who cope with them. One of the few even darkly joyous passages found in *The Bluest Eye* depicts a black father, perceived through the eyes of a black son, as godlike. Cholly and Blue hover on the periphery of a church picnic, when the father of a family takes aim to break open a watermelon: "Tall, head forward, eyes fastened on a rock, his arms higher than the pines, his hands holding a melon bigger than the sun," his presence raises goose bumps on Cholly's arms and neck. When the boy wonders whether this might be an image of God, the white gaze overwhelms him as he recalls that God is a "nice old white man." Therefore, the figure "holding the world in his hands, ready to dash it to the ground and spill the red guts so niggers could eat the sweet, warm insides," must be the devil. If so, Cholly prefers this "strong, black devil" who, unlike God, inspires him (134).

Excitement will forever be associated for Cholly with the sensual music of a mouth organ mixing with the sharp scent of pine. Both sad and pleased that the melon breaks badly, allowing its blood-red heart to roll free, Blue and Cholly taste its juiciness together. A generous offering to them from the laughing father, the watermelon's "nasty-sweet guts of the earth" becomes "too obvious, almost obscene, in the joy it promise[s]" (135). Here Morrison clearly celebrates the sensuality, vigor, and fraternity of black men, the triumphant "badness" of the unbound heart as it escapes its confining rind, the bonding of the men as they take communion over it. Gender is troped as food, the field-grown, nasty-sweet watermelon associated with masculinity and kitchen-fixed sweet bread or oven-baked peach cobbler with femininity. Cholly overhears the old women at his aunt's funeral murmuring that she would still be alive if she had eaten pure sweet bread instead of Essie's peach pie, a dish more difficult for Jimmy to digest. A lifetime of giving over her juices, of serving white people and black men, gives her a "cold in [her] womb" and finally kills the tough old woman (137).

While Morrison delights, then, in black male "juice," she also recognizes that the black women who try to contain its spillage can often become squeezed dry. They project their contractions onto the children, and the cycle continues as the boys resist and the girls repress. The females at Jimmy's funeral shroud Cholly in a cocoon of solicitude. Although no one talks to him, treating him "like the child he was, never engaging him in serious conversation," they "anticipated wishes he never had" (140). The old women's "lullaby of grief" literally numbs Cholly, whose subconscious breaks free by transforming the feminine into the masculine and rejecting a sad God for a strong devil: "In his sleep the foul odor of an old woman's stools turned into the healthy smell of horse shit, and the voices of the three women were muted into the pleasant notes of a mouth organ." Even his soft penis changes into "a long hickory stick," caressed by the hands of a conjure woman (139). Of all the women in his life, only M'Dear, the midwife who enables birth but lives outside the traditional community of women, touches Cholly's manhood lovingly.

Rape by the white hunters complicates even further his adolescent confusion about his sexuality, masculinity, and identity. Consequently, thirteen-year-old Cholly steps down off the restrictive security of the porch and seeks his father to find himself. Morrison depicts running away from home for a Georgia black boy as presenting few difficulties. Hungering to fill his senses, Cholly is happier on the road to Macon than he ever remembers being, except eating watermelon with Blue. His "dry-mouthed apprehension upon meeting his father" giving way to the "saliva flow of excitement," the boy inhales a "rife and stimulating man smell" coming off the crowd gathered at the back of the pool hall "for and about dice and money." This becomes a crucial moment in Cholly's self-development. Like Hurston's young Janey, he cannot remember "what his own self looked like," and he has idealized his unknown father as a devil/god. Searching in the crowd for the man who represents a larger image of himself, he sees cold, pleading, flat, or fearful eyes focused only on the dice. Locating the eyes of his father affords both relief at the end of a long journey and shock at realizing that at fourteen he is taller than his god and that his god worships playing for money. Samson Fuller's bald spot inspires a short-lived affection as the man turns a "hard, belligerent face" to the boy and defensively assumes that a woman has sent him to collect child-support payment. Afraid of his father's eyes, unable to recall his mother's name, Cholly appears to an impatient Samson like Cholly's mother did to Jimmy: "Something wrong with your head?" Samson's ensuing outburst, "Tell that bitch she get her money. Now, get the fuck outta my face!" stops cold any confused attempt on Cholly's part to state his name, much less identify his need for his father's recognition (154–56).

Repressive adult ideas about money, sexuality, and power take their toll on a boy's burgeoning manhood. Rejection by his father leaving him literally unable to walk, concentrating every muscle on trying not to cry, Cholly soils his pants like the infant he has been reduced to. He lies curled in a fetal position, his world a hollow of silence, finally releasing his tears when he remembers his Aunt Jimmy. Cut off from the fraternity of men, Cholly responds to the women leaning out of windows who see "the long clean neck of a new young boy and call to him." They "give him back his manhood, which he takes aimlessly" (158–59). Morrison gives ironic baptism to what she calls a "dangerously free man," the virile male cut off from the black community whose eclectic life can be interpreted only by a blues player. Only the musician would know how to connect the notes of joy, anger, pain, and love that are Cholly's life and give them that "final and pervading ache of freedom." Cholly is "free to live his fantasies, and free even to die, the how and the when of which held no interest for him" (159). Abandoned by his mother, renounced by his father, he has nothing left to lose and becomes absorbed by the juices of his perceptions and appetites.

This strong black devil comes to Pauline with yellow eyes, flared nostrils, and his own music, awakening in her a joy that makes him desire to nest with her. "Strutting right out of a Kentucky sun on the hottest day of the year," his godlike state satisfies her yearning for a savior, and the two go up north to make a world of laughter until they, too, succumb to the white gaze and turn love into longing (114). Morrison generally refuses to demonize any character, focusing the narrative gaze on the forces that distort them. However, she does hold black women's adaptations of middle-class white values responsible for much of the tension in African American male-female relationships (14). She does not call Cholly's father Samson without some thought about who cuts his hair. A one-note marriage to Pauline does for Cholly what the white men's flashlight on his behind does not do: its "sheer weight of sameness" freezes his imagination and drives him to despair. To be "required to sleep with the same woman forever was a curious and unnatural idea to him," and he wonders at the "arrogance of the female" (160).

His curiosity pressed out of him by the constancy in his marriage, nothing interests Cholly: not other people, not even his own self. Drink alone provides respite and oblivion. Blows from his wife, however, periodically rouse him from his stupor. Unlike M'Dear, the outlaw woman who caresses his manhood, a passive Pauline, brainwashed by Western notions of beauty and romance, tries to cut it off. Her dependency on him becomes as destructive as Aunt Jimmy's dismissal of his parents. Morrison certainly holds Pauline as accountable as Cholly for the disintegration of their family. Losing her front tooth to the candy she craves from the big screen reflects Pauline's capitulation of self to the white gaze. Afterward, she settles down "to just being ugly," and her "meanness [gets] worse." Cholly pokes fun at her, she tries to kill him, and fights constitute their sole mode of communication. In one of her increasingly infrequent reveries, she acknowledges: "[Cholly] begin to make me madder than anything I knowed, and I couldn't keep my hands off him" (123).

Cholly's binges and orneriness provide both Pauline and him with "the material they needed to make their lives tolerable." Each drunken escapade concludes in a ritual of violence that gives substance to tiny, undistinguished days. These "violent breaks in routine that were themselves routine" allow Pauline to "display the style and imagination of what she believed to be her own true self. To deprive her of these fights was to deprive her of all the zest and reasonableness of life" (41–42). Cholly becomes a scapegoat for vengeance and betrayal as she forces "him to indulge in the weaknesses she despised." Like Aunt Jimmy before her, she holds her children's father up to them as a model of sin and failure (126–27).

The unrelieved desecration of their marriage is rendered even more terrible by Pauline's occasional memory of the rainbow it once was, the spontaneous comradeship they offered each other. Then, sex compares to june-bug green, berry purple, and lemonade yellow; orgasm suggests "laughing between [the] legs" and the power she feels when her husband "has let go of all he has, and give[s] it to [her]" and she becomes "strong enough, pretty enough, and young enough to let him make [her] come." Sleep includes Cholly's leg "throwed over [hers]" so that she "can't move and don't want to" (131). Pared from "lust and simple caring for," Pauline's girlhood dreams about beauty and romantic love are reduced to fanatical judgments about other people's shortcomings. The narrowing of her self occurs in direct proportion to the transformation of Cholly's beautiful yellow, sun-drenched eyes into mean red ones (122). Morrison clearly separates Cholly's ugliness from that of Pauline. While his wife handles hers as a prop to support her self-perceived role as martyr, Cholly's form manifests itself in abusive behavior; hating weaker people like Pauline, and previously Darlene, he can leave himself intact.

His children stupefy Cholly even more than his wife does. Parentless himself, without training or experience in child-rearing, he has no frame of reference in which to comprehend a parent-child relationship. In Cholly's case, Morrison rejects as even possible two typical, though questionable, Western male positions assigned to children—material heirs or vicarious trophies. She also rejects the feasibility of a positive relationship between Cholly and child: "Had he not been alone in the world since he was thirteen, knowing only a dying old woman who felt responsible for him, but whose age, sex, and interests were so remote from his own, [Cholly] might have felt a stable connection between himself and the children" (160–61). Without any such support, he simply reacts to his offspring as impulse dictates.

With his childhood as background, Morrison foregrounds Cholly's rape of his child. Unlike Mr. Henry's "picking" at Frieda, restrained both in degree and by its comic tone, the writer uses all her feminine power to create a scene charged with poetry and pain. Morrison herself finds interesting that, "where I thought I would have the most difficulty subverting the language to a feminine mode, I had the least: connecting Cholly's 'rape' by the whitemen to his own of his daughter. This most masculine act of aggression becomes feminized in my language, 'passive,' and, I think, more accurately repellent when deprived of the male 'glamour of shame' rape is (or once was) routinely given" (215).

Staggering into the female sphere of the kitchen, Cholly is so drunk that he can barely make out Pecola humped over a sink of dirty dishes, much less sort out the jumble of feelings her small back arouses in him. Morrison elucidates the sequence of his emotions as "revulsion, guilt, pity, then love" and goes on to explain the source of each feeling as dim images elicit striking reactions in Cholly's psyche. Reduced to the elemental: "What could a burned-out black man say to the hunched back of his eleven-year-old daughter? . . . What of his knowledge of the world and of life could be useful to her? What could his heavy arms and befuddled brain accomplish that would earn him his own respect, that would in turn allow him to accept her love?" Impotence and guilt rise "in a bilious duet." Pecola's haunted eyes irritate him; her trust moves him to fury. Then the "timid, tucked-in look" of her toe scratching the back of her calf reminds him of a young Pauline, and a protective tenderness floods with sexual excitement as Cholly reels from one stimulus to another, responding on all fours like an animal. The "border of politeness" surrounding his lust renders it even more terrifying. He wants "to fuck her—tenderly" (161–63).

The horror of the scene climaxes as pent-up male power launches against the delicacy of the child. Cholly can no longer contain the "shit that weighs [him] down" (*Song of Solomon* 179). His soul "seemed to slip down to his guts and fly out into her, and the gigantic thrust he made into her then provoked the only sound she made—a hollow suck of air in the back of her throat. Like the rapid loss of air from a circus balloon." As he finally connects with Pecola in the only way he knows how, one which denies her very consciousness, he finds it painful to remove himself from her. The sight of her sad, limp grayish panties once again fuses hostility with affection; Cholly's "hatred would not let him pick her up, the tenderness forced him to cover her" (163).

Even more damaging to Pecola's psyche, however, is the association of the pain between her legs with the "face of her mother looming over her" (163). Unlike Frieda, Pecola finds support from neither father, mother, nor sister. Pauline has already knocked her daughter down repeatedly, physically and psychologically, a habit that crescendos when Pecola accidentally spills their housekeeper's hot berry cobbler onto the Fishers' kitchen floor. In a strikingly symbolic and painful scene, the mother violently rejects her child to affirm the baby-doll white girl. We learn from Pecola's mad ramblings at the end of the book that her mother does not accept her story about her father's attack, never again, in fact, speaks to or looks at the daughter she describes from birth as ugly, and that an increasingly desensitized Cholly rapes Pecola again while she sits reading on the ripped sofa, the seat of so many of his humiliations.

Morrison allows readers to blame Cholly at the same time her narrator forgives him. A grown-up Claudia contends that love is "never any better than the lover." Pauline's love is passive and possessive. Thus, while Sammy and Cholly corporeally flee the community, Pauline, still performing the white man's housework, disappears from memory. It becomes Cholly's love that prevails on the last page. Though he dies in the workhouse, Cholly is "the one who loved [Pecola] enough to touch her, envelope her, give something of himself to her." However, his touch turns "fatal, and the something he gave her filled the matrix of her agony with death." Because it contains "no gift for the beloved," the love of a dangerously free man "is never safe." The lover alone "possesses his gift of love," and the loved one remains "frozen in the glare of the lover's inward eye" (206). As Paul D concludes about Sethe's love for Beloved, Cholly's fertilizer is simply "too thick" for the thin American soil already hostile to common flowers like Pecola (*Beloved* 164).

Morrison creates one other leading man in *The Bluest Eye* whose connection with Pecola turns toxic to her because the blue-eyed gaze has poisoned him. Following hard upon Cholly's chapter, Soaphead Church's artistic abuse complicates our outrage at her father's mistreatment of Pecola. While Cholly's lower-class raising is too bleak, Soaphead's "upper-class" rearing is too lush. According to Claudia, black children distinguish between the deprivation of winter and the luxuriance of spring only by "a change in whipping style." The "nervous meanness" in the sharp sting of new green switches makes children long for a dull winter pain, for the "steady stroke of a strap" or the "firm but honest slap of a hairbrush" (97). Cholly's touch and Soaphead's "salvation" differ as ignorant but well-intended brutality and cruel but creative sadomasochism.

Middle-class Louis Junior, stocked with Cholly's vitality but grafted onto Soaphead's sterility, provides a youthful bridge figure between the two men. As Cholly's distortions entwine with the bent love of black women, the portrait of a strong but subdued sugar-brown girl precedes Junior's perversions. Geraldine embodies one of the tall, thin girls from small southern towns who establish "quiet, black neighborhoods where everybody is gainfully employed." Unlike her flamboyant Flip Wilson namesake, this Geraldine is never fretful or shrill but moves through the streets without a stir, anchored by the firmness of her middle-class convictions. She does not drink, smoke, or swear, still refers to sex as "nookey," and sings a clear second soprano from the second row in the choir, though she is never selected to solo. In short, the sugar-brown girl is as "sweet and plain as buttercake" (82).

Learning at a land-grant college to perform the white man's work with refinement, this girl finishes there the lessons begun in muted houses with potted plants and cultivated lawns: how to eliminate the dreadful black funkiness of passion and nature. Never known to have boyfriends, she always marries, mating with "certain men" who surreptitiously notice her domestic skill and seek from their wives the pleasant security of their mothers. Children will sense that they cannot come into her yard to retrieve a ball, but her husband remains unaware that this plain brown wren has invaded his castle and made it her home. Comically inverting the clever, individualistic attitude of Flip Wilson's survivalist, Morrison describes her Geraldine: she "will build her nest stick by stick, make it her own inviolable world, and stand guard over its every plant, weed, and doily, even against [her husband]" (83–84). Unlike Flip's unembarrassed, transvestite "natural woman," fiercely faithful to her Killer, androgynous Geraldine, absurdly self-contained, gives her body partially and sparingly to shadowy Louis Senior ("What the Black Woman Thinks" 63). Because she recoils from intimacy with another person, her favorite creature becomes her sleek, black, blue-eyed cat.[9] As clean and quiet as she, reflecting her order, precision, and constancy, he purrs warmly in her lap, eliciting from her erotic, masturbatory sensations. The cat represents her cross-dressed alter ego: imitation vanilla, feminine Geraldine's bittersweet chocolate, masculine Geraldine.

Although her hips indicate, rightly, that she will bear children easily and painlessly, repressed Geraldine responds no more naturally to children than generously with men. She cannot be a loving mother because she is obsessed with suppressing irrepressible Geraldine. For propriety's sake, however, she does have one child. A son. Junior. A wonderful mother from the perspective of the home economics department, Geraldine does not allow her baby to cry. She satiates immediately Junior's every physical need but can offer him nothing of herself or allow him his self; thus, he desires only to dominate both. Junior soon discovers that his mother's affection is bound up in the black cat. He reacts by becoming angry at her all-consuming subjugation of all their selves, redirecting his hatred of her toward her cat, and spending "some happy moments watching it suffer" (86). Morrison depicts the quietly seething life of Geraldine, Louis, and Junior in the saccharine-sweet language of the Dick-and-Jane primer and effects a darkly humorous indictment of black families who attempt to replicate restrained, middle-class white ones to their own detriment.

It is not the black cat that brings bad luck to Geraldine's family but her twisted reactions to both.

Geraldine extends the conundrum of her repressed sexuality and racial self-hatred into child-rearing. Building her Ohio nest next to the comically named Washington Irving School, this conscientious, stay-at-home wren ensures that Junior reads only white, male classics and watches like a hawk for any lapse of his training on the playground. Junior manifests the energetic yet isolated boy's desperation for a gang, but his mother's prejudices thwart his attempts to make friends. Separating prospective candidates into white kids, niggers, and colored people, Geraldine defines niggers as dirty and loud and colored people as neat and quiet. Grooming him carefully as the latter, she will allow him to play only with white kids. Junior, however, longs to roll in the dirt with the black boys: "He wanted to feel their hardness pressing on him, smell their wild blackness, and say 'Fuck you' with that lovely casualness." Gradually he succumbs to his mother's insistence that these nasty boys are not good enough for him, makes do with passive white "geeks," and begins to enjoy bullying girls, with the exception of the "nigger girls" who travel in packs and retaliate quickly. In effect, while insubstantial Louis Senior "just kept on reading the Lorain *Journal*," Geraldine methodically educates her son to abuse females like herself (87–88).

Unlike the masculine war dance of the "nigger boys" surrounding Pecola, overt brutality that threatens her physically, Junior's tactics are covert, ingenious, and psychologically deadly—in short, middle-class "feminine." Alternately "bored and frightened" at home, he is delighted to find on his playground territory segregated prey in the form of an "ugly" Pecola. One alienated child who already manifests the cunning of the beta predator entices another lonely child into his den under the guise of showing her "real kittens." As Pecola tries to absorb the astonishing array of Geraldine's pretty house furnishings, especially the gaily decorated portrait of Jesus, Junior throws her blackness in the form of a "big black cat," claws unsheathed, right into her face. Entertained by his cruelty, he becomes enraged when Pecola, like his mother, strokes the cat more than she does him. He snatches it from her and swings it wildly in circles by its hind leg. When a screaming Pecola tries to intervene, he accidentally releases it full force against the window pane (89).

The real damage occurs, however, when Geraldine enters to survey the scene and Junior, pointing to Pecola, says, "She killed our cat." Devastated by the abuse of her secret self, overwhelmed by memories of needy black children, Geraldine's mild "Who is this girl?" becomes a savage "You nasty little black bitch. Get out of my house." Morrison shows the swath of destruction cut as black people cope with the white desecration of their selves by crushing the next black self down on the pecking order. Geraldine picks up the limp form of her cat, "its blue eyes closed, leaving only an empty, black, and helpless face," and rubs her face in its soft fur. Then she turns her gaze to Pecola. She sees what she has incorporated all her life: the great, uncomprehending eyes of poor little black boys and girls that "questioned nothing and asked everything." In an accurate and unforgettable ode to black children who endure unforgivable neglect, the narrator champions their irrepressible vitality. Helplessly unable to feed all these crying babies, their mothers cope with frustrated guilt by telling them to "Shet up!" Geraldine, having sacrificed her entire being not to be them, ejects them all from her nest. Morrison does not so much blame as hold the mirror up to mothers like Geraldine who deny their best selves and their children and, under the sad but unsurprised eyes of Jesus, enable Junior to torture Pecola (91–92).

If Cholly represents the poor but dangerously free black man, Junior is the male whose natural black self becomes enslaved to unnatural, middle-class white values. Morrison's black male "aristocrat," then, appears as an old West Indian named Elihue Micah Whitcomb, renamed Soaphead Church by the Lorain women for his primitive but dainty fanaticism. While Junior's distortions result from his relationship with a conflicted black mother, Elihue's perversions derive from a sadistic biracial father. In portraying Junior, Morrison spends more time on Geraldine than on Junior, showcasing matriarchal control of and responsibility for the son's behavior. Elihue is certainly a by-product of upper-class—therefore patriarchal—training, but as an adult he also remains accountable for his own actions. Thus, he takes center stage in his savagely inverted fairy tale.

In what may be her most brutal response to Western cultural attacks on black men, Morrison presents Soaphead as a parody of T. S. Eliot's privileged, sterile, white male intellectual. Associating the self-loathing of the manipulative, middle-class bully with neutered Junior's hatred of his mother's unnamed but pampered black cat, Morrison connects the effete Soaphead's disgust with himself to his aversion for an exhausted, mangy old mongrel called Bob. The mutt's eyes run with a "sea-green matter around which gnats and flies clustered," indicating, like the peeling green paint of the MacTeer house, an encroaching disorder (171). Identified ironically as "what one might call a very clean old man," Soaphead cannot stand the sight of the repulsive but frail and harmless Bob, who sleeps most of his days in front of the entrance to the old man's apartment (167). Morrison engages in some delightfully irreverent wordplay here with the terms "dirty old man," meaning pervert, and "dirty dog," suggesting both a sexually potent male and a sexually provocative dance. Physically and emotionally unable to perform the life-affirming dirty dog, Soaphead is reduced to a sick, debased dirty old man. Like Junior, he projects his self-disgust onto his nemesis. Discriminating, decaying, biracial Elihue is a literally tidy but figuratively very dirty old man who yearns to poison the ostensibly dirty but genuinely inoffensive, and unpedigreed, dog.

Despite his travel and education, Elihue reveals no instinct for self-awareness. The town women, however, discover his anal-retentive impotence shortly after his arrival. Unable to comprehend his fastidious rejection of them but impressed with the way he speaks English, they decide that he is "supernatural rather than unnatural" and call him Soaphead Church. Morrison defines *soaphead* as the "tight, curly hair that took on and held a sheen and wave when pomaded with soap lather. A sort of primitive process" (167). Soaphead quickly sizes up and capitalizes on his nickname by becoming an interpreter of dreams. Such actions testify to his affinity with language and his parasitic resourcefulness yet complete uselessness. Instead of creating original word pictures like the people's delightfully concrete "Soaphead," Elihue's fine education teaches him to adopt abstract labels for himself like "misanthrope" and to rationalize that naming an evil will neutralize if not annihilate it. The old man obsesses with odd, worn things because "the slightest contact with people produced in him a faint but persistent nausea" (164). His appetite for the "residue of the human spirit smeared on inanimate objects," all of humanity he can withstand, leads him to "casual but habitual examination of trash barrels in alleys and wastebaskets in public places" (165–66). Unlike the instinctual, unschooled, yet realistically tolerant townspeople who realize that an evil must be allowed to run its course, Soaphead takes comfort and courage from the knowledge of the ineffectual intellectual: language without purpose, the moral company of and consolation from critics met in books, the furtive pleasure drawn from sorting through other people's garbage, the false pride available when he suspends his revulsion long enough to help somebody out.

Soaphead inherits his preference for words and things over human beings from a family "proud of its academic accomplishments and its mixed blood—in fact, they believed the former was based on the latter." His lightly browned skin and cinnamon eyes are bequeathed to him from Sir Whitcomb, described as "some decaying British nobleman, who chose to disintegrate under a sun more easeful than England's." Morrison aims both linguistic barrels at dicty blacks whose pride derives from miscegenation with whites. Dubbed a gentleman by order of the king, Sir Whitcomb provides the mother of his "mulatto bastard" with a civilized three hundred pounds sterling, for which mother and son feel immensely grateful. The bastard regards "lightening up the family complexion and thinning out the family features" as his life's purpose and marries a "good Victorian parody" of similar parentage who will enable him to pass his Anglophilia—that is, racial self-hatred—onto his children (167).

With the brittle confidence born of racial superiority, these children perform well in situations, like school, that require industry, order, ambition, and conformity to (white) authority. Approving schoolmasters reward them for good behavior. The boys are recommended for study abroad, enter such socially acceptable professions as medicine, law, and theology, and "[emerge] repeatedly in the powerless government offices available to the native population." Taking what solace they can from petty corruption in their public and private lives, the male Whitcombs imitate the lascivious behaviors of the "nobles" and, to protect their whiteness, intermarry. With their usual astuteness, they blame their inclination toward eccentricity—the appearance, for example, of "one or two old maids or gardener boys"—on the outcome of such ill-advised unions, not, as Morrison dryly concludes, on "the original genes of the decaying lord" (168).

Among such aberrations exists a religious fanatic who founds a cult and begets four sons. One becomes a schoolmaster "known for the precision of his justice and the control in his violence." The schoolmaster mates with a "sweet, indolent Chinese girl," who dies from the fatigue of giving birth to Elihue Micah Whitcomb. If Geraldine's manipulation via satiation of an energetic child creates a bully, the disciplined violence Elihue's father exerts on a frail one effects a flagellant. Elihue responds to his father's theories about "education, discipline, and the good life" with "hard habits and a soft imagination. A hatred of, and fascination with, any hint of disorder or decay." He reads widely but understands selectively, "choosing the bits and pieces of other men's ideas that supported whatever predilection he had at the moment" and perfecting the fine art of self-deception. Thus, he recalls Hamlet's abuse of Ophelia and his "frivolous politics" but not Christ's love of Mary Magdalene and his "serious anarchy." Acknowledging only the narrowest interpretation of the best minds in Western culture, vastly preferring Dante to Dostoyevsky, he finds his Beatrice in the person of "lovely, laughing big-legged" Velma, a clerk in a Chinese department store whose good nature and zest for life do not eliminate the sickly Elihue from it (169).

While middle-class Geraldine spends all her vigor quietly coercing her son into submitting to the blue-eyed gaze, Elihue, as Morrison's black male aristocrat, exerts all his energy scourging his own desire for Western-style physical beauty and material things. Whether it attracts or repels, the magnetic force remains white. Trained for no useful vocation, Elihue learns to love small, useless things. He so represses aesthetic gratification that his natural asceticism becomes a craving for solitude, celibacy a "haven, silence a shield" (165). Frail himself, he elevates robust health to celestial status, beyond the reach of human touch. Velma's vitality is yang to the yin of Elihue's melancholy.[10] Moved by his daintiness and lack of humor, she longs to teach him about delight. However, when she discovers two months into their marriage that he is more interested in "altering her joy to a more academic gloom," that he "equate[s] lovemaking with communion and the Holy Grail," she makes like one of Morrison's feisty male specimens and leaves (170).

His wife's refusal to spend her life in "the soundless cave of Elihue's mind," regarded by him as desertion, becomes the defining event in Elihue's life. Velma was to have been the answer to the unacknowledged question he had learned "on the flat side of his father's belt": "Where was the life to counter the encroaching nonlife?" (170). Saved from virtual collapse at her loss by the "steady hand" of his father, young Elihue grows old trying to "find" himself, to locate an ego that can only be forged. Sterile intellectualism merging with flower-child self-indulgence, he wanders from job to unsuitable job, a disdain for people drawing him to professions designed to serve them. Advised that he has no vocation for the ministry, incapable of withstanding the cold truths of psychiatry, drifting into sociology, then physical therapy, then desk clerk, insurance agent, salesman (only at black businesses), Elihue finally finds himself cut off from his father's allowance, unable to earn money, and, now in America, sinking into "rapidly fraying gentility" (171).

As with other Lorain community members whose lives collide with Pecola's, Soaphead's contribution to her destruction results from his reactions to white contempt. In this case, his primitive fanaticism turns lethal because of sexual and racial self-hatred. Although prissy Elihue would critique his nature as an "arabesque: intricate, symmetrical, balanced, and tightly constructed," the townspeople would simply call Soaphead uptight. In either case, he can alleviate tension only by succumbing to rare but keen sexual cravings. Morrison comically ticks off the outlets unavailable to a homosexual who lacks the courage to practice: bestiality (doesn't occur to him); sodomy (can't sustain or stand erections); bisexuality (abhors physical contact). Disquieted by the natural excretions of the human body, he settles his attentions on those bodies least offensive to him: children's. Also, since he views his intentions as anything but lewd, his sexuality the innocent "greentime, noontime of the archipelago," and since he is too shy to confront homosexuality (not to mention that unruly little boys might hurt or insult him), he patronizes the generally more manageable, and clean, little girls.

Morrison is less interested in detailing the attacks on Pecola than in analyzing their causes and effects. Attempting to cope with American culture, Elihue Whitcomb's African American character rationalizes sexually preying on children with the finesse of an Enlightenment intellectual; Soaphead Church seizes the opportunity for perverse redemption by playing an Old Testament God whose "business is dread." The child remains caught in the crossfire. With child by her father, Pecola appears on the doorstep of the "true Spiritualist and Psychic Reader," who silently holds out his card as he inquires about her business. Quite the opposite of the skillful counselor who promises no miracles but attempts to guide confused clients through the difficulties of self-analysis, Soaphead offers immediate gratification to the angry, lonely, defeated, miserable, or hungry but simple souls who stand before him, alone, in various states of dread. The sophisticated gentleman of intellect makes his living by milking the anxieties of ignorant black people. His practice is to do what people ask—to advise dread—not to suggest that the request might be "unfair, mean, or hopeless." Then, blaming an abstract, impersonal Originator of Life for all life's imperfections, he regrets that God did not seek his counsel and manifests the perfect psychosis to grant Pecola's request for blue eyes (172–73).

In the logic of the mad humanist, Pecola's appearance represents a miracle of sorts. Converted into Soaphead's instrument of destruction, she eliminates the need for rage or blinding revulsion to spur his own action. The task he assigns her to prove herself worthy of the blue-eyed gaze requires her to give Bob the poison Soaphead lacks the courage to employ and the decency to tell her she uses. Instead, like a good Transcendentalist, he presents Bob as the possibility of contact with God through nature. The dog's choked convulsions, as his body reacts to the poison, serve as a sign of God's promise to the horrified twelve-year-old and proof of the old man's power. As Soaphead's nemesis, Bob becomes the "simple creature" through which a perverse God speaks (175). Morrison's brutally poignant description of the little girl gently stroking the decrepit dog's head before feeding him the poisoned meat makes clear that the spiritualist's "gift" to the pregnant child provides, with the certainty that she has taken yet another life, a share in the giver's madness. While she typically defends folk traditions and superstitions vigorously against Western scientific rationalism and celebrates individuals who possess inner sight, Morrison creates Soaphead Church to illustrate the depravity of a person who manipulates such a gift for profit or personal power. He reduces himself and his insight to that which sophisticated intellectuals generally label it: cynical con-artistry.

Soaphead seeks the power surge of godhead when he agrees to be the instrument through which Pecola might receive the blue eyes of the white god they both worship. His emotions toward the "unattractive" black child replicate Cholly's: love and understanding quickly replaced by rage because he has no power to help her. If Cholly's ignorance and sexuality lead him to express love in the only way that he can envision, Soaphead's self-deception and sexuality cause him to con himself into believing that he commits an act of love when he actually attempts from a safe distance to cultivate illusions of power (173–74).

Tongue fondling the worn gold inlay encapsulating his coveted class snobbery, Soaphead sits down at his writing table after Pecola flees the yard. Exultant that intellect has triumphed over mortality, he takes a bottle of ink from the same shelf that contained his poison and, "relishing his penmanship," writes a poison-pen letter justifying the ways of man to God. He painstakingly identifies himself as one of the colonized living "greenly and youngish" on the greater of the two Antilles. He offers an accurate assessment of the self-destruction that black people have wrought upon themselves by emulating the worst of white cultural traits and retaining those of their own that are "most gratifying to sustain and least trouble to maintain." Soaphead's letter becomes his grotesque demonstration of penmanship as mightier than the sword. "Consequently we were not royal but snobbish," he writes, "not aristocratic but class-conscious; we believed authority was cruelty to our inferiors, and education was being at school" (176–77). However, while Soaphead's eloquent and elevated language rings dramatically of truth, he, as usual, accepts no responsibility for his blind arrogance, assumes no humility for his stupidity, and blames all his actions on Velma's desertion and God's unforgivable design flaw—an imperfect universe.

With breathtakingly fluid sophistry, Soaphead connects Velma to empty hotel rooms, to the aggressive breasts of little girls commanding him to touch them, and to proselytizing, lying, and extorting money, all the while asking God why and how he could allow it to happen: "How is it I could lift my eyes from the contemplation of Your Body and fall deeply into the contemplation of theirs?" At one point he even depicts God as a fellow pedophile, who colludes with and vicariously participates in the enjoyment Soaphead's hands and mouth steal from "salt-sweet" breasts. Assuring God that he never for a moment loved the lies or the money, and at least never entered the church, Soaphead argues that the breasts were "not just an easy luxurious human vice; they were, for [him], A Thing To Do Instead. Instead of Papa, instead of the Cloth, instead of Velma, and [he] *chose* not to do without them" (179).

Morrison includes in her depiction of Soaphead's insanity certain qualities characteristic of literary madmen. His letter to God juxtaposes fantastic delusions of grandeur and an inverted perception of reality ("it is because I weep for You that I had to do your work for You") with bursts of brilliant if bizarre insight: "I needed a comfortable evil to prevent my knowing what I could not bear to know" (180). She also individualizes his brand of lunacy with a chuckle at what Hurston calls the "niggerati." It may well be madness for African Americans to adopt the Western intellectual models that have so often been used against them, especially by the literati. Even in his ravings, Soaphead illuminates the power connections between creation and language, light and word, being and naming. He revels in the knowledge that Pecola came to *him* for help, derides God for being afraid to reveal his name, but can recall only the derivations of his own white lineage, not those of the name given him by the black community. Upbraiding God for abandoning his creations and leaving his lackey to take up the slack, Elihue Micah Whitcomb writes bitterly that the last person to hear from God was Job (who, of course, also complained constantly). The biblical Elihue became one of Job's confidants, a man who defended the status quo in the platitudes of his day and, in essence, dumped Job's problems onto Job. Suggesting a similar conservatism and facility for blaming the victim, the patrilineal name of Morrison's Elihue is certainly "the real thing . . . the person only what his name says" (180). Fancying himself a reformer and coveting a place as the king's adviser and the title of prophet, Morrison's Elihue adds Micah to his comic triple play on names.[11] Her joke tags Elihue in that, unlike the rest of the Old Testament prophets who were aristocrats, Micah was a commoner.

Morrison also distinguishes Soaphead's brand of madman's logic by contrasting the tactics of African American inversion with Western distortions of reality. To survive white oppression, the sanest of black Americans have resorted, frequently with humor and usually without damaging others, to turning bottoms into tops. Even those who lose their bearings, such as *Sula*'s Shadrack, generally behave in ways accepted by and tolerated within the boundaries of the black community. Using ritual to control fear and invert an intolerable reality, Shadrack's peasant's madness, unlike that of Soaphead, is strange but humorously harmless. Imitating aristocratic white models of competitive colonialism, Soaphead's method of coping becomes not merely defensive, nor funny, but offensively destructive to African Americans. The unentrenched West Indian essentially colonizes Pecola, rejecting her self by implanting blue eyes in the face of a black child.

Morrison thus attributes Soaphead's disintegration, and ultimately that of Pecola, to an inability to withstand the strain of white abuse. Trained by his father's "love" simultaneously to hate and please white authority, Elihue views the Father as white. By giving a black child a streak of cobalt blue right out of God's own heaven, he, like Prometheus, steals from the gods the fire of creation, presumably for the benefit of his kind. And, like Prometheus, he pays dearly for his misguided intentions, ending his days rummaging about in his cigar box full of insignificant nothings and his nights slipping into ivory, dreamless sleeps. Although Morrison portrays Soaphead Church as a horrible madman, she also allows us to understand that he, like Cholly, re-collects through Pecola the innocence in himself. Like her, he embodies the delicate, vulnerable sink of everyone else's garbage. While her madness keeps her fluttering her arms hopelessly in a futile effort to reach the blue void of freedom, Soaphead's transforms him into the Father of Darkness. Attempting to be the power that despises him, poisoned like old Bob by a black child's need for blue eyes, Soaphead cannot create, only destroy. His sole act of "creation" inflicts his madness onto Pecola. The terrible salvation handed down to Elihue Micah Whitcomb by his white ancestors sends her over the edge, not Cholly's brutal love. The buck stops, after all, with the original genes of the decaying lord.

In keeping with the black figures in the final version of the white primer, Morrison's novel concludes with its characters angling crazily, madly. The breakdown occurs when the Dick-and-Jane story, ostensibly intended simply to introduce codes embedded in the reading process, begins subliminally to instruct all children in the primacy of white cultural "norms." Morrison's response to this Western *primum mobile* familiarizes all adults with the codes of black culture and warns us about the destructiveness of certain white codes. *The Bluest Eye* thus becomes a book not in the least intended merely for adolescents. It is a novel written for adults and an African American primer calculated to educate people not only about the plight of black girls living in America but about that of black boys. The book-design artist who maintains the possibility of Pecola as androgynous is Morrison herself.

CHAPTER 3

An Elegy on Black Masculinity

The Beautiful Boys in *Sula*

Morrison dedicates her second book, praised for its celebration of girls' intimacy, to boys. She inscribes *Sula* (1973) to her young sons, whom she "miss[es] although they have not left [her]." Based on Sula's absence, Morrison's novel, like her dedication, illustrates that it is "sheer good fortune to miss somebody long before they leave you." *Sula* embraces inversion, doubling, opposites, and others, attributes which, together with community and a sense of humor, constitute the secrets of African American endurance captured in its opening "nigger joke." Despite the community's collective good humor, however, *Sula* also reveals that most African Americans are not ready to assign a man's freedom to a woman. Because "they were neither white nor male, [Sula and Nel] had set about creating something else to be" (52). Sula's attempts to remain that precariously free something go "too deep, too far" for her community (164). Even Nel finally rejects her friend, and therefore the other part of herself, challenging her alter ego: "You can't act like a man" (142). Only a man who leaves the Bottom Community stays uncaught.

Thus, the traditional black community cannot wholeheartedly endorse its free black male and does not yet miss its masculine female. Along with the inversions and conundrums essential to its survival and a credit to African American ingenuity, its taboos ultimately critique power and injustice in America. Clyde Franklin attributes the ambiguity shrouding contemporary black masculinity to "the legacy of a nondefinition of the Black male slave sex role, and continued reluctance to perceive the Black male as a man—at least in the hegemonic sense of the word" (276). Morrison concurs and reminds us to rethink how histories of tops and bottoms, ups and downs within American social structures become convoluted into the ironic hierarchies and differences in African American society. She also warns us to miss our beautiful black boys before they leave us, to consider any difficulties between black men and women in a cultural as well as racial and sexual context.

In *Sula*, Morrison turns intermittently from her study of a black female scapegoat to focus on the men. A description of dislocation, for example, follows hard upon the relief experienced by residents of the Bottom with Sula's death. The figure for Christmas-after-Sula is the "curled bodies of men who chose to sleep the day away rather than face the silence made by the absence of Lionel trains, drums, cry-baby dolls and rocking horses." Teenagers sneak into the local theater to let Tex Ritter "free them from the recollection of their fathers' shoes, yawning in impotence under the bed" (154). Such scenes encapsulate what sociologists Kimmel and Messner identify as a "blind spot" in American vision. We generally perceive the forces that oppress or marginalize us because these are "the ones . . . most painful in daily life." However, the mechanisms "that afford us privilege are very often invisible to us" (x). The African American community remains terribly aware of what amounts to a war against its males. A more empowered white American culture, on the other hand, may tend to blame its victims for their reactions. Although she joins her people in their deep concern about their boys and about the disintegration of black male and female relationships in the twentieth and twenty-first centuries, Morrison denies that the crux of the problem is gender: "Many of the problems modern couples have are caused not so much by conflicting gender roles as by other 'differences' the culture offers" (McKay 404).

Sula also anticipates Mary Pipher's popular psychological study of the cultural abuses that contemporary America inflicts on its adolescent girls. In *Reviving Ophelia*, Pipher remains convinced that we will revitalize our girls when we encourage women to reconnect with and preserve the androgynous wholeness of their childhood. To do this, they must address the men in their lives in order to accept the masculine in themselves. Sula's very name, connoting peace, bird, or sun, merges the dynamic energy of the son's fiery yang with the daughter's tranquil yin. Virginia Woolf imagines a space the size of a shilling in the back of one gender's collective head, which must be described by the opposite gender because it cannot be seen except by the other. Nonetheless, many of the writers in Woolf's white canonical tradition upstage men in favor of a central female character or backstage women to spotlight men. Morrison insists that her male characters share center stage with her females to perform the story of male-female relationships in the African American community.

Even minor male characters in *Sula* function as far more than mere cues for leading women. The novel opens with an elegiac lament for a community systematically pulled out by its roots. Immediately after comes the history of a "nigger joke," which turns things upside down and gives that community its name, the Bottom. Allusions to a faceless white "they" that tear down pear trees where children perch to yell their greetings to passersby segue into a concrete image. *Sula*'s first reference to an adult member of this eradicated black community is male: "feet in long tan shoes once point[ing] down from chair rungs" (3). The bottommost part of the body and directed downward, these stylish male feet become a synecdoche for the entire community, the segment left to speak up for the whole gone missing.

The "nigger joke," told wryly on themselves by these "feet" and by downtrodden black and discouraged white folks seeking "a little comfort somehow," portrays a good white farmer who promises his slave freedom and some fertile bottomland if the slave will complete certain tasks. After he does his chores, the slave receives his freedom. However, his master tricks him into choosing rocky hilltop instead of rich valley property because the slave master calls the hill land the "bottom of heaven—best land there is" (4–5). Relayed from the community's perspective, this joke represents Morrison's analogy for African American "signifyin(g)," a rhetorical self-defense that protects the integrity of the black self through a clever inversion of the context in which (white) society defines value. African American boys engage in signifying rituals from an early age as a kind of verbal jujitsu. Humorous like Shakespeare's fools, frequently prevented only by his wit from being insolent, the signifier is allowed license.

The boys draped gracefully over chairs in front of the Time and a Half Pool Hall begin their passage into manhood by mastering such rites in Morrison's Bottom Community. Instead of the slack, sullen-eyed loafers they frequently seem to the outside world, she presents them as alert creatures with panther eyes and creamy vanilla haunches, virile pool haunts of a "sinister beauty" (49). Those who remain framed and tamed by the community, their lust tempered to kindness as they move into elder-hood, take on names, powers, and duties as comrades to the women. These elders include Mr. Buckland Reed, who appears eight times in the novel as Eva's longtime friend, adviser, and retainer. He of the gold teeth and practical wife cautions Eva against "naming" the deweys but encourages her talent for dream and fortune-telling by taking her lottery numbers in to play. While he has little success in subduing Eva's godlike arrogance and merely stands aghast when Sula commits her grandmother to a home, the sturdy community elder escapes the final apocalypse when people go too deep, too far.

Hospital orderly Willy Field is another of the old guard faithful to Eva. Finding her blood staining his just-mopped floors, Willy saves her from bleeding to death by shouting for the nurses who have ignored the one-legged black woman in their fascination with Hannah's charred flesh. His good deed wins him Eva's curses. The Mr. half of Mr. and Mrs. Suggs joins his wife in taking Eva's children for the year and a half Eva is gone and in hoisting and throwing the tomato-filled water tub onto Hannah, a last-ditch effort to put out the flame-crazed woman. Reverend Deal provides rituals like Chicken Little's funeral ceremony as he leads the community women in venting long-suppressed pain, and Uncle Paul brings Hannah two bushels of Kentucky Wonders to can. Even male elders in the extended community offer support and nurturance to the women who need them. Mr. Henri Martin writes Helene about her grandmother's illness, conveying the dying woman's silent plea that her granddaughter make the trip to New Orleans. When Helene and Nel arrive at a black-wreathed house, he, alone inside with Cecile's body, opens the door and goes quietly about completing funeral arrangements.

Ignored or disdained outside the community, these elders acquire usefulness and dignity within its framework, apart from yet connected to the women. The Bottom is not powerful enough, however, to arrest the destructive influences of the outside white world on young black male development. Increasingly fewer of its beautiful boys remain or return to take their place as elders. Psychologist Michael Gurian echoes Morrison's observations about boys. Morrison comments that "men love the company of other men . . . [and] enjoy the barber shop and the pool room." Hence, relationships among men are "based on something quite different [from those of women]" (Stepto 387). Gurian defines this "something" to be often not "talk-dependent" but "proximity- and activity-dependent" (53). As such, male adolescents, specified by Gurian to range from approximately nine to twenty-one years of age, need a "nurturing system, male-driven, in which discipline, morality teaching, and emotional sustenance are provided *by* males, *for* males" (72). Morrison notes that black males relate to each other regardless of class, implying that such interaction does not always occur in white male culture (Stepto 388). She also observes that the "rhythm of [male] lives is outward, adventuresome" (McKay 399). Whether or not Bottom forces prevail upon them to stay, Nel's "beautiful boys in 1921" or any other time are probably biologically hardwired to venture out.

The community can provide a self-respecting place for its male children and elders, but its boys on the threshold of manhood need to "go on off the porch." The white male world that awaits it outside the Bottom, however, does little to nurture, sustain, or guide the masculinity of the "smooth vanilla crotches" spread invitingly wide on chairs in front of the pool hall. Those whose virility urges them outward all too frequently become the black soldiers with the "closed faces" and "locked eyes" who can offer Helene no compassion for her humiliation by the white conductor on the southbound train. Initially watchfully indifferent to her apologetic voice and eagerness to please, the soldiers' expressions become increasingly stricken with her every submissive "Sir." An insolent male redneck cows the elegantly attired Helene simply by calling her "gal" and ordering her to move her "butt." As he reduces the proud, class-conscious woman to a foolish street pup smile, the muscles in the soldiers' faces tighten, and Nel senses that they "were bubbling with a hatred for her mother that had not been there in the beginning but had been born with the dazzling smile" (22). The "po' white's" unchecked disrespect of a "dictie" black woman strips the furious soldiers of any claim to the white, upper-class knighthood they resent yet covet. Simultaneously pitying and shamed by her damsel-in-distress behavior, they make no effort to be gallant to Helene even after the conductor disappears. The "white m[a]n, period" uses a black woman to emasculate black men. White and black men reduce Helene from a thoroughbred to "de mule uh de world." The animosity between the African American woman and men in this situation arises not from gender conflicts but from complex issues of race and class.

While white female characters may not be present in *Sula*, Morrison creates, in addition to the conductor, a chorus of minor white male characters suggesting the range of treatment African American boys can expect to experience from white men outside the Bottom. With few exceptions, white males operate as plagues. These afflictions range from pests to predators to vultures to excess: from the manipulative white farmer of the "nigger joke," evolving into the more directly aggressive entrepreneurs who tear down a community to put up a golf course, to Mr. Hodges, owner of the funeral parlor who will bury anybody, including Sula, if a substantial enough death policy exists. There are variations on the redneck bully: the balding male nurse whose care for Shadrack in the army hospital consists of intimidation; the loafers with their "muddy eyes" and "tongues curling around toothpicks" standing like "wrecked Dorics" on train station platforms to prevent black female travelers from using the toilet (24); the Irish Catholic schoolboys who help to secure their immigrant parents' place in the new world, and entertain themselves, by harassing black schoolchildren.

There are ambitious, underoccupied lawmen. One peace officer arrests and beats a drunken Tar Baby because the white mayor's niece swerves her automobile to avoid hitting him only to sideswipe another car. Another example of absolute power corrupting absolutely, this constable then forces his charge to lie in his own excrement. Two other sheriffs and the bargeman who discovers Chicken Little's body become scourges on the community by virtue of neglect or distorted kindness. The sheriff who jails the shell-shocked Shadrack for drunkenness quickly recognizes his prisoner's mental trauma. He then assumes his position as a cog in the white-controlled machine that fails black veterans when he sends Shadrack home, untreated, amid the squash in a farmer's wagon. The sheriff who reluctantly receives Chicken Little's body suggests that the bargeman who delivers it throw it back in the river. Regretting his decision to involve himself because the body is that of a child, the bargeman complains all the while about niggers killing their young. Nonetheless, he complies with the sheriff's second suggestion to dump the small form in the burlap sack onto a ferryman who will take it to Meridian the next day. Last on the plague list are the patronizing missionaries who come with Christmas candy and castoffs to glean barely a nod from sullenly resentful natives.

Morrison presents, however, one slight exception to *Sula*'s cacophony of white male voices. Disdaining to pay respect to someone it believes has caused it so much pain, the Bottom refuses to participate in Sula's final disposition. When even Nel waits two days to report her friend's death to the hospital, then the mortuary, then the police, white men finally take responsibility for the dead pariah. Police question the community for hours to ascertain Sula's given name. White men silently remove, prepare, dress, and bury the body. With this codicil to her narrative on white engagement with the black community, Morrison both refuses to contribute to oversimplified race propaganda and underscores the moral ambiguity that rests at the core of the novel.

Set against this clashing chorus of black and white male voices, Morrison creates a number of more fully realized yet still secondary African American male characters. First, she explores how the absence of several men affects Nel and Sula's childhood. While the Wright and Peace households showcase the women, they are replete with men but noticeably lacking in husbands and fathers. Morrison represents the Wright line of women by the "disgust on the face of the dead [Cecile]," expressive, in other words, of a distorted physicality (28). The tiny, soft Rochelle works as a whore, primarily in reaction to her mother's Catholic repressions. Naturally, Helene reacts against her mother in turn and follows Cecile's stifled, class-conscious path, rearing her own daughter to "pull" her nose to make it pointed. None of the Wright women comfortably expresses affection, either to men or to children. Helene's reaction to both becomes manipulation and Nel's a "cumbersome bear-love" (138).

The sole man who participates in the lives of all three women, Wiley Wright, does so by default. Pressured by his Great-aunt Cecile and her granddaughter to turn his enchantment with Helene into a marriage proposal, the middle-aged ship's cook takes his young bride away from the Sundown House to put her "in a lovely house with a brick porch and real lace curtains at the window" (17). He worships his graceful wife, mostly from afar, and Helene remains quite content that he docks only three days out of sixteen. Wiley is, in fact, simply Helene's sometime "john." The niceties of marriage elevate both in community status; the wife's beauty, manner, bearing, or possessions protect neither from white male disrespect. Although Cecile attempts to extricate her granddaughter from the influences of the Sundown House, Helene continues to prevail upon her daughter to accept the view, reinforced by Wiley's absence, that wives trade sex for security.

Ironically, Helene's absent but unmissed husband gives the patronymic W(right) women their name. The matronymic Peace (piece) household derives its name from women who embrace maleness. Wiley Wright cleverly avoids becoming a sketch in small of the more fully realized Jude Greene, Nel's husband. Eva's boyish husband predicts the allure of Sula's lover for the opposite sex but not his respect for women. Gone like Wiley during most of his five-year marriage to Eva, when Boy Boy comes home, he does "whatever he could that he liked, and he liked womanizing best, drinking second, and abusing Eva third" (32). He leaves her not because of the woman's possessiveness, as Ajax does Sula, but because he futilely seeks white male approbation through the acquisition of "shine" (36). Another community female forced by hard times to postpone her pain, Eva has no idea what she should or will feel when Boy Boy returns for a visit. As he struts into her house, the picture of shine, but makes no reference to his children, she realizes that underneath his aura of leisure and new money lies "defeat in the stalk of his neck and the curious tight way he held his shoulders" (36). She diverts her pain into a pleasurably intense hatred of her husband, however, only when the raucous laughter of the woman waiting for him outside reminds her suddenly of big-city ruthlessness. Eva's children and grandchild become prey to the twisted love at the center of her life, created in large part by Boy Boy's absence.

These marriages illustrate the manifold scapegoats designed by African American men and women to cope with unsatisfying relationships, often caused by the defeats they suffer from white discrimination. Morrison places ultimate responsibility for many of the community's problems, however, on its emulation of Western cultural values about romantic love and acquisition, continuing to denounce concepts introduced in *The Bluest Eye* as the "white gaze" or "master narrative." Using her sexuality to gain position and possession, Helene welcomes the distance from her husband that Wiley's pedestal allows her but which damages her child. Defeated by his quest for shine, Boy Boy projects his frustrations onto his wife, who then converts her anger at him into fuel for a meanness that gives her life meaning but damages her children. Connections severed, the men roam, the women remain, and the children react. Only in Rekus and Hannah do we find the fleeting potential for a nurturing marriage. Similar to Hurston's playfully antiestablishment Tea Cake, Rekus is a "laughing man"; tellingly, like Tea Cake, he dies young. Comfortable with her sexuality like Hurston's independent Janie, Hannah has the generosity, self-reliance, and courage to see to her own physical needs. After Rekus's death, without the "slightest confusion about work and responsibilities," she makes love to a man and washes his wife's dishes in the same afternoon (41). Hannah considers male touch natural, not shameful, and not associated with money or necessarily with marriage. With the loss of her husband, however, she loses interest in "caring for" and settles for sex. While a number of Morrison's male characters do provide stability for the community, she maintains that self-possession differs from possessiveness. In fact, her novels suggest that one partner's desire to dominate the other destroys male-female harmony.

Because the Peace women welcome but do not try to captivate masculinity, their household stays full of beautiful boys. However, because Eva's love has been twisted by the need to sacrifice "[an arm and] a leg" so that everybody can survive, her love distorts those boys. The relatively few male characters delineated by Morrison as "ribs" to her females, combined with the idea that this Eve loves maleness though she lacks a leg, signifies on the concept of penis envy with delicious irreverence. A god among men, she collects and then renames them according to a private scheme of affection, whim, dark humor, and meanness. Originally called Ralph, Eva's last child and only son is, in accord with his color, the "Plum" of her eye. During the hungry first months after Boy Boy leaves, Plum takes his father's place in bed with Eva while the two girls sleep on the floor. The little boy absorbs so much of his mother's milk that he becomes physically unable to eliminate on his own, so, in a desperate attempt to unblock him, Eva shoves "the last bit of food she had in the world (besides three beets) up his ass." Afterward, she articulates her association of food and freedom with an oath grotesquely reminiscent of Scarlett O'Hara's radish epiphany just before intermission in the film version of *Gone with the Wind*. Miss Scarlett's melodramatic "I'll never be hungry again" becomes Eva's understated "Uh uh. Nooo" (34). Her saga resumes with Eva having mysteriously obtained the money to build her idiosyncratic Tara, so that Plum, to whom she hopes to bequeath everything, can float "in a constant swaddle of love and affection, until 1917 when he went to war" (45). After he returns a shadow of his sweet self and addicted to heroin, Eva dreams that he tries to climb back into her womb. Though she copes grimly for years with her own suffering, she cannot bear her boy's, and, godlike, she sacrifices him in a baptism of fire. Plum represents the son protected but prevented from maturing by the love of the powerful black matriarch.

Eva takes in several other males whom she also paradoxically saves and destroys. Giving a small room off the kitchen to a beautiful, fair-haired mountain boy who never eats and speaks only in a whisper, Eva insists that he is white and gleefully calls him Tar Baby. On the one hand, his name is wonderfully incongruous with Tar Baby's milky complexion; on the other, it becomes a ruthlessly penetrating application of the African American folk tale to signify on his silence and passive acceptance of abuse. Although his "blood" remains a matter of debate, the community welcomes his mournful tenor twang and tolerates without interference his single-minded intent to drink himself to death. Raised in the hills, Tar Baby has not been acculturated into the Bottom's signifying tactics of humor and subversion as antidotes to pain. Thus, its indifference to his self-destructive behavior results partly from the community's contempt for an individual who takes himself seriously enough to commit suicide. Eva accepts responsibility for the boy but does not give him the skills necessary for his survival.

However, she does provide three other strays with an innovative means of taking care of one another, though her technique stunts their growth, too. Displaying a folk wisdom that anticipates such psychological studies as Gurian's, Eva understands that, unlike girls who tend toward pairs, boys need extensive clans or "gangs" to identify with in order to realize individuality (70–71). Ignoring obvious differences in physical appearance, name, and age, she perceives from their wildness three boys' need for a system and, calling each one "Dewey," leaves them to form the decimals. Slowly, each child comes out of the cocoon he formed when somebody gave him away and ties his shoelaces to the laces of the others in the deweys' favorite game of chain gang. Although Morrison recognizes the limitations of communities, she also acknowledges the value of community to ensure human survival. In addition, she has some fun with the propaganda that (to many white people) all black people look alike and that all black men are headed for prison. Individually each Dewey is a lost boy; collectively, as the deweys or Lost Boys, they locate an identity together. Even their white teacher comes to be astonished at how much the deweys, who initially look nothing alike, become gradually indistinguishable.

While the dewey system and chain gang serve the group well by protecting its collective self, they simultaneously consume the individuality of Lost Boys and prevent their maturation. The Library of Congress eventually rejected the Dewey Decimal System because catalogers found it too limited. Chain gangs represent obvious constraints within an already restrictive prison culture. Gurian notes that the ideal clan requires adult male participation as individual role models for its boys. A mysterious god of three in one, the deweys form a gang that is "inseparable, loving nothing and no one but themselves" (38). With the absence of committed adult males to bond with or emulate, the deweys remain "Stouthearted, surly, and wholly unpredictable" children (39). Attaining an adult height of exactly forty-eight inches, they develop only the skill of nurturing one another by biting everybody else. They essentially stop growing except for "their magnificent teeth" (74).

Morrison creates one last minor male character who, though not a member of Eva's clan, has a significant influence on her granddaughter and, through Sula, on Eva. We meet Chicken Little just after Sula overhears Hannah declare she loves but does not like her child. Bewildered and hurt, Sula flees to find Nel. Together they deal with her pain by acting it out. Lying flat on the grass, foreheads almost touching, the two methodically attack tiny pieces of the life around them—grass, twigs, earth. Then they collapse their separate "depressions" together and throw all the "small defiling things" they can find into the hole, refilling it with soil and smoothing over the grave (58–59). The ritual does not completely pacify them, however, and a little boy dressed in oversize knickers wanders conveniently into range, picking his nose. Hannah's declaration has excited as well as wounded her daughter. Adrenaline pumping, Sula invites Chicken to view the world from a detached perch high in the branches of a tree. Excited in turn, the child descends safely, escorted by Sula, who then swings him wildly out over the river. Chicken Little can neither swim nor fly. He becomes merely "something newly missing" in the water (61).

Here Morrison rewrites another folktale to illustrate the destructive chain reaction set off by fear and hysteria and to emphasize the vulnerability of children as the excitement feeds on itself. Like his namesake, Chicken Little is gullible. While no sky falls on his head, water, the element associated throughout the novel with Sula, engulfs him. Christian believes that the "overflowing release of Sula's hurt emotions . . . results in her accidental drowning of Chicken Little" (59). Certainly her use of someone more vulnerable than she as a sink for her fear foreshadows her putting Eva away because the old woman frightens her. Like Eva, when Sula is afraid for her Other(s), she cuts off part of herself; when she fears for herself, she spills her "meanness" onto others. Chicken Little becomes, as does Pecola, "a total and complete victim" of the chain of abuse surrounding him (Stepto 384). He also becomes the means by which Sula is set dangerously free from any context, any community. Having killed, albeit accidentally, and not held responsible, Sula no longer fears death. Although the treatment of males by such characters as Sula and Eva provides fuel for critics who accuse Morrison of portraying castrating females, Morrison actually focuses more on the forces, inside and outside the African American community, that mutilate both women and men.

She does, however, create boys in *Sula* to illustrate how community influences male individuation, both positively and negatively. She also designs three representative masculine types into which many of these boys develop. The types are characteristic of but not necessarily restricted to the African American community, nor even to men.

Jude Greene represents the first type. His surname suggests money and symbolizes the white male power about which he is green with envy. True to his first name, twenty-year-old Jud[as]'s "craving to do the white man's work" betrays him; he, in turn, breaks faith with his wife and children (128). If Morrison associates the color yellow with sexuality and vitality, green indicates degrees of restraint: from the male nurse in the "apple green suit" who confines Shadrack; to the "green pitcher" containing the yellow lemonade Eva serves to Boy Boy upon his return visit; to Boy Boy's trophy woman in her "pea-green dress" leaning against the smallest pear tree as she waits for him outside; to the green silk ribbon that signals to Ajax Sula's newfound feelings of possession for him; to the shabby green coat Nel wears as she turns to leave Sula for the last time thinking how much her old friend has cost her. Because he has not "touched the borders of his own life," has not freed himself to create his own order, Jude remains easily threatened and has everything to prove (Stepto 385). Abundant signs betray his discomfort with his masculinity, his overdependence on the group, his lack of self-control. "Well-liked" by the community, he sings tenor in the Mount Zion's Men's Quartet; his job waiting tables at the Hotel Medallion is a "blessing" to his parents and siblings. Longing, however, to exchange high notes, thin-soled shoes, and "woman's work" for the physical demands and camaraderie of the road men, Jude wants to help build the New River Road, not travel it. When his hurt at having his labor rejected in favor of "thin-armed white boys" turns into shame and rage, he turns to marriage with a pliant and nurturing Nel as a means of proving his manhood. Marriage causes both Jude and Nel to deny their separate needs. Through Jude, Nel acquires vicarious pain; with Nel, Jude becomes "head of a household pinned to an unsatisfactory job out of necessity." To the detriment of her individuality as well as his, the "two of them together . . . make one Jude" (83).

While the narrator speculates about and Nel finally asks Sula why she has sex with Jude, the novel addresses only by implication the reasons Jude has sex with Sula. One answer is that, here, form follows function; the absence of an answer equals the answer. Along with Plum and Tar Baby, Morrison depicts Jude as one of the most passive male figures in *Sula*, and, true to form, he allows Sula to use him merely to fill up some space. A second answer is that, since he cannot usurp white male power, he will conquer the masculine black female. A third is that the masculine in Sula attracts his incomplete masculinity. When a whiny Jude looks to his wife for support about some petty insult done to him at work, Sula interrupts to instruct him in the defensive tactics of signifying, offering him not "milkwarm commiseration" but the self-mocking irony of another "nigger joke" (102–4). He then acknowledges to himself that Sula does not provide conventional feminine marriage material: she "stir[s] a man's mind maybe, but not his body" (104).

Jude is simply not whole enough to be a real partner for anyone. He has not integrated the feminine with the masculine part of himself and therefore stays a boy. Gurian describes four elements that represent the core of manhood and ten "integrities" taught to both boys and girls around the world as the foundations of adulthood.[1] Because he lacks several of these, Jude's self remains undeveloped or damaged. The white community prevents him from participating in healthy, life-sustaining enterprise. The black community does not provide him with psychological, emotional, or sexual integrity, so he turns to a woman for the kind of support and "developmental experience that extended families are supposed to give" (229–75). As Morrison comments, "a man like Jude, who was doing a rather routine, macho thing, would split" because difference or disapproval threatens him. Just the "requirements of staying in the house and having to apologize to his wife were too much for him" (Stepto 385).

If Morrison associates Jude with the order and containment of earth green, she connects Ajax with the chaos and freedom of sky blue. The last image we have of Sula as a girl presents a "slim figure in blue, gliding with just a hint of a strut, down the path toward the road" (85). When the woman returns to the Bottom, Ajax recognizes his affinity for her and picks two bottles of milk "off the porch of some white family." Framed by "a slick blue sky," he holds them up to her like a trophy through the blue glass of her front door. Ajax senses that Sula is one of two women he knows "whose life was her own, who could deal with life efficiently, and who was not interested in nailing him" (124–27). He toasts her androgyny by drinking the feminine milk and handing her the clean, masculine lines and aesthetic solidarity of the bottles. Anticipating his *Song of Solomon* successor, Milkman, Ajax respects the feminine. Like Kingfish of the *Amos and Andy* radio and television series, he embodies, depending on one's perspective, the outlaw or free man, the anarchist or victim. He is certainly, like Sula, the artist seeking his form.

Ajax incorporates the African American version of the Ulysses theme in literature, the figure of the male in motion, the traveling man looking not to acquire the pot of gold at the end of the rainbow but to find out what lies over the rainbow. Historically, African American men have had no land, held no dominion; agency involves moving. Like Sula, Ajax has limited ties with community. Like Sula, he is curious and fearless and adventuresome, and in the process of finding and knowing, he is also making himself. While Morrison admits that social critics describe this tendency to leave their homes and families to be a major failing of black men, she views it as "one of the most attractive features about black male life," part of their interesting magic (Stepto 392).

Morrison expresses Ajax's curiosity, sense of adventure, and need for freedom in his fascination with airplanes, the sky-blue form of transportation that supplanted trains as lovers in the black male psyche, captured in such stories as James Alan McPherson's "A Solo Song: For Doc." Even more than planes, however, Ajax's mother, an "evil conjure woman" enchants him. As such, he draws his artistic power from his feminine side. Unlike Sula, he likes the milk Morrison associates with women, and his kindness to females in general is a habit he acquires from dealing with a mother who inspires thoughtfulness and generosity in her sons. Because his feminine model is an articulate woman absorbed in the folk arts, whose absolute tolerance allows him the freedom to be himself, he becomes attracted to and curious about Sula's elusiveness and indifference to established habits of behavior. Because, other than his mother, "he had never met an interesting woman in his life," Ajax seeks in Sula the intellectual stimulation that disturbs Jude, and Sula, in turn, finds pleasure in "the fact that he talked to her" (127).

Traditional work "don't do nothing" for Ajax, who grows up admiring the creativity of the occult artist. His playful gifts to Sula, chosen for their aesthetic, not monetary, value, reflect her views about labor (142). Morrison notes that their history leads white women to call work an opportunity for "liberation." Forced to work, black women dub it "responsibility." Sula takes greater pleasure in Ajax bringing her blueberries, butterflies, and a whistling reed than a steady paycheck ("What the Black Woman Thinks" 64). Her "lawless" nature responds to this complex individual who reflects the "tremendous possibility for masculinity among black men" found frequently among musicians and artists, the unemployed and imprisoned for "going all the way within [their] own mind[s] and within whatever [their] outline[s] might be" (Stepto 386).

Contrary to Demetrakopoulos's statement that most men never really know a woman, Ajax understands more about women than Sula and Nel do about men (86). He recognizes that Nel searches for her own "misery" through Jude, and he listens to Sula more than he speaks. Unintimidated by her, he elicits the brilliance he expects from her. His "clear comfort at being in her presence, his lazy willingness to tell her all about fixes and the powers of plants, his refusal to baby or protect her, his assumption that she was both tough and wise—all of that coupled with a wide generosity of spirit only occasionally erupting into vengeance" allow him both connection to and separation from Sula's psyche (128). Because Ajax is "secure enough and free enough and bright enough," threats of emasculation by anyone disappear. Because he possesses a complete self, he treats Sula not as an extension of himself, a vessel, or a symbol but as a whole person. Their sex becomes "not one person killing the other" but mutual enjoyment (Stepto 385). It is Sula who takes Ajax by the wrist and pulls him into Hannah's pantry, freed forever by Eva's absence from the clutter of accumulated goods, to pull pleasure from his "track-lean hips" (125). It is Sula who mounts Ajax, swaying over him like a tree as he calls soft obscenities up to her. Her thighs "swallow" his genitals just as he swallows her mouth. Her water moistens his earth; his earth contains her water. Sula's analytical speculations sound the only jarring notes in this scene of harmonious feeling, as she wonders, "When do the two make mud?" (131).

Her question goes unanswered when Ajax leaves without a trace. Unlike Jude, he retreats not because he feels humiliated but because Sula upsets the balance of self and other in their relationship. The very thing that attracts Ajax to Sula in the first place, her rejection of community control, is the one thing she relinquishes when she experiences Nel's lesson of love as possession. Ajax simply refuses to assimilate community mores about marriage and fidelity, which Sula incorporates when she gives herself over to be consumed by him. When she discovers "not love, perhaps, but possession or at least the desire for it," and Ajax detects the scent of the nest, their sex becomes a killing thing: she asks him to "lean on [her]"; he "drag[s] her under him and ma[kes] love to her with the steadiness and the intensity of a man about to leave for Dayton" (133–34).

Because Ajax owns nothing, Sula can find proof of his presence only through his "stunning absence." Her newfound loss of self turns her house into a shrine to him. She finally locates concrete evidence of his stay, ironically in his license to drive, and discovers that his real name is Albert (A.) Jacks. Sula interprets this as a clear sign that she never really knew her lover, and perhaps she doesn't. Under the influence of romantic convention, she began to visualize him as the strong and swift Greek warrior, or even the all-purpose cleanser, when his name actually suggests the playfulness of a child's game. Unlike Jude, who uses Nel to complete him, and unlike Nel and Sula, who complete each other, Ajax is intact within himself. Integrating the feminine with the masculine, able to connect yet be separate, his complex completeness draws Sula's attraction and respect. She recognizes the gold leaf underneath the blackness of his face, and underneath that the cold alabaster, and underneath that the fertile loam. In Morrison's complicated world—created to resist easy definitions of good and evil—Ajax is no more an absolute villain for leaving Sula than Sula is an absolute villain for having this insight: "Soon I would have torn the flesh from his face just to see if I was right about the gold and nobody would have understood that kind of curiosity" (136).

Both Jude, as product of order and community, and Ajax, as representative of freedom and individuality, deal with conflict from the perspective of what Morrison describes as a gender-determined social construction of reality that renders space "specific" for women, as well as specifically feminine, but unrestricted for men. Transcending conflict in the form of flight defines a male exercise of power because men "always want to change things, and women probably don't," approaching "conflict, dominion, and power" differently (Tate 122–23). Because he is not whole, Jude attempts to find himself by leaving home; Ajax leaves home to keep himself free.

Shadrack, however, copes with trauma and marginally retains his self while remaining on the fringe of community—but only through madness. As Cedric Bryant points out, madness is "power to the black community" (733). The inhabitants of the Bottom "knew Shadrack was crazy but that did not mean that he didn't have any sense or, even more important, that he had no power" (15). Unlike Jude and Ajax, but like Sula, Shadrack returns to the "soft voices" of his people to re-collect his power and maintain his identity. Together with Sula, his oddness shapes the Bottom. Opening and closing *Sula* by focusing on Shadrack, Morrison writes that residents of the community became "mightily preoccupied" with what Shadrack and Sula were all about and, by understanding their difference, with what "they themselves were all about, tucked up there in the Bottom" (6). She agrees with Michel Foucault that the civilization and humanity of a community can be measured by the way it treats its "disjunctions" or misfits (ix–x). She recalls eccentricity and freedom in the individual habits of her community but conformity when the survival of the village was threatened. Interested in who endures and why, Morrison is "enchanted, personally, with people who are extraordinary because in them [she] can find what is applicable to the ordinary" (LeClair 374). With Shadrack she creates a totally self-contained and ordered world, an organized form of madness, to contrast with Sula's strangeness. Their applicability to the ordinary suggests why the Bottom tolerates Shadrack's resistance while it shuns Sula's lawlessness.

Although Shadrack cannot always distinguish between reality and fantasy, he does ironically balance Jude's penchant for order and community with Ajax's need for freedom and individuality. Moreover, Shadrack's reaction to the horrors of "other people's wars," like Wright's *The Man Who Lived Underground*, inverts assumptions about sanity and insanity (160). Perhaps sanity includes the mind's refusal to accept a creed, endorsed by those in power, that values possessions greater than life. Perhaps this sanity can be maintained only from the perspective of those underground or, in Morrison's fiction, those up in the Bottom. In *Sula*, Shadrack and Sula are up in the bottom of the Bottom. However, because people can predict it, they understand and thus assimilate Shadrack's madness in a way that they can never accommodate Sula's unexpected strangeness. They will buy Shadrack's fish but will neither wash nor bury Sula. Nonetheless, they do not exile or destroy either one.

Another of the community's "beautiful boys," Shadrack, like Ajax, learns to signify on the steps of the pool hall. At twenty-one Ajax delights women with his virile grace and incurs envy from men of all ages for his "magnificently foul mouth." His fame lies not in the viciousness of his curses but in the creative nastiness and imaginative phrasing of harmless epithets such as "shit" and "pig meat" (50). At the same age Shadrack finds himself running with a headless comrade in 1917 across the fields of

France and at twenty-two returns to Medallion "handsome but ravaged," still able to move even the most fastidious to reminisce about his prewar beauty (7). At twenty-five and literally raving mad, he fights off the derision of the "tetter heads" with curses that become "stingingly personal" and is the "only black who could curse white people and get away with it" (15, 62). Through Shadrack, and Ajax afterward, Morrison contrasts the black male method of verbal sparring with the white male mode of physical battle and implies that the difference in tenor of the two boys' curses results directly from the manner of combat Shadrack experiences in the world outside the Bottom.

Even in the midst of dirty, gray explosions, Shad wonders at the purity and whiteness of his cold breath. Shell-shocked, he focuses on the color and arrangement of his unappetizing hospital food, taking comfort from the containment of its repugnance by the tray sections and absorbing the soothing equilibrium of its balance. He is terrified of the voice of the male nurse in the apple-green suit and what appears to him as the Jack-in-the-beanstalk sprouting of his own fingers, associating one with military order and the other with the uncontrollable destructiveness of his hands. When he finds himself safely back among his soft voices and Sula recognizes his harmlessness by the graceful arc of his fingers around wood (as he does hers by the "tadpole" over her eye), he will walk about with his penis out but will "never touch anybody, never [fight], never caress" (15). Relaxing in the hospital only when a straitjacket restricts his hands, released because of his disruptive panic or the hospital's lack of space, Shadrack must confront what has become a bewildering chaos of grounds and floating paper-doll people. His imagination, coupled with a complete freedom to cut out in a direction of his own, overwhelms him.

Frantic that his monstrous hands cannot unloose his sore feet from the crippling double knots tied in his shoelaces by the white male nurse, he continues on the road to try to "tie the loose cords in his mind," uncover the secret of who he is, and discover why the nurse labels him "Private" (10). His bizarre behavior when officials force him to abandon his confinement, similar again to Wright's fred daniels, causes passengers in "dark, square cars [to shutter] their eyes at what they took to be a drunken man" (12). Feet "clotted with pain," paralyzed by a blinding headache, in the world outside the military shelter Shadrack can neither find a comfortable way to walk nor see himself clearly. His headache subsides and his hands become "courteously still," however, when the police lock him in jail and he recognizes a familiar command to "fuck himself" painted on the cell wall. He joyfully greets the blackness of his "indisputable presence" as he glimpses his reflection in toilet bowl water

(12–13). In the tradition of Wright's and Ellison's invisible men and their allegorical journeys to selfhood, Shadrack finds enlightenment in darkness, sanity in madness, and freedom when the white authorities send him back up to the black Bottom.

Like a character from Hemingway's fiction, Shadrack copes with an immense exterior space of unpredictable death, where order equates to military precision with the details of destruction, by retreating to a small, peaceful interior space over which he has complete control. His outwardly ramshackle but inwardly pristine shack suggests his state of being; his aesthetic nature and love of water connect him to Sula. A "permanently astonished" Shadrack holds himself together by dreaming of soft voices and a river full of fish (7). Recalling that he no sooner crossed the border of a frozen stream in France when the world explodes around him, he builds his shack on the far side of the river but maintains his relationship with the community on the opposite bank via a handmade bridge. Sensual attention to the delicate rituals of fishing, a reminder of its tranquilizing effects on Nick in "Big Two-Hearted River," helps him heal his wounded psyche. Despite his disruptions, he perceives that contained water enables creative power; unregulated water reverts to destructive force. Such manifestations of madness, caused by, rejected by, yet saner than the war going on outside the community, are accepted by, accommodated by, and imaginatively assimilated into the flow of life up in the Bottom.

As he struggles to emerge from his psychological hibernation, Shadrack joins his invisible colleagues in their compulsion to speak out on the lower frequencies. Finally free of white-imposed death, his message to his Bottom people takes the form of introducing National Suicide Day, a ritual that "had to do with making a place for fear as a way of controlling it" (14). Trading the Grim Reaper's sharp scythe for a comic cowbell and a hangman's noose, realizing that death's power lies in its unexpectedness, he proclaims to his people in the voice of the street preacher that the third day of the new year is "their only chance to kill themselves or each other" (14). Even Shadrack's name validates his prophetic purpose and acknowledges his insight as a shield against fiery furnaces. His nickname, which alludes to the shad or small, quick bottom fish, both applauds the humaneness of the black male's agile method of survival and recognizes his susceptibility to larger, more ruthless, and ultimately less civilized predators.[2]

Like Sula, who is buried as a witch, Shadrack's gift to his community provides its people with a scapegoat to contain their destructive fear and then lead them to freedom from it. Unlike Sula, whose threatening awareness alienates her from a people who will love her when "Lindbergh sleeps with Bessie Smith," Shadrack's childlike instinct allows the community to institutionalize his ritual and to love him now. Their messages reflect two sides of the same symbol. Interpreting Shadrack's declaration of "Always" to be his doom for her part in Chicken Little's drowning, Sula resigns herself to the permanence of chaos and death, acknowledging that all of us are dying all the time. For her the difference lies in "dying like a stump" or living "like one of those redwoods." In this context, "Being good to somebody is just like being mean to somebody. Risky. You don't get nothing for it" (143–45). By telling her "Always," however, Shadrack intends to ensure that Sula will not have to be afraid of "the change—the falling away of skin" to assure her of the permanence of order and life (157).

With Sula's death, the Bottom Community's reactionary effort remains unnecessary, dislocation sets in, and even Shadrack becomes frightened. Nonetheless, he sticks tight to "his habit—singing his song, ringing his bell and holding fast to his rope." Some people decline to respond for one reason or another. Helene Wright, for instance, merely observes "the ruckus with characteristic scorn." Others, who already understand the "Spirit's touch" or the solace of multiple families "bending their backs in a field while singing as from one throat," resist this "curious disorder, this headless display and so refuse to go." In their desperation, some finally heed the "befuddled" Shadrack's call but do so, unfortunately, in Sula's voice. Freeing themselves briefly from the weight of adult pain and fear, they laugh at death and embrace chaos. Pausing at the site that symbolizes their connection to the outside world, they "killed, as best they could, the tunnel they were forbidden to build." Sula's path to freedom is, indeed, a risky one. Some go "too deep, too far," joining her in death. Crazy old Shadrack, however, stays standing above the furnace, still astonished, still ringing his bell (159–62).

Morrison reunites her outcasts at the end of the novel through memory, with Nel bearing witness. At sixty-eight Shadrack represents the last of the Bottom's "beautiful boys," the virile individuality of 1921 having given way to the homogenized dewey look of 1965. Remaining "energetically mad" but separated from his river, Shadrack focuses now on hauling trash instead of the tremor of fish on the line. He and Nel pass each other in opposite lines of direction, "each thinking separate thoughts about the past" (173–74). Reduced to lines, all three of *Sula*'s masculine models become, by its conclusion, disassociated from the feminine circle. However, the book does not so much attack the "pathology" of masculine linearity as censure the dis-ease caused by the master narrative. *Sula* actually affirms human differences and the commonality of human sorrow.

It also ultimately asserts: "Sometimes good looks like evil; sometimes evil looks like good. . . . It depends on what uses you put it to" (Stepto 381). Nel's wholesale acceptance of the community's laws heightens her status within it but leaves her alone and essentially noncontributing; Jude's compliance means voluntary exile. Sula's radical lawlessness unifies a community, which then isolates her within it; Ajax's noncompliance means voluntary exile. Only Shadrack's creative assimilation, connected but resistant to a social frame of reference, allows freedom of choice within place. However, even the Bottom's place for such an androgynous vision is madness.

Sula proposes that class and racial constructions may ultimately collapse preconceptions about gender. While Jude, as order and community, Ajax, as chaos and individuality, and Shadrack, as Dickinson's "divinest sense" in much madness, illustrate the Bottom's masculine types, these roles could as easily be represented by its women—Nel, Sula, and Ajax's conjure mother. Sula retorts to Nel's admonishment that a sister "can't act like a man": "I'm a woman and colored. Ain't that the same as being a man?" (142). Concerned with the integrity of male/female individuality and the harmony of their relationships as well as the roles that black and white communities play in sustaining or damaging both, Morrison consistently refuses to elevate female above male or male above female. Nel's fine, final cry of sorrow, for Sula not Jude, is both long and round. Though "it [has] no bottom and it [has] no top," it completes Morrison's elegy on masculinity (174).

CHAPTER 4

Flying without Ever Leaving the Ground

Feminine Masculinity in *Song of Solomon*

The Bluest Eye is Morrison's manifesto. It pecks away at those aspects of the "white gaze" abusive to African American masculinity: distorted sexuality, ownership, physical beauty, romantic love. *Sula* extends Morrison's outrage at the attempted annihilation of that manhood by rough white hands who "tore the [protectively poisonous] nightshade and [thornily sweet] blackberry patches from their roots" to make room for the paltry sound and fury of a golf course (3). Portraying Sula and Nel as the adult women that Claudia and Frieda grow into, it laments the erosion of the Bottom's complex androgyny from without and within. While Morrison's first two novels attend to the females in the black community, they do not dismiss its male figures as completely isolated, alienated, or irrelevant, nor do they blame all of the community's ills on them. *Song of Solomon* (1977) becomes unequivocal testament to Morrison's praise of men as it celebrates the vitality and truth of what she calls the free black male. It encourages his impulse to step down off the communal confinement of the porch, seek his ancestral fathers, and locate his ancient properties. Dedicated to "Daddy," the novel embraces a culture in which "The fathers may soar."

Morrison herself says of the book: "Men are more prominent. They interested me in a way I hadn't thought about before, almost as a species" (Watkins 50). She applauds the feistiness or "magic" inherent in such classic black male stereotypes as Kingfish, who "did anything he was big enough to do" (Stepto 384). She also acknowledges that the male's manifestation of power resides in his ability to change situations or places, reflected in his fascination with trains and planes. Morrison finds flying "one of the most attractive features about the black male life. . . . It's part of that whole business of breaking ground, doing the other thing."

The men's love of confident speed—their willingness to split at the drop of a hat—takes its toll, however, on children who are left with overburdened mothers and no stable connection to their fathers. Identifying flying as the central figure for masculinity in *Song of Solomon*, Morrison juxtaposes this metaphor with a trope connected to women and children: song. She states that "the fathers may soar, they may triumph, they may leave, but the children know who they are; they remember, half in glory and half in accusation. That is one of the points of 'Song': all the men have left someone, and it is the children who remember it, sing about it, mythologize it, make it a part of their family history" (Watkins 50). Appropriating a deliberately ambiguous pronoun, the other half of the book's mantra affirms: "The children may know their names."

Several scholars comment on Morrison's attitude toward a pattern of migratory men. Demetrakopoulos commends Morrison for examining this archetype from the women's and children's points of view but finds the loss to the men's own spiritual development an even more devastating ramification. Flying with no real point of return costs black men "maturation, individuation, connections," creating a polarized, soulless masculine (Holloway 86–90). Hovet and Lounsberry categorize Morrison's characters into three kinds of fliers: propertied nesting birds, daring but dangerous fliers, and soaring whole fliers. They conclude that her black men can fly free only when they establish a strong self-identity yet simultaneously maintain a positive connection to the community. All three critics acknowledge that flying as a commonplace in African American literature takes on connotations beyond the mere thought of escape or freedom, suggesting physical, moral, or spiritual heights and symbolizing intellect, imagination, or sexual potency. However, none extends the metaphor to include basic survival.

Morrison often claims a fascination with who endures and who does not and why. Black communities have outlasted immeasurable trauma by calling on flexibility, or flight, expressed physically and through humor, story, and song. *Song of Solomon* explores the gendered manifestations of these forms of survival. It then accords the status of griot to those individuals who, drawing from both masculine and feminine wellsprings, master the life skills and pass them on.[1] Assuming griot responsibility herself by writing in a conversational mode, Morrison clarifies her intentions by naming her story after the biblical Song of Songs, also associated with erotic love, the myth of its singer's ascension, and the preservation of tribal identity. Both texts essentially represent flight or survival manuals for their respective communities as related through song. Rooted in oral composition, both achieve unity through dialogue between male and female and through repetition of scenes told from both perspectives. Solomon, a masculine variant of the female name Sula, related to Sulaimaan and Sulayman, suggests such androgynous wisdom.

Despite the fact that *Song of Solomon* showcases the men whom Demetrakopoulos describes as "pathological," it remains the most affirmative of Morrison's first four novels. This occurs, in part, because it may be read, like its namesake, as celebrating the special characteristics of a chosen people. As significantly triumphant, however, is a central character who finds his voice through this heritage. The female songs and the male stories of his people cultivate in Milkman what might be called feminine masculinity, a maleness connected to women, anchored by delicately balanced dualities, and based on flying without ever leaving the ground.[2]

Milkman Dead, at four, loses "all interest in himself" when he discovers that only birds and airplanes can fly, leaving his imagination "so bereft that he appeared dull even to the women who did not hate his mother" (9). He is one of several characters in the novel that, individually, are off balance or buffeted by extremes. In fact, the book's structure consists of the contrasting and/or complementary stories of multiple pairs of characters who attain clarity, find meaning, or maintain equanimity primarily when set against each other: Macon and Pilate Dead; Ruth Foster and Pilate Dead; Magdalene called Lena and First Corinthians; Guitar Bains and Macon Dead. Mobley insists that *Song of Solomon* functions to deconstruct the prevailing yet reductive perception of the black community as a single-voiced whole while it reconstructs it as "a dynamic, complex, multivoiced network of ongoing dialogues." Thus, Milkman's initiation is "not merely a matter of acquiring his own voice but one of recognizing that the relationship between the voice of the self and the voices of the community is not either/or but both/and" (42). What keeps these characters off kilter is the intrusion of sterile, white, middle-class notions of property, propriety, and competition; their struggle for selfhood involves not only gender differences but conflicts of race, class, and age.

Black men do leave and their children do grieve but often because the men, and their women, succumb to or spin their wheels against prestige and power. Morrison simply declines simple statements about the behavior of black fathers and husbands, acknowledging that she does not find "men who leave their families necessarily villainous" (McKay 402). Ajax, for example, leaves Sula only when she gives her self over to ideas about ownership. Flight for the community, then, depends on the reciprocal ballast that black men and women provide for each other as, together, they transcend the dead weight of foreign values forced upon and destructive to them. While possession and position weigh down and isolate many white fathers and dangerously free black males float far adrift of the feminine community, Morrison's free black man has a unique opportunity to balance masculine with feminine, sky with ground.

When they are unfettered by Western ideas about patrimony or children as vicarious trophies, black fathers traditionally teach their sons how to be men by "talking that talk." Flight instruction involves lessons in oral language games that encourage boys to play right alongside the men.[3] Unlike white American culture, which rears too many boys to accept the adage that he who dies with the most toys wins, African American boys survive owning no toys or having their toys taken from them through their skill with language, until making becomes more important than stuff, process as important as product, work a form of play. Instead of accumulating things or firing weapons, they are schooled to catch an opponent off guard, to hit and run via verbal acrobatics, and to arm themselves with flexibility and self-deprecating humor.

Sula opens with an example of such strategy in the form of a "nigger joke" that black people ruefully tell on themselves when they feel downtrodden or misused. Depicting a slaveowner who talks his male slave out of the rich farmland promised him, it reflects one of the lessons in self-defense that Pilate shows Milkman when she insists on wearing a brass earring containing her name written on a piece of paper: manipulative print cultures can easily outmaneuver oral ones unless people keep their wits, and self-awareness, about them. Another example of the vulnerable strength possessed by men taught to value play as power, *Sula*'s war-ravaged Shadrack uses knowledge and symbol not for acquisition or domination but to distance or to contain external chaos—that is, to keep his own balance. *Song of Solomon* opens with a variation on the Bottom's nigger joke: Not Doctor Street. Illuminating the negative illustrates what Ellison's Invisible Man learns from the elusive Rinehart, that perhaps the truth "was always a lie" and that, if so, "his world was possibility" (498). Calling something what it isn't maintains that a creative mind can free itself by mapping out its own reality. Seeing and saying can become being, as Baby Suggs reminds her *Beloved* people in the Clearing. Morrison's revision of a popular black archetype, Flip Wilson's Geraldine, highlights the particular necessity for African Americans barraged by stimuli destructive to their selves to practice visual and verbal re-creation. Because stereotypical portraits construe the virtues of black people as vices, the male comic's portrayal of a single set of traits within his campy female character provokes, according to Morrison, both hatred and affection:

> Geraldine is defensive, cunning, sexy, egocentric and transvestite. But that's not all she is. A shift in semantics and we find the accuracy: for defensive read survivalist; for cunning read clever; for sexy read a natural unembarrassed acceptance of her sexuality; for egocentric read keen awareness of individuality; for transvestite (man in woman's dress) read a masculine strength beneath the accouterments of glamour. ("What the Black Woman Thinks" 63)

We read Morrison's semantics in *Song* for ingenious possibility and for deconstructed and reconstructed accuracy as geography. Guitar offers Milkman some history along with his tea: "Goddam, Milk, I do believe my whole life's geography" (114). Pilate takes nothing with her on her journey across America but a fourth-grade geography book, rocks gathered from every place significant to her self-development, and a sack containing her father's bones. Forbidden by snobbish white town fathers to call a street in an upscale part of a Michigan city "Doctor Street" for the black physician who breaks through the color line to live and die on it, black people of both genders retaliate with a chuckle by renaming it "Not Doctor Street." Barely warmed up, these Southside residents then dub the charity hospital situated on it, where the doctor is not allowed to practice nor they to be treated, "(No) Mercy Hospital." Here Morrison turns white sophisticates' rejection of black folk modes of communication into ignorant illiteracy. Official white maps register a public way as the high-sounding but imagistically dull Mains Avenue, though black people prohibited from living on it know it as plain but picturesque Doctor Street. The latter, having no formal address nor access to government documents, begin to use the street as a point of reference for residency and the U.S. mail as a means of transferring messages. Envelopes arrive at the post office addressed to people on Doctor Street. The name acquires a quasi-official status, which threatens the authority of the town fathers. As a result, postal workers banish the messages to the Dead Letter Office. In its humorous, pictorial bluntness, the name "Dead Letter Office" has more in common with the hieroglyphic black dialect described by Hurston and Gates than with the alphabetic Standard American dialect. Morrison's allusion to Melville's association of Bartleby with the Dead Letter Office suggests that the practice of passive resistance and its reliance on semiotics are not confined to black communities but common to peaceful minorities of all hues who would prefer not to.

Thus, large-print culture reductively restricts the unofficial and supposedly inappropriate language of the smaller oral or word-picture community. A battle for dominance ensues. The white fathers mount an active, aggressive attack; black citizens retaliate with passive resistance and mother wit. City legislators, whose principal political life, according to Morrison's narrator, involves a concern for proper names and the maintenance of their historical landmarks, plaster written notices all over town to the effect that "the avenue running northerly and southerly from Shore Road fronting the lake to the junction of routes 6 and 2 leading to Pennsylvania, and also running parallel to and between Rutherford Avenue and Broadway, had always been and would always be known as Mains Avenue and not Doctor Street." Acknowledging this information wryly as a "genuinely clarifying public notice," Southside residents fall back on their flexibility, humor, and skill with wordplay to maintain their integrity and keep their myths alive (4). At the same time, like modern Portias disguised as Doctors, they turn the fanaticism of their metaphorically challenged Shylocks back on its originators while they satisfy the letter of the law and rub authoritarian noses in their own silliness. In large part because of white male objection, the street remains fixed in communal memory for perpetuity as "Not Doctor Street."

This elusiveness, so integral to African American survival and captured so brilliantly in *Song of Solomon*, has puzzled even black critics. Confessing her difficulty in grasping a "single solid sense" of the novel, Karla Holloway finally consults the collective of her racial heritage. In a marvelously personal critical essay, she articulates the multifaceted and shifting identity of *Song* by providing analogies to her children's summer flight simulations and the singing at the funeral of a beloved uncle (101–14). As she looks to black spirituals for the source of the text's symbolic patterns, she realizes the extensiveness of the network intertwining flight and song. Many spirituals perpetuate a mythologized "escape" of subject peoples as inspiration for those who would follow; as such, the very theme of *Song of Solomon* rests deep within racial memory. Holloway also concludes that the rich and complex spirituality of these African peoples "paralleled what they understood as a miraculous liberation with a similarly miraculous event—the power of flight as transformation and transcendence. Christianity may have offered a religious ground for the displaced African to replant the symbols of his spirituality—but the growth from that soil was distinctly Black and African" (102).

Observing accurately that the "physical power of both flight and song is woven together at every crucial juncture in this novel," Holloway's comparison of the text's "shifting presence" to the call-and-response structure of her uncle's funeral service reveals an important overlooked distinction. She describes the musical cadence of the minister's voice in prayer, an antiphony to audible sobs and heavy sorrow from those gathered. As if to relieve pressure, someone hums; then another sings, several sigh into the music, and finally the minister's voice becomes not only rhythmic punctuation to the song but actually calls out its words. Unlike the white town fathers in *Song* who attempt to impose their authority on black citizens, this black ministerial father invites, supports, and then adapts to the calls of his church family. Remembering literally being spiritually lifted out of her sorrowful place, Holloway views this kind of collective emotional ascension as the aesthetic identity of *Song of Solomon*.

She fails to note, however, the gender difference in the individual expression of this passion, power, and transformation. While she identifies the minister clearly as male, she implies that the singers, and probably most of the hummers, are female. African American church history and American music history, as well as Morrison's own novels, certainly support this supposition. The majority of black preachers and most jazz and blues instrumentalists have traditionally been male while the vocalists, particularly those performing solo for choirs or bands, are female. In *The Bluest Eye*, Morrison depicts Mama trying to assimilate Mr. Henry's assault on Frieda by cleaning her house and singing "something about trains and Arkansas," all the time wearing her hat (98). On the other hand, Morrison asserts that the pieces of Cholly's eclectic, "dangerously free" life could be understood and given true form only by a male blues player. The woman survives by staying and singing about leaving, the man by leaving and playing about what he has left. In *Song of Solomon*, Milkman, who "knew no songs, and had no singing voice that anybody would want to hear," speaks the words of the song that the dying Pilate, a wonderful contralto herself, asks to hear: "Without the least bit of a tune, he sang for the lady" whose constantly moving lips have fallen still (936). In her descriptions of three types of voices dialogized in *Song of Solomon*, Mobley distinguishes between the responsive voice as we hear it in the community of men and that associated with women. She cites the conversations in the barbershop as an example of the male responsive voice. The same position in Morrison's community of women, however, forms not a speaking voice but the choral singing performed by Pilate, Reba, and Hagar. The current rap phenomenon, which merges the chanted word with pulsating music to evoke hard-driving inner-city life, exists as a predominantly male one, and its roots derive from the rhythmical verbal dueling, common among the black male folk community, known as signifying.

In short, Holloway correctly assesses that the association of flight or transcendence with song remains deeply embedded within the African American racial consciousness. The implications of song, however, become as gendered as those of flight, the vaginal/phallic associations with feminine/masculine flight equipment comically apparent. Solo singers are frequently female; flight equipment (i.e., a voice) contained within their bodies keeps them metaphorically close to home. Male vocalists tend to band together and often combine music and oratory into songs, sermons, and spoken stories. Likewise, male instrumentalists usually jam in groups, taking turns at taking off alone via flight instruments connected externally to their bodies but returning to harmonize with their brothers. Voices beating time, some men preach, some rap, some tell "lies." Some "talk their talk through the gold of curved metal, or in the touch of black-and-white rectangles and taut skins and strings echoing from wooden corridors" (*The Bluest Eye* 159). Whatever their bag, these men show each other how to lift it, how to achieve, protect, and finally transcend self, not so much by solo or choral singing as by playing or preaching or storytelling within the sphere of a clan.[4]

Hurston records such male communal activities in *Their Eyes Were Watching God.* Janie asserts her selfhood and independence, literally speaking herself free from male dominance, when, encouraged by Tea-cake, she begins to participate in the performance rituals forbidden her by Joe Starks. Hurston's description reveals that Joe's resistance to Janie's involvement in the porch-talking involves class as much as gender prejudices. His rules of etiquette imitate those of propertied white males with big voices: setting his wife in a high chair apart from what he considers trashy town women emphasizes his superiority. Although "ragtaggled" women join in the rough play more often than either church women or the mayor's wife, the "big picture talkers" are far more apt to be male than female. Mobley finds instances of female characters in *Song of Solomon* who speak in the signifying voice. Nonetheless, she claims that it appears most often in male discourse at predominantly male gatherings. Performance rituals for the sisters, which include shouting and singing and "getting happy," are more often restricted to church-related situations.

Thus, black men are traditionally more likely than black women to use tall-tale-telling as a contribution to child rearing, to relate magnificently exaggerated exploits to their sons. However, stories that depict unrealistically overblown accomplishments or outlandishly daring deeds sometimes leave such boys as Cholly Breedlove feeling ignorant, inadequate, or bereft. Although fatherless Cholly loves hard-drinking Blue Jack and his stories about the women he's had and the scrapes he's gotten out of, the boy feels too ashamed to confess his own growing pains to Blue the experienced woman-killer. Morrison admits to choosing a man to make the journey in *Song of Solomon* because she believed a man had more to learn than a woman. Assuming that males acquire their knowledge about being men from other men, she was "amazed at how little men taught one another in the book." The book taught her that Milkman needs two sets of information in order to become a complete human being, one from Guitar and one from Pilate, so that "there is a balance between what he learns from a man and what he learns from a woman." She concludes that this kind of harmony makes it possible for her African American Everyman "to do something important instead of figuring how he can live better and more comfortably, and easier" (McKay 410).

In his 1998 study about ways that parents, mentors, and educators can help shape fragile boys into exceptional men, psychologist Michael Gurian insists that American boys are in crisis. He affirms the importance in all cultures of a clan to lead the boy through adolescence, ancestral voices to encourage him on his journey to manhood, and stories that will call him home. Noting that boys without clans or lineal integrity do not hear the voices of present and past guiding them toward the self-discipline of manhood and that image-creating machines currently usurp the sacred and profoundly subtle storytelling function, Gurian extends Morrison's concern that modern American culture is failing its boys. Anticipating his call-to-action by some twenty years, she intended *Song of Solomon* as a literary intervention into what she perceives to be a cultural crisis in the African American community.

For Morrison, the danger involves black people losing the roootedness that an oral tradition provided when their community was less geographically dispersed: "We don't live in places where we can hear those stories anymore; parents don't sit around and tell their children those classical, mythological archetypal stories that we heard years ago. But the new information has got to get out, and there are several ways to do it. One is in the novel. . . . It should have the ability to be both print and oral literature . . . to make you stand up and . . . feel something profoundly in the same way that a black preacher requires his congregation to speak . . . to make that connection" ("Rootedness" 340). Gurian echoes Morrison's use of song as a metaphor for self-expression: "Everyone in the family line who has come before the boy hums a song of self in his blood and cells. The boy wants to hear this song clearly throughout his journey to manhood. He wants to be a person of his own race, creed, and culture—a person who *belongs* in the world because he has a *birthright*" (257). Every male child possesses the urge to become the product of the energies of his family and its past and is thus instinctively drawn to enter realms of time and culture that predate him, to "hear the long song of his bloodline and ethnic origin" (257).

Gurian also connects storytelling with human identity and delineates the importance for this male child of tales describing the hero's journey, told not by machines but by human beings. Joseph Campbell's seminal work on the similarities among cultural story patterns, *The Hero with a Thousand Faces*, includes the worldwide myth in which the boy travels through three family systems and then into the fourth and fifth realms of strange kingdoms and the nonliving, initiating himself and being initiated into manhood. By the end of his amazing journey, the boy comprehends that even the exotic creatures of the outer worlds actually represent pieces of the man himself. No matter where the hero goes to prove his manhood, he finds himself back home. Home may look different as the boy's perspective evolves into a man's. However, "it is only when he recognizes that the human family is everywhere" that he becomes "a responsible man, a hero, a king, capable of caring for his community" (Gurian 216). Gurian marvels at the "depth at which the human psyche lives in the same interior landscape, no matter its cultures, creating stories through which to teach its young how to live, its adults how to thrive, and its elders how to pass on what they have learned before they themselves pass on" (215). Scholars have long recognized the pattern of the hero's journey in *Song of Solomon*. Less attention has been paid to Morrison's assertions, supported by current research, that the mode of storytelling remains as important as the stories themselves.

In essence, her novel models for the African American community what it advocates; it loves what it criticizes. Morrison's subject is a black man/boy who tries to slide by, who does not want to go anywhere, and, consequently, who is ignorant despite his thirty-two years. Detached from his clan, unaware of his ancestors, uneducated about his cultural myths, he chases his own tail and, as Guitar contemptuously growls, that of any accommodating woman. As such, he possesses, like the white male peacock that fascinates him so, "too much tail" to fly and becomes a danger to himself and a detriment to his people (179).[5] *Song of Solomon* holds Milkman's retarded boyhood up for censure. By nourishing him with the male stories and the female songs of his clan, both living and dead, it also offers not only Milkman but the other boys in Morrison's neighborhood something valuable to chase. It bestows upon all the gift of androgynous flight.

Milkman Dead's wings stay clipped for thirty-two years because he remains caught between two collections of stories, one of them paralyzing and the other polarizing. The first has been passed down to him by his father, the second passed along by his friend. As Guitar retorts when Milkman accuses the older boy of criticizing where Milkman lives, "Not where you live—where you hang out. You don't live nowhere. Not Not Doctor Street *or* Southside" (103). For Morrison, both places are inherently flawed and incomplete: too rigidly masculine and racist and in need of a woman's sweet touch. Like Gurian, who argues that the masks and voices of the tellers of stories exert as much influence as the stories they tell, enumerating the destructive effects of image-creating machines on today's boys, Morrison seeks for her community a strong, wise, generous teacher and historian, in short a modern griot who embodies both yang and yin.

A dead man walking transfers the stories of Not Doctor Street to Milkman.[6] Articulating Macon Dead's tones as a muffled imitation of the white male master narrative, Morrison compares his manner of address to a dormant volcano:

> Solid, rumbling, likely to erupt without prior notice, Macon kept each member of his family awkward with fear. His hatred of his wife glittered and sparked in every word he spoke to her. The disappointment he felt in his daughters sifted down on them like ash, dulling their buttery complexions and choking the lilt out of what should have been girlish voices. Under the frozen heat of his glance they dropped the salt cellar into the yolks of their poached eggs. (10–11)

With a "high behind and an athlete's stride," the young, ruggedly built Macon walks tall (17). His smoldering passions and appetites, stifled beneath the cold mask of the decorous businessman, seethe dangerously close to the surface. He takes a top-down management style. He communicates with others by instilling dread. Family and tenants fear his eruptions into violence yet become animated by the anticipation and drama of the possibility of his released energy. Driven systematically to kill the child in himself in order to outdo the white man at his own work, Macon represents the prototypical Type A abuser found frequently in the closet of the executive suite. Resenting his self-enforced repression, his emotions build up unbearable pressure. To let off steam, he shoots unpredictably intermittent sparks of anger at his wife and projects the ash of his disappointment in them onto his daughters, dulling their expressions and inhibiting their words. Macon's "frozen heat" dries the very femininity out of the female members of his family. His speech pattern, which dominates his household, may thus be parsed as low-grade but continually intensifying rumblings of discontent punctuated by the periodic sparks of hatred and soot of criticism climaxed by violent outbursts of rage ebbing once more into throbbing dis-ease. Into the absences within his parts of speech fall the silences of the women, a quiet that "was not peaceful, for it was preceded by and would soon be terminated by" Macon's presence (10). Macon Dead's is the story of the dead-end draw of absolute power, unchecked by communal restraint, corrupting absolutely.

The ingrown vitality of his public address reflects Macon's sexual proclivities. The energy required to stifle such outrage cuts short his ability to sow and grow, to father and husband; a drunken Porter refers to him as a "baby-dicked baboon" (26). As a boy he capably and kindly cares for his younger sister. Repressed nurturance, however, converts to nausea. The tightly controlled but slightly veiled disgust that smothers his Dead women renders them unsure of and thus harmful to themselves. Like many battered women who doubt their femininity, they sterilize their creativity, spilling salt into their own poached and encroached on eggs. Macon frustrates even Ruth's last-ditch effort to ward off living death and reinstate her sex life. Her husband does everything short of killing her to force her to abort their son.

If Macon's style of management is top down, his approach to sex is missionary position. It is also perversely fetishistic. He becomes far more aroused by removing his wife's expensive white underthings than exploring her naked body lying "as moist and crumbly as unbleached sugar." Morrison's elaborate description of Macon's deliberately lingering foreplay, involving not Ruth's person but "the most beautiful, the most delicate, the whitest and softest underwear on earth," leaves her reader in stitches and comically indicates the cloaked but complex white colonialism that turns Macon on. Never speaking during sex, though both occasionally giggle like children playing "doctor," and saving Ruth's stockings for last, he finally enters her to ejaculate quickly. Though both "[like] it that way," Macon has not seen Ruth's naked feet in twenty years and misses only the underwear. Having married his wife to co-opt her physician father's social position and pursuit of light skin color, Macon goes about undoing her lovely, complicated undergarments, including her perspiration shields, as methodically as he attempts to unlock the most intimate secrets of white male dominance.

Appropriating the mask of white-collar professionalism but residing oddly on Not Doctor Street, Macon's mace becomes his bunch of Southside rental property keys. Habitually curling his fingers around their soothing solidarity, he fondles them like a favorite teething ring. Morrison continues to display Macon's comic childishness as he struts down the street to his converted storefront office, formerly known as "Sonny's Shop." Eager for folks to take him seriously, he neatly paints the more impressive word OFFICE on the front door, copying the white town fathers' literate, authoritarian mode of signing. Collective memory conspires against him, however, aided by peeling gold letters associating his business establishment with its previous owner. Southside residents view him as just another sonny, presumably doing "something or other" in that shop of his (17). Macon's association with a masculine print culture also appears in his obsession with his wall calendar and account book. Unable to see Guitar's grandmother except as overdue rent, he reduces all of life to linear time and money. Thus, he allows a dried-up old woman attempting to shelter two young boys "till Saturday coming" to come up with rent money she does not have and cannot get. Mrs. Bains speaks for all of Southside when she tells her grandsons: "A nigger in business is a terrible thing to see. A terrible, terrible thing to see" (22).

Unlike Mrs. Bains, whose juice has been sapped by 1945 to a mere glitter of tears in her eyes, Macon uses the war years to expand his waistline. Knowing that "as a Negro he wasn't going to get a big slice of the pie," he scoops up the considerable pie filling "oozing around the edge of the crust." Unable to satisfy his sweet tooth, however, he spills filling into his lap, stickies his hands, and weighs himself down with a sagging paunch. Like the fat cat he has turned into, he is too stuffed to play, buying up beach property and automobiles not for recreation or transportation but for investment and prestige. Morrison depicts Honore Island as a wealthy black version of Fitzgerald's West Egg, and Gatsby's car becomes Macon Dead's hearse.

Because he cannot play, Macon creates no life. For Morrison the business of living is serious play. As such, she re-envisions the childish idleness traditionally attributed to poor African Americans by stern white businessmen. A shift in semantics once more locates the accuracy; irresponsibly childish becomes responsively childlike. While white town fathers scoff at Southside men for their unwillingness to do their work, Southside men snigger at white town fathers for their inability to have any fun. The absence of playfulness, then, renders Macon childish in Southside and, as a black man, an even readier target for ridicule.

The Dead family ritual of Sunday afternoon drives in Macon's plush Packard encapsulates Morrison's pointed irony. These pleasure rides are "much too important for Macon to enjoy." The only fun he makes results from the reactions of black people who spot the automobile spinning through the rough part of town called the Blood Bank toward the wealthy white neighborhoods. Some sigh with "good-humored envy at the classiness, the dignity of it"; others watch the Dead family glide by with "a tiny bit of jealousy and a whole lot of amusement, for Macon's wide green Packard belied what they thought a car was for." The passage that follows represents a marvelous rendition of what Morrison thinks things are for: to offer personal refreshment and collect human memories. Her readers find out what cars are for by what Macon's is not: for gunning engines, blowing tires, roaring by in first gear to thrill pedestrians, hailing friends, running out of gas, giving a lift to teenagers perched on the running board, drinking beer, eating ice cream, making love in the back seat, and providing windows for baby boys to pee out of. The only "real lived life at all" produced by Macon's funereally silent machine becomes the quip it inspires among Southside residents who dub it Macon Dead's hearse (31–33).

Macon Dead remains childish because he kills the child in himself that would allow him to play with others. In his urgency to rewrite the master narrative, he separates himself from family and friends, cuts himself off from male stories and female songs. Apart from Freddie, the "gold-toothed bantamweight," born flunky, and town crier, he makes no contact with black men.[7] His cool manner discourages the casual or spontaneous conversation that is the heart of black male talk, and his hard-nosed business tactics, as well as his snobbery, prohibit him from haunting the pool halls and barbershops that are the sites of black male storytelling. Feather will not even allow Macon's son into Feather's pool hall. Macon connects with Southside and the Blood Bank, the novel's twin pulses of male life, only by collecting rent, a distasteful chore he turns over to Milkman as soon as possible. Instead of joining forces with Porter and the other members of the Seven Days against white oppression, he arms himself to shoot a drunken Porter out of his apartment window to obtain his rent money and maintain his own status as landlord.

Although Freddie, who loves "gossip and the telling of it," acts as Macon's eye and ear, he is an unreliable close reader and witness; he relays factually accurate but interpretively flawed stories. Thus, Macon has no coach to advise him, no buddy to criticize him, and the unobjective perspective of a janitor who spends all his time in the basement of people's lives. Because he wants to be told only what he wishes to hear, Macon, like Machiavelli's bad prince, listens with half an ear to "a fool and a liar" who sells favors for right of familiarity (23–25). His mind already "sharpened by hatred," his lack of brothers and association with a sycophant merely spur his cynicism (15). In essence, the single male story in Macon's life becomes the one he tries to plagiarize—the white male capitalist narrative.

Like Eliot's Prufrock, Macon also deadens his ears to the sounds of the mermaids; he can hear them "singing, each to each" but is too afraid, and too literate, to let them sing to him. He essentially writes himself out of the song that symbolizes woman. He dehumanizes Southside women like Mrs. Bains, disdains his daughters Magdalene called Lena and First Corinthians, and despises only one woman more than his wife—his sister Pilate. Two scenes in particular render Macon's isolation from women and the complicated puzzle illustrating African American paternity. The first poignantly describes Macon departing from his usual evening routine to stand outside Pilate's window and listen to the harmonies of the three women inside. Tired and irritable after a hard day of rent-gouging, he is not soothed even by the melting light of first dark. Instead, its trembling illumination displays his properties like "squat ghosts with hooded eyes," and he responds as though "the houses were in league with one another to make him feel like the outsider, the propertyless, landless wanderer" (27). Initially turning away from Pilate's small house on Darling Street, whose basement "seemed to be rising from rather than settling into the ground," he stops cold when he visualizes the picture of his destination: his wife's "narrow unyielding back," his daughters "boiled dry from yearning," his son "to whom he could speak only if his words held some command or criticism." In his alienation from any home, he is drawn to "a bit of music—from the person who had been his first caring for" (28).

Here Macon reveals a fleeting but disturbing premonition into the full understanding that Milkman will finally acquire: that "anything could appear to be something else, and probably was," that sight may be the least reliable of the senses, that feminine intuition might be real, and that home becomes whom you care for (331–32). Seeking no masculine talk, only a glimpse of the source of the singing that reminds him of "fields and wild turkey and calico," he lets the stress of the day drain from him and drinks in "the effortless beauty of the women singing in the candlelight" (29). Sensing himself "softening under the weight of memory and music," Macon cannot leave even when the song fades away and the air becomes still (30). He pursues not just the sensuality of the women but the feminine part of himself, which has for so long had no voice. Under the relentless light of a work day, however, he quickly recovers what he conceives as his masculinity and compensates for what he views as his weak lapse by vigorously resuming his paternal responsibilities to his son, lecturing him about what is real. Assuring Milkman that Pilate has nothing to teach him about this world, he presents him with the only important thing he needs to know: "Own things. And let the things you own own other things. Then you'll own yourself and other people too" (55).

Macon's dismissal of feminine discourse and resumption of the white male lecture mode culminate in one of the two stories that he knows to pass down to his son, his version of the relationship between Ruth and her father. Informing Milkman, who has just knocked Macon into the radiator for assaulting Ruth, that Milkman needs to hear the whole story, Macon can offer his son only half the story—his own. In brief, Macon "sees" Ruth committing incest with her father. He describes her lying "naked as a yard dog" next to Doctor Foster in his sickbed, where she kisses him: "Him dead and white and puffy and skinny, and she had his fingers in her mouth" (73).[8] While the sight of her mouth on the dead man's fingers eventually fades from memory, Macon sustains his outrage by imagining details and remembering her underwear. Ruth recalls the incident, however, as kneeling in her slip at her father's bedside and kissing the only part of him not disfigured by his disease—his beautiful fingers. She explains that her father alone cared about her, that she is not strange but small. Because she lives in a big house that "pressed [her] into a small package," Ruth, like her daughters, has no songs to sing, and her one life-denying story articulates a loneliness that forces her to seek unnatural connections to father, husband, and son.

Spillers and Hirsch comment on the implications of incest as it applies to the African American family. The terms *family*, *father*, and *mother* "signify differently in an African American context than they do in a Eurocentric one. The laws of captivity recognized neither maternity nor paternity . . . but they made the status of paternity particularly distant from the patriarchal domain reigning in the dominant culture" (Hirsch 71). Having repressed the Africanist perspective and seized on the Eurocentric one, Macon so fears what he views as an improper distance between father/daughter, mother/son, or brother/sister that he cannot comprehend much less cope with the complexities of filial or sibling relationships in black communities, forced on them by former enslavement. He appeases his anxieties by having no conversation with women at all.

Thus, Macon's voice becomes not only commanding and critical; it drowns out other sounds: "And you're my own son. And you will do what I tell you to do. With or without explanations"; "As long as your feet are under my table, you'll do in this house what you are told"; "Watch your mouth!"; "Don't you raise your voice to me" (50). Sensitive listeners might infer from such negative tones that Macon functions in the novel primarily to teach his son how not to speak. As Nellie McKay comments, "We don't admire Milkman's father." His creator, on the other hand, defends her character. "Why not?" she responds, citing Macon as an example of a stable black man when McKay describes Morrison's male figures as unsteady and constantly in motion (402).

Such ambiguity can partly be explained by Morrison's effort to render complex individuals who embody "bits of both [good and bad]." However, Gurian sheds further light on Macon's behavior with his analysis of male compassion (McKay 402). Describing men equally as capable of showing compassion as women but with instinctually different ways of doing so, his research suggests that what some critics define as Macon's negative qualities are sometimes merely "natural ways of showing compassion, some of which appear to run counter to what is taught in the female model." Gurian maintains that males often reveal compassion through silence. He offers examples that remain "no longer very respected, much to the confusion of adolescent boys and men": efficient resolution of distress through problem-solving, giving the gift of space by leaving others alone, "leaving home for weeks and months on end to go to work and provide the resources by which their wives and children can survive" (235–36). While much of Macon-speak may be attributed to its deadening white male model, Morrison is not averse to inverting her own inversions so that "dead" becomes "silent" in both negative and positive senses. Macon does have several gifts to pass on to his son: he is stable and responsible; he works hard to satisfy Milkman's physical, material, and aesthetic needs; and he provides Milkman with a positive rendition of his grandfather's story.

Although the brutal circumstances that conclude his father's history cause Macon Dead the Second to misread Macon Dead the First, Milkman's father buffers Milkman's first draft of the saga of Macon Dead. We learn from Macon's story that he "worked right alongside [his] father. Right alongside him" (51). However, Milkman must piece together out of snatches gathered from Pilate and from the old men in Danville, Pennsylvania, that Macon I's murder by white people leads Macon II to mis/reinterpret the concept of work. Macon's violent loss of his beloved father kills his idealism and his creativity and turns serious play into nonproductive work.[9]

Morrison compares the quasi-inspiring story of Macon Dead Senior with that of his son not just to criticize Macon Dead Junior. By showcasing what she views as the significance of fathers in their children's development, she also defends him and encourages us to love him.[10] In his first life, Macon Dead Senior is Jake, youngest son of Solomon, the legendary flying slave who flew off carrying his baby boy but dropped him near the porch of the Big House. Thus, Jake has the distinction of being both his father's favorite child and the one his father left next to rich white people. The very knowledge of Solomon's love sustains Jake. The son combines this affection with information gathered from the Big House to climb his own ladder and create his American dream—the beautiful farm he calls

Lincoln's Heaven. Renamed Macon Dead by a drunken white clerk when Jake goes to register at the Freedmen's Bureau, Macon Dead Senior keeps his new name to wipe out his slave past and start afresh. Unlike his son, however, who maintains his name but rejects his past, the father retains his community ties.

Exuding a natural sexuality, this new American Adam tries to grow things on his land, not own them or cut them down for profit. Unable to read or write, he knows "only what he saw and heard tell of." However, he ingeniously communicates the significant facts and truths of his culture through the tools he has available. His farm horse becomes President Lincoln because Lincoln "was a good plow hand before he was President and you shouldn't take a good plow hand away from his work." His hog is General Lee, finest general around because, when slaughtered, he makes "the best pork outside Virginia. . . . Even his balls was tasty" (52). His name game entices his children to decipher his sly, encoded humor and simultaneously remember their history. It also offers them a playful way to learn survival skills.

Isolated by illiteracy on a predominantly literate mainland, Macon Senior survives by creatively turning islands into streams. Deconstructing print, he relies directly on his senses to locate the accuracy. For example, he reconstructs the written word as a picture on a page and appropriately names his daughter Pilate: not after the man who killed Christ but for the sheltering way the large, majestic figure in the group of letters bends protectively over the smaller ones. Because the ex-slave rejects the power and possessions of the literate majority for the opportunity to nurture, he goes on protecting his children after his death. Pilate's father whispers to her to stay grounded and to sing; she keeps the comfort of his bones close to her always. As usual in *Song of Solomon*, the advice Macon Dead Senior gives his daughter may be interpreted in more than one way. However, the words "You just can't fly on off and leave a body" since a "human life is precious" certainly encourage Pilate to keep her feet on the ground, to assume responsibility for all of life (208). Seeking sincerely to enact Polonius's cynically motivated maxim, "By indirections find directions out," Macon Dead even accompanies his grandson on his journey to selfhood. Jake appears in Danville as the man in the brown peaked cap and old-fashioned collar who helps Milkman find Circe by directing him to Reverend Cooper's yellow house in Stone Lane.

Although Milkman embellishes tales of his father's masculine exploits, he finally realizes that any sustenance his stories can provide the old men in Danville will be ephemeral and gossamer. Gazing at Milkman with their rheumy eyes and their regrets, these men have turned into the living dead; they are the ghosts of Macon Dead's future returned to his past. Rigidity and white interference reshape Macon Senior's legacy. The beautiful freedom of Lincoln's Heaven reverts to owning a piece of the rock, and Macon's murder fuels the black men's desire to steal a home in it. Their mistaken dream, and their outraged impotence, speaks like a sermon, extolling them to stop sniveling and "picking around the edges of the world." Vowing to "take advantage, and if you can't take advantage, take disadvantage," they promise to "Take it, hold it, . . . shake it, squeeze it, turn it, twist it, beat it, kick it, kiss it, whip it, stomp it, dig it, plow it, seed it, reap it, rent it, buy it, sell it, own it, build it, multiply it, and pass it on" (235). Their rap tune sounds sour, however, because its arrangement is futile and its lyrics prosaic—to win, to own, to dominate. As Milkman tells Guitar, Macon Junior "doesn't care whether a white man lives or swallows lye. He just wants what they have" (224). The drive to "worry them white folks to death," which perpetually emasculates the old men, causes them to overlook a small but significant detail about Macon Senior. While he can "plow forty in no time flat," he can also "sing like an angel while he [does] it" (235–36). Unlike the insubstantial zombies who warn against his son's mode of manhood, the dead grandfather lives by embodying the feminine masculinity that the grandson seeks.

Macon's false inheritance results partly from the forced absence of his real father but also from the unwilling presence of his foster father. As Spillers emphasizes, the mostly illiterate African slave father, dispossessed of his culture and subordinate to the "captor father's mocking presence," transmits neither patronym, logos, nor law to his progeny (80). Morrison's description of Macon's courtship of Doctor Foster provides some grim fun with its perverse twists on Faulkner's already wonderfully strange story of southern dispossession, "A Rose for Emily." Miss Emily Grierson's aristocratic father stands straddling and silhouetted against the entrance of his great house with front door flung back but horsewhip in hand to fend off his daughter's gentlemen callers. Doctor Foster, on the other hand, undramatically opens the door with the lion's paw knocker to his daughter's suitor, but not because of any magic in Macon's keys. The not-so-good Doctor, or father, responds rudely to Macon's "honorable" intentions and polite request to "keep [Ruth's] company," saying that he knows nothing about Macon other than his name, which he dislikes. His apparent concession to accede to his daughter's preference actually disguises his gratitude toward a young man who proposes to divert her attentions away from her father. Ruth's "steady beam of love," "slow-witted" good-night kiss, and ecstatically shining face as he bends reluctantly over her unsettle her father (23).

Doctor Foster serves as Macon's substitute father under more than one false pretense. He allows Macon to continue believing that male potency resides in property. He verifies his son-in-law's pretentious gentility and his delusions of grandeur while he covers up his own core sterility. Morrison symbolizes the internal decay in the Foster family with the increasingly pronounced watermark staining their mahogany dining room table. Caused and concealed by the bowl of fresh flowers or leaf arrangement that decorates the table every day, it indicates the elegance that Doctor believes distinguishes his family from "the people among whom they lived" (12). He demands such flora not because he has a green thumb but in order to thumb his nose at other people. The single flaw in the otherwise fine, dark wood, the watermark stands as the mooring by which to locate the Fosters; Doctor Foster's expensive imitation of white gentility forever mars a solid black family.

Morrison provides another symbol of Doctor's internal vacuousness in the ether he sniffs to deaden his sensibilities and become his own patient etherized upon a table. His actions epitomize the hypocritical practitioner of the Hippocratic Oath who, instead of healing himself, numbs himself to and even increases others' pain. While this physician remains physically present, he is emotionally elsewhere.

Doctor Foster's disgust with himself spills over into an "absolute hatred of this woman who would not grant him peace, but kept her shining lightish eyes fixed on him like magnets holding him from the narrow earth he longed for" (134). Ruth's serene efficiency at stirring up the already dead, also apparent in her coolly deliberate provocation of Macon Dead, causes her husband to "wonder who she was married to—[her father or him]" (72). Unlike Macon Dead Senior, whose legacy nurtures his daughter after his death, this imitation vanilla father cannot rise from his grave even when his daughter lies on top of it. Ringing changes on the emotional, sexual, and moral perversions that Faulkner explores in "A Rose for Emily," Morrison depicts the black father imitating but rejected by the white one. In both versions, however, the ultimate victim is a daughter, starved for affection from the father, satisfying her hunger for male connection in grotesque ways.

Both stories also comment wryly on decaying cultures and destructive notions about manhood. As Faulkner associates Emily's bloated body with the dissolution of the Old South, so Morrison describes the dying Doctor Foster as its failed black experiment: "Helpless, fat stomach, skinny arms and legs, looking like a white rat" (73).[11] Thus, Morrison inverts Faulkner's description of rotting white gentility to examine its diseased black counterpart and to illustrate the "puzzle" that is African

American paternity (Spillers 80). Arguing that it amounts to racial suicide for black daddies to imitate white patrons, she acknowledges that Macon Dead has lost his balance but agrees with him when he tells his son: "I am not a bad man" (74).

If Macon is a fat cat and Doctor Foster a skinny white rat, Guitar Bains is a lean but mean lynx. Sons of Solomon all, all tainted by Big House contact, Macon and Doctor want what white men have. As a result, Macon becomes a smoldering volcano and Doctor a not-doctor not allowed to heal. White interference turns Guitar's stories into sermons on racial hatred and his serious play into a lethal weapon.[12] Nonetheless, the primer Guitar provides for Milkman's survival is generally more useful to him than his father's lectures about owning things and people and, ultimately, selves. Both his buddy and a royal bane of Milkman's existence, Guitar introduces the younger boy to the signifying speak of Southside, teaches him the ABCs of black male urban survival, and, most importantly, inspires his dormant imagination.

Guitar first encounters Milkman as Ruth goes into labor for her son on the steps of Mercy Hospital and at the age of five stays bound to him forever by the sight of Mr. Smith flying off its roof on homemade blue silk wings and the sound of Pilate singing "Sugarman gone home"(6). The tension between visual and auditory images defines Guitar, but his circumstances tip the scales in favor of what he can see.

The essential skills Guitar sees fit to signify on to Milkman include pointers about geography (Guitar's trope for place-is-race), a subject that Milkman has thus far studiously avoided. Sheltered from birth, Milkman remains so naïve about the facts of race in America that, when Reverend Cooper describes Macon Senior's murder by whites, the grandson raises everybody's eyebrows by wondering: "Did anybody ever catch the men who did it?" (231). During one of his many escapes to Guitar's locked apartment, this time to avoid Hagar's ice pick, Milkman enjoys, with his tea and over his objections, a geography lesson that represents both a humorous attempt to lift his sagging spirits and a challenging debate about the insidiousness of Western racism. Guitar's banter, ostensibly countering Milkman's mockery of his host's kitchen habits, actually engages serious race issues. The repartee skips lightly but intensely from tea-making (the domination of black workers in India by British tea growers) to Guitar's current location (the myth that the North treats African Americans more humanely than does the South) to teapots (Milkman's superficiality) to teabags (white colonization of northern blacks) to the exclamation "Jesus!" (the strange fruit that is black people hanging from southern trees) to eggs (not among the multiplicity of racist epithets for niggers and, if brown, the complexities of miscegenation). Concluding his lesson by warning his friend, "somebody got to bust your shell," Guitar exclaims: "Goddam, Milk, I do believe my whole life's geography" (114–16).

Once he clarifies the heated local racial climate, Guitar goes on to signify about how to cope with the temperature. When Milkman reassures his worried friend, "Everything's cool," Guitar responds: "Even the North Pole ain't cool" (117). Annoyed by Milkman's indifference to his own fate and that of his race, this experience-toughened male rejects the clichéd 1960s panacea and, with the controlled grace of a cat, emphasizes his frustration by slamming his fist into a wall. On the other hand, he also explains to Milkman that, because the geographical deck remains so stacked against them, simply trying to stay alive and in the game distorts African Americans, causing them to cheat one another. His remedy for pain reads: "Don't carry it inside and don't give it to nobody else. Try to understand it, but if you can't, just forget it and keep yourself strong, man" (88).

When Milkman wallows in self-absorbed self-pity, withholding the support that Guitar demands each black man offer his brother, Guitar signifies the relationship between selfhood, compassion, and survival, insisting: "Niggers get their names the way they get everything else—the best way they can." And when his friend complains, "Why can't we get our stuff the right way?" Guitar retorts: "The best way is the right way" (87–88). Even as a young person, Guitar embraces three of the four elements that Gurian identifies as the heart of manhood: compassion, honor, and responsibility. Morrison confirms, however, that even the definition of these terms depends, for Guitar, on geography.

However a man gets "his stuff," Guitar upholds the importance of getting some, chipping away at Milkman's reluctance to commit to something meaningful beyond himself. When Milkman objects to "a bullshit lecture" and his friend's tone of voice, Guitar distinguishes between lecturing and talking. He then proposes that Milkman do less talking and more listening because he spends "fifty percent of [his] brainpower thinking about a piece of ass." When Milkman accuses Guitar of being "mad at every Negro who ain't scrubbing floors and picking cotton," he responds: "If things ever got tough, you'd melt. You're not a serious person, Milkman" (103–4). Milkman defends himself by comparing what he perceives as Guitar's inclination to blow everything out of proportion with that of Macon Dead. He cannot yet see the difference between the two men's concerns—Guitar's for his people and Macon's for his paperclips. As Milkman wonders, "What's happening to everybody?" Guitar makes one more attempt to enlighten his thirty-one-year-old buddy, suggesting in an ironic but still conversational tone: "Looks like everybody's going in the wrong direction but you, don't it?" (106).

Maintaining the need for a significant destination, Guitar claims that African American males have to get there by balancing on the catwalk between the flexibility of nine lives and the ability to pounce, claw, and bite. Despite fashionable feminist views, Morrison acknowledges, and Gurian concurs, that most men are natural fighters and hunters. As he observes the children in Shalimar at play, Milkman recalls that his "velvet suit separated him from the other children" until Guitar pulls four boys off him. Corduroy knickers or straight pants help to dissuade white and black children from taunting and torturing him, but they never ask Milkman to join their circle or singing games until a grinning, whooping Guitar becomes his blood brother. Guitar's enthusiasm represents "the first time Milkman saw anybody really enjoy a fight," and it teaches him that males bond through physical contact (264). Contemporary studies on conflict resolution recommend various approaches to achieve compromise and prevent violence. They also suggest that healthy competition can clear the air, redefine respectful boundaries, and even make fast friends.[13]

Guitar informs Milkman that people have described Guitar from childhood as a natural-born hunter, that he could "hear anything, smell anything, and see like a cat" (85). As a small boy in the South, he will take a shot at any available game and is never afraid, not even to kill. Nonetheless, he accepts and acts on the code of honor endorsed among the respected hunters of his tribe. He might not obey the white-imposed laws restricting hunting seasons, operating instead by the seasons of natural balance, but, unlike white men and the domestic house cat, he does not kill for power or pleasure but for survival. When he and Milkman, plotting to steal Pilate's inheritance, spot a pure white peacock spreading its tail on the hood of a flashy Buick, Guitar yells for Milkman to catch it. Milkman asks his friend what he wants to do with such an exotic, and Guitar shouts gleefully, "Eat him!" (179).[14]

The peacock scene illustrates two additional survival skills that the hunter signifies for Milkman: take risks but pack light. His conspiracy with Guitar to cop Pilate's sack of gold releases the salty taste in Milkman's mouth that he associates with his friend's ability to create a sense of life lived on the cutting edge. It recalls their childhood when they "swaggered, haunched, leaned, straddled, ran all over town trying to pick fights or at least scare somebody: . . . When they succeeded they rode the wind."

Even as men "the terror they needed to provoke in others, if for no other reason than to feel it themselves, was rarer but not lighter. Dominion won by fear and secured by fear was still sweeter than any that could be got another way" (177). Though Guitar's appetites exceed his, Milkman thrives on the danger and joy that Guitar brings to living. When Milkman holds back, ticking off the risks of breaking into Pilate's house, Guitar urges him to take a chance: "You can't get no pot of gold being reasonable. . . . You got a life? Live it! Live the motherfuckin life!" (183). Conceding that such intensity requires an incredible lightness of being, however, Guitar points out that the white male peacock cannot fly because it has "Too much tail. All that jewelry weighs it down. Like vanity. Can't nobody fly with all that shit. Wanna fly, you got to give up the shit that weighs you down" (179).

These scenes may appear to have more in common with some tenets of the National Rifle Association or *Field and Stream* magazine than with those of animal-rights activists. However, Morrison may also merely be reflecting the biological hardwiring that Gurian describes as part of masculine development and acknowledging certain laws of nature. Qualifying his definition of the "male brain" as a "spectrum of possibilities" but explaining that some features of the "male emotional system" seem to be uniquely male, Gurian asserts that the male brain is designed for such spatial activities as hunting and playing ball. He defines it as an object-oriented brain that, "as an outgrowth of its spatiality, loves to experience *objects moving through space*." This brain does not concentrate on the emotional core of its object because to do so would make the brain less efficient at fulfilling its function, which is "to gain dominance over and, through dominance, to transform the object into something useful to self and community" (31–40). Morrison's narrator simply notes: "To win. There was nothing like it in the world" (251).

Using the humanization of objects in space and the cyclical approach to time that Gurian maintains is more typical of the evolved "female brain," Morrison returns Guitar to his beloved South as one of the hunters Milkman meets in Shalimar, Virginia. Seeking direction and a fan belt, Milkman arrives on the porch of Solomon's Store and, still ignorant, manages within seconds to insult the young black men lounging about. Like the velvet clothes of his childhood, his three-piece suit, fine leather shoes, snap-brim hat, silk tie, and gold watch set him apart from the others, and his cavalier manner of "buying a car as if it were a bottle of whiskey" only irritates them further. He does not bother to introduce himself or ask their names, referring to them as "them." As such, he is "telling them that they weren't men, that they relied on women and children for their food," and that money measures manhood (266).[15] Milkman partially redeems his blackness by calling on the street-fighting skills taught him by Guitar to fend off a toothless, knife-wielding local named Saul, after which he exchanges a broken bottle for a shotgun and an invitation from the older men to hunt in the woods. Faces masked, sitting quietly on the porch throughout the fracas as if nothing were occurring, these four men represent the gurus Gurian insists middle adolescent boys be turned over to, the uncles who trained Guitar to hunt, and the griots who will help Milkman find his manhood.

Milkman's initiation by the old men into "coonhunting" caps the instruction by Guitar that will see his protégé halfway home.[16] The men remove Milkman's city clothes, symbols of white civilization, replacing them with muddy brogans, army fatigues, and a knit cap like Pilate's. Told to "take that change out your pocket, . . . Makes too much noise," he lets go of his money and gradually leaves off focusing on the burning lamp held in front of him until he "grow[s] accustomed to the dark" (272–73). Morrison makes her obvious allusions to Faulkner's "The Bear" even more apparent when Milkman, overly nonchalant, inquires, "Any bears out here?" (272–73). However, her twist on the tale of a boy initiated into manhood as he releases the trappings of civilization and communes with nature reveals her usual comic, and black, signature. Like Hurston's Janie, who identifies her African American self by playing games and going deeper into the black muck, Milkman must discover how to walk that walk. He has to find out how to pick up his feet in order to miss roots and stones, how to distinguish a tree from a shadow—in short, how to read the landscape. As the man whose "whole life's geography" begins to unlock the secrets of rural black male survival, he simultaneously locates human nature and, ultimately, himself (114).

Morrison also distinguishes her male initiation story as her character comes to appreciate the pre-literate culture of his ancestors. Alone in the dark, unencumbered by anything other than "what he was born with, or had learned to use," reduced to breath, thoughts, senses, and endurance, his "self—the cocoon that was 'personality'—gave way." Freed from the burden of ego, the last of "the shit that weighs [him] down," Milkman is now vulnerable enough and light enough to discern the instinct that will allow him to "separate out, of all the things there were to sense, the one that life itself might depend on." Like a child suddenly gifted with the miracle of reading, he can break the hunters' code with a shock of recognition. He understands that the men communicate with the dogs, that in "distinctive voices they [are] saying distinctive, complicated things. . . . And if they could talk to animals, and the animals could talk to them, what didn't they know about human beings? Or the earth itself?" (278). Morrison follows Milkman's epiphany with a passage that associates the noises of the dogs and men with the musical conversation of jazz instrumentalists, acknowledging that instinct and passion effect creation and communication as often as do logic and reason.

She also allows Milkman the precious understanding that creativity flows from humility, the result of quieting the ego in order to listen. Hunters whisper to trees and ground. They "touched them, as a blind man caresses a page of Braille, pulling meaning through his fingers" (278). This becomes the shared knowledge, the common sense that will enable Milkman to bond with the other men in mutual compassion, responsibility, honor, self-deprecating humor, and love. He now possesses the awareness of his brother's pain that Guitar tried so hard to teach him—and Guitar appears in the woods as the bobcat that challenges him and imprints this pain onto his body. The skills acquired during the serious play of "coonhunting" permit Milkman to save his own life. His prize, depicted as the hunters' literal killing, skinning, and gutting of the lynx, performs the metaphorical transcendence of son beyond father, student beyond teacher. Contained and restrained by the reverence of ritual, Milkman bites into the bloody heart of the bobcat and takes for himself the manhood of the master.

Morrison certainly controls no patent on releasing characters into a "green world." Like the Forest of Arden or the woods outside Athens or Prospero's island, Guitar's South resembles James Dickey's "country of nine-fingered people," the land of the primitive, the sensual, the imaginative (52). And like other stories in which the inexperienced or "already dead" awaken their slumbering imaginations by descending into and then transcending the underworld id, the scenery does not always look pretty. Fascinating, exciting, enticing, dangerous, the woods are "lovely," as Frost would have it, but also "dark and deep." Even in Shakespeare's lush, erotic forest, the deer, anthropomorphic tears welling in its liquid eyes, dies cruelly by the archer's hand. Acknowledging the creative/killer instinct as essential to the hunter's survival, Guitar nonetheless objects, like Uncle Ike in Faulkner's "Delta Autumn," to the killing of a doe. Telling Milkman, "A man shouldn't do that," this man conveys his respect and love for and his responsibility to women in various ways.

For example, after Milkman describes his "dream" about his mother's encounter with blood-red killer tulips, revealing that he senses but will not confront the smothering toll that even fresh flowers have taken on her life, Guitar asks with a smile: "Why didn't you go help her?" (105). Milkman, lacking the compassion to realize when those closest to him get into trouble, rationalizes with date rapists that Ruth "was having fun. She liked it." Guitar, on the other hand, possesses the intuition that Sarah Orne Jewett calls the "gift of sympathy." Though he claims political activism prevents him from making a long-term commitment to a woman, he reprimands Milkman for his friend's callous treatment of Hagar. Recognizing Milkman's responsibility for his cousin's self-destructive behavior, Guitar discerns the difference between calling off a relationship between two consenting adults and so hurting a girl that she becomes one "messed-up lady" (152).

He also attempts to talk Hagar through her "graveyard love." Repelled as he is by "mindlessness in love," Guitar becomes overwhelmed by sorrow as he literally carries Hagar home from his apartment, speaking quietly to her over the roar of the old car's engine. He suggests that, because she wants to belong to Milkman, she thinks she owns him. He tells her that *belong* is a bad word, especially when associated with love for human beings. Employing signifying tactics more gently than he does with Milkman, he shows Hagar how the clouds softly encircling the mountain never cover its peak. Cautioning, "You can't lose what you don't own," he questions whether she can possibly love a person who is not a person without her. He points out that, if her life means so little to her that she could give it away, she cannot expect someone else to appreciate it. His final words, "He can't value you more than you value yourself," falling on Hagar's deaf ears, Guitar muses sadly about the pride, the conceit of "doormat women" who would kill or die for love. Always spoiled as children, they grow up to be "the stingiest, greediest people on earth and out of their stinginess grew their stingy little love that ate everything in sight" (305–7). Certain that the universe is out of kilter when they are not loved, these girls need a chorus of women to offer them the facts of life. A man like Guitar, however, empathizes enough with women to talk to Hagar like a sister would.

Guitar's final warning to his brother explains how "Everybody wants the life of a black man." Rapping "It's the condition our condition is in" when Milkman complains that people require something from him they can get nowhere else and think he has, Guitar goes on to elaborate: white men "want us dead or quiet"; white women want us " 'universal,' human, no 'race consciousness.' Tame, except in bed"; and black women, "they want your whole self" and call it love, responsibility, and understanding. Asserting that women demand a man's full attention, refusing him the right to risk his own life unless it revolves around them, and affirming the value of brotherhood, he scoffs at his friend's denial that anybody can choose what to die for: "Yes you can, and if you can't, you can damn well try to" (222–23). His message exudes the feistiness that Morrison applauds in the free black male, the "magic" that no one can contain though everyone has tried.

The only thing that can kill the free man, at least according to Pilate, is his own ignorance. In Guitar's case, this becomes blind obsession with black justice. Like Macon's dead voice and Saul's missing teeth, Guitar carries the scar of the white father's abuse of the black father. He reacts by rejecting any part of himself not mean and lean enough to avenge the mistreatment. Already endowed with a propensity to hunt and conquer greater than that of Milkman, he locks himself off from his anima by a means other than Macon's keys and reduces himself to yang, body, action, logic, and will. Macon overstuffs himself with excess pie filling; Guitar is nauseated by the mere smell of sweets.[17]

Confiding to Milkman that sugar "makes [him] think of dead people. And white people. And [he] start[s] to puke," a young Guitar reveals that he has felt this way since his father was sliced in half during work at a sawmill and the foreman responded by giving the children a sack of divinity candy made by his wife (61). In lieu of life insurance, the sawmill owner hands Guitar's mother forty dollars, which she "happily" accepts to buy her children a peppermint stick on the day of her husband's funeral. His child's mind cannot grasp the pain and despair that finally drive his mother away. The oldest son misinterprets his mother's gesture as disloyalty to the black man and capitulation and subjugation to the white one. Clutching but refusing to eat the "bone-white and blood-red stick," Guitar endures the mockery of his brother and two sisters at what they believe is his miserliness until he can drop the candy into the "stinking hole" of the outhouse (224–25).

Forced to develop "an inside and an outside" and to understand "how not to mix them" in order to cope with a big, white-sounding voice, Guitar must confront a divided self at too young an age (Hurston 68). For Morrison, the trope reads "sliced in half and boxed backward" (224). A boy learns how ruthless competition leaves the two parts of his father's body to face each other in their coffin. He remains haunted from childhood by the nightmare that "when his father was wakened on Judgment Day his first sight would not be glory or the magnificent head of God—or even the rainbow. It would be his own other eye" (224). Because white male control imposes a split or incomplete self on black boys like Macon and Guitar, their understanding of compassion, honor, and responsibility becomes distorted, so they engage in unhealthy, life-denying enterprise.[18] Guitar's father, like Guitar, cannot buy into the mystery of the Father because he has been prevented from playing the father.

Searching for the wholeness of manhood, Guitar instinctively seeks out older men who appear to possess that gift. Separated from their natural habitat, however, the southern hunters of his boyhood turn into the violently activist Seven Days. The Days' enterprise involves dispensing revenge. While these men reveal the same modesty and self-deprecating humor as their southern counterparts, they are compelled to use the part of the night Corinthians associates with men who hunt, not to survive but to terrorize. They become secretive, forfeiting their griot status, and the signifying voice becomes "a litany of personal humiliation, outrage, and anger turned sicklelike back to themselves as humor" (82).

The coping mechanism that converts horror into humor also twists love into hatred. When Mr. Smith decides to fly off the roof of Mercy Hospital, he both sacrifices himself to protect the Seven Days' identities and transcends his participation in depravity. Either way, he concedes his dedication to insuring Mutual Life. Morrison takes pains to emphasize the complexities of love and hate for African American men by having Mr. Smith's flight or descent act as catalyst for the first black child to be born in Mercy Hospital. In addition, the bland little insurance agent signs his suicide note: "Please forgive me. I loved you all" (3). Porter's drunken binges, also signs of the dehumanizing responsibilities of being a Seven Day, allow him to express frustrated love. As he urinates over the women's heads and shoots blindly into the crowd or at himself, he screams: "You women . . . Don't you see I love ya? I'd die for ya, kill for ya . . . Gimme hate, Lord, . . . But don't give me love. I can't take no more love, Lord" (26). This volatile behavior, along with the calendars that fill the walls of his tiny apartment and mark the days on which he strikes back at white people, contrast ironically with the gentle restraint of Porter's lovemaking with Corinthians.

Two other Seven Days, co-owners of a Southside barbershop, express a similarly distorted sensitivity. Hospital Tommy notices Guitar and Milkman sitting dejectedly on the curb while on "sabbatical" from school, having been ejected from Feather's pool hall. Taking the time to give them their first lesson in imperfect justice, Railroad Tommy ticks off a comic litany of things Guitar will not have. These men tell hard truths through humor, promising the boys they can count only on a broken heart and a whole lot of folly. Perhaps the most tragic of the Seven Day comedians, however, is Empire State. Happy and industrious after marrying a woman in France and bringing her home, he discovers six years later that his white wife loves not only him and not only another black man but "the whole race." Thereupon, he "sat down, closed his mouth, and never said another word" (128–29). Saved from the "poorhouse, workhouse, or nuthouse, one" by a janitor's job in the Tommys' shop, a drooling, silent Empire State channels his thwarted love into avenging Emmet Till's murder. State is the "colored man what killed that white boy in the schoolyard" (111).

Shaped by these misshapen mentors, Guitar turns into the most fanatic of all. His voice full not of money but of the ringing of the hunter's horn, he becomes a killing machine in the name of love. Although a model of the self-discipline that Gurian cites as the mark of manhood, he focuses intensely but with one eye closed. Avoiding alcohol, cigarettes, and tobacco and drinking only herbal teas, he hones his body for battle, keeping himself strong for what he calls "the big crunch" (225). He eschews work other than the manual labor with which to cover basic necessities, he cannot afford marriage or children, and he dreams about money merely to pay for "the wonders of TNT" (181). Attributing the beauty of the Days' terrorism to its secrecy and smallness, describing time and his days as "very satisfying," Guitar answers Milkman's accusation that no love can thrive in such a life: "What I'm doing ain't about hating white people. It's about loving us. . . . My whole life is love" (159).

As do most idealists, however, he loves ideas more than individuals. He expresses his disillusionment best through his attitude toward women. Categorizing them as doormats, smothering clouds, Jemimas, or white, Guitar comes to view females as "Other" because, like Macon, he remains too scarred to endorse his own feminine nature.[19] The disconnectedness surfaces clearly in his distaste for his mother and his disgust with Pilate. Sickened by the memory of his mother smiling at the white man who reduced his father's death to four ten-dollar bills, he recalls more than gratitude in her eyes: "not love but a willingness to love" (224). His hostility toward her forgiveness carries over to his relationship with Pilate. Guitar's childhood fascination with Milkman's aunt gives way to bitter resentment at what he terms the "Jemima" act she puts on to get Milkman and him out of jail. Silent anger "like heat shimmering out of his skin" spreading to a "jeweled hatred in his eyes," he defines the willing public humiliation on his behalf from this flexible woman whose home he has just broken into as "voluntary slavery" (207, 210, 224). While he treats Pilate's granddaughter gently, his kindness to Hagar is detached and driven by the very possessiveness he cautions her against. Guitar responds to Milkman's inability to distinguish the demands black women place on men from those of white women by flaring his nostrils. To "Why worry about the colored woman at all?" he snaps: "Because she's *mine*" (223).

The fanatical rigidity about racial justice that causes Guitar to turn on his mother and Pilate finally forces him to turn against his brother. And as with Macon Dead and Doctor Foster, an obsession with white culture turns into black suicide. He strikes ultimately at himself. Opting for fight instead of flight as defense against white attack, he employs terrorist tactics, informing Milkman: "Fair is one more thing I've given up" (224). As such, he exists by adopting what he defines as white methods of killing. Southside residents refer to "crimes planned and executed in a truly lunatic manner against total strangers" as "white madness." Believing that black people kill one another for "good reason," they justify only crimes committed in the heat of passion (100). The Seven Days' brand of violence, however, counters white madness with like-minded indifference, determination, and cold-blooded logic. Describing Hitler as "the most natural white man in the world," Guitar denies that any black man would kill for fun and maintains that it takes considerable "effort of the will to overcome an unnatural enemy" (156). Arguing that he has "better" motives for murder because they do not involve enjoyment, power, public attention, money, land, or anger, Guitar kills to keep the black-white ratio "balanced" and to "make a world where one day white people will think before they lynch" (160). In other words, and from his perspective, he kills to survive (160).

Demetrakopoulos describes Guitar as "one of Morrison's most appealing male characters" and expresses "a real loss" when he continues to pursue his vendetta (89). Such ambiguity distinguishes Morrison's memorable characters, however, and in Guitar's case it has to do with the "magic" of the free man. At the core of his fearlessness toward death lies, ironically, a reverence for life. American Indian culture likewise maintains that the hunter must respect and pay homage to the animal he kills because, in order to value life, he must possess the courage to seize it. As Milkman learns, "Perhaps that's what all human relationships boiled down to: Would you save my life? or would you take it?" With the exceptions of his mother and Pilate, those close to Milkman "seem to prefer him out of this life." Even Macon Dead tries to kill his son before his birth, and afterward to own him. Only his dangerously free black brother is "exceptional." To both questions, Guitar, the deadly hunter who defends black life, could answer "yes" (331).

Guitar and Macon represent two of the relatively static models of black manhood that Milkman incorporates into what will become his own flexible masculinity by the conclusion of the novel. Until his rebirth, Milkman represents a third. Although it "promises everything," the gold sought by all three symbolizes something distinct to each man. For Macon it offers "complete power," for Guitar "perfect justice," and for Milkman "total freedom" (185). Disconnected from the practical idealism that defines the traditional female community, however, the men pursuing these separate visions are incomplete and subject to perilous extremes. Once he assumes the masculine freedom of flying without leaving the feminine ground, Milkman becomes the American male whom Morrison envisions as successfully moderating masculine paradigms to his benefit and to that of his posterity. Mercy, which Morrison views as the resolute core of black womanhood, makes possible the black male's fluid wholeness.

Morrison indicates Milkman's limitations—along with his potential for self-awareness, flexibility, balance, creativity, and leadership—when he notices, at fourteen, one of his legs appearing shorter than the other. Using her signature overlaying of fantasy on reality that owes more to the black folk tradition than to magical realism, she creates from a cliché a sympathetically accurate portrait of the fragile and conflicted male adolescent. Milkman's deformity occurs mostly in his mind, though it pains him on the basketball court so crucial to black boys. His "burning defect" causes the "strut of a very young man trying to seem more sophisticated than he [is]," a distinguishing trademark designed to cope with his lack of distinction. Copied by his peers, it suggests the boys' struggle for balance. The narrator describes various reactions to this affected slouch in order to measure her characters' compassion, or lack thereof, for the disabilities that make male adolescent development uneasy. Like most boys, Milkman acquires habits to disguise what Ruth explains to an unsympathetic Lena as growing pains. He leans on bravado to threaten his sister: "I'll walk any way I want to, including over your ugly face" (62). He never stands straight but favors his left leg, cultivating for pretentious reasons a secret affinity with the white, liberal FDR, whom he publicly rejects. Threatened because Macon appears to have no imperfections but merely strengthens with age, he makes no attempt to hide his moue at his conservative black father.

Even at twenty-two Milkman worries, with good reason, that his face lacks coherence, a "coming together of the features into a total self." He is still too much like the child kneeling between his mother and father on the front seat of the Packard, riding awkwardly backward in order to see anything at all out the rear window. Like "flying blind" or a man "peeping around a corner of someplace he is not supposed to be," he remains uninformed, uncertain, and thus unable "to make up his mind whether to go forward or to turn back" (32, 69–70). At thirty-two he continues to live with his parents and to walk over the women who have cared for him, never so much as asking one of them if she is tired or sad or making any of them a "cup of tea" (331).[20] Milkman wants the humble confidence born of self-knowledge, which Morrison and Gurian connect with a respect for women. In addition, he lacks an appreciation for the contributions of race, class, and gender as well as an ability to transcend their limitations. However, when his fuller awareness finally surpasses the partial understanding of Macon and Guitar, he grows into the "lithe young man with onyx skin and legs as straight as cane stalks," the man who has "a name that [is] real" (17).

Morrison uses multiple names to illustrate that Milkman benefits from learning to transform into strengths the infirmities passed on to him by all his male influences—black and white, rich and poor. Realizing that, because of his faulty leg, he cannot emulate such perfectionists as Macon and Guitar, he endorses difference even as a boy and appears "deep," even "mysterious," to his mother's friends. His father's son in spite of them both, he carries his father's and his grandfathers' names along with the nickname so many black men acquire from "yearnings, gestures, flaws, events, mistakes, weaknesses" (330). His initials, as Ruth reminds him, reflect the M.D. of his physician grandfather, and he takes his middle name from Doctor Foster's surname, a word that means nurture or cherish as well as substitute. Although he laughs off his mother's wish that he enter college and attend medical school in favor of working for the father he both respects and fears, he also dissociates himself from Macon in many ways. Nonetheless, he inherits some positive values from Doctor and Macon; he also converts certain of their more destructive ideas into constructive ones.

Rejecting Macon's avoidance of tobacco and obsession with money, he shares with him his "love of good shoes and fine thin socks." And as his father's employee, he does try to "do the work the way Macon wanted it done" (63). For Morrison, addiction to money kills more people in American culture than smoking or hard work. Because he enjoys the useful, pleasurable, or beautiful, Milkman can resist the more destructive values that Macon adopts from white culture. Having had access to the comforts money brings, he can appreciate the luxury of freedom more than the stationary things Macon and Guitar dream about. Having been catered to, he does not feel the acute craving for respect that drives Doctor Foster.

While middle-class privilege allows Milkman to begin life free from the scars of his predecessors, it also prevents him from understanding their disabilities so that he can move beyond his own. He must develop compassion for Guitar's dreams and Doctor's yearnings while acknowledging their shortcomings. Finally interested in the road signs during the last leg of his long journey to selfhood, he wonders for the first time what underlies the names of places and pays tribute to his grandfather as the "first colored man of consequence in that city." He comprehends that the black people who name a street after Doctor overlook the fact that he is "arrogant, color-struck, snobbish." They "didn't care about that. They were paying their respect to whatever it was that made him *be* a doctor in the first place, when the odds were that he'd be a yardman all of his life" (329).

Echoing Maya Angelou's passionate declaration that nobody can make it alone, Morrison claims that boys need even more instruction than girls. If Doctor illustrates for his grandson the painful significance of self-esteem, Macon Dead Junior lectures his son about its connection to work and introduces him to Macon Dead Senior, rechristened son of Solomon who, with the help of Pilate and the children of Shalimar, will become Milkman's model for serious play. Guitar shows his friend how to be a hunter and what it means to be a poor black man in America. Black women sing to Milkman about mercy. Thus, while he learns to be a man among men from his black brothers, the youngest son of Solomon must learn from his black sisters (and mothers and aunts and cousins) to reconstruct Macon's notions about power, Guitar's about justice, and his own about freedom in order to be a man in a community.

Morrison envisions Milkman evolving beyond even *Sula*'s Ajax, who loves his conjure mother first and "after her—airplanes," the free black man who can appreciate a woman "whose life was her own" (126–27). If the childhood nickname given him by his father's flunky predicts a certain milk-white assimilation despite an onyx skin, it also indicates an attraction to women. Struggling between complicitous looks and appreciative laughter to find the right expression, Freddie the janitor signifies with his usual gutter mentality on the long-legged four-year-old who still, if reluctantly, nurses from his mother: "A natural milkman if ever I seen one. Look out, womens. Here he come. Huh!" (15). Refusing to acknowledge a name that "sounded dirty, intimate, and hot," fastidious Macon suspects that it is not associated with the cleanliness or honesty of a dairyman. Repressed male adults thus cause the boy to feel ashamed and guilty about his closeness to his mother, and Macon transmits his disgust with the Dead women to his son. Milkman then ignores Ruth as "too insubstantial, too shadowy for love," pisses on Lena, patronizes Corinthians, destroys Hagar, and steals from Pilate (75).

Despite his unintentionally destructive behavior toward them, as Pilate says, "Ain't nothing going to kill him but his own ignorance, and won't no woman ever kill him. What's likelier is that it'll be a woman save his life" (140). Unlike Guitar, who will fight either for or against him, women preserve Milkman's life in both senses of stifling and protecting. Pressed small by Macon and Foster, Ruth, Lena, and Corinthians are silenced into passive aggression or "displayed" and then "splayed," essentially telling tales only of terrifying males. Hence, they nurture by negating themselves. Ruth must surrender the secret power and pleasurable fantasy of her nursing self as a "cauldron issuing spinning gold," fully "half of what made her daily life bearable," and Milkman must stop nursing from (feeding off of) his mother in order to nurse (care for) Ruth (13–14). He has to separate himself from her in order to see her as a "pale but complicated woman given to deviousness and ultra-fine manners" who has a "life apart from allowing or interfering with his own" (75).

When Milkman strikes his father after Macon hits Ruth, he partly establishes his own dominance, protecting his mother out of the same wide-eyed ignorance that causes him to accidentally urinate on Lena's twig and to break up Corinthians's relationship with Porter.[21] Nonetheless, Ruth enlists Pilate to help her fend off Macon's dangerous effects on Milkman, and the two "tear her up" for what both know are Hagar's futile attempts on Milkman's life, "just for the tryin" (139). Even mousy Lena's magnificent pronouncement that the little "hog's gut that hangs down between [his] legs" does not make him a man becomes the much-needed catalyst that encourages Milkman to leave home. Declaring that he has yet to "wash [his] own underwear, spread a bed, wipe the ring from [his] tub, or move a fleck of [his] dirt from one place to another," Lena warns her brother: "I don't make roses anymore, and you have pissed your last in this house. . . . Now get out of my room" (215–16).

Along with learning to take his mother and older sisters seriously, instead of mindlessly taking the milk they provide but leave out on the table too long, Milkman must also view women as something apart from an aid to autoerotic stimulation. Inspired at age twelve by his first sight of Hagar, he "had no need to see her face; he had already fallen in love with her behind" (43). At seventeen he readily responds to the older girl's desire to pass the time by watching "the lump grow in a little boy's pants" (97). However, after more than a dozen years of sex "so free, so abundant, it had lost its fervor," he regards her as "the third beer," the one "you drink because it's there, because it can't hurt, and because what difference does it make?" (91).[22] Guitar repeatedly criticizes Milkman's cavalier treatment of black women. Pilate's defense of her daughter, juxtaposed against the offense taken by the men in Shalimar toward Milkman's presumptive ease with their females, supplies context for Guitar's words.

Pilate has no difficulty whatsoever with Reba's giving away everything she has or living "from one orgasm to another" (150). She will, however, skillfully jab a knife blade into the heart of anyone who "fool[s]" with her belongings. Requesting a "little talk" with Reba's abusive newcomer boyfriend as he literally sweats blood under the pressure of her kitchen knife, she dryly explains her predicament to him: because women lack the strength and self-control of men, "Mamas get hurt and nervous when somebody don't like they children" (94). Thus, while she hates to pull her knife out of him and risk his further hurting her child, she also hates to push it further in, empathizing with the man's mother, who would experience similar pain about her child's suffering. Comically but pointedly illustrating the painfully delicate balance between obligation to self and responsibility to community, this conjure woman, who "never bothered anybody" and is "helpful to everybody," asserts her power by speaking softly but carrying a big blade. Moving easily between male and female modes of persuasion, she reinforces Guitar's instruments of destruction with her constantly moving lips, ominously still now, until the boyfriend "chooses" to flee. Unlike Guitar and the young men of Shalimar who are territorial about their women, however, Pilate refuses to extend her concept of ownership beyond what Morrison calls "caring for." She also shows a young Milkman that every woman remains some mother's child.

Although he is a "natural milkman" whose inability to hold liquor and "waking dreams" verify his affinity with the fluid female, the third Macon Dead needs a griot to help him distill these gifts. Born without the navel that normally links people to the collective, already disconnected from her mother, Pilate is the wine-brewing outlander who makes up her life as she goes along and who, guided by her father, shares with Milkman the recipe to create his. If macho Guitar teaches his friend how to play with outdoor hunting equipment, an androgynous Pilate keeps a sharp knife on her kitchen shelf. She prepares for discord but prefers the harmonies of singing by ear. She exhibits the strength and endurance coupled with intuition, imagination, nurturance, flexibility, humility, and forgiveness that, for Morrison, define the African American woman. Having been walking on water for years, this black Pilate not only does not kill Christ; she represents the Pilot, the Christ/griot model to which her nephew can aspire.

Unlike the other Dead women, Pilate knows inspiring songs to sing. Contrary to Macon's opinion, these songs make more available to Milkman than Macon's materialism. Milkman tries to milk from his aunt what she has been freely giving him all his life, obvious from the first time he seeks her out. Morrison's colorful "lady," who has "one earring, no navel, and [looks] like a tall black tree" and whom an unusually deferential Guitar refers to as "Miss Pilate," reveals the talent of *Sula*'s Bottom community for turning bottoms into tops. Feminizing her father's signifying tactics, she effortlessly dispels any misconceptions her nephew has about her ugliness, poverty, filth, and drunkenness. Just as easily she converts his secret shame of her into a vehement defense of the name he has always been embarrassed about. Cleverly tricking him into maintaining his position and that of his mother and sisters in a family that she states has "but three Deads alive," Pilate subtly forces a bewildered Milkman to claim his special inheritance, support the Dead women, and redefine reality. A mere shift in her semantics confirms that there is more than one way to be dead or alive. At the same time, she tests the mettle of the one she has chosen to wake up.[23] While the natural hunter in Guitar catches on more quickly that, in order to keep up with this woman's indirect directness, he must stop "feigning indifference" and "pay careful attention to his language," he lacks the empathy for women that comes naturally to the milkman (37).

Appearing to climb steps as if she were holding her crotch and constantly changing rhythm to keep the boys off balance, this female Pilate laughs at their awkwardness but offers to feed them. Requesting water, Guitar and Milkman curiously enter her two-room wine shack, which looks "both barren and cluttered" and in which everything "had been made for some other purpose" (39). The sunny kitchen, narcotic fruity "piny-winy" fumes, and Pilate's gravelly voice hypnotize her guests. They succumb in "pleasant semi-stupor" while she cooks up her parable of the egg. Promising a yolk akin to "wet velvet," she describes imprecisely but in great detail her quirky pedagogy for producing a perfect soft-boiled egg. Unlike the soft-fried egg that Guitar informs Milkman he cannot be, Pilate's manifestation becomes possible if "the water and the egg . . . meet each other on a kind of equal standing." Their temperatures have to be assessed and moderated so that one "can't get the upper hand over the other." More importantly, once it boils gently, the egg pot must be removed from the fire and covered with a newspaper for the time it takes the cook to "do one small obligation." Pilate goes to the toilet: "Not for a long stay, mind you. Just a short one" (39–40).

As Milkman listens, enchanted, Pilate deftly folds into her homemade scholastic recipe a portrait of the "good friend" that his father was to her as a boy, the murder and resurrection of his grandfather, and the tale of a man she saves from falling off a cliff in his own house. Here Morrison imaginatively illustrates her theories about African American folklore and highlights the significant role in the community of the artist/storyteller: in addition to preparing him a simple meal from scratch, an old aunt passes along to her young nephew practical advice so that he might himself be prepared to cook plain but nutritious food with the grace of a chef. She garnishes his masculine plate with a cornucopia of more typically feminine modes of creativity and communication, which include hospitality, intuition, sensitivity, charm, unpredictability, patience, ingenuity, subtlety, contained passion, useful knowledge, and the ability to do more than one thing at a time. On the side she serves her guest a fresh image of his father, a spicy introduction to his grandfather, and piquant ideas about the complex affinities between mind and body, thought and reality; the insignificance of fact but the importance of detail in depicting truth; and the variety of colors that blackness can take. Artfully modifying her temper to suit that of her audience, the cook/storyteller/griot delicately renders all this nourishment in the aesthetically pleasing and delightfully feminine guise of making a perfect soft-boiled egg.

Milkman will continue for longer than she lives to absorb refreshment from the woman who cooks plain fare for him while she sings him her stories. If he gets his masculine stuff from Guitar, he pilfers from Pilate the skill to incorporate feminine into masculine. Anarchists both, the two outlaws finally take offense at the world's rejection of them and reject the inessential. Unlike Guitar, however, Pilate includes assumptions as well as objects among the lost and missing. She cuts her hair but seeks knowledge of what makes her happy, what rings true, and what is necessary to survive. She gives up apparent interest in table manners or hygiene but acquires a "deep concern for and about human relationships." She dresses outrageously but respects other people's privacy; she stares but never makes an impolite remark. She practices passive resistance and nonviolent self-defense, but she always, always offers food before engaging a visitor in one word of social or business conversation. She utilizes her natural ability to heal and pays close attention to her griot father, who "appear[s] before her sometimes and [tells] her things" (149–50). Unlike Guitar, who has been cut off from a supportive father, Pilate subtly hums to instead of aggressively rapping on Milkman. While innumerable variations become possible on her blues rendition of "O Sugarman done fly . . . O Sugarman done gone," it contains four major metaphorical verses intended to provide black boys with feminine flight instruction.

The first verse presents an outline of shape-shifting. Though they value commitment equally, Guitar raps risk for the group while Pilate sings slide for the individual. Collecting only rocks from every place she visits, she is a wide-spirited, walking woman who makes places her own without possessing them. When she discovers that Hagar is less lucky than Reba and less strong than she, however, she gives up the traveling life for someone who belongs to her and seeks contact with her people. She forces herself on no one, leaving without a protest but "with a last fond look at the baby [Milkman]" when Macon rudely rejects her. Her loss of physical movement represents an opportunity for interior journeys. An illiterate Pilate turns for possibilities to the pictures in her fourth-grade geography book and to passing on the stories of her travels to those who come to listen.

From her verse on shape-shifting, Milkman acquires the power of change within stasis, flexibility within commitment, the home that exists within. He must resist not living anywhere. However, he must also refuse to stay in one place so that he embraces living everywhere. As does Guitar's secrecy, the mysteriousness of this unpredictable flexibility serves double duty as defensive camouflage. Pilate can, like the grounded angels in a paradise lost, shrink or expand herself, depending on need. In awe of her difference, her people believe that she has "the power to step out of her skin, set a bush afire from fifty yards, and turn a man into a ripe rutabaga," leaving her and hers alone and certainly not daring to bother her "sweet sugar lumpkin" (94, 318). Her ordinarily burning bush becomes a shrinking violet, however, when she needs to disentangle from white law another of her babies. She avoids violence but enrages Guitar, who will kill or die before he cowers.

Verse two of her song adds to the power of flexible humility that of patient attention. If Guitar preaches to Milkman to talk the talk, then walk the walk, Pilate persuades him to listen and wait. To signal this skill, Pilate must pilot Milkman back into the romantic Old South and resume her shape there as the witch Circe. Milkman's first solo flight spirits him away from "all those other people's nightmares" to find his own personal demon, a terrifying woman "older than death" who inhabits a haunted, rot-eaten mansion (219–20). The thick green maw of woods through which he must fight to satisfy his Hansel-and-Gretel hunger eats his hat and wets his pants, but he prevails to mistake for peeking children the intelligent golden eyes of a pack of strangely humming Weimaraners. As her sensually exotic fairy tale unravels, Morrison challenges Milkman and her readers to engage in a close reading of the seductive world of romance and to examine the nightmare reality—the life that crawls, slinks, creeps, watches, burrows, scurries, and lies still—beneath its superficial glamour. Inverting the usual pattern, she tells her tale from the witch's perspective, rendering this filthy hag capable of overpowering the nauseating, suffocating smell of beautiful but dangerously penned animals long enough for Milkman to hear her version. Smelling of Pilate's spicy sweet perfume, the old woman who frightens children and grown men is also the midwife who delivers everybody, shelters Macon and Pilate as children, and protects Milkman now.

So old that she looks colorless, her features indistinguishable beneath the "pleats and crochetwork of skin committed to constant change," Circe relates the transformations she has endured in the "strong, mellifluent voice of a twenty-year-old girl" (240). She tells the story of a black slavewoman who wills herself to live long enough to see the Butler Big House not only gone with the wind but so rife with stink that people dare not go anywhere downwind of it. She has prevailed over the murder of her people by Butlers she has birthed, the flight of children she has nurtured, the death of masters she has served, and the suicide of the last remaining daughter of the house of Butler. Through all this destruction, she watches, waits, and enables creation, having lost only Milkman's grandmother. While a sympathetically incensed Milkman wonders whether she remains in such crumbling disease because the Butlers willed her their property or because she loved them that much, Circe retorts cryptically that she stays because "all the money was gone, so [Elizabeth Butler] killed herself" (242).

Not trusting his ears or her girlish voice, Milkman misjudges Circe's combination of daintiness and savagery and regards her as simply simple. He angles for any information she can give him about his family and the Butlers, but because he condescendingly idealizes her as the stereotypical self-sacrificing mammy, he cannot fully grasp her meaning. Exasperated, Circe finally snaps: "Your ear is on your head, but it's not connected to your brain." She explains sharply that Elizabeth killed herself rather than do the work Circe has done all her life and that if Milkman thinks she stays on because she loved a woman who thought so little of her, then he has "about as much sense as a fart!" (247). Birthing dogs now instead of babies, she deals with the pain of dead bodies by keeping alive even the horror stories that fuel a flagging spirit. Morrison's own cutting irony hums ominously along with the sleek, handsome, obedient, barely contained German dogs as Circe describes how the Butlers loved, stole, lied, and killed for their house, how she will never again clean it or one thing in it, and how she delivers the vicious, steel-gray animals to destroy it and to ensure that no one can enter it to rebuild.[24]

Circe encompasses past, future, and present. She epitomizes the prophetic Queen Margaret of Shakespeare's civil war plays, Faulkner's American Civil War curse come again to terrifying life. Vowing that "everything in this world they lived for will crumble and rot," she represents the fate that ensures the cycle of evil will play itself out. Appearing ancient and modern, madly aggressive and rationally submissive, her humming, like that of her dogs, is as dangerous as it is pleasant. Her revenge by inches, however, falls not on an individual but on the house of murderers, on the system that shelters them. Cautioning Milkman against personal vengeance, Reverend Cooper claims that Circe took care of "any evening up left to do." He explains that nothing rich white folks "stole or killed for did 'em a bit a good" and states: "Things work out, son. The ways of God are mysterious, but if you live it out, just live it out, you see that it always works out" (232–33).

To patient vision Pilate contributes a third verse on caring but light responsibility; she sings Sing's sad song but carries Mr. Solomon's funny bones. Gradually piecing together the various strands of his grandparents' story, Milkman gathers from enigmatic Circe and his snobbish cousin Susan Byrd that his grandmother was of mixed blood but singular in her attachment to her beloved. Like Hagar's obsession with Milkman and Ryna's with the legendary Solomon, Sing's passion for the son of Solomon is "overcrazy," a "nervous love" (243). In addition, the youngest son of Solomon learns by memorizing and listening carefully to the children of Shalimar's (Solomon's) song of Solomon that he belongs to "that tribe of [flying] niggers" (328). When he pays close attention to the multiplicity of voices shaping his ancestral history, Milkman finally possesses the secret of his African American heritage: he descends from a man who "lifted his beautiful black ass up in the sky and flew on home" (328). He is also delivered of a woman who either pushed "too hard" or "lost [her] mind, or died or something" from "trying to take care of children by [herself]" (243, 323).

Unlike Solomon, who returns free but alone to Africa, going home for the son of Solomon becomes the possibility of acquiring a feminine masculinity and grounded American flight. After he fights Guitar to win his manhood, Milkman can take from and bathe Sweet in mutually harmonious care:

> She put salve on his face. He washed her hair. She sprinkled talcum on his feet. He straddled her behind and massaged her back. She put witch hazel on his swollen neck. He made up the bed. She gave him gumbo to eat. He washed the dishes. She washed his clothes and hung them out to dry. He scoured her tub. She ironed his shirt and pants. He gave her fifty dollars. She kissed his mouth. He touched her face. She said please come back. He said I'll see you tonight. (285)

Because he is finally comfortable with his masculinity, Milkman's "neck skin" no longer "crawled with fear" under the threat of male attack; his pulse remains steady when Guitar appears out of nowhere to take his gold (206). His reward comes as a dream in which he sees himself flying "not with arms outstretched like airplane wings, nor shot forward like Superman" but "floating," relaxed like a man on a couch reading a newspaper (298). Cruising at times over a womblike sea, he does not fear drowning. Alone in the sky, he hears someone applauding him from the ground. Milkman has accepted the good news that stories are real. He has become a man who knows that nothing can be taken for granted, that he bears responsibility for everything. He can now seek a grounded woman like Pilate who carries her responsibilities easily and who will encourage him to fly.

While Macon will "die not understanding one thing about [his sister]," Macon's son lives long enough to appreciate why Pilate totes Mr. Solomon's bones (206). Believing them to be those of the old white man she complies with a frightened young Macon to kill, she remains unaware that they are, in fact, the remains of her brave black father, murdered by cowardly white men. Nonetheless, Pilate has learned from her father that the name doesn't matter, that she "just can't fly on off and leave a body" (147). She uses the bones to reenact her humble responsibility to all the precious living. Her load is light as dust, however, because she bears it with forgiveness—of herself and others. It "frees up your mind," she says, "to have the bones right there with you wherever you go" (208). Though Milkman must keep with him always a lock of Hagar's hair, the last verse of the song Pilate sings to him prays for mercy for him.

During the powerful scene in which Hagar dies literally of too much makeup, figuratively of too little self, she murmurs to Pilate that Milkman despises her hair. Pilate responds to her granddaughter: "How can he not love your hair? It's the same hair that grows out of his own armpits. The same hair that crawls up out his crotch on up his stomach. . . . It's all over his head, Hagar. It's his hair too. He got to love it." Unconvinced, the girl succumbs to the inferiority attributed to her biblical namesake. Hagar falls victim to Madison Avenue hype, Reba and Pilate's anaconda love, and Milkman's stupid neglect. Pilate reacts to the death of her beloved by bursting into song. Although she embarrasses the sparse but respectful attendees at Hagar's "decent funeral" and startles with her trumpeting contralto the "sympathetic winos" hovering in the vestibule, she unabashedly shouts for mercy "in the morning," begs for mercy "in the darkness," prays for mercy "on [her] knees." With Reba's sweet soprano as response to her call, mother and daughter ease their pain, despair, and rage at the loss of their "sweet sugar lumpkin" (315–18). Selecting Hagar apart from any other Dead, Pilate employs ritual instead of violence to cope with her grief, assuage her guilt, and forgive her nephew.

Morrison affirms that the possibility of compassion lies in the capacity for self-love and in humility without humiliation. Pilate must locate mercy for herself before she can forgive Milkman. Milkman must find pity for his sins before he can offer it to others.

When interviewer Bill Moyers asks her to describe her vision for the contemporary black community, Morrison replies: "Love. We need to love ourselves." When Milkman's carelessness toward Hagar (and the fact that a young woman dies so that a young man can rise) disquiets readers, Morrison responds: "That generally is the way [a mistake] is—there is nothing that you can do about it except do better, and don't do *that* again" (McKay 403). By breaking a wine bottle over his head and throwing him into her cellar, Pilate reminds Milkman, ecstatic over his newfound self-knowledge but still missing the last piece of his puzzle, about his responsibilities. Accepting Hagar's hair, he finally thinks of the children: "Jesus Christ, [Solomon] left . . . Ryna behind . . . and twenty-one children! Guitar and the Days chose never to have children. Shalimar left his, but it was the children who sang about it and kept the story of his leaving alive" (332). Acknowledging his responsibility as a father to all the children, Milkman now has a life to give. In the fullness of himself, he is willing to die at the end of the novel, and the person he will die for is a woman. In doing so, he demonstrates that black manhood includes the capacity to "challenge patriarchy and embrace the core aims of black feminism which revolve around gender equality" (Leak 100).

As paradoxical as the phoenix rising from its ashes, Milkman takes Pilate's place as she relinquishes her load of bones.[25] Together they bury them in a small grave on Solomon's Leap marked by "Sing's snuffbox with the single word Jake ever wrote": Pilate's name (335). While Pilate must suffer by Guitar's hands to illustrate the violence of violence, she never truly dies just as she is never really born. She willingly yanks her earring from her ear. She falls to the ground before Milkman hears the shot fired. Returned home, her sack of bones releases a "deep sigh" and her signature "spicy sugared ginger smell"; birds lift into the air the snuffbox containing her name (335).[26] Having carried out her father's legacy, she and he live on in their love for their people. She leaves to her nephew her father's gifts for song and for seeing what is possible. To ease her passing, he recalls the "worn old words" and "without the least bit of a tune" sings in a strong speaking voice for the lady who can fly without leaving the ground (336). The multi-ethnic association of buried bones with freed spirits is plentiful, as is the connection of a lock of hair with undying love. In Morrison's folk idiom, the concept would be: "Them bones gonna rise again."

Milkman must "give up his ghost," however, "in the killing arms of his brother" (337). Having let go of the "shit that weighs [him] down,"

Milkman as imagination and possibility meets Guitar as action and reality in a savagely joyful leap of faith (179). Smiling over the barrel of his rifle, Guitar lays his gun on the ground before he stands to receive his blood brother.[27] The scene joins the potency of competition, reminiscent of the hunt for the bobcat, with that of flight. In all its ambiguity, their reunion suggests the potential for universal human transcendence; it also notes the particular flight/plight of the African American male. Unlike many, Milkman unites Guitar's playing, rapping, hunting, fighting with the complex rhythms of the woman who has been teaching him her tunes all his life. The words resounding from the rocks over both their heads echo: "Tar tar tar," "Am am am am," "Life life life life." With properties as black and powerful as the ancient tar pits, Milkman takes ownership of his American self by taking on the secret of its African griot. Mastery of life resides in submission to its spirit: "If you surrender to the air, you [can] *ride* it" (337).[28]

Morrison creates a multiplicity of voices to tell her black boy that, though he cannot own any life, a man must possess a life to live and to give. At the same time, he becomes responsible for all lives, including his own and especially the children's. Capturing these paradoxes beautifully, her final simile, which describes Milkman "as fleet and bright as a lode(load)star," suggests he has met the balance of her requirements (337). Merging talk/play/fight with song, he assumes the feminine masculinity of the griot to "[whirl] about and [touch] the sun" (303). As he listens to the voices he has been conditioned to ignore under the weight of patriarchal hegemony, however, Milkman incorporates unto himself even more than androgyny. His song stretches for what Hirsch calls "the space of contradiction," the space between male and female, young and old, black and white, rich and poor, work and play, heard and seen, closeness and distance, community and individual, past and present, African and American (86).

Hirsch interprets the book's dedication, a simple "Daddy" without the customary "to" or "for," as a child's plea rather than an adult's presentation. She also finds "disturbing" Morrison's statement "the fact that they [black men] would split in a minute just delights me" (72–74). Crediting *Song of Solomon* with "deconstructing the dichotomy between the material presence of the mother and the legendary symbolic absence of the father," Hirsch laments that it does not offer a way to "share the son's knowledge with the daughter." Her conclusion, that "African American masculinity is still too deeply threatened and endangered," captures precisely what Morrison's novel attempts to address (90). Its epigraph ("The fathers may soar / And the children may know their names") may be read simultaneously as a tribute, a statement of possibility, and a grant of permission. Likewise, its dedication may be interpreted as a cry of appeal, a call of warning (the title's acronym signals SOS), and a note of triumph. Although some Deads never learn to live, Pilate soars and shows Milkman how to spread his wings. Toni Morrison advocates perpetual possibility. Her world allows boys and girls to fly in different but mutually supportive ways. Her feminine masculinity occupies Morrison's space of transformation.

CHAPTER 5

The Nigger in the Woodpile

Sons and Lovers in *Tar Baby*

The image resonating at the core of *Tar Baby* (1981) projects a hungry, dirty, dark-skinned young man located on a fantasy island near Haiti in the bedroom closet of a red-haired, pale-skinned, well-heeled older woman. Relayed separately by the various black and white voices reacting to it, the image fluctuates, taking its power from and suggesting positions of power with the nuances of descriptors selected. *Dirty* could as easily be *filthy; hungry* also means *starving; located* becomes *crouching*, *hiding*, or *sitting on the floor as calm as you please*. Combined with *white woman*, *kept* or *well-kept*, *terrified* or *abusive* create distinctive portraits. As she dusts off the trope of the nigger in the woodpile, used by the red-headed woman to encapsulate the scene, Morrison chuckles at its clichéd racism while she deconstructs the mythmaking process itself. More significantly, however, she exposes and then inverts the heart of male darkness in Western civilization and what Melville called "the power of blackness" in American literature.

Tar Baby opens with a man whose "skin blended well with the dark waters" jumping from a cargo ship comically dubbed H.M.S. *Stor Konigsgaarten*. Associated throughout the novel with slave ship escapees, this man of many names and with savannas in his face reduces to her knees by his mere appearance a red-and-white Valentine candy woman, her hand covering her mouth in speechless horror. Critics have found such scenes notable as they argue over whether or not *Tar Baby*, with its fully realized white characters, marks a logical development in Morrison's artistry or an abrupt departure. Whatever the case, the book remains oddly disturbing to most readers (more so, for many, than the rape and pedophilia displayed in *The Bluest Eye*) although it has gained in popularity from its original lukewarm reception. This quality of disruption looks to be calculated on more than one level.

Morrison's preface to *Playing in the Dark: Whiteness and the Literary Imagination* describes her reading of *The Words to Say It*, Marie Cardinal's autobiographical novel, which documents the latter's descent into madness. Intrigued especially by when the writer knew herself to be in trouble, the precise narrative moment that "convinced her she was in danger of collapse," Morrison quotes Cardinal's "first encounter with the Thing." This "Thing" turns out to be the young woman's reaction to a Louis Armstrong concert. The pounding acceleration of her heart overwhelming the climbing, improvisational notes of Armstrong's trumpet, she is "gripped by panic at the idea of dying there in the middle of spasms, stomping feet, and the crowd howling" and flees into the street "like someone possessed" (vi–vii). With the comic deflation typical of her prose apparent in her personal response, Morrison remembers smiling at her own reaction: "What on earth was Louie playing that night?" What did the sublime poise of this music contain that drove a sensitive French Algerian girl hyperventilating into the street "to be struck by the beauty and ravage of a camellia 'svelte in appearance but torn apart inside' "? *Playing in the Dark* becomes Morrison's assertion that the cultural associations of jazz and black manhood contribute to the white woman's breakdown. It traces the sources of, and shorthand for, black people and images in American letters and their effects on the literary imagination. In this monograph and earlier in *Tar Baby*, she enumerates the ways "black people ignite critical moments of discovery or change or emphasis" in stories not of their own making (viii). In *Tar Baby*, a black woman writer reenvisions the figure of the nigger in the woodpile, an image usually perceived as male, to enlighten her readers about the "disrupting darkness," the masks and distortions imposed on black men in American literature and culture (91).

Playing in the Dark wonders whether the "major and championed characteristics of our national literature—individualism, masculinity, social engagement versus historical isolation; acute and ambiguous moral problematics; the thematics of innocence coupled with an obsession with figurations of death and hell—are not in fact responses to a dark, abiding, signing Africanist presence" (5). Lauren Lepow recognizes that *Tar Baby* represents its creator's attempt to recast Milton's misogynist version of the Genesis myth in a feminist mode. However, her insightful essay fails to connect this revision of original sin, loss of innocence, and presence of death and hell with Morrison's evaluation of the character of American culture and its literature.[1] Morrison remains emphatic that "just as the formation of the nation necessitated coded language and purposeful restriction to deal with the racial disingenuousness and moral frailty at its heart, so too did the literature, whose founding characteristics extend into the [twenty-first] century, reproduce the necessity for codes and restriction. . . . A real or fabricated Africanist presence was crucial to their sense of Americanness. And it shows" (*Playing* 6).

With the male characters especially in *Tar Baby*, Morrison challenges this white concept of Americanness. She sets loose the nigger in the woodpile by removing her Americans from homeland culture to relocate them in the French Caribbean and allow them the isolation and detachment required for self-discovery. Gurleen Grewal views the island setting as Morrison's rewriting of Shakespeare's play *The Tempest*, one that effects a "disidentification with Prospero's ordering of the world," and *Tar Baby* as postcolonial fiction (94). As apt, however, would be a comparison to Shakespeare's *Othello*, with its scenic shift from city to island, its exploration of sex and race, and its presentation of the Moor as the figural enactment of the Fall, repository of truth, sink of uncertainty and error. If it be such, however, Morrison's Fall occurs upside down. The paradoxes of falling to fly, dying to live already inherent in its myth become further complicated so that blackness, darkness, dirt, chaos are signed as ascendant and the hegemony of whiteness renders descent. The writer records with her fourth book "unphotographable beauty" (46). Instead of *Othello*'s dramatization of wilderness and wildness threatening civilization, *Tar Baby*'s white civilization bears the guilt of attacking black wildness. The dark, blind, and naked horsemen on Isle des Chevaliers roam in league with the swamp women and the champion daisy trees to defend its natural lushness against the encroaching swords and stiff, ornate epaulets of glittering Napoleonic chevaliers.

Morrison unloads her nigger in the garden off the king's storage boat to stir up the ironic contrast between spontaneous island funk and the calculated artifice of L'Arbe de la Croix.[2] The figure itself implies an association with and disruption between natural and human. Referring to the something sinister but comic that jumps out unexpectedly, this provocateur, like the medieval Vice character or the family skeleton stuffed for years in a back closet, finally escapes to wreak gleeful havoc among household members. The garden or woodpile exists as nature carefully accumulated, cultivated, measured, and groomed, arranged neatly for future warmth, promising order, possession, control. The human hidden in its midst is grotesquely misplaced, and the trickster figure of the nigger introduces comic disharmony, with its usual sexual overtones. Certainly the woodpile indicates white male ownership, potency, and mastery of a tight ship; to him the nigger represents the frightening possibility of emasculation, mutiny, or miscegenation. Margaret Street appropriates the term when, exhausted by anticipation of her son's Christmas visit and the wilderness creeping into the seasoned and regulated arguments between her and her husband, she takes to her bedroom and opens her closet door wide to find Son Green inside. The morning after leaves her like Marie Cardinal, drained of panic and sleep, acknowledging, "Things were not getting better. She was not getting better. She could feel it and right smack in the middle of it, with Michael on his way, *this* had to happen: literally, literally a nigger in the woodpile" (83).

Just as pulsating jazz triggers Cardinal's sexual and racial fears and guilt, Margaret becomes at once roused and repulsed by the black man in her bedroom. Even as she is "shaking like a leaf" and thinking of her closet as "a toilet now where something rotten had been and still was," a sink where "black sperm was sticking in clots to her French jeans or down in the toe of her Anne Klein shoes," she feels most insulted by her husband's courteous reception of the intruder and cavalier dismissal of her hysteria (86). References throughout to order and disorder, both external and internal, emphasize this conflict between the uncontainable and the restrained, so disturbing to Margaret and codified by her reference to the nigger in the woodpile. Like his outwardly nonplussed reaction to Son's unruly presence, Valerian Street's winter house encloses his effort to superimpose coolly sophisticated grace over the summer exuberance of the island.

Morrison presents Isle des Chevaliers as a noisy, colorful, live thing, its rich vitality and irrepressible movement stunned into defensive reaction by white male invasion.[3] Her paradise is very much an earthly one bearing an uncanny resemblance to her traditional black community. In this place, extremes of life and death, containment and freedom, signified by her usual colors of green and blue, shade fluidly into each other. However, her description of the island and its creatures highlights what no longer exists. Along with the absence of the "sea-green green of the sea and the sky-blue sky of the sky," the exotic animal and plant life is endangered, a disruption not the result of such natural events as death, disease, or starvation but manmade by rough white hands. As does *Sula*'s Bottom, the island community tolerates the cruelty of natural selection because it ensures survival. Hungry children will always try to stone wild parrots that must then seek another refuge, and poisonous snakes remain part of paradise. They are not as in Milton's version, however, segregated for their evil, if evil it is; the champion daisy trees cradle the sleeping diamondbacks gently in their arms. The paradisiacal aspect of Isle des Chevaliers lies not in the nonexistence of extremes but in the counterbalance of destruction and loss with creation and growth. Deluge occurs along with overbearing sunshine, but the rains are "equal." They visit for a polite daily hour, not an intrusive season, until the men's reconstruction "folded the earth where there had been no fold and hollowed her where there had been no hollow" (9).

Except for the blind horsemen, the creatures of the island exist for the most part as metaphorically female.[4] The river and rain forest represent its matriarchs. Ballasted by a masculine sturdiness, their undeniably feminine force becomes Amazonian so that gender approaches the powerful androgyny that Morrison applauds in her griot figures. Left unbothered, the river forms life-giving pools, and the trees rise serenely sheltering.[5] Their protective tendencies grow distorted and turn dangerous only under duress. Although the huge champion daisy trees usually calmly rock rattlesnakes, those who escape being gnawed through by the men's saws drive their roots further into the earth, clutching it "like lost boys found." They have nightmares for years about their "wild-eyed and yelling" fallen comrades, and their incoherent mutterings annoy their diamondback partners, who leave them in disgust for new growth that "came to life in spaces the sun saw for the first time." Crashed headlong into by the insulted river—run crazy by the rude rains set loose by the shocked rain forest that is cut down by white saws—the lone surviving giant trees reconnoiter and marshal threateningly for war. The river becomes equally destructive. Like a scatterbrained woman, this demented body of water scuttles about the forest floor, crests, loses its course and finally its head. Evicted from its embankments and unable to collect its waterfalls, it, too, gets nasty. Because it must sit in one place like a grieving grandmother, its clear nourishing liquids sour into the swamp water called Sein de Vieilles or witch's tit. With the chilling power of a conjure woman's charm, its "shriveled fogbound oval" seeps with a "thick black substance that even mosquitoes could not live near" (9–10). In wry Morrison code, abuse of the black locals by rough-edged white stiffs renders island life perverse and mean and, as with the African American communities she depicts in *The Bluest Eye* and *Sula*, leads ultimately to their turning on each other.

In addition to the river and tree matrons, a cornucopia of lesser airs, sprites, and creatures populate the island, all of which Morrison depicts as traditionally black and female. These include a pushy waterlady, prophesying fish, testifying clouds, alert moon, oppressively affectionate maiden aunt fog, complacent bees, gossipy angel trumpets, nosy emperor butterflies, seductive teenaged avocado tree, arrogant swamp women, and workaholic soldier ants, plenty of sisters to fill the church pews. She intersperses blind, wet, and naked black horsemen galloping wildly about and among this plethora of women. Pictured like Caliban as half spirit/half human, these mythic beings are the three-hundred-year-old descendants of African slaves who go mysteriously blind the moment they see the domination awaiting them on Dominique. Morrison deliberately juxtaposes the plainspoken *horsemen* against their more elegantly coined counterpart *chevaliers* to defend what she has consistently called the free black male, determinedly unbound by Western cultural or class restrictions and bred simply to breed and play. Although she applauds all of Shakespeare's insightful fools, Morrison elevates his earthy Calibans above his airy Ariels. She also echoes his praise of plainness but converts his faith in sight into the value of hearing.

Interpretations of the horsemen/chevaliers myth vary with listener and teller. As relayed by easygoing local fishermen, a race of blind people descends from the blacks suddenly struck blind onboard a French-owned slave ship, which foundered and sank with its cargo of Frenchmen, horses, and slaves. Forced by their blindness to float instinctively with the tides, the slaves wash up on Isle des Chevaliers along with the horses. Those only half blinded are "rescued" by the French and returned to Dominique and servitude. Morrison makes some fun here, turning "struck dumb" into "struck blind." She also experiments with various paradoxical connotations of *blind:* sightless, unable to see, refusing to see, instinctual, insightful. While the term usually suggests a disability, blindness becomes an asset in *Tar Baby*'s topsy-turvy world. Sightless slaves cannot be used for slave labor; blind seers stay unenslaved. Among the stranded but still standing, blind horsemen yet ride.

Appropriating the story she hears from the first family to whom her husband sells property, Margaret Street insists that his island's rightful name is Isle de *le* Chevalier. To this distressed damsel there can be only one masculine model, a gallant knight, preferably on a white horse. Septuagenarian Valerian prefers his friend Dr. Michelin's version, which maintains that one hundred French chevaliers remain in the saddle, all as old and tired as he. Only the ageless natives Gideon and Therese and the young black visitors Son and Jadine perceive the riders to be forever young, strong, naked, and black. In Gideon's words, they race one another blindly but freely through the hills, avoiding the possessive clutches of "trees and things," and sleep for sport with the self-possessed swamp women in Sein de Vieilles. These horsemen see only with the mind's eye and "can't stand for sighted people to look at them without their permission" (152–53). Weaving the stories adroitly together, Morrison unravels

Western rationalism and its linear notion of history, illustrating that the position of the listener (or what she calls the "gaze" of the reader) determines the outcome of the story.

The different worldviews created by race, class, age, and gender crystallize in the horsemen/chevalier scenarios imagined by Son and Valerian as they face off against each other across the winter house dining room table. Valerian sits at its head and Son at its foot:

> Somewhere in the back of Valerian's mind one hundred French chevaliers were roaming the hills on horses. Their swords were in their scabbards and their epaulets glittered in the sun. Backs straight, shoulders high—alert but restful in the security of the Napoleonic Code.
>
> Somewhere in the back of Son's mind one hundred black men on one hundred unshod horses rode blind and naked through the hills and had done so for hundreds of years. They knew the rain forest when it was a rain forest, they knew where the river began, where the roots twisted above the ground; they knew all there was to know about the island and had not even seen it. They had floated in strange waters blind, but they were still there racing each other for sport in the hills behind this white man's house. (206)

In the binary opposition of these fixed faces, Morrison ridicules flag-flying masculine absolutism. She emphasizes once more that perspective can alter not only the moral of a story but its direction. Comically revitalizing yet another worn phrase, she insists that, with a little feminine intuition and flexibility, horses can indeed be changed in midstream.

Morrison's gaze continues to subvert Western ideals of masculinity as she reveals that smooth Valerian, not unpolished Son, represents the sinister but comic threat not to civilization but to wildness. The master of the house turns into the white nigger in the unpiled wood of the island. She persists in twisting her nigger inside out by appointing the lightly concealed restraint of Valerian's wide, bright, and airy house to weigh down the androgynous and unsubtle exuberance of Isle des Chevaliers. L'Arbe de la Croix mockingly models the publicly casual but privately tightly rehearsed recklessness that Renaissance courtiers aspired to and called *sprezzatura*. Even its name appears humorously ironic. Although Morrison's French, as spoken through Valerian, is usually flawless, she deliberately misspeaks enough words, through Margaret's bumbling efforts, to suggest playful digs at nouveau-riche Americans who establish their pedigrees by imitating things Parisian, including its French.[6] She spells *L'Arbe* phonetically. Sounding like a cross between the French word for tree (l'arbre) and the English abbreviation for a financier who engages in arbitrage (arb), the misspelling of the symbol of his island takeover indicates that Valerian's impeccable bearing is vulnerable. He designs his paradise to bear any number of crosses, some anticipated, but the heaviest arrives unexpected.

The first entails the burden of ownership on nature as well as art. While debates about the supremacy of nature versus art are ancient ones, Morrison inevitably sides against the aesthetic purists to tout a balanced usefulness. Her work, and *Tar Baby*'s Sydney, testifies to Philip Sidney's assertion that poesy should delight *and* instruct. When art becomes property, however, dollar signs overpower semiotics. Western-educated art historian Jadine embarrassedly confesses to Western art collector Valerian that "Picasso *is* better than an Itumba mask. The fact that he was intrigued by them is proof of his genius, not the mask-makers' " (74). However, she also acknowledges to herself that the work of a Stateside black whose talent towers over lesser artists like a sequoia over weeds goes largely unmarketed. Valerian's magnificently understated house merges the talents of a fashionable Mexican architect and nondescript Haitian laborers who have no union and "therefore could not distinguish between craft and art." What the builders find useful or value as traditional, such as natural air-conditioning or tongue-in-groove flooring, they finish "lovingly to perfection" (10). What they see as intrusive, nonfunctional, or inessential, such as hand-kilned Mexican tiles or indoor plumbing, turns out shoddily done. Morrison insists that art is freely made for love and use, not coerced for money.

As with most commissioned art, Valerian's house comes to be a not completely disguised façade for its owner's personality. Its form reveals as much about him as do its contents, its oversights or imperfections as much as its successes. Arranging graceful landscaping to keep the house "just under a surfeit of beauty," he makes every effort to avoid the gaucherie of "designed" and becomes adroit at the art of concealing the art, and the pain (11). Even the smallest, most calculatedly casual island touches take on the appearance of practicality although they are actually sentimental indulgences by which he deflects childhood hurts or emotional voids. Having withdrawn to his island garden to cultivate neither growing nor retiring but dying, Valerian shuns his neighbors, refuses to entertain guests, and simulates the only things he misses of life in the city of brotherly love—hydrangeas and the postman. He brings with him from Philadelphia his five other things of value: a tennis shirt, garden shears, classical records, a sixty-four-bulb chandelier, and the "Principal Beauty" of Maine. He attaches to his coolly tropical house a hothouse in which he reads mail-order seed catalogs and refines ordinary northern plants. Descended from a workaholic German grandmother whose four sons convert her rich candy confections into a financial empire, Valerian Street is named for an emperor and access to ordered, grounded motion, reared with the cotton-candy detachment that swathes *petits princes.*[7] He swaps his cocooned childhood for a loveless, childless first marriage. Then, exchanging vows at thirty-nine with a seventeen-year-old beauty-pageant winner because something in him knelt down to her, he is relieved when she produces a male heir. After he knows for certain, however, that his son will never be more than another stranger to him, he builds his greenhouse "as a place of controlled ever-flowering life to greet death in" (53).

Morrison barely conceals her irony, and pity, as she constructs Valerian's hothouse to suggest the terrible cipher to which property values have reduced his emotional IQ. Protected by two servants, mountains of ineffectual business correspondence, and oceans of expensive cognac and Chablis, he reigns over temperature-controlled life on a hill high enough to view the sea from three sides, though he prefers his miniature garden to the vast deep. Like the practiced banter with teeth that reflects the husband's habitual mode of communication with his wife, Valerian has been schooled to keep his innermost feelings in check with gestures that Morrison describes as perpetually treading water. He seeks to recapture through his son the youth he never had. The son, however, seems to him indefinitely and disappointingly childlike. Valerian, therefore, wants "his own youth again and a place to spend it" (54). Thus, he adds yet another emotionally warped appendage to his big house—a washhouse from which he can draw occasional backward glimpses out of the one glass window of the greenhouse.

If Morrison's greenhouse becomes a trope for the impossibly pristine permanence idealized by white male American dreamers, her washhouse represents the receptacle of their sludge, the elimination of which remains necessary to keep their ideal afloat. It suggests the black American scapegoat. For Valerian it contains the memory of a drunken woman who launders the dirty linen of his childhood and helps him to wash away the grief of which his suddenly *"serioso mammas"* try to cleanse him after his father dies (54). Indulging his narrow view of the nigger in the woodpile, Valerian likes to imagine that no washer exists in his island washhouse and that the native "Mary" who feeds "Billy Blass" towels into the dryer is a thin, toothless, birdlike woman rubbing pillow slips on a scrub board with a bar of orange Octagon soap. He spends the last ages of his manhood recalling his boyhood backyard down to its fat, brown hydrangea, his father lying in state inside a funereal house, and the unnamed servant in the shed who greets his childish chatter with the "pointless conversation of an adult without stature to a child who had some—'What your daddy doin today?' " A preliminary to the canned but only companionable conversation allowed a lonely child, the question is finally answered, "He's dead today," and the seven-year-old first experiences limitlessness, the too big, too deep "bottomless bucket of time into which his little boy legs were sinking and his little boy hands were floundering" (141).

After an awkward silence, this tiny woman—never identified as such but obviously black—blinks, makes Valerian fetch, unwrap, and rub a bar of soap on a wet pillowcase until his knuckles are raw, and is then sacked by George, his current butler, for making the prince wash his own clothes. Out of kindness for something small and wounded, Valerian's pet friend gives him the difficult and important work he needs to scrub his heart out and accepts the rescission of her wash bucket as her reward. Valerian is left to tread water in the bucket with no bottom. His adult self attempts to re-create this childish reassurance not by doing the hard work of attending to himself and touching bottom but by gazing from the protection of the greenhouse constructed by others into the washhouse built and operated by others, "knowing there was a woman in there doing something difficult but useful in peace" (142). Morrison's powerful scene asserts that patriarchal dreams of safety, American or otherwise, amount to nothing more than the emperor's nonexistent new clothes.

The presumed safety of hegemonic inheritance becomes the cross Valerian carries that cuts him off from the most personal parts of his paradise. Morrison describes his attitude toward various intimacies to suggest the pathology of his need for controlled form. If Valerian sees only what he cares to see, he hears only the echo of the vacuum in his head. Carefully orchestrated music, underscored by the drum of the greenhouse air conditioner, creates white noise to deaden sound and inhibit hearing. Preferring to work in reflective silence, Sydney is grateful that his employer contains the swarming classical notes within his greenhouse. Valerian's obsession, however, does not include original compositions but appreciates the exactly correct musical arrangements that will ensure the broadest production among his green charges. He experiments with various composers to reject Chopin and some of the Russians because his Magnum Rex peonies, "overwhelmed by all that passion, whined and curled their lips." He settles on Bach's meticulously structured *Goldberg* Variations for germination and a fertilizer of classical Haydn sprinkled cautiously with romantic Liszt for "strong sprouting" (12).[8] Morrison's comically rounded reference to [flutist Jean-Pierre] Rampal's Rondo in D, with which Valerian easily satisfies his straight-stick, tight-stemmed northern plants, ironically suggests the limited musical, and sexual, appetites of upwardly mobile

Westerners, frightened, like Marie Cardinal, by achingly sensual blues and spontaneous jazz. Morrison's study of hothouse music concludes that if white boys can't jump, the emperor's green boys got no rhythm.

Valerian certainly shows a static beat in his feet. Never the dancing fool, he refuses to let his toes breathe in sandals or the comfortable huaraches of the tropics, stubbornly encasing them in hot leather Ballys. The condition of their feet, hands, and backs tells a great deal about *Tar Baby*'s characters. Both Valerian and Sydney have sore feet; mock-hostile debates over corns versus bunions, perspiration versus sweat provide the two of them with entertaining class collisions. Valerian advises Sydney, who complains about his bunions, to avoid Thom McAns and wear either slippers or the decent shoes handed down to him by Valerian. Sydney insists that he knows his work, that he cannot be a first-rate butler in slippers, and that he has never worn cheap or cast-off shoes in his life. Sydney advises Valerian to remove his Philadelphia shoes, to which Valerian retorts that perspiration, not imported Ballys, contributes to his corns and that he would as soon be in a straitjacket as huaraches. Sydney crows that it is, indeed, sweat that causes bunions and that hacking at his toes with a razor will leave Valerian begging for a straitjacket. Both men defend expensive shoes at the expense of aching feet but for reasons that reveal the vast space between them. Sydney stands on his feet all day in a job that requires sturdy but unobtrusively elegant shoes. Valerian, who spends most of his day sitting busily idle, demands the same shoes not for their practicality nor for their beauty but because the partners in his family business have always worn them. Useful flexibility in the black servant appears as nonfunctional rigidity in the white master.[9] Morrison points out, however, that the conflict revolves not so much around caste with Valerian (his gray evening eyes appraise indifferently the criticism of his peers) as a craving for permanence. His selection of shoes becomes merely one more stroke to keep him treading water above death.

Another ongoing battle between employer and employee, as well as husband and wife, involves eating habits, also an intimacy by which Morrison identifies Valerian's infantilism. While blind seer Therese thrives on the apples of knowledge that land Milton's Eve into so much hot water, Valerian's stupid diet stunts his growth. The subject of calories supplies constant table talk, with Margaret compulsively limiting her intake and Valerian eating freely of things that are bad for him. Ondine sneaks Postum into her boss's coffee, Sydney edges the box of saccharine tablets closer to and the salt out of Valerian's reach, but he inevitably demands strong coffee, plops in sugar cubes, and asks Margaret to pass the salt. Eschewing light croissants because the flakes are messy, he happily downs heavy but artfully presented ham and eggs or mashed potatoes and gravy with liberal quantities of fine wine and "medicinal" cognac, then tells "the boy" to pick up a bottle of Maalox to assuage the ulcer he insists is occasional irregularity. Ondine comments tartly that if he would "leave that liquor alone" and eat foods that would naturally "open him right up," Valerian could "eat like regular people" (37). Perceiving himself to be normal, decent, balanced, simple, modest, fair, generous, and, above all, not abusive, her self-described Boy Scout employer, however, actually finds it vain and inelegant to stay in shape and remains content to impose his constipated life on others.

Valerian's hang-ups about eating also stem from the family business. Street Brothers' original confections showcase a huge, heavy chocolate concoction Grandmother Stadt made as a treat for her youngest son, Theodore. She shaped Teddy Boys like gingerbread men with broad-brimmed hats, which buyers associated with the rugged virility of Theodore Roosevelt. This hat evolves into an unintentional but fortunate advertising gimmick that causes the candy to sell widely even as it diminishes in size, in contrast to the "faggoty" candy named by Valerian's uncles after their sole heir. Manufactured from the syrup sludge left over from the sugar and cocoa used in their financial mainstay, "Ooooh. Valerian!!" is strawberry and mint flavored, red and white gumdrops packaged in a red and white box. Their tough-minded (white) sales reps advise the uncles to close out these "fairy candies" and "give [them] something with nuts." The uncles, however, refuse to give up on sweet, pretty Valerian. Even when told that neither easterners nor midwesterners will touch the candy, only southern "jigs," the uncles fight to keep it, an effort that Valerian appreciates but "recognize[s] as sentimental and not professional" (50–51).

This clear-eyed business sense and his love of music and books allow Valerian to be firm about quitting the firm at exactly sixty-five, before he becomes the "industrial nuisances his uncles had" (50). Thus pressured to eat hearty but temperamentally inclined to more delicate fare, Valerian must measure his manhood by the amount he consumes. His "professionalism" conditions him to bite the hand that feeds him, which happens to be his own. Retelling the gingerbread man story to contrast the appetites of black and white consumers, Morrison forwards her assertion in a 1994 filmed interview with Bill Moyers that her people are being devoured. White wolves gorge obsessively on the flesh of chocolate gingerbread men while "jigs" exhibit a sweet tooth for mild fruit flavors.[10] Morrison also uses their caloric intake and quality to suggest her characters' level of self-awareness. While his tastes are liberally cultivated and his travels cosmopolitan, Valerian remains, like *Song of Solomon*'s Milkman, guilty of innocence; he possesses the means to libraries of facts but comes to produce no useful knowledge. He even fires Gideon and Therese for stealing apples.[11]

Valerian's sole intimate in the Caribbean reflects his manner of eating and drinking. An abscessed tooth "so brutal it lifted him out of bed and knocked him to his knees" effects his introduction to "that fat dentist," Robert Michelin (26, 14).[12] Unprepared for emergency travel, Valerian rings for a quick-witted Sydney, who makes arrangements to borrow a boat from the neighbors his employer hates. While Valerian suffers silently in a Dominique cab, Sydney bangs on the door of the French dentist who sought island sanctuary after being run out of Algeria and who remains outraged that he might again be assaulted by local blacks "whose teeth he would not repair." Allowed to collapse "limp and craven" in the dentist's chair, Valerian "[gives] himself up to whatever the Frenchman had in mind." This turns out to be a needle full of Novocain shooting "straight into his nostril on up to the pupil of his eye and out his left temple" and afterward, under Valerian's persuasion, brandy through a straw. Hurled by agony from visions of a death grip that contained "the crushed balls of a D.D.S." to grateful weeping "for the absence of all sensation in his head," Valerian once more reveals the ridiculously painful contortions he will undergo to avoid pain. He fails to perceive the irony of his extremely dependent independence. Although he is self-aware enough to smile later at the silly picture of "two elderly men drunk and quarreling about Pershing [perishing?]," neither Valerian nor Michelin will acknowledge what they really have in common: advanced age and lonely exile, voluntary or not, from uncomfortably telling situations (15).

Michelin and Valerian also share the memory of "years of grief in the wake of a termagant" and a second marriage that has "done nothing to make either forget his first" (16). Morrison understands that an excess of repressed pain must eventually abscess. She relies on what is perhaps the most personal of human habits to reveal how much of himself Valerian's inherited patriarchy destroys. Like the Macbeths, he has murdered sleep. However, his sleep disorders manifest themselves not so much as active insomnia or sleepwalking as passive but equally disruptive distortions. First of all, and over his sarcastic objections, Valerian and his wife sleep separately. They marry because the knight in him kneels to Margaret's youthful red-and-whiteness, and she likes the safe solidarity of his voice and his nice square fingernails. Valerian's association of his wife with the red-and-white candy named after him is too obvious for anyone but him to ignore. He has married a young woman to recapture not his lost youth but the youth he never had. It becomes difficult, however, to make love to a past one has yet to experience, and like the sweet but lightweight Valerians, Valerian turns out to be a flop in the appetite department. Unlike the mutually satisfying lust depicted between Son and Jadine, Valerian emerges only once from his cool hothouse to have sex with Margaret; and this occurs as another by-product of the nigger in the woodpile—Son's presence. Even their sex appears autoerotic. Because his attempt in the master bed the night before proved unsuccessful, Valerian kneels to perform cunnilingus on his wife the next day, an action which, given the nature of their relationship, amounts to giving himself oral pleasure.

If Margaret cannot dream the dream she ought to have, disturbing conjurations bombard Valerian. Clogged up, however, by "the surfeit and bounty of excess," he stupidly resists the messages he receives (*The Dancing Mind* 13). At one ironic point among the carnage of World War I, a feeling overwhelms him indicating something momentous, but he "was never sent with the message the world was waiting for." He possesses enough insight to recognize that "the message was not his," that he does not have the insight required to dream it up, but he also believes that "he was worthy of delivering it" (54). While the postman always rings twice, this emperor never answers the bell. Valerian has access to the signs, but he will not read them and so cannot carry them. His beloved greenhouse, for example, doubles as a "nice place to talk to his ghosts in peace," including that of his first wife. Dismissing her as an "unlovable shrew," he refuses to listen to her rant even as she returns to glide among his seed flats. With his usual poor timing, he begins to miss this wife at precisely the point she dies (14, 143). Determined to love Margaret simply to prove himself capable of the love his first wife lacked (enough to abort his unborn children), he continues to remain detached from his second wife. He can wish only in the first one's absence that she had felt something else. Unlike Macbeth's witches, the regular visitations of Margaret's predecessor tell her former husband unequivocally that she was unlovable merely because he would not love her. Numb Valerian now wishes she felt nothing at all.

If his greenhouse ghosts roam any which way but peaceful, so, too, the messages unravel that Valerian whispers into his pillow or wrist. An indirect but exactly spelled message interrupts his deep brandy sleep: *"These iceboxes are brown broken perspective v-i-o-l-i-a-x is something more and can't be coal note"* (49). Once again his fine education fails him. Just as he rejects modern literature because its language has "changed so much—stained with rivulets of disorder and meaninglessness," he avoids a close reading of his own confused and disturbingly swirling thoughts. Valerian's encoded message to himself manifests all the symptoms he needs to diagnose the cause of his dis-ease; it also marvelously represents Morrison's concept of the nigger in the woodpile. Hidden among allusions to frigidity (*"iceboxes"*), distortion (*"broken perspective"*), violation (*"v-i-o-l-i-a-x"*), curbed curiosity (*"something more"*), stunned disbelief (*"can't be"*), and abbreviated but understandable communication (*"note"*) are references to the dislocating darkness she describes in *Playing in the Dark* (*"brown," "coal"*).

Valerian Street has the skills but not the selfhood needed to decipher the code. A habitual fondness for verbal duels and wordplay sharpens his already perceptive powers of association. He quickly points out, for example, that Margaret speaks in "food measurements" and connects her language with "having too much" (67). On the other hand, the morning after he "rattles" to Jadine, his homemade nigger in the woodpile, he cannot imagine why he would attribute withdrawing to the Caribbean to the relationship between Margaret and their son (142). Self-deluded that he simply declines to remain a stranger in his own rapidly changing hometown, he cannot decode the message that beats at the heart of his alienation: unable to cope with limitlessness, conditioned to tread water, seeking the unrealistic safety of paradise, he commits the sin of innocence. Another solitary American Adam choosing his place of rest not east but west of Eden, Valerian participates in and becomes, therefore, responsible for his own destruction.

If Valerian's not-brave, not-New World comprises half of *Tar Baby*'s white/black male equation, it hath not other such people in it. Hegemony allows room for only one Prospero. However, additional absent masculine figures take his part in the chevalier/horseman duality. First, the hearty uncles, the Old World men on both sides of the family, establish and maintain his patriarchal lineage. While Valerian's uncles are German and Margaret's Italian, all view America as a stairway to economic opportunity and a desirable young woman as the trophy at the top of the steps. Both prince and princess suffer as a consequence. Because his family lacks male stock, Valerian's executive uncles "took over his education" and his childhood, reducing him, like his namesake candy, to sit on shelves or in display cases until he is "hard as marbles" (50). Likewise, Margaret appears as the only blue-eyed, redheaded girl in a blue-collar, dark-haired, male-dominated family. Her strikingly unexpected beauty sets her apart from the ordinariness of the other Lordis, calling her very legitimacy into question. The adults in her family distribute their energies among those children who are not beautiful and on "the problems of surviving in a county that did not want them there" (57). Doubt in the eyes of her uncles and the nuns, coupled with the inattention of her parents, clinches her isolation. Margaret finds herself always "going up or down stairs" while the Lordi Brothers stroke their thumbs and build houses with their own hands and her new husband's male friends talk about "music and money and the Marshall Plan" (58). As she reveals the destructive toll that patriarchy takes on the emotional well-being of male and female heirs alike, Morrison also exposes the complex solidarity among the various exiled Europeans who emigrate to the United States. Not only does climbing the New World stairwell harden them; they cluster "together like grapes" (50). Closing ranks regardless of class against the nigger in the woodpile, they find their most obvious common denominator by rejecting his black manhood.

The masculine figure absent from Valerian's camp who most tellingly defines the Old World new male is Ryk, Jadine's French lover, to whom Margaret refers as "Mr. Sealskin" (277). Separated from the other "handsome raucous men" who want to "marry, live with, support, fund, and promote her" only by his Christmas gift of an expensive sealskin coat made from the skins of ninety baby seals, Ryk acts as a sexual acrobat, a "foreplay expert" and "nonverbal equipment" man (225). A combination of Valerian's cool maleness and the hearty kind of Margaret's uncles, he becomes so sophisticated, or hardened, that he is amazed at Jadine's objection to his weekend liaison with a mutual friend.[13] Ryk conceals his shallowness by touting openness and honesty in relationships and behind such grandly symbolic gestures as buying a new mattress "for [them] to grow old on." The placid mistress thrown out with his former mattress is Chinese American, tied to a history of being bound. Rick, coyly spelled Ryk, represents what writer Pam Houston wryly calls a "hunter," the predatory male who collects and objectifies women as trophies; and this one apparently has a fetish for exotic flesh. Jadine herself wonders whether or not "the person he wants to marry is [her] or a black girl." Relationships with such men make her feel "lonely and inauthentic," as though she wants to "get out of [her] skin and be only the person inside—not American—not black" (47–48). Giving even Valerian's "antique grace" a run for its money, Ryk is raucous enough to mail Jadine her own skin, the sleek, glossy, jet-black coat that she finds so frighteningly seductive (91). Valerian shows more style in his audacity, describing his affairs as "two or three girls who had helped him enter the fifties (lovely, lovely). Nothing to worry Margaret had she known." Lovers offer these suave but insensitive men "merely life preservers," enabling them to bob on the surface of their emotions (54).

If Valerian represents a white version of the something unexpected and out of place that gnaws away at life on Isle des Chevaliers, his only begotten son, unbeknownst to him, develops into the nigger in his very own woodpile. Michael, too, has gone corporeally missing in action. His introduction occurs in the form of his fire-red footlocker with a bull's-eye painted on the lid, "Dick Gregory for President" stickers, and a lock that opens with a hairpin. Supposedly signaling his arrival, the traveling trunk, like its anarchistic owner, never shows. The trunk's color suggests danger. As the disruptive archangel in his father's Eden, Michael, albeit also as the unpresent target of abuse, escorts Valerian out of his hothouse. The son causes his first commotion by abandoning the family fantasy island via the bridge of poetry. Valerian again uses a black woman to vent pent-up anger at both son and wife, smiling sweetly at Jadine that Margaret is "giving [Michael] his favorite poet for Christmas. Isn't that so, love?" (66). B. J. Bridges is a poet and former teacher of Michael, who took all of Bridges's classes. To entice her son to come home for Christmas, Margaret, in her usual clumsy manner, alludes to Bridges's visit with a line she thinks she borrows from one of his poems: "And he glittered when he walked." Although Valerian immediately recognizes Robinson's "Richard Cory" as the source and mocks Margaret's ignorance, his arrogant sophistication prevents him from comprehending that his son's favorite poem depicts a wealthy suicide. Even as a student, Michael senses the lonely hollowness in Valerian's imperial paradise and burns his bridges before he, too, opts to put "a bullet through his head" (Robinson 10).

Valerian does unwittingly see in his son, however, a reflection of himself. To mask his disappointment that his heir refuses to take over the chocolate factory, he drops coated insinuations about what he regards as Michael's protracted adolescence. From digs at his bohemian dress to his career metamorphoses as "band manager, shepherd, poet-in-residence, film producer, lifeguard," and snake dancer at a school for the Hopis to his penchant for organizing "a race of exotics skipping around being picturesque for him," Valerian accuses Margaret of making a "perpetual loser of one of the most beautiful, the brightest boy in the land." Claiming that he cannot be responsible for things outside his control, he blames his wife for convincing Michael that "poetry was incompatible with property" (27, 72–75). Associating Son's appearance in his dining room with the image of his absent son smiling at him not in derision but in reconciliation out of a bowl of peaches, Valerian invites the black intruder to have a drink. If the invitation derives partly from a childish display of audacity (like the Petit Prince, the emperor thoroughly enjoys wreaking havoc among his complacent people), it is also a gesture designed to please the thirty-year-old socialist on the reservation as well as the "winsome two-year-old under the sink" (143).

Once more Valerian possesses all the indicators. Under the influence of his after-dinner port and a black woman's reassuring presence, he recreates finding Michael crouched singing to himself in the cabinet under his father's bathroom sink. He recollects the child searching in the dark for something soft, Margaret declining to talk to her son, the song sounding so heart-wrenchingly lonely. He muses about the little boy's odd slavishness to his mother and her emotional manipulation of him. He remains puzzled by his second wife's refusal, like his first wife's abortions, to have another child. Although he always tries to defend an overly defensive Michael, Valerian simply will not interpret clear signs of dysfunctional behavior. He does not see that Margaret projects the rage she cannot contain toward an emotionally abusive husband, who dumps his overflow into her, onto what she later calls *his* baby. Valerian closes his reverie with the maudlin sentimentality that he purports to detest. Glad that Michael "got out from under [Margaret, the Sink]," he regrets losing his son. He explains to his bored but captive audience, "I haven't seen him for three years, and the last couple of times I didn't like him or even know him. But I loved him. . . . That beautiful boy. With a smile like . . . like Sunday." This perfect "S[o]nday," which Valerian sounds out with "the bell-full voice of ownership," was a vulnerable baby into which a flawed mother stuck voodoo pins. To cap off the irony, Jadine, her mind in "automatic park," responds to the memories of an old man too preoccupied with pouring his wine to offer her any with a barely concealed yawn (77–78).

When his wife finally spoon-feeds Valerian the truth about her child abuse in small sound bites, he knows what to do: "Go to Michael. Find him, touch him, rub him, hold him in his arms. Now." However, marooned on "frail new legs" that have no strength to transport him anyplace, he is reduced to a "waxen horror" that not even Margaret can penetrate (232–34). Demetrakopoulos identifies Margaret as Morrison's first fully developed white woman and "the first full-fledged portrait of a child abuser in all of literature" (138). Nonetheless, Morrison treats her, as she does Cholly and Guitar and Valerian, with understanding and sympathy, focusing on the environmental conditions that swamp her into another Sein de Vieilles. Morrison also emphasizes the son's affection for his mother. Despite the fact that an adult on whom he depends causes him unspeakable pain out of her own pain, the child grows into an adult who will risk love. In his agony, Valerian demands above shuddering hands, "Why does he love *you*?" Margaret's initial response, "Because I love him," crumbles under his usual pressure into a helpless "I don't know" (238). The answer certainly includes a combination of love/loathing from his mother and loving care from the black woman in the kitchen as contrasted with a father who narcotizes himself against pain and, therefore, love. Valerian perceives Michael searching for people through whom he can vicariously experience the sorrow he is embarrassed to feel for himself. The emperor despises this kind of "cultural orphan who sought other cultures he could love without risk or pain." Viewing his son, who converts his childhood abuse into a desire to heal bruised people, as a Peter Pan–ish "purveyor of exotics," Valerian remains every bit the aimlessly wandering Lost Boy (145).

If Valerian and Son face off across the distance of the dining room table, Sydney softens the space between them. Discreetly excellent in his service as he stands unobtrusively in the background to attend both men at either end of the long table, he sits down only at the "perfectly round" table in the kitchen, his place at which immediately becomes its head (33). Proud of his long-standing position as Du Bois's "Phil-a-delphia Negro mentioned in the book of the very same name," Sydney becomes an easy target for accusations of Uncle Tomism (163). He certainly maintains a "classy silence" in the presence of the native blacks whom he and Ondine rename Yardman and the Marys. Jadine notes somewhat condescendingly that her uncle and aunt are " 'making it' " "steadily and carefully" (41, 126). Morrison, however, confesses to feeling "enormous respect" for the Sydneys of the world (McKay 405). She appreciates his appreciation for work well done, his comfort with himself, his ability to take over when necessary, his tenderness toward his wife, his intolerance of bad behavior. Adroit at multitasking, he maintains a mask of "alert serenity" behind which he manages a complicated household with an "easy silent tread" (74).

Sydney knows that caring for people in the midst of tentativeness is difficult and makes a few silver platters serve for the nuts and fruits as well as the petits fours. Pilate's choice of household furnishings in *Song of Solomon* comparably privileges versatility. Like that of his androgynous predecessor, Sydney's flexible tolerance extends fine care (silver trays) to eccentrics (nuts and fruits) and Lilliputians (petits fours) as well as to the tools of his trade. He effects order but seeks a fluid, cooperative arrangement unlike Valerian's rigid, imposed containment. Accepting, for example, Margaret's need to maintain the illusion that they merely winter in Dominique, he always sends something back with her on her trips to Philadelphia in exchange for the return of carefully selected, multipurpose items. While Ondine sleeps "up to her neck in percale" to defy the heat, her husband goes to bed without a pajama top in deference to it (43). In contrast to the other household members, however, both partners sleep tranquilly because they have earned their rest.

Their personal space reflects the gap between Sydney's approach to housekeeping and Valerian's method of gardening. Unlike the publicly precise casualness of L'Arbe de la Croix, Sydney and Ondine's rooms remain off-limits but lived-in. If Valerian's living room has a coming-and-going hotel feel, their kitchen takes on a look of permanence though their quarters permit few guests. Morrison describes the big house, designed impressively enough to warrant its own name, in great detail and as early as page 10 of her novel. She makes no mention of the servants' rooms, however, until well over halfway through and then with few specifics. She limits her description to the marked difference between the tiny apartment "up over the downstairs kitchen" and the rest of the house (100). Containing well-used, secondhand furniture, family mementos, and "the smell of human beings," it has a "tacky permanence to it, but closed" (160). It offers no chairs for outsiders. Valerian blames his empty chairs on his distaste for the new breed of "bright couples," who close in "wide-open porches" and enlarge windows that "had been tiny, private and sweet." These intrusive newcomers privatize "their houses by turning them backward away from the street" but publicize "their lives and [talk] about wine as though it were a theology instead of a drink" (142). Exhibiting more in common with servants whose race and class forbid fraternizing, the emperor commissions his palace to awe guests he does not care to receive. Drawing little sustenance from his home, he lives outside it with his hothouse plants and shuns both public accountability and personal intimacy. Sydney, on the other hand, carefully separates his inside and outside selves, viewing his public space as his responsibility and using his formality both to foster its air of *sprezzatura* and to protect himself. Fiercely cultivating the privacy from which he draws nourishment to perform his excellent work, he shares living arrangements only with loving intimates.

When Jadine suggests that Son apologize to her uncle and aunt, he goes instinctively to their personal realm, in full knowledge that Sydney will be the most difficult to convince. Unlike the mask of style that Valerian never allows himself to remove, Sydney's face "zigzag[s] like lightning" at Son's presence in his home. As Ondine explains and Son moves quickly aside so that he does not stand between husband and wife, Sydney erupts hotly that only he can invite someone into his place and he does not welcome a wild, underground "swamp nigger." Freed by his own domain from all pretenses to civility, the butler says unequivocally that "if you looking to lounge here and live off the fat of the land, and if you think I'm going to wait on you, think twice!" (163).

Morrison continues to applaud the distinction between public and private selves with Sydney's eating habits. Unlike Valerian and Margaret's erratic and unhealthy diets, the servants regularly sit down in their kitchen to three very full meals a day, and their menu has absolutely no association with what is being served in the dining room. A change in eating behavior indicates a reversal in political climate. Although Son interprets the Christmas dinner fiasco to indicate that "white folks and black folks should not sit down and eat together," Sydney ultimately feeds Valerian his hot potato, cooling it with the butler's own breath, and drinks his employer's fine white wine. Morrison admits to sheltering her privacy in order to carry out her community service. She is "grateful" that black writers are no longer "fashionable" so that it will be possible for some really brilliant ones to surface. Arguing that "once you get off the television screen, you can go home and do your work because your responsibilities are different," she intends no diminution of political activism—simply the opportunity to be more discriminating: "And it's open, it's just freer, that's all, and there's room, there's lots of room" (Stepto 393). A huge, publicly casual space such as Valerian's, however, demands exhausting perfectionist performance, prohibiting public sacrifice. Sydney's small private space, on the other hand, may be unimpressive, but it remains relaxing, promoting outstanding public service.

If Sydney periodically resents trying to run a house with "everybody doing whatever comes to mind" and tires of "refereeing everybody," he steadfastly provides individuals with what they need (97, 35). He understands that the emperor must rule. He puts up with Valerian's pretensions to understated elegance although his obsession with European rhythms sets the butler's "teeth on edge" (12). He alleviates his employer's depressed ennui, entertaining him with a formidably accurate verbal dueling partner but letting him win often enough to divert his thoughts from Michael. He defends beleaguered Margaret to her husband and his wife. He tells Valerian that Margaret is bored, that he, not she, suffers from alcoholism. He adroitly covers up the awkwardness that her husband's sarcasm facilitates. He appeases Ondine's need to be needed, rubbing her sore feet as he allows her to criticize what she loves. He observes that part of Michael's problem is too much affection, that with Ondine and Margaret "spoil[ing] him stupid," the boy "can't fix his mind on nothing"; he also notes that Michael's attempts to "liberate" the servants "[mean] well" (35–36). He puts Son decidedly in his place, quite willing to put a bullet in his head if he behaves badly, then accepts his apologetic change of attitude and calls him Son. He fusses at his niece in the privacy of the kitchen about her table manners and what she defines as "work" while affectionately patting her knee; he serves Jadine in the dining room as regally as he does Valerian and Margaret, never making even eye contact with any of them.

Sydney comprehends that too much can be as bad as too little, and he turns to his wife as an equal. Unlike the emperor who will have no match, Sydney and Ondine remain comrades in arms. Sleeping back to back, each half of the "pair of married servants" senses safety radiating from the "steady, able spine of its partner" just a "hip turn away" (43). Unlike the relationship between Valerian and Margaret, neither aging nor an age gap prohibits lovemaking from their marriage bed. Informed by her husband that Son's arrival has been the catalyst for conjugal sex in the imperial bed, Ondine sniffs: "They ought to sleep together. . . . Whoever heard of married folks sleeping any other way but together" (191). Although Sydney usually plays the deferential yin to Ondine's defiant yang, the situation is reversible on demand. When the husband becomes enraged about sleeping arrangements that place Son upstairs above his downstairs room over the downstairs kitchen, the wife takes over. She affirms his discomfort with the nigger in the woodpile, confirming that Son's presence makes everybody grind their teeth, but tells Sydney this is not his bone to gnaw. Temporarily able to reassure her husband, Ondine stays solidly realistic. If she surprises herself when Sydney becomes "shook" by talking "good sense" that she "didn't know she had about a situation that both frightened and disoriented her," she also admits to herself that race is indeed Sydney's bone but that at present he must toss it aside (102). Her heavy braids coiled on her head like a silver diadem, her voice oddly flat, she regrets not their struggle to move on up but the fact that she lacks the strength to chase chickens anymore, much less wring their necks. Practical about the ongoing precariousness of their situation, Ondine, like her mate, balances idealism with the realities of everyday survival.

Even in the soundness of his earned sleep, Sydney still dreams. His is a tiny, recurring image of a rust-red Baltimore that, though unrecalled upon awakening, curiously refreshes him. Because the city of his childhood always remains "a red city in his mind—red brick, red sun, red necks and cardinals," it has merely rusted gently with age. Although he gives up his city as a young man to become one of those proud, industrious Philadelphia Negroes, Sydney's most vivid dreams for the last fifty years recollect the fish, trees, wagons, music, and fruit stands of that "red rusty Baltimore of 1921" (61). When Jadine, admitting to her benefactor the inferiority of African clay masks, remembers that Michael wanted all the Childs to return to Baltimore and "be thrilling," Valerian glances at Sydney and laughs: "*Sydney? A potter?*" (75). Jadine smiles in turn but does not turn to look her uncle. Unlike the emperor who never dreams that his butler might imagine himself an artist, Sydney understands more about Valerian's nightly visitations than does Valerian himself.

This old black man takes care of things with a gun and the gift of sympathy. "Unbidden but right on time," his shadowlike figure circles the table with steps of felt and nerves of steel (62). He reassures his wife that nothing can change, that they have stock certificates and Social Security. When things do change, however, he changes with them. It is Sydney who confronts the nigger in the woodpile and who leads his sobbing wife, her "diadem braids turned into horns," from the table after her shocking Christmas revelation (209). If his own form of class blinders allows him to be fooled, over his wife's cautions, into believing that Son covets Valerian's patronage and not Sydney's niece, he and Ondine both come to realize that even a Jade in their crown will not allow them to sit down on a throne (102). Remarking "[Jadine] didn't do well by us," he responds to Ondine's comment that a child (Childs) is not an interest-bearing savings account: "Seem like folks used to take care of folks once upon a time. Old black people must be a worrisome thing to the young ones these days." Resolved that if L'Arbe de la Croix is not his home, then "nothing is but the grave," he retorts when Ondine acknowledges they will have to bury themselves: "Well, in that case the shroud may as well be comfy" (283–84).

We last see Valerian sitting down alone, fanning his hands dreamily in the controlled air of his greenhouse in a bizarre parody of an orchestra conductor with nobody playing his song. Margaret, having finally dreamed the dream she should have, serenely folds his shirts and considers cutting his hair. Morrison's ultimate portrait of Valerian depicts a big baby boy. As helpless as Samson blinded and shorn, he tries to peer behind the mask his servant wears, chooses to see kindness there, and wants to go home. Sydney, still standing, takes over. Gently blowing on the hot potato that he hand-feeds his master, he drinks Valerian's wine, orders huaraches for the emperor's corns, and, turning up the volume on the classical music, announces the permanence of their place in an imperfect paradise. Sydney, in other words, endures.

Most canonical American literary texts emphasize the dangers of order threatened by chaos. *Tar Baby*, on the other hand, highlights the dangers of disrupted disorder. From this perspective, Son sits at odds with Valerian as bucket boy for the bottom of the table. Morrison relates both versions of masculinity to the feminine figure of water. Valerian struggles to stay on top of it; Son yearns for immersion within it. Unlike the white male entrepreneur who spends his life either treading water in the bucket with no bottom or using women as emotional sinks, even the Old World free black male swims easily and, like the blind horsemen, floats with the female current. The novel opens as Son, "crazy with homesickness," jumps feetfirst off the *Stor Konigsgaarten* into warm, pulsing, ammonia-scented waves (138). Pushed gently but firmly by the "water lady" into the velvet darkness of a "wide, empty tunnel," he becomes reborn—or comes out of the closet where he has stored himself—to bolt like Br'er Rabbit for Valerian's garden patch. He believes from the beginning that "he [is] safe," even though he whirls "counterclockwise" from the rest of the landscape (3–5).

Directed by the lady's insistent palm away from the shore, Son locates the women onboard the *Seabird II*, anchored in the blue, not green, realm that Morrison associates with freedom. Although he protests way too much that he does not follow the women, William "Son" Green is clearly awakened like Prufrock by a mermaid's voice saying, "I'm never lonely," as he sleeps in one of the *Seabird*'s storage spaces (6). A volatile combination of *Sula*'s Jude Greene turned *Song of Solomon*'s Guitar, this dark-skinned young man prepares to emerge as the nigger in the woodpile of L'Arbe de la Croix. He tastes the salt in his mustache, equivalent to hearing Guitar's hunter's horn, and sets out to "ma[k]e one Jude" (or Son) by mating with an egg queen (*Sula* 83). In so doing, he wears what Morrison calls his "most effective mask," which is none at all, and violently upsets the fruit basket of Isle des Chevaliers, bringing to life the masks of all those who do not eat the apples it does not produce ("Unspeakable Things Unspoken" 30).

Indentured by the consequences of previous violence to the wandering life, William Green fades from view to emerge as one of the great "uns," an international legion of the uncounted "underclass of undocumented men." He becomes an unidentified, unlicensed crewman on "ships with volatile cargo," terrified of Social Security cards, refusing to "equate work with life," and unable "to stay anywhere for long" (166). Like Guitar and Milkman at the end of his journey, however, Green remains rooted in black cultural pride even as he rejects the rituals of white middle-class success. A provocateur with "a lot of space around his eyes," this man of many names is most comfortable as "Son," the "him that he never lied to, the one he tucked in at night and the one he did not want to die" (80, 139). The other selves that appear on forged documents exist as "fabrications of the moment, misinformation required to protect Son from harm and to secure that one reality at least" (139). Son's fight to maintain his self suggests the black male counterpart to the tar-black female in vibrant yellow who holds up three white eggs and spits at Jadine. This woman in yellow represents Jadine's betrayal in Paris of her authentic, original self along with the ebony skins of ninety baby seals. Son associates himself with the ninety yellow houses of Eloe, Florida, whose white doors are opened by black women shouting, "Come on in, you honey you," and with the fat black ladies in white dresses minding the pie table in the church basement (119).

Son is simply a horseman of a different color. This Old World free black male has fixed ideas about gender roles, quite different from but just as firm as Valerian's visions of chevaliers kneeling to ladies on pedestals.[14] For Son, women should be sexual pleasure and nurturing comfort, though they can be challenges or smothering threats. When he smells spicy food then hears Jadine's voice on the boat, he does not know whether her tones ring warm on the inside and cold at the edges or the other way round; he does sense that he is the only man on board. Morrison's italics emphasize Son's amazement that the women on the *Seabird* "had not *cooked*," reheating instead takeout they had ordered in (8). He attempts to avoid what he perceives as Margaret's sharp tips, counting for support on her marshmallow center. He shows his respect for Ondine by sitting down in her kitchen to eat so much of her food that she softens considerably toward him. He crouches unbidden night after night in Jadine's room, trying to overlay his dreams of pie tables and icehouses and nickel nickelodeons and "white wet sheets flapping on a line, and the sound of a six-string guitar plucked after supper while children scooped walnuts up off the ground" onto the transparencies of "gold and cloisonné and honey-colored silk" that a Parisian haute couture model projects onto the screen of her imagination (119–20). Unlike Valerian's cerebral hothouse cool, Son moves sensuously in tune with his environment, including the women in it. Both men, however, desire women who dance to their music.

The crash of a bottle of Bain de Soleil onto the deck of the boat announces that its sunny island destination will be the bane of Son's wild existence, as he becomes the bane of its civilized interlopers. Instead of tasting the white man's imported garden apples, the nigger in the woodpile greedily devours the boat's homegrown, bitter oranges of knowledge and steals the bittersweet chocolate and [Eve]ian water from Ondine's downstairs kitchen. Ondine is the first to sense the disruption that his arrival will bring. Thoughts about the uninvited intruder in the upstairs guest room cause her to ponder a bit of blue sky breaking through a crack in the shutters. She receives the impression of "a small, smooth sound, like a well-oiled gear shifting" and slowly returns to plucking her white hen. Having already attributed the loss of her chocolate to a hungry rat reminiscent of Wright's Bigger Thomas, she tells Sydney that she has seen Son's eyes when he thinks no one looks. When her husband asks her what she finds there, she responds gravely: "Wildness. Plain straight-out wildness. He wants [Jadine], Sydney. And he'll do what he has to do to get her and what he has to to keep her" (192).

Morrison associates Son with wildness throughout *Tar Baby*. Philip Page argues that, apart from *Jazz*'s Wild, Son is "the wildest of Morrison's wild characters." A trickster figure, he represents "both good and bad," a bringer of good and bad luck. He befriends and provokes, lives outside but subverts the community he enters. He is "freer and hence more dangerous than Cholly, Sula, or Guitar" (123). Jan Furman, on the other hand, maintains that Son "is not a chronic wanderer by nature and by choice"; but for his wife's affair, he would "probably have remained at home in Eloe" (59). If so, Morrison connects a reversion to wildness to her character's relationships with women. This Son is "mammy made" and "Mama spoiled," the baby boy of the black community who has been so accustomed to being well fed by the pie women that he becomes bewildered, even enraged when a woman does not want to cook for him (269).

Urged out to sea by the water lady but following the boat women inland, Son is drawn by them to an island where "things went back to their natural state so quickly" (94). Morrison comments that the Tar Baby folktale she chose to reinterpret seemed to her to be about masks coming to life, about the tensions between masks and the representational life they displace ("Unspeakable Things" 30). Its texture required a worn, exaggerated leanness so that, like the stark symmetry of a mask sculpture or the deep eaves and light-filtering curtains that counter the heat-heavy sky over L'Arbe de la Croix, no distractions exist to prevent occupants from concentrating "on whichever of their personal problems they wished" (81). Jadine muses that Isle des Chevaliers magnifies everything, producing "much too much sleep," and that "such tranquility in sleep made for wildness in the waking hours" (68). Unlike Valerian, who nods daily so often in his greenhouse chair that he requires brandy to force himself to sleep even fitfully in the master bed at night, and unlike Sydney, who earns his nightly rest in his upstairs bed with Ondine over the downstairs kitchen, Son sleeps mostly in the daytime and prowls in the dark, foraging for food.

The sleep he gets is sporadic and spread out: in a bunk on a cargo ship, in a utility closet on a boat, under a bench in a gazebo, on the floor in Jadine's room, in a hammock on the patio. As he wanders the estate grounds like a wild thing taking what he needs when he needs it, he trails the mark of his scent. Therese first detects the "chocolate eater's" presence from the unmistakable smell of a starving human, akin to "the smell of human afterbirth that only humans could produce" (105). Son worries that the animal odor he fights to control in the room with Jadine permeates so powerfully it will wake her. His other behaviors appear equally raw. When Sydney discovers him and escorts him downstairs at the point of a gun, he asks to "take a leak." Invited by the emperor to dine, he "burrow[s] in his plate like an animal, grunting in monosyllables" and insulting the butler by calling out "Hi"(94).[15] Under the stimulating effect of island calm, Son reverts to his most savage tendencies, eating, sleeping, and eliminating instinctually like an animal or a child.

While Sydney routinely shaves and cuts Valerian's hair and the two argue over what shoes to wear, Son walks off the boat with feet uncovered and hair unkempt. He relinquishes his shoes to the water lady and steps into Jadine's shower with the soles of his feet encrusted by black dirt. Like his fingernails, his hair grows long. It looks to Jadine "physically overpowering, like bundles of long whips or lashes that could grab her and beat her to jelly. And would" (113). Soaped squeaky with her bath gel, his "uncivilized, reform-school hair" and beard "crackled like lightning," more vital than her sealskin coat. When he looks at his watered-down reflection in the mirror, Son observes that even void of its personal dirt, "black people's hair . . . was definitely alive" and, unattended, his "pelt" as springy to the touch as foliage (132). In New York with Jadine, he tells her he wants some body hair. Nommo, however, denies the lovers the time needed for Jade's smooth-shaven surface to refoliate.[16]

Son's instinct leads him to touch first Jadine's bare foot, after he begs her to bring both out from where she has tucked them underneath her so that he might merely admire. Unfolding them cautiously "as though she was about to do something wild" while informing him that he really needs professional care, she nonetheless remains as quiet under his hand as the bitch she recalls in Baltimore. Son puts his "forefinger on her sole [soul] and held it and held it and held it there" (179). His power over living things results from his natural way with them, unmasked and unimpeded like Valerian by impressions of *sprezzatura*. When Valerian archly asks his disheveled dinner guest whether or not he believes in spirits of nature, Son answers directly and without apology: "In a swamp, I believe" (93). Shape-shifting like the spirits, and Pilate, to provide everyone with the Son they seek without losing his identity, Son realizes that all are afraid of him except Valerian, who assumes superiority to the lackey dialect the minion puts on for his master and the "guest's" rough jokes about black whores—at which the host laughs "to beat the band" (149). Son quickly seduces the others in spite of their fears, disarming even Sydney, and then looks to get himself on Jadine's mind. In the form of wild man, swamp nigger, horseman, baboon, river rat, or even gorilla, the threateningly unpredictable energy of a "big strong-looking man" in the craftily designed woodpile of L'Arbe de la Croix is alluring (107). As Sydney finally concedes, Son "made something grow that was dying" (192).

This uncontainable masculine magnetism both attracts and repels Jadine in the way her model's glossies clash with her unphotographable femaleness, "that mother/sister/she" (46). Embarrassed when Son enters her bedroom at the memory of rubbing her nipples into her sleek sealskin coat, she wonders whether it or he looks the blacker or shinier but vehemently opposes the thought of him touching her (alter) skin. She holds on tight to the leashes of "small dark dogs galloping on silver feet" as he whispers "Go-oddamn" at the sight of her mink-colored eyes and her wet and open lips on the cover of a fashion magazine (113, 116). Though the civilized part of her feels insulted and ashamed when he presses his loins into hers to "smell" her, the primitive part is enchanted by his uncultivated, unabashed exuberance. The leash of her sophisticated education helps her subdue arousal by making Son look naïve when he accepts her claim of wearing earrings belonging to Catherine the Great. On the other hand, she sinks up to her thighs in the swamp women's ancient, powerful tar after only one day beached with Son on the waterfront.[17] Surrounded by the sea-green sea and the sky-blue sky, she can no more capture with her charcoal the essence of his "laughing heaven-raised face" than he can previously look her in the face, explaining his reticence: "The [posed] pictures are easier. They don't move" (170, 119). Returning to Valerian's house, however, Jadine scrubs her legs raw to remove the sticky tar: "The little feet [Son] wanted so badly to see were clean again, peachy soft again as though they had never been touched and never themselves had touched the ground" (186).

Unlike the "perfect conversations" that take place between Sydney and Ondine, the "hooks" Son and Jadine hang on prevent their wordless communication (McKay 406). In Son's case, memories of pie ladies and original dimes mess up visions of breathtaking beauty. In Jadine's, dreams about night women with breasts and large hats that leave her orphaned, juxtaposed against a picture of an African "woman's woman" wearing canary yellow and carrying eggs, take the comfort out of cloisonné and sponges and honey-colored silk and large hands (119). Hooked by the heart-stopping beauty of what Gideon calls Son's first "yella," the nigger in the woodpile accepts a makeover that includes a soft homemade haircut, borrowed Hickey Freeman suit, white shirt unbuttoned at the throat and cuffs, and a little Paco Rabanne cologne.[18] Jadine is by turns startled, impressed, and frightened at his sudden "gorgeous" change in appearance. Morrison's readers, on the other hand, remember her warnings in *The Bluest Eye* about the dangers of succumbing to white images of physical beauty and romantic love (156). Son is likewise torn between the unhinging seductiveness of his beautiful, light-skinned tar baby and the recollected safety of his Florida briar patch and original dime.

The Eloe of Son's "rememory," as *Beloved*'s Sethe calls imagined recall, involves not only the femininity of the pie tables but also the masculinity of the original dime. Left by her "deliberately unappetizing" picnic lunch "yearning for more," Jadine asks Son what he wants out of life, and he unhesitatingly responds, "My original dime." Morrison's trope for his authentic maleness, the shiny coin represents Son's reward for cleaning a tub of massive sheepshead fish for an irascible "nothing kind of dude" named San Francisco. After this the "best" and "only real" money he ever had, with which he buys his "first personal, store-bought purchase," five cigarettes and a Dr. Pepper, he can no longer work just for money (169–70). The magic happens in the simplicity of the experience and the value of fraternity, not in the sophistication of appearance or a respect for industry. Son remembers Frisco and fraternity when he sees Yardman's back out of Jadine's window. He studies backs because, unprotected and unmanipulable like a smokehouse cot open to vagrants for the night, they "told it all." Son associates Gideon's back with the endured physical and psychological pain of his people, and "the angle of the old man's spine" elicits unshed tears (139). He contrasts his present indoor, Easter-white cleanness with the other kneeling outdoors in the dirt and mourns a fading past in the form of Yardman's back. The comfort Son feels at Gideon's house restores momentarily the welcome of the cot. The yardman grooms the horseman's hair, after the butler refuses; fed by Therese and adored by Alma Estee, Son allows himself a fireside sentiment "free of postures and phony accents." He feels for the first time in years like a "well-heeled man" (150–51). While Valerian's past is informed solely by an unnamed black washerwoman whose sons he patronizes, Son romanticizes all of his past, especially the black men in it.

Vietnam and a flapping fish cement his attachment to memories such as Miss Tyler's piano. Flooded at the sight of Valerian's piano by the feeling he had "swum seven seas for seven years only to arrive at the place he had started from," Son recalls being afraid during the war for the hands that stroked Miss Tyler's keys, despite the razzing of Drake,

Soldier, and Ernie Paul, because "nothing else mattered" (136). He longed for hands doing "something nice and human for a change." After his dishonorable discharge, however, he simply exchanges the "slaughter of whole families in their sleep" for watching lambs, chickens, tuna "die by the ton" (136, 131). Morrison captures the distortion that killing inflicts on Son's nature with his violent reaction to a dying snapper that slaps him in the face. Fishing off the coast of Argentina, everyone but Son having spectacular luck, Son finally reels in a "huge glitter of froth and steel," which asserts itself by flipping him a final, dazzling flourish of its tail as he bends to remove its hook. Enraged, he bashes the snapper's head in with his fist. While the Swede laughs, the Mexican, a fellow fisherman, quietly hands him a drawing done in prison of Uncle Sam crushing the corpses of children. Guiltily accepting the Mexican's observation that Son is "*Cierto Americano*" in his outrage at the "claim of a snapper on its own life," its refusal "to want, goddamn it, to surrender itself for his pleasure," he decides that the time has come to go home not to America but to his home in it—the green Elysian fields of black pie ladies (167).

This display of violence deserves comparison with Son's previous killing of his wife and subsequent treatment of Jadine. Playing piano badly after Vietnam in a small jazz joint, he returns home to find his mate in bed with a thirteen-year-old boy. He runs his car through the house, and Cheyenne burns to death in the ensuing fire. Son does not regret his action, though he acknowledges that he went too far. He is, however, ashamed that he did not have the courage or the compassion to look the woman in the eyes as she died. Preferring stills of Jadine's face to its living state, Son now requires life to hold still. He controls the tail of the flying fish with his knee as he strikes its head. He does not want Jadine to "talk back" or, worse, insert her dreams into his and snatches her camera out of her hand as she takes pictures of Eloe (120). He insists that he *can* tell a black woman what she is or ought to be, and, like Guitar, he likes her fear: he "basked in it like a cat in steam-pipe heat and it made him feel protective and violent at the same time" (177). He calls "free stuff" a "pain" because it requires the subtlety of seduction (213). He wants Jadine, but he "want[s] to smash something too" (301). Various critics have debated whether or not Son rapes Jadine toward the end of their relationship.[19] Given the pattern his frustration takes, rape becomes a credible scenario. After he sees disgust on her face and tells her the tar baby story as he tears open his shirt, Morrison describes Jadine as "slippery, gutted" like the battered snapper. Moreover, Son, once again, fears he has gone too far.

However, Son also helps everybody to ollieballen (all a ya ballin'/ bawlin') at Christmas. When he flicks Valerian's cyclamen stems into bloom between thumb and middle finger, he smilingly informs the emperor that plants resemble women: "You have to jack them up every once in awhile" (149). In his big hands the island community "vomit[s] up color like a drunk," and everybody enjoys sex (187). His sometimes gentle, sometimes jarring revitalization of repressed things, what Valerian calls "black magic," takes its strength from the truth behind it.[20] When innocent people are threatened, the man with "savannahs in his face" meets straight on the evening eyes of the man who threatens out of willful innocence. Refusing in a voice that clicks "like a key opening a lock" the emperor's order to leave the table, Son inspires life into the masks of all the people sitting round it (206). This rough magic wielded by the nigger in the woodpile brings the possibility of both death and growth; moving silently and stealthily in the dark, he "fuck[s] like a star" (292).

Freed by disrupted order to meet and mate, Son and Jadine attempt to mix water and oil into the soil from which each finds most comfort. Jadine remembers New York as a black woman's town where sisters "Talk shit. Take none." While Son waits anxiously in the bathtub for her to arrive, as close as he can get to water in a hotel room, she giggles happily in the cab to be back on the island that refreshes her and "oils her joints" (221–22). Although there "wasn't a permanent adult job in the whole of the city" for Son, they find his virility to be an account transferable into Big Apple sophistication. Upon meeting him, Jadine's friend Betty even foregoes her lesbian lifestyle (227). Instead of thriving on city energy and noise, however, Son feels disheartened by its emptiness and crying silence. Looking in vain right and left for children and old people, he discovers childhood gone underground, old age in kennels, and the girls mutely crying. He becomes most depressed, though, by men on "tippy-toe" staring straight ahead because they cannot stand to see the crying girls and by "beautiful males who had found the whole business of being black and men at the same time too difficult and so they'd dumped it, . . . snipp[ing] off their testicles and past[ing] them to their chests" (216). Nonetheless, the lovers forego their separate worlds and reinvent another Eden through each other until Nommo declares no more in New York and they leave, like Milton's couple, "hand-in-hand" for Eloe (230).[21]

The original dime he "ain't got" draws Son to the place he remembers as having "plenty of nuffin" (171). Unlike snappy New York City, Eloe contains children that Jadine entertains by snapping pictures of them, an old woman who calls Jadine daughter, an old man named Old Man whose son is Old Man's Son, and the fraternity of black Soldiers. To Jadine, however, its sisters take shit and talk none. When Son's father, Franklin G. Green, known as Old Man since he was seven, refuses to violate taboo by allowing the unmarried Son and Jadine to sleep together under his roof, his son argues that Jade is "special." Old Man retorts, "So am I, Son. So am I," and his son capitulates (249). Although father and son do not embrace because they "didn't know how," Soldier and Son affectionately "hit each other on the head, the hands, the shoulders," laughing and talking and ignoring the women and children clustered silently outside (246–47). The worshipful stares and nonconversation of the female neighbors along with the disapproval of the old folks annoy Jadine, who reluctantly receives a nightgown but refuses to accept a name when Son's Aunt Rosa refers to her as "daughter." Soldier, however, most directly challenges her composure (255). Bluntly demanding who "controls" her relationship with Son while he touts his friend as marriageable material, describes Cheyenne as dangerous but the "best pussy in Florida," and warns her that Son hates being controlled, Soldier fights to keep his buddy behind the bunker of fraternity. He admits freely to Son's "hot one" that her lover "wouldn't know a good woman from a snake" and won't take advice, that he "thinks with his dick," and that restraint makes him "wildlike" (254–55). When Jadine rails against his sexist "cradle," Son responds by recalling the physical and emotional endurance of his mother, aunt, sisters, and wife: "Anybody who thought women were inferior didn't come out of north Florida" (267–68). Nonetheless, the Eloe of Son's rememory remains a black man's town.

The conclusion of *Tar Baby* finds the lovers convinced, like Soldier, that one is saving the other, and the rescue does not go well. Son perceives himself responsible for tearing down Jadine's "blinding awe" of whiteness, then escaping the plantation of L'Arbe de la Croix, and finally maintaining a moderate climate in which to contain her fragility (219). Instead of delicate wind chimes tinkling in the breeze of his breath, however, Jadine proves to be an Amazon soldier ant queen whose life becomes so regimented that there is "little need for males and they are seldom produced" (290). Instead of sleeping safely nestled in his large hands, she allows no time for dreaming and says hands off to the night women with breasts, "who had seduced him and were trying to lay claim to her" (262). In between loving him, she fights him. Each pulls "the other away from the maw of hell—its very ridge top. Each knew the world as it was meant or ought to be. One had a past, the other a future and each one bore the culture to save the race in his hands. Mama-spoiled black man, will you mature with me? Culture-bearing black woman, whose culture are you bearing?" (269). Morrison asserts that Son and Jadine have "no problems as far as men and women are concerned. They knew exactly what to do." The issues that divide them have less to do with conflicting gender roles and more with "other 'differences' the culture offers" such as class and racial consciousness. The question for each comes down to "whether he or she was really a member of the tribe" (McKay 404).

When it comes to sex, then, Jadine and Son speak wordless volumes. Apart from lust and sometimes simple caring for, however, they have to explain their selves away. She thinks it impossible for anything to be as black as his Eloe and refuses to spend her life down on Hurston's muck. He takes back from her his original dime, gotten, she spits at him, when some black woman "like me fucked a white man for it and then *gave* it to Frisco who made you work your ass off for it" (272). Shamed, like Adam, by the woman's nakedness that the man created and then soils, Son stares at Jadine's sad pictures of Eloe, tossed carelessly on the coffee table along with her keys to their place. Morrison remains convinced that her male character lives in Eloe only imaginatively. If that place were real, she comments, Jadine "could not destroy it with a camera" (McKay 405).

Stranded in the middle of no-man's-land, Son, like Milkman, is saved by a woman who gives him a choice of where he wants to be. Following Jadine, he returns to Dominique and finds Gideon and Therese. Warned by both to stay away from the yella who has "forgotten her ancient properties," he tells them he has no choice. Blind Therese offers to take him in the dark to Isle des Chevaliers, pulls the *Prix de France* up to a bridge of rocks on the opposite side of the island from L'Arbe de la Croix, and announces that now he can choose: he can search for Jade, live in "the garden of some other white people house," or locate his home in the hills where the blind and naked horsemen wait to ride with him. At the end of her novel, Morrison's nigger abjures the woodpile, elects the possibility of perpetual fraternity, and resumes his mythological place in his-story. Carried by a woman through another black, watery passage, her sturdy feet next to his all the way, the "small boy" turns his traveling bag over to deconstructionist Marie Therese Foucault, crawls over the sister rocks away from the nursing sound of the sea, and feels his way onto solid ground. Stumbling initially over pebbles and roots of trees, he takes his first few halting steps. Suddenly the fog lifts, and the trees "ste[p] back a bit as if to make the way easier for a certain kind of man." Then Son scampers like Br'er Rabbit "lickety-split. Lickety-split. Lickety-lickety-lickety-split" (305–6).

Jadine is en route to land in Paris and start over at the same time Son is running out of control through the swamp. Both must sacrifice their dream of past or future safety to gain their present freedom. She accepts her crown as ant queen; he dons his mask of wild hare. Each must leave off the safety of the other to become the safety for which the other longs. The increasing distance between their perspectives can be measured by their reactions to Therese's niece Alma Estee. Meeting her as she cleans the ladies' room of Dominique's pale-yellow airport, Jadine, startled by the contrast between the girl's green uniform and the "black pearls of hair" visible under her russet wig, checks her own eyelashes in the mirror (289). Responding to the charge of having killed the chocolate eater by saying she has to go, she drops her loose francs into "Mary's" plastic pail (289). Here Morrison suggests that this yella remembers the vibrant woman in yellow whose "force has burnt away [her] lashes" but chooses to exchange ancient for current properties while a staring, doe-eyed Alma Estee remains awed by Jade's rarity (46). Son, however, becomes dizzy at the sight of Alma Estee "in a wig the color of dried blood." Believing that he could forego fraternity and forsake the pie ladies for the woman, he immediately regrets being "corrupted by cloisonné" when a "bougainvillea in a girdle . . . an avocado with earrings" refuses to let him remove her wig (299). Given a choice at the end of the novel, Son, "looking neither to the left nor to the right," opts to go home the only way he can (306). He will represent the kind of man who runs with the horsemen and sports with the swamp women, the man who drives through houses and jacks up potted plants, the man who draws soldier ants to him with chocolate and drives them away with a mirror, the man who fucks like a star.

The lone male left actually living in the world of Son's wild kingdom is Gideon. Yardman does not rate a place at Valerian's table at all. In fact, he never enters the house unless followed by Ondine. Flexible enough, however, to fool around with most any outdoor job, he endures even dispossession twice a year when a professional, white male maintenance crew comes "in a launch with machines" to make enough money to "drive Mercedes and Yamahas all over Queen of France" (41). Although he "pull[s] his own oars in his own mud-colored boat," the faded blue of *Prix de France* embossed on its prow suggests that with age Gideon has mellowed more than Son. Like the blind horsemen, he survives through guile the claims on him from white and black people alike. Pretending not to read so that Ondine cannot hand him a long list of chores to finish or things to install, he also removes one of the panes to the pantry window she orders him to repair so that the starving Son has access to food. He lets Therese lie when she takes hand-kissing credit for the idea. When the Americans dismiss one of the annoyingly inattentive "Marys," he brings Therese "right back and tell[s] them it's a brand-new woman" (153). Only this wet nurse of the "magic breasts" can outwit him "(of all people)" with thirty-four letters written in perfect French by a local priest and acolyte. Two years Gideon's senior, his mother's baby sister successfully finagles apples and money from her nephew and entices him with visions of handling family property the old lady does not have into leaving the United States after twenty years' residence there.

Subterfuge, including a stolen visa and marriage to an African American nurse, gets Gideon into the States via Quebec. He comes to assess the advantages of U.S. citizenship, however, as the "ability to send an occasional ten-dollar money order, buy a leisure suit and watch TV" and is delighted to return to his homeland from the country he calls "a bad place to die in" (154). Most natives of Dominique do not bother to disguise the "contempt they felt in their hearts for everybody but themselves," including haughty Therese, who ignores the presence of the killer "white bosses" as simply irrelevant to her romances. Gideon, on the other hand, considers "what they thinking about it all" as integral to his version of things (110–11). Immigrant life and the humiliation of abandoning his U.S. ship minus money or degrees as well as the insults heaped on him by family afford him patience, humility, and tolerance. His shame is offset when his English and affability earn him an easy job at L'Arbe de la Croix. His happiness at being home prevents him from "hold[ing] a grudge or sustain[ing] anger for more than an hour" (110). Unlike Valerian's Eden or Son's Eloe, Gideon's Dominique stays real. The land for which he comes back having been confiscated by the French, he nonetheless eats splendidly from the sea. Together with the rest of the poor, he takes advantage of wild avocado trees, forages in private and communal kitchen gardens. His "laughing, lying crone" of an aunt provides ready entertainment, along with waiting for carnival, drinking and "relaxing" with women, and playing with "the boys" in paradise (109, 155). Freely blowing about land and sea, he lives with Therese and sometimes Alma in Therese's powder-pink house on Place de Vent where hurricanes require him to replace the roof four times a year.

If Valerian and Sydney remain earthbound and Son thrives in water, Gideon is neither gone with nor blowing in the wind. He already knows there is no safety. There is, however, home. Longing for critics who can understand the black cosmology or decipher the African American codes that undergird her novels, Morrison explains that for black people Sula's or Gideon's return home represents not a defeat but a triumph "because [they come] back to where [they were] at the beginning" (McKay 407). Although soldier ant queens refuse to come out of their kingdoms in the night wind, Son, ensconced in a hammock rocked by the breeze outside L'Arbe de la Croix, relies on wind resistance to force him to confront his solitude. Recognizing that Valerian's hothouse stifles the rush of air required to shake things up, he also knows that dwelling too long adrift has made something come loose in him.

This is why he chokes up when he stares out Jadine's window at Gideon's smokehouse-cot back. Despite the world's dismissal of it, Son understands his magical power and chooses solitude because he "never wanted to live in the world their way. There was something wrong with the rites. He had wanted . . . [s]ome other way of being in the world that he felt leaving him when he stood in the white towel watching Yardman's—Gideon's—back" (166). However, this other way may be as impossibly unrealistic as Son's memories of Eloe, the "kind of thing that one takes when one leaves, and harbors it in the heart" (McKay 405). Gideon loves his home, but he also lives there. While Son holds back unshed tears as he watches the old man working, Yardman has stopped pretending to be uninterested and is "openly enjoying the possibilities" as he describes Jadine "naked as a worm" and, later, Son in a towel framed against the window of Jadine's bedroom. Telling Therese that when Jade jumped back it "didn't do no good" because he "got eyes in the top of [his] head," he avoids being seen seeing Son: "I pretended I was taking off my cap to scratch my head and looking off up in the trees" (107). Thus, as Son overflows with tearful sentiment about Gideon's poor back, Gideon is having a good time not having to put on a front. The yardman continues to exist in the space between safety and freedom by putting back on yet another temporary roof to be blown off the pink cement house in Place de Vent.

He also resolutely refuses to romanticize women. Advising Son from the beginning against accepting the "stuff" yallas "put down," he offers his experiences with his own wife, whom he marries for all practical purposes, as additional caution about the wiles of women (155). If yallas must choose to be black, and most do not, black American nurses exhibit "abnormal sexual hunger." Had his wife's faithfulness not countered her "mean, arrogant and insatiable" behavior, he would "never have left her out of gratitude" (303). Gideon looks to his relationship with incorrigible Therese to provide him both family and fraternity. Although he will eat with and entertain her on Isle des Chevaliers, at home he does not socialize with her, staying to himself or visiting old cronies. Very much the king of the castle when other men are about, he lies about his accomplishments, talks, eats, and generously offers the run of her house as Therese silently and tolerantly serves. Nonetheless, the house is hers. Each allows the other a removable protean mask of maleness or femaleness while they also attend to their private needs. This balanced attitude toward gender roles explains Gideon's skepticism about romantic love: he "never got over being amazed at that kind of passion, though he had seen it enough." For Yardman, Jadine is "[a] woman, man. Just a woman" (301–2).

Militant Son objects passionately when the Childs call Gideon "Yardman." However, Morrison maintains that renaming occurs routinely among males in African American communities: "I never knew the real names of my father's friends. Still don't. They used other names." Partly the result of "cultural orphanage," partly a refusal to let slavery prevent blacks from "owning" their names, the best revenge is to "take another name which is yours because it reflects something about you or your own choice" (LeClair 375). Unlike Son, Gideon remains "accommodating" enough to accept Yardman (41). His character embodies, indeed, the insignificant biblical farmer who conceals food from the oppressors of his people, defeats a huge army with a small force by cleverly breaking jars and blowing trumpets, and, believing only God can rule, refuses to become emperor. He incorporates the businessman whose goal is New Testament distribution. He contains the caretaker who looks after things outside the house while Sydney takes care of the inside. Like Sydney more craftily flexible than the others on Isle des Chevaliers, Gideon can have on hand at home fraternity, community, and a journey instead of a job.

Sharks and free black men swim or die. Everybody at the end of *Tar Baby* is moving either forward or backward, apart from Valerian who treads water and goes nowhere. Sydney and Ondine still stand and wait, Jadine flies, Margaret folds, Therese rows, Son runs, and Gideon puts the roof back on. Isle des Chevaliers is returning to its precolonized wildness. While some readers might well agree with Demetrakopoulos that Morrison's black men are twisted, their position in this book could also be described as especially durable. The nigger in the woodpile has come out of the closet to send ants flying, rabbits running, and everything else every which way. He has exposed the emperor's new clothes. He has countered classical form with romantic feeling, industry with fraternity. The novel ends in ambiguity because Morrison cannot now envision a harmonious juncture for authentic African American men and women or for black and white Americans. She does conclude, however, that Americans of either gender or any color cannot dwell altogether in the past or look only to the future. The overflow from the abscess on American history has not yet been absorbed, nor has the scar of slavery healed. At present there can be no safety for African American males. They prevail, though, through possibility.

CHAPTER 6

Circles of Sorrow, Sites of Memory, Forms of Flooding

Colored Men's Time in *Beloved*

Among the memories that send Son scampering lickety-split at the end of *Tar Baby* is the site of a smokehouse cot. Wrapped in an Easter-white towel, having watched his personal dirt swirl down somebody else's shower drain, he stares out the window of a beautifully kept bedroom at the back of an old black man on the ground below "stooping over some cutting or digging chore" (139). The association of the black man's back with a vacant bed for vagabonds leads Son to imagine a life for Yardman that echoes the essence of his own experience. He has spent his adult years on the road seeking fraternity and studying backs because they are "simply there, all open, unprotected and unmanipulable . . . stretched like a smokehouse cot where hobos could spend the night." Unlike eyes or mouths, backs "told it all," exposing the canker pains, pinched nerves, empty mailboxes, missed trains home, and this-seat-taken signs so familiar to African American males. Fighting back unshed tears at the sight of the back that signals something leaving him, temporarily reprieved when Gideon stands up, Son whispers inaudibly to the man he does not see watching him look: " 'Thanks. . . . One more second of your smokehouse cot might have brought me there at last' " (139–40).

Beloved (1987) brings Morrison's men there at last. If *Tar Baby* associates Son's experience with backs, *Beloved* captures the lives of Stamp Paid and the last of the Sweet Home men through impressions of hands and feet. If the lovers in *Tar Baby* occupy totally different time zones, Son preoccupied with his past and Jadine obsessed with her future so that they deny themselves a present together, Paul D and Sethe circle about each other in an equally unsatisfying perpetual present. They have survived enslavement by burying their pasts and ignoring their futures. If *Tar Baby* concludes with limited possibility for African American gender balance, *Beloved* is the book required to lance the poison from the abscess on American history, penetrate the walls of the separate circles, and bring the potential in line. As an innocently callous Miss Amy Denver, her good hands roughly smoothing out Sethe's swollen feet, cheerfully informs the half-dead slavewoman: "Can't nothing heal without pain, you know" (78). Images of battered black bodies are central to this reconstructed slave narrative.[1] Memories of slavery's brutality surface through the characters' senses; re-membering, understanding, and reconciliation arise as individual and collective bodies painfully become sound. Morrison's Pulitzer Prize–winning novel notes that Jadine needs to "rememory" the past of her people and that Son should "lay all that mess down" (36, 86).[2]

While *Beloved* represents a re-vision of the slave narrative, the gothic novel, and the romance—relayed primarily from a black female perspective—it is also the most postmodern of Morrison's first five books. It specifically addresses what occurs when individuals reject a postmodernist world, clinging stubbornly to a single interpretation of time and history: Sethe copes with her past by refusing, ever, to move again, Paul D by declining to stay still. Past and present in *Beloved* clash and converge, divide and merge, so that a future is possible only when conflicting perspectives coexist peacefully. This means that the black male story must be placed neither above nor below but alongside that of the black female. Zora Neale Hurston confirms: "Now, women forget all those things they don't want to remember, and remember everything they don't want to forget. The dream is the truth." She identifies the life of men, however, as less imaginatively personal and more outwardly fixed and rationally theoretical. To explain, she signifies on Frederick Douglass's apostrophe to the ships: "Ships at a distance have every man's wish on board. For some they come in with the tide. For others they sail forever on the horizon, never out of sight, never landing until the Watcher turns his eyes away in resignation, his dreams mocked to death by Time" (*Their Eyes Were Watching God* 1). Claiming to have been unaware of Hurston's work until well into completing her own, Morrison views their similarities as undeniable evidence of a vibrant black tradition and alludes to an observation from Hurston that predicts her successor's process of veil-lifting or truth-telling: " 'Like the dead-seeming cold rocks, I have memories within that came out of the material that went to make me.' These 'memories within' are the subsoil of my work. But memories and recollections won't give me total access to the unwritten interior life of these people. Only the act of the imagination can help me" ("The Site of Memory" 111).

In the eyes of Hurston and Morrison, then, even younger women generally perceive postmodern pluralism as a comfortable position. Men, however, may have to come to it more gradually. This would explain why Paul D and Stamp Paid, the most compelling males in *Beloved*, are, respectively, middle-aged and old. Their age enhances the novel's exploration into how often we "choose to put ourselves someplace else, outside, rather than in here, inside." Morrison believes that men "can hide easier because they can always be men. They can be abstract, in a crunch, and they seem to know what maleness is [but] . . . they don't talk about the vulnerable 'me.'" Only when they "get very much older, then they can stop posturing" (Naylor and Morrison 571). Paul D and Stamp Paid mature enough to stop posturing, get specific, and go inside. They represent the seeds of what may become a full-blown, pluralistic, postmodernist black masculinity.

If readers consider the male figures in the novel as we come across them, we find ourselves compelled to adopt postmodernist pluralism, shifting back and forth in time, following their tracks as the men circle the sorrow of slavery that weighs on the heart of African American history and the undulating truths of their personal fictions. Associating this process primarily with women, contemporary psychologists call it rumination. Black men, however, learned long ago from enslavement how to transform what eats at them inside into blues songs; "blues," in fact, is just another word for black male rumination. Imitating a blues mode of repetition, suggestion, and indirection that derives pleasure from fingering the jagged grain, *Beloved* introduces us on its opening page to our first male figures with the abbreviated troubles of Sethe's sons, Howard and Buglar (3). Then as various inhabitants of 124 Bluestone Road and their neighbors appropriate the riff and voice their ruminations about the ramifications of past and present pain circa 1873, the canvas of male portraits expands.[3] Fading impressions of Howard and Buglar lead Sethe to rememory the young son of a tombstone engraver as well as the character known as schoolteacher's nephews (5–6). Baby Suggs vaguely recollects her husband Suggs and her eight children, half of whom were boys, by six fathers (5). Sethe, transported to Sweet Home by a sight such as Here Boy lapping water, feels ashamed that her memories of its beautiful soughing sycamores remain clearer than the boys hanging from their branches (6).

Walking "anywhere these days . . . they let [him] sit down," Paul D stands up to smile his greetings at Sethe on the porch of 124 and follows her through its door into a pulsing red wave of sadness (6–8). He immediately envisions the Sweet Home men, including Mr. Garner, Sethe's husband Halle, Paul F, Paul A, and, himself, Paul D Garner, his favorite tree Brother, his friend Sixo, and, by association, the nameless white driver who lashed his buggy whip unsuccessfully at Sixo's bare haunches (9–11, 21, 25). Beloved's appearance, the dazed insistence of a "young colored woman . . . drifting from ruin," prevents Paul D from questioning her about her past because he cannot forget that "elsewhere, solitary, hunted and hunting for, were men, men, men" (52). Beloved's intense devotion to and insatiable craving for information from her cause Sethe to recall the reason she is named for her father: he was the only man her mother called by his name, having thrown unnamed onto the island or into the sea all her children fathered by nameless whites (62). Doubts about his virility remind Paul D of the cocky rooster he saved from extinction at Sweet Home and named Mister (72). Sethe connects distorted masculinity with absolute power as Amy Denver matter-of-factly describes the beatings she received from Mr. Buddy (79). Baby Suggs and Stamp Paid spend their last years attempting to authenticate and transcend the abuse of their early days. In so doing, Baby calls on black men to dance in the Clearing (87), and Stamp provides his nephews the possibility of liberation by showing them how to draw a line under their debts and convert defeat into affirmation (90). Denver simply stops hearing when Nelson Lord inquires whether or not her mother murdered her sister (102). Paul D reluctantly recollects the eighty-three days straight that he trembled in a prison camp after he tried to kill Brandywine (106), remembers the resistance and resilience of the chain gang community cared for by Hi Man (107), and recalls the ill Indian outlaws who tended the fugitive buffalo men (111).

Ella cynically considers all of life to be colored by uppity white men who are "the lowest yet" while Baby Suggs sacrifices her great heart to redeem black people from white men, only to have both break it, too, at last (119). On her way to Cincinnati and freedom from low whites, Baby ruminates about Mr. Whitlow, the slaver who sold her to Mr. Garner (142). She then re-creates Whitlow's overseer, whose present to her was the perpetual sight of two of her children, Nancy and Famous, suffocating in the hull of a slave ship before it even left for Savannah. Its captain had stayed put three weeks in a hot Virginia port to ensure a full cargo before setting sail. The overseer makes it his business to inform Baby about the death of her "pickaninnies" more "from a wish to have his way with her than from the kindness of his heart," and she covers her ears to avoid hearing the names of her children come from his mouth (143–44). She readily accepts information about Woodruff, the Bodwins' yard man, after she arrives at their house and encounters Brother Edwin Bodwin (144). Her first independent act spears the writing skills of Reverend Pike in order to fish out the children who went on down the highway (146–47). Baby's trawling expedition turns up plain bad luck.

As it dwells on a past of phenomenally bad luck, usually in the form of white men, 124 Bluestone turns out to be a broken record resounding the upbeat rhythms of the present black community. Two white preachers, a journalist, and a jailer follow in the tracks of the four apocalyptic horsemen (183, 148). Bad luck forces Stamp Paid to endure emasculation by his young master (184), Sawyer to resist anything too sweet (188), and Beloved to cope with the dead man on her face and the frightening men without skin (210). The last of *Beloved*'s initial male sketches depicts the stiff neck and departing back of a stern rider who needs no specific identification as white (231). Like a sensuously pulsating blues tune, the remainder of the book, including the 241 pages surrounding first-takes, fills in the gaps, fleshes out the bones, and straightens up the contours of its players' lives, male alongside female. Morrison's analogy for the creative process becomes an apt one for the structure of her novel: she compares writing to what people call the "flooding" of the Mississippi into areas where it had been rerouted to make room for livable acreage. Convinced that the "act of imagination is bound up with memory," she asserts that the river is not flooding but rather remembering where it used to be. Like the perfect memory of water, writers and the bluesmen of *Beloved* forever try to get home. This emotional memory, the rush of imagination, represents their form of flooding—and determines each male slave's rendition of manhood ("The Site of Memory" 119).

While Morrison's order of appearance for the male figures in her novel is primarily associative and each introduction generally brief, full understanding of them involves tracing the men's memories back to their original source. If imagining and writing and playing the blues require returning again and again to the site of memory, then truth, as Guitar points out to Milkman, can be located in geography. The first places about which a postmodern audience should have knowledge comprise the passage across the Atlantic from West Africa to the West Indies or America that became the route of the slave trade. Re-creating the voyage called the Middle Passage returns us to the wellspring of African American consciousness. It also calls to mind the sixty million or more unidentified captives who died on the ships or in the sea en route. As the ghosts of these unloved reveal, the Middle Passage constitutes a position of no place and a place of no time. It is neither here nor there; it remains, like the grave that it resembled and frequently was, a time out of time. Morrison, however, lovingly fills in the space/time vacuum with the mostly terrible details of imagined truth. She also juxtaposes present with past events.

The eyes, mouths, and hands of men especially haunt a Beloved "always crouching" within the restrictive containment of womb, ship's belly, bed, or grave (210). She relives scenes from either/both a slave ship or a "cemetery as old as sky" and remembers: "The man on my face [who] is dead his face is not mine his mouth smells sweet but his eyes are locked . . . [as well as] the men without skin [who] bring us their morning water to drink" (155, 210). Her soliloquy confuses faces and times as she tries to "say things that are pictures" (210). We hear about signs of her emancipation out of water: after arriving from the amniotic fluid of birth in a boat before being reborn, she walks, this time reborn fully formed, out of a stream nearby 124 Bluestone.[4] Or could it be Beloved who rides the winds above the Atlantic Ocean or growls with a voice "just outside music" on the banks of the Licking River next to the graveyard (60)? We learn about the "agitation of dead Miami no longer content to rest in the mounds that covered them" (155). Or could we be hearing protests by inhumanly crowded black prisoners, forced to eat feces and drink the urine of white guards to stay alive when they can no longer even vomit or contain enough fluid to cry, sweat, or urinate. Then who are those unborn, alive, or dead souls that tremble "trying to leave [their] bodies behind"? Whether she stays on the ship or in the grave, Belóved especially misses the wide shoulders, filed teeth, and soft song of the dead black man on her face after the loud-talking white men pole the pile of black bodies into the sea. His face, neither above nor below but on her face, both obstructs and joins Sethe's and hers: "When he dies on my face I can see hers . . . which is mine." She does not miss but cannot separate herself from the man who is either/both Paul D or one of the lowest yet who sexually abuses her, "hurt[ing] where [she] sleeps," "put[ting] his finger there," calling her "beloved in the dark and bitch in the light" (210–12, 241).

Thus, the vision of men expressed by the visitation of Sethe's daughter takes us to close, dark places of distorted pleasure or degrading pain. Likewise, Sethe's real and imagined mothers associate men with ambiguous feelings, and likewise these emotions spring from "thought pictures" of shamelessly, gorgeously fertile plantations producing corn, rice, indigo, cotton, tobacco, sugarcane—and slaves (36). An apparently beautiful if rebellious spirit, Sethe's mother throws away unnamed all of her children fathered by white men. Keeping only the child born of and named for the black man she "put her arms around" (62), she gives to her daughter the feminine form of the male name that, according to St. Augustine, means resurrection (Scruggs 185).[5] The circle of sorrow branded under the breast of Sethe's mother, which burns along with her body and bit-forced smile, is unbroken by Sethe's mother-in-law, in a manner of speaking. Baby Suggs recollects the men connected with the Whitlow plantation: the master whose bill of sale acknowledges her as his own Jenny Whitlow but who sells her children, the overseer who trades for her sex the story of two of these children dying in a stifling ship prevented from sailing by a captain of capitalism. Then she sees her husband in a "manner of speaking," the "serious, melancholy man who taught her how to make shoes." Having made a pact that whoever could run would run and not look back, he apparently makes good on his chance. Hope that Suggs will find or hear tell of her when she goes compels her to insist on retaining as rightfully hers "Baby Suggs," the name selected as suiting her by the husband who knows how to size up unsteady situations and run in sturdy shoes (142–44).[6]

The son of another plantation master unwittingly causes Stamp Paid to change his name. Young master's selection of Stamp's wife, Vashti, as a temporary concubine frees the slave to re-create himself for all time. Born with the name of Moses's successor and the supervisor of Israel's conquest of Canaan, Joshua means "Jehovah is salvation." Joshua assumes the name Stamp Paid and the right to redeem his own self when he submits to emasculation without killing himself because his wife asks him to stay alive. With this gift he deems himself debt-free. Finding a total lack of obligation, however, to render him not so much "rambunctious" as unsatisfied, he extends his debtlessness to others, rendering them their bill of sale: "You paid it; now life owes you." The receipt he requires for handing his wife over to a white man while choosing life so that she has a place to come home to when "the boy was through" is a "welcome door that he never had to knock on" (184–85). Morrison's retelling of the biblical story of Joshua suggests that deliverance rests not so much in tumbling Jericho's walls of responsibility as in the choice of what to be responsible for.

After sharing space with Morrison's men as they endure the Middle Passage in the bowels of a tall ship and following them to generic sprawling southern plantations where they reenact the atrocities of slavery, her readers begin to focus on the specific as they bump into rememories of the best of the worst: a small but exquisitely beautiful spot in Kentucky called Sweet Home. Her rendition of the Garners' family farm sounds like a distorted remix of Stephen Foster's nostalgically romantic *My Old Kentucky Home* and Morrison's ironic reminder, At what price this beauty? Acknowledging that the Garners are "kindhearted people," Terry Otten adopts Hannah Arendt's term when he refers to them as "nice Nazis." By their "accommodation of slavery, they made possible the prototypal evil of schoolteacher" (86).

The man running Sweet Home determines Sweet Home masculinity. The before-and-after portraits of Halle, the Pauls, and Sixo mean "before schoolteacher" and "after Garner"; a change in white male ownership effects a corresponding alteration in black male self-definition. The boyishly godlike Garner acts like "the world was a toy he was supposed to have fun with" and enjoys circulating the myth that he creates men (139). Because he tells his slaves to act like men, they can control their appetites when Sethe comes to Sweet Home and they run "smack into their nature" (140). Young and so sick with desire they had "taken to calves," they let the iron-eyed girl take her time in choosing "in spite of the fact that each one would have beaten the others to mush to have her." Combining the brutal facts of male biology with the irony that thirteen-year-old Sethe has no choice but to choose, Morrison expresses the magnitude of the boys' restraint as a "year of yearning, when rape seemed the solitary gift of life" (10).

While Garner brags, and other farmers frown, on his claim to raising "nigger men," his experiment in buying and rearing boys actually measures his own stunted manhood and becomes not much less pernicious to the boys' selfhood than schoolteacher's questions. Smiling broadly at his disapproving neighbors, "if you a man yourself, you'll want your niggers to be men too," he looks forward to their reaction: "I wouldn't have no nigger men round my wife." His prepared retort, "Neither would I," enables him after a stunned silence to pick a fight. The encounter also proves to the pummeled but pleased Garner his masculinity once more. A "real Kentuckian" to his mind is one "tough enough and smart enough to make and call his own niggers men" (10–11). So called, they become men but only in Garner's wide brown eyes and on his pristine property. Ordered not to stray from Sweet Home except in his company, "men-bred slaves" must suffer the hard fall from innocence when they do leave the garden and the tough lesson that their maleness is not given over but garnered (141).

This slave master's masculine model includes a genially charming if thick-skinned fraternal order, which initiates its members by laughing, teasing, and fostering fights on the playground. The appeal of its exuberance and competitive energy, however, turns out to be illusory, limited, and temporary, and Garner himself just an overgrown, self-centered though likable baby. His standing joke is not only racist but sexist; he is blind to age and physical disability. So sound in body and self-esteem that he jumps out of his wagon carrying Baby Suggs to freedom and strides halfway up the Bodwins' sidewalk before the ignored, crippled old woman can set her feet on the ground, Garner dwells secure in his enthusiastic, isolationist innocence. Responding to the Bodwins' criticism that they do not "hold with slavery, even Garner's kind," he asks "Jenny": "Did I let Halle buy you or not?" The woman at least twenty years his senior defers, "Yes, sir, you did" but reminds herself, "you got my boy and I'm all broke down. You be renting him out to pay for me way after I'm gone to Glory" (146).

Treating only his male slaves like respected paid labor, encouraging them to correct or defy him, to invent solutions and attack problems without permission, and refusing to "stud them out," Garner still plays with people's lives, oblivious to the danger in which he places them all. And he pays for his arrogant naïveté with his life, the lives of his wife and slaves, and the dissolution of his dream. While Lillian Garner explains her husband's death as a stroke that brings on an exploded eardrum, Sixo insists that the hole in Mr. Garner's ear results from gunpowder and disgruntled neighbors. Whatever the cause, he finally has to hear with a vengeance the messages about free will and dangerous freedom.[7] His absence means that a crying Mrs. Garner, rendered speechless by the cancer of benign slavery at her throat, must sell the oldest Paul (F) to pay off their debts and that the arrival of schoolteacher will break those Sweet Home men left home alone.

If Garner is a laughing lord and a nice Nazi, schoolteacher, as his name suggests and like literature's nastiest villains, is intelligent, rational, detached, and even more convinced than Mr. Garner that he is right. Always accompanied by his notebook and particularly fond of the ink that Sethe mixes, schoolteacher feels called to prove the logic of slavery through the scientific study of slave behavior. The irony that "the Age of Enlightenment was at the same time as the age of racism" intrigues Morrison (Carabi 89). Presenting their ideas via anthropology, biology, theology, and the Darwinian theory of evolution, researchers pursued racism with rigorous methodology; in 1850 schoolteacher would have been a mainstream scholar.[8] Although Morrison offers few details about the "short," "little" man with a big hat and spectacles, who insists on wearing a formal collar in the fields, schoolteacher's presence, even with its lowercase *s*, pervades *Beloved*. He arrives with two nephews and a "coach box full of papers" to take over Sweet Home because, as Halle observes, "people said she [Mrs. Garner] shouldn't be alone out there with nothing but Negroes" (197). Mrs. Garner is also foolishly flattered that her "husband's sister's husband had book learning and was willing to come farm Sweet Home after Mr. Garner passed" (36). Her racist fears and class snobbery deplete her power. Despite the loss of Paul F, the Sweet Home men remain willing and able to care for Sweet Home, and Sethe is dedicated in her duties to her ailing mistress. Like her servants, Lillian Garner becomes diminished by schoolteacher's science, deprived literally and figuratively of her voice. Unlike the others, however, she chooses to renege on her responsibilities.

Schoolteacher is as fanatic about being socially correct as being scientifically right. Sethe tells Denver that all three of the guests had "pretty manners." Gentle in "a lot of ways," they speak softly and spit genteelly into handkerchiefs. Familiar from Frederick Douglass's 1845 slave narrative as the church deacons who rank among the cruelest slavers, they embody "the kind who know Jesus by His first name, but out of politeness never use it even to His face" (37). The rest of what we learn about schoolteacher and company occurs literally in bits and pieces as Paul D and Sethe circle around the subject. These "gentle" colonialists rape Sethe repeatedly: one nephew with mossy teeth sucks the milk from her breasts behind the barn while the other holds her down and voyeuristic, book-reading schoolteacher watches and takes notes.[9] Then when she informs a helpless Mrs. Garner, tired-out from barely talking, he directs his nephews to dig a hole in which to carefully place Sethe's pregnant belly so as to protect his unborn property and to open up her back with cowhide. Not as "strong as Mr. Garner," schoolteacher is also not even perversely virile enough to participate in the physical abuse, leaving that play to his nephews. Like Soaphead Church, schoolteacher's lewd pleasures come primarily from peeping, pinching, and posing apparently innocuous questions.

It becomes these questions more than the beatings or the bit that tear into pieces for all time not only Sixo but Sethe. The Sweet Home slaves discover that schoolteacher's journal contains his painstaking notes for an account weighing their animal features more heavily than their human traits and that he indoctrinates his nephews with a similar theory about African American humanity: "No, no. That's not the way. I told you to put [Sethe's] human characteristics on the left; her animal ones on the right. And don't forget to line them up" (193). Her scalp prickling as it does when she spots schoolteacher's oversized hat and flies to kill her children, Sethe stumbles blindly backward and goes to Mrs. Garner for an explanation of *characteristic*. Told that it defines a "thing that's natural to a thing," the word instructs her that she is little more than a beast of burden. When schoolteacher measures Sethe's behind, she cannot sleep. Jolted by the realization that his Lilliputian method leaves no room for possibility but determines all blacks as breeders and that her children will be sold like cattle, she learns to line up schoolteacher against the Garners, noting to Halle that the latter are not like the whites she knew in "the big place . . . before [she] came here." When he asks her, "How these different?" she replies that they "talk soft." This leads to one of the final lessons she learns from her husband: "It don't matter, Sethe. What they say is the same. Loud or soft" (195). Using intuitive Halle as spokesman, Morrison resolves with flawless syllogistic reasoning that racism on the smallest of scales is every bit as brutal as slavery. She also concludes that the slaveowners, not the slaves, are the narrow-minded brutes.

Twenty-year-old Halle already understands that a black man whose manhood can be modified by the white men who own him is not much of a man. While he remembers little but Garner's brand of slave life, he nonetheless knows it to be fatally reductive: "If all my labor is Sweet Home, including the extra, what I got left to sell?" (196). Having been allowed to labor off Sweet Home, he perceives alternatives to slavery. Of the two hard things that Baby Suggs has to do in her life, "standing on her feet till she dropped or leaving her last and probably only living child," she chooses "the hard thing that made him happy." She asks herself why, however: What does "a sixty-odd-year-old slavewoman who walks like a three-legged dog need freedom for?" The beloved son forty years her junior senses what the exhausted, knocked-down, knocked-up, broken-down, mind-numbed, self-less old woman cannot feel until she "step[s] foot on free ground." Having never drawn "one free breath," he imagines rightly "there was nothing like it in this world" (141).

Despite his imagination, however, Halle does not survive. Because he fails to learn, like Paul D, when to love small, even Sweet Home's slavery crushes him. Overly hardened by the savage training of the lowest yet, Ella tells Sethe: "Don't love nothing" (92). Called a man by "one who would know," named by his mother for a special man, Halle Suggs, on the other hand, becomes too gentled by being chosen (125). The youngest of Baby Suggs's eight children, he is the only one permitted to live with her. He is also allowed to honeymoon with Sethe in the cornfield and to interact with her and his three children enough, even in the dark, to bond with them. So "in love with his mother" that he buys her freedom with five years of Sundays just to "see her sit down," he possesses the kind of masculinity that Sethe, and Paul D, sees as "a serious recommendation" (11).

In essence, Halle has been lovingly instructed to show empathy and to do something hard for others. His gift of sympathy employed within a slave system, however, destroys him. Tempered by the "nastiness of life," Baby Suggs's measure of manhood takes into account that her children can be played as pawns in somebody else's chess game. So for her: "A man ain't nothing but a man. . . . But a son? Well now, that's *somebody*" (23). Both the woman who gets to keep him for twenty years and the girl who stops stuttering when she first meets him idealize the strong but shy Halle, Sethe so much that she wants to sanctify their union with ceremony. Hiding behind honeysuckle, she is fascinated by how different the usually subdued men act in her absence, how they "laughed and played and urinated and sang" (23). Confident that she can make Sweet Home hers by bringing wildflowers into the white woman's kitchen, she desires similarly to cultivate Halle by having a formal wedding. Her proposal of slave marriage makes Mrs. Garner smile. Nevertheless, entering the spirit of the occasion as though it were a pet's affair, the mistress dresses up her faithful servant with crystal earrings while Sethe and Halle mark it with respectively meaningful if plainer signals. Here Morrison juxtaposes a male perspective on desire alongside a female one. Fluidly turning her dream into the truth, as Hurston says women do, Sethe pulls together a makeshift "bedding dress" out of disparate pieces of cloth that have to be taken apart and put back afterward; Halle, holding his wish at a distance, hangs his hitching rope on the wall of her cabin. He judges the husk-filled mattress on its dirt floor, however, as more comfortable but less tender than the tiny cornfield he takes Sethe to for privacy. Reared by a woman to be a milkman, Halle becomes so impressed with the mightiness of the leap between a calf and a girl that he fails to fortify himself against their similarities.[10]

Morrison confirms this fusion of human and animal, which, white supremacists' opinions to the contrary, remains a fact common to human nature, with Paul D and Sethe's memories of waving tassels of corn. Mr. Garner maintains a small field of corn because the crop benefits both animals and people. Morrison confesses that a "picture of corn and the nimbus of emotion surrounding it became a powerful one" in *Beloved* ("The Site of Memory" 118). She recalls associating the planting, harvesting, and eating of corn during her childhood with mystery, liberation, sexual excitement, pleasure, and community. She envisions her parents holding hands as they walk into the garden forbidden to her and her sister, the freedom the girls enjoy in the absence of authority, the daytime naps her parents take after which they appear very rested, the sweet, butter-dripping corn eaten as finger food and shared with family and neighbors.

The connotations with which she surrounds corn suggest the human need to satisfy both physical and spiritual, sensation and imagination. Because "Nothing could be as good as the sex with [Sethe that] Paul D had been imagining on and off for twenty-five years" and "[Sethe's] deprivation had been not having any dreams of her own at all," their coupling disappoints him as well as her (20, 25). Paul must resolve his illusions about the iron-eyed girl with the barefoot woman she has become, and Sethe has to trust that a man is more than a man. While fastidious schoolteacher tries to separate the animal out of the human, Morrison's lovers integrate both properties. Her example of how she transforms a picture of corn into a scene in a novel, how image invokes memory that inspires imagined truth, not only re-creates the process of writing a book; it offers an explanation of how Paul D and Sethe finally incorporate spiritual into physical, possible into actual, past into present so that they have a future together. This poststructuralist blues process also makes possible their fluid gender balance.

Morrison conveys with achingly good humor the postmodern isolation of their memories and imaginative processes despite the lovers' physical union. In their individual worlds again after the long-delayed but soon-over lovemaking, Paul D no longer remains so enamored of Sethe's breasts. Sethe is insulted that Paul D still wears his shirt: " 'Dog,' she thought" (22). However, not wanting each other, as Paul observes, actually feels good. Free of desire, both can recollect in tranquility the picture of Halle's sublimely ridiculous cornfield, his romantic touch of privacy that turns into public display. For Paul D, it had been "hard, hard, hard sitting there erect as dogs" watching "corn stalks dance at noon" in the field below. For Sethe, staring at the retracted back of her present lover melts into a memory of clutching "husk and cornsilk hair" on the uncovered back of her past one. For Paul, only the "feast of new corn [the men] allowed themselves that night" could appease his "jealous admiration": "parting the hair to get to the tip, the edge of his fingernail just under, so as not to graze a single kernel." For Sethe, the "ripping sound," which accompanies the "pulling down of the tight sheath," always "convinced her it hurt." For Paul, the "ear yielded up to him its shy rows, exposed at last." For Sethe, how "jailed down the juice." For Paul, how "quick the jailed-up flavor ran free." For both, at last, how "loose the silk. How fine and loose and free" (27). Separated from each other by conditioned, gendered response, the two nonetheless come together through the common bond of slavery to embrace the concept of individual freedom.

Associated in Sweet Home memory with lavishly buttered, too-tender corn, Halle becomes lost not just as a man but as manufactured desire—

for a somebody son, a caring husband, a loyal brother, a loving father.[11] Those who survive 124 Bluestone must relinquish their illusions as well as their nightmares, translating them into rememories that weather well enough to make a life together and apart. This is especially true for Denver. To the lonely daughter who never sees him, Halle exists as a fiercely cherished absence. Desiring to possess somebody to belong to, she claims this absent father and waits in secret eighteen years for him to return to help her "watch out for Ma'am and anything come in the yard." She resents that she has been forced all her life to give over his absence to others: first to her grandmother as the "son, deeply mourned because he was the one who brought her out of there. Then it was her mother's absent husband. Now it was this hazelnut stranger's absent friend" (13). Even the image that allows Denver access to memories of her father and signals his nature, a soft-fried egg, must come through the grandmother who tells her "all [her] daddy's things" (207–9).[12]

Denver hears that Baby Suggs stays "a little scared" of Halle because he is "too good for the world," loving "animals and tools and crops and the alphabet." She learns that her father could "count on paper" and "look at you and tell where you hurt and he could fix it too." The "angel man" of Denver's dreams, Halle is too sensitive, too sweet, too domesticated, simply not wild enough to "make it through nothing." His credo concludes: "If you can't count they can cheat you. If you can't read they can beat you" (208). Despite, even because of, his refinement and his fine semiotic education, the sight of schoolteacher's nephews sucking his wife's breasts breaks him. Paul D recalls seeing Sweet Home's sweetest man squatting by the churn smearing butter and clabber over his face because "the milk they took is on his mind" and he is driven like Lady Macbeth to reenact the picture (70). Paul last glimpses his friend "greased and flat-eyed as a fish" (224). Halle resembles Sethe in that he dares to love large and, when threatened, to take his best thing out of harm's way—in his case, his mind's eye. It is, however, the woman who refuses to look away who "lasted" (201). Halle's soft form of feminine masculinity, possible and desirable in Garner's paradise, is not tough enough to survive the abuses of schoolteacher's slavery.[13]

If Halle becomes too tame to last, Sixo is not civilized enough. The man with a number for a name, Sixo stays constantly at sixes and sevens, but his word is his bond.[14] If Halle comes to be associated with sweet, buttered corn and a soft-fried egg, Sixo turns into one hot potato: "Indigo with a flame-red tongue," he experiments with night-cooked sweet and white varieties. While he adroitly digs his own hole in which to roast them at all hours, he can never get his temperature successfully adjusted so that the results are "undercooked, overcooked, dried-out or raw." He never gets it quite right because he has no one to show him how and so finds himself continually out of synch; he is either at the wrong place at the right time or the right place at the wrong time.[15] Paul D's memory of Sixo's hypermasculinity can be captured by the story of a trip that he plots down to the second to visit a woman thirty miles away. Leaving on a Saturday when he judges the moon to be in the right place for love, he arrives at her cabin shortly before church on Sunday and has exactly sixty minutes to sit down and say good morning before he must start out on the seventeen-hour walk back to Sweet Home. The shiny blue tinge of his black skin and his hot red tongue indicate not only his African origin and his suitability for African American legend and song. These are also the colors Morrison connects with freedom and danger.

Associated like Guitar and Son with nature, Sixo operates according to natural rather than manmade time and as a wild thing exhibits a propensity to "creep" at night, acquiring a useful knowledge of direction and the local terrain. During one of his evening crawls, he discovers a stone structure abandoned by Indians. He requests its permission to enter and, absorbing its sacred aura, deems it suitable for a tryst with Patsy, the Thirty-Mile Woman. Receiving the blessing of its Presence and persuading fourteen-year-old Patsy to meet him there, Sixo gives her painstaking directions about timing and location but, again, fails to take into account the human factor: he arrives on time, but she does not. Frightened for her, he asks the wind for help and hears her forlorn whimper. Shouting, "Breathe, I can find you," he does and, once more out of time, they drop where they stand (24). His preference in romantic rendezvous a primitive place of ancient stones instead of Halle's cultivated field of young corn, Sixo relies on inartificial remedies for human problems and exhibits an affinity with American Indian ritual, including its reverence for snakes.

Morrison's emphasis on Sixo's agile tongue and the alliteration of *s* sounds in his name suggest the hissing of a snake. While his relationship with Patsy prevents his desire to copulate with calves, he punctures her calf to simulate snakebite so that she will have an excuse for being late to pick worms off tobacco leaves. Locating the road home at daylight, his clothes in his hands, he confronts one of two male characters in *Beloved* that Morrison identifies without racial signifiers as white: the driver of an oncoming wagon, "wide-eyed, raised a whip while the woman seated beside him covered her face." The uncoiling of the whip matches the ease with which Sixo fades into the woods to avoid its bite on his blue-black behind. Although he laughs only once, Sixo evolves into a marvelously humorous storyteller by combining his quick tongue with a sardonic wit.

In his distinctive African American manner of relating darkly comic tales with a straight face, he fashions narratives that make his listeners want to laugh and cry at the same time. He shares recitals such as his buck-naked story openly with the other Sweet Home men; he will not make public his practice of going alone among trees at night for "dancing . . . to keep his bloodlines open." He remains private about what he takes seriously, allowing not even close friends to observe. They, however, are able to imagine and eager to laugh at the "picture they pictured . . . in daylight, that is, when it was safe" (25). Fascinating yet dangerous, attractive yet revolting, fluid yet fast, Sixo becomes the paradoxical narrow fellow in the grass of Garner's garden. Both in nature and in myth he is never met "Attended, or alone / Without a tighter breathing / And Zero at the Bone" (Dickinson 170–71).

His stories about the treatment of blacksnakes in places other than Sweet Home unveil as dark as his skin. Before schoolteacher, however, Sixo is gloomy but gentle. Schoolteacher's restraining orders and lessons in fear turn him absolutely savage. Morrison creates her black male to represent what Stamp Paid calls "the secret spread of this new kind of whitefolks' jungle." Stamp observes: "Whitepeople believed that whatever the manners, under every dark skin was a jungle. Swift unnavigable waters, swinging screaming baboons, sleeping snakes, red gums ready for their sweet white blood." Noting the perniciousness of such a self-fulfilling prophesy, that the more "coloredpeople spent their strength trying to convince [whites] how gentle they were, how clever and loving, how human, the more they used themselves up to persuade whites of something Negroes believed could not be questioned, the deeper and more tangled the jungle grew inside." African Americans, however, do not import this wilderness; it sprouts from "the jungle whitefolks planted in [blackfolks]." Growing "In, through and after life . . . it invaded the whites who had made it. Touched them every one. Changed and altered them. Made them bloody, silly, worse than even they wanted to be, so scared were they of the jungle they had made. The screaming baboon lived under their own white skin; the red gums were their own" (198–99). Stamp stumbles upon a symptom of the silent, hidden disease that infects Sixo when the old man removes a red ribbon hanging from the bottom of his boat: "knotted around a curl of wet wooly hair, clinging still to its bit of scalp," this scrap of little girl lost turns him dizzy and takes his breath away until he can finally recapture enough air to gasp to the road and the river: "What are these people? You tell me, Jesus. What *are* they?" (180).

Although Sixo is the only Sweet Home man already jaded enough not to be sorry to see Garner go, he lives to regret his attitude. His instincts about danger become overly acute. He suspects that Garner was done in by his neighbors. He believes that Mrs. Garner's doctor poisons her. But schoolteacher's slavery shocks even Sixo. Until schoolteacher, Sixo tells atrocious tales primarily to instruct and to delight; after schoolteacher, he speaks only to survive. He comes to understand before the others do that without Garner's presence, there can be no manhood for Sweet Home men. Schoolteacher confiscates their guns, their strength, their ideas. He calls their suggestions backtalk. He experiments with various forms of rehabilitation, which he records in his notebook. He complains that the slaves "ate too much, rested too much, talked too much, which was certainly true compared to him, because schoolteacher ate little, spoke less and rested not at all," and he succeeds at breaking "into children what Garner had raised into men" (220).

One of schoolteacher's most successful experiments shows Sweet Home men the significance of stealing. Accustomed to taking what they need without asking, the slaves are inhumanely deprived when schoolteacher arrives. He considers everything they touch, even "two yard eggs the hen herself didn't even remember," to be stealing. The loss of their shotguns means they lack game, and a steady diet of vegetables, beans, bread, and hominy will not sustain a life of hard labor. Sixo resorts to his forked tongue to rationalize to rational but prejudiced schoolteacher why Sixo slaughters a shoat. Because schoolteacher's questions reek of simply "going through the motions," Sixo merely sits with the streak-of-lean in his hand, "not even getting up to plead." Denying he stole the pig but keeping his eyes trained on his plate, he admits to killing, butchering, cooking, and eating the pig. He explains his actions as " 'Improving your property, sir': 'Sixo plant rye to give the high piece a better chance. Sixo take and feed the soil, give you more crop. Sixo take and feed Sixo give you more work.' " The narrator comments wryly on this virtuoso performance: "Clever, but schoolteacher beat him anyway to show him that definitions belonged to the definers—not the defined."[16] Taught that stealing represents not only survival but a sign of African American manhood, the men "began to pilfer in earnest, and it became not only their right but their obligation" (190–91).

The mutual distrust and disrespect initiated by schoolteacher escalate to the point that he puts locks on every available storage door and Sixo keeps a nail in his mouth to undo the rope that binds him at night. Schoolteacher's most successful instrument for schooling his slaves to run, however, becomes not deliberate physical abuse but unintended psychological trauma, the so-called objective data about their animal characteristics that he records in his notebook. At this point Sixo assumes the role of wildcard in schoolteacher's stacked deck. His mind no longer on Sweet Home, the slave's eyes are on the horizon. While he has always declined to laugh and consistently rejects Halle's offer to teach him to read, write, and cipher because it "would change his mind," he now refuses to speak English. Informing his friend that the alphabet and counting on paper would "make him forget things he shouldn't and memorize things he shouldn't and he didn't want his mind messed up," Sixo avoids like the plague the language of the men who try to rewrite his character (208).

Just as the Seven Days' Sunday man loses his cool with Milkman, accusing him of not being serious enough, hot-tongued Sixo speaks English once again to urge his friends to join him in a dangerous bid for freedom. Because he has been stealing away for years to see the Thirty-Mile Woman and Halle has lifted bales off the farm to let Baby Suggs sit down, these two know what lies outside Sweet Home and which way to travel. They arrange to transmit information through sound and song. Patsy tells Sixo that a train is leaving to go up yonder. A woman will signal to get on board by a rattle in the cornfield. Halle hears the rattle "that is not bird or snake" and sings to the others: "Hush, hush. Somebody's calling my name. Hush, hush. Somebody's calling my name. O my Lord, O my Lord, what shall I do" (224). The slaves swing into (s)low motion a sweet but constantly shifting plan calculated to carry them home but totally vulnerable to white whim. Once more, Sixo's timing proves off, and the most fascinating parts of his story include its missteps.

Again like Guitar, Sixo's love for his people, distorted by racism, drives his destruction. "Hell-bent to make [a family] with the Thirty-Mile Woman," his connection with children can be discerned in his attention to Sethe's. Sethe begins her confession of the "perfect death of her crawling-already? baby" by crediting Sixo for being the biggest help with her children of anyone at Sweet Home (219, 99). Confiding in Paul D the difficulties of bringing up babies by yourself with no woman to "help you get through," she describes Halle as "good" but exhausted from working off debt. It is Sixo who "heard [Howard] screaming and come running" when Red Cora mashes his hand in the cow barn (160–61). It is Sixo who resets the little boy's dislocated thumb. Although he stands stoically firm in his refusal to help Paul D decide what to do when they wait for the others in the creekbed, Sixo remains sensitive to the whereabouts of Sethe's children and perceptive that the mother would inevitably be close to the quarters because her young ones still sleep there. Sixo is not calloused to a brother's confusion; he merely conserves his energy to protect his progeny. Likewise, as Paul D hides with her in the dry creek, the

Thirty-Mile Woman seems "dulled to smoke," the unfocused "nothing" of a "shape in the dark breathing lightly." With Sixo's arrival, however, Patsy lights up like star glow. Morrison highlights the intensity of their relationship, the wattage of which beams as powerful as Sethe's love for her children: the "shining [for him alone] that comes from inside her" reflects his ability to locate her solely by her breathing (65, 225).

It becomes appropriate, then, that naturally passionate Sixo dies with his feet held to the fire. While he can hear from far away something as normal as the breathing of his mate, the strange spectacle of schoolteacher and company bearing down just above the ditch catches him unawares. He pushes Patsy to run on down the creekbed. He and Paul D divert her captors by sprinting in the opposite direction. Surrounded and bound, Sixo grabs the mouth of a rifle pointed at his head, fails with hands tied to position it to his advantage, and starts to sing. Judging him unsuitable by the tone of his voice, the men knock him unconscious, stake him to a tree, and attempt to burn him alive. Morrison's story unfolds as darkly humorous as one of Sixo's own: schoolteacher's men struggle with stubbornly puny flames in grass slick with dew. Sixo begins to laugh for the first time, and while the grass hisses as his feet smolder and his trousers smoke, he calls out gaily "Seven-O! Seven-O!" Although neither the white men nor Paul D understands completely the meaning of his words, everybody recognizes the sound—"hatred so loose it was juba"—and the men "shoot him to shut him up. Have to." Sixo's song and his laughter trumpet his grim triumph far louder than his language. While the whites fool themselves into believing they got his number, the black man throws a seven.[17] They think to burn him a good one, but he craps out to save his "blossoming seed," emitting a laugh so "rippling and full of glee it put out the fire" (226–29).

If Sixo perceives that the best defense is a good offense, turning even an offensive name to his advantage, the three Pauls, like *Sula*'s deweys, seek safety but find merely anonymity in number. Signifying a man by a number instead of a name effectively emasculates him; to call three half-brothers by the same name with their sole identifying characteristic a letter attached almost as an afterthought becomes unmistakably dehumanizing. As offspring of slavery, Paul F, Paul A, and Paul D Garner are children of the same mother, whom they do not remember, and by different fathers, whom they have never met. The alphabetical arrangement of the letters following their names does not even indicate their birth order. Morrison carves their primary distinctions from the different manifestations of pain they suffer. After Garner dies, Mrs. Garner sells Paul F to pay off Sweet Home's debts. Paul D's last memory of his oldest brother is a picture of him sitting in the bed of a wagon, chicken in his pocket, tears in his eyes as he waves good-bye to his family and home of over twenty years. His new owner takes him to live in what the others have only heard called "the trace." They have not seen a trace of him since. Until he places Sethe's stories alongside his, Paul D knows simply that his second brother goes missing during the day of the disrupted escape plan. His last memory of Paul A pictures him moving cut timber after dinner. He never shows up at the quarters for supper, nor does he appear that night in the designated creekbed. Sethe complicates the image as she recollects Paul A beaten, not long or hard but for the first time, by a schoolteacher who talks soft but watches hard. She also rememories a boy "with Paul A's shirt on but not his feet or his head," hanging from a pretty tree that escaped being hacked (198).

Unlike the clearly marked Halle and Sixo, who stand separately with their women ready to die for family freedom, the two Pauls remaining at Sweet Home huddle alone together, struggling to make the slightest of decisions about how to hack anything. Saying they "need time to think about it," they engage in a full evening's discussion to decide whether or not they should join Sixo and Halle in the plan. They wonder "where they will end up; how they will live. What work; who will take them in; should they try to get to Paul F?" After the fact, Paul D realizes that the brothers hesitate because they have been "isolated in a wonderful lie . . . [p]rotected and convinced they were special." They are so afraid of not being that they will put up "with anything and everything" just to stay alive in a beautiful place where they have no right to be (221–22).

Even a tree and a chicken take on with their names more character at Sweet Home than do the amorphous Pauls. Pondering postcoitus the "revolting clump of scars" on Sethe's back that Amy Denver perceives as a lovely chokecherry tree, Paul D remembers the beautiful tree he selects to sit under while he eats his midday meal, sometimes alone but mostly with Sixo. Although Sweet Home has "more pretty trees than any farm around," Paul D singles out one to shelter him that is "old, wide and beckoning" and calls it Brother (21, 221). He also names a rooster. The youngest Paul pays close enough attention to apprehend life inside what appears to be an empty egg left after the hen walks off with her newly hatched chicks. Tapping it open, he enables a helpless, crippled "peep" to escape its shell. Despite the fact that the "son a bitch" would have died without his aid, he dubs the tiny rooster Mister. As he watches Mister "grow up and whup everything in the yard," he begins to realize the prophetic power of language and to wonder whether Garner, in announcing his slaves as men, was "naming what he saw or creating what he did not" (220). Described as "hateful," "bloody," and "evil," Mister rules the roost "bad feet and all" (72).

If schoolteacher looks for the lowest common denominator in a human being, Paul D seeks out the nobility in a chicken. He affirms his prodigy's potential maleness with its name and locates its potency in its huge, bright-red comb. Taller "than tall men" but collared at the "peak of his strength," Paul compares his masculinity to Mister's. He muses that, even with bad feet but without the bit in its mouth, the bird "looked so . . . free. Better than me. Stronger, tougher" because he "was allowed to be and stay what he was" (220, 72). Schoolteacher's iron weighing down Paul D's tongue does not drive him wild-eyed; he panics only when "walking past the roosters looking at them look at me." Until he sees Mister, he focuses on the humiliation of Sixo, Halle, and the other Pauls. When he spots the unencumbered and tub-enthroned rooster "smiling" at his forced smile, the last of the Sweet Home men understands that it is "not just them, [but] me too" (71–72). Twenty-year-old Paul's lack of identity and self-control, apparent in his need to name things and his fascination with family trees, results from the slave system's abuse of language, its desecration of black manhood, and its degrading gaze.

Until their separation, the attitude of the owner of Sweet Home determines the Pauls' selfhood. Garner calls them men, so they become men—but only according to his frontier codification of their masculinity. Schoolteacher believes that he alone knows their worth, and he tells them apart by how much they cost. Paul D thinks he has always realized his value as a laborer, but listening to white men talk after they burn Sixo allows Paul to discover his worth. That is to say, "he learns his price," the "dollar value of his weight, his strength, his heart, his brain, his penis, and his future": nine hundred dollars, if schoolteacher can get it (226). Until he gets his own pain, however, Paul D remains simply one of the Pauls, and "never for a minute did he believe he could escape. Until it rained" (221). The last images Morrison leaves of Sweet Home are Sethe's vision of headless, feetless, and nameless black boys hanging from soughing sycamores and the sound of Paul D saying, "It wasn't sweet and it sure wasn't home" (14). Garner's socialist fantasy simply does not work when the workers are slaves; being broken into children makes the men "run off" (220).

If Halle and Sixo constitute the black males who dominate but do not survive Sweet Home, Paul D survives its abuses to dominate Morrison's impressions of men during her slave narrative's middle passage. After his displacement and subsequent escape to no-place, Paul joins Sethe, Denver, and the rememory of Baby Suggs at 124 Bluestone. The four encounter several minor but no less distinctive male figures, however, during their disparate journeys to freedom. Behind the disapproving, morning-after odor of Baby Suggs's excess in celebrating not her freedom but the sight of her grandchildren freed hangs the smell of a "dark and coming thing." The only identification Baby can locate for this other offensive odor is its association with "high-topped shoes she didn't like the look of" (138). An image of shoes, then, ironic since most slaves went shoeless, leads Baby to ruminate about her recollections of Brother Bodwin, Mr. Woodruff, and Reverend Pike.

The story of Baby Suggs's escape reveals a variation on the typical slave narrative. Slave life having worn out her hands, legs, hip, eyes, head, kidneys, womb, and tongue, everything but the heart that "started beating the minute she crossed the Ohio River," she makes her free life on the back of her son's labor by offering up her great heart (147). Unlike the plight/flight of fugitive slaves, Halle gives his mother her bill of sale, Garner escorts her onto free soil, and Edward Bodwin and his sister provide her with a legal safe house. Quakers and abolitionists, the latter spend their prime years participating in rescue and sedition and rent out the family homestead to Negroes since the siblings moved to town as children with their father and grandfather. Morrison appreciates the charity of public servants like Brother Bodwin, but she also chuckles at the naïve hypocrisy and romantic self-righteousness that frequently accompany the evangelistic missionary spirit.

Although he has been on Bluestone Road only once since he left at age three, Bodwin will forego rent to maintain 124 since it represents what was precious and sweet about his childhood. There he learned to bury his privacy from an overbearing but deeply religious father who taught him to respect the holiness of all human life. Now in his seventies, the lifelong bachelor also remembers 124 as the house where women died—his mother, grandmother, aunt, and older sister. Thus, Bodwin's primary motivations for giving over his life to abolitionist activities (debates, meetings, petitions, recruitment, letters, quarrels) involve as much the distracting stimulation and headiness of the public contest and an excuse to avoid sexual entanglements with women as philanthropy. Indulging himself in theatrical contrasts, such as the one between his shock of white hair above a young face and his big black mustache set off by a clean-shaven chin, he thrives on the constant visibility and publicity that accompany his engagement in local political antagonisms. While Brother Bodwin's heart might be in the right place, it beats for the wrong reasons: he just loves to fight. It is Baby Suggs, not Bodwin, who serves the public straight from the heart.

Morrison uses the black and white of Bodwin's coloring to link his abolitionist sympathies with his vanity and showmanship while suggesting that human beings cannot be classified, racially or morally, as merely black or white. Since his head is white, and the hair surrounding his mouth is black, she also implies that he speaks out for the human rights of slaves in order to whitewash his own public image. Morrison reinforces her irony with a return to Baby Suggs's memory of shoes. Brother Bodwin's appearance, earning him the title of "bleached nigger," coupled with competition from black boatmen, enrages some white Mississippi rivermen enough that they "shoe-blackened his face and his hair" (260). Despite his rather unexpected affinity for boot polish, however, Baby's new patron, along with his snowy-haired sister who raises her bushy black eyebrows in surprise, expresses doubt that Baby could be an accomplished cobbler. No longer in blackface, Bodwin says uncertainly: "Well . . . that'll be something, but you'll need more" (147). He reveals the ambiguity of his patronage as hospitality turns patronizing. Calling the woman twenty years their senior by a wrong first name, the siblings make sure "Jenny" has eaten (in the kitchen), inquire about her skills (too old for the slaughterhouse, she might take in wash), offhandedly tick off the numerous tasks she will be expected to complete for them (though they will acquire free upkeep of their property from her), and grant permission for her presence in their abandoned home (as long as she is clean).

A young man named Woodruff makes an apt escort for Baby over to the blues tone of 124. Although Morrison does not specifically single him out by race, he is undoubtedly black and on the lam. Young Janey, the Bodwins' Negro housekeeper, refers to him as Mr. Woodruff, who comes in several days a week to do the outside chores. Omitting his title, the Bodwins tell Jenny that "Woodruff" will "carry her out there." The man himself says very little. His appearance, however, shows a burn on his jaw, a brand that his heavy beard will not hide. Calling Baby "ma'am," he declares himself from Virginia and recently relocated to Ohio. She merely responds, "I see" (144–46). He speaks in black vernacular, he does not talk down to his charge, and he understands the intricacies of the local church. Skilled like *Tar Baby*'s Yardman, endowed with a similar name, Woodruff undeniably represents one of Morrison's outdoor black men, albeit, as a fugitive slave, a wanderer without shoes.

When Baby confesses she has not been inside a church for ten years, Woodruff tells her that Reverend Pike will reacquaint her. Morrison's brief reference to the reverend during this crucial part of Baby's narrative reveals the importance of the church to the black community not only as a source of song and solace but as a means of networking with missing or widely scattered family members. While Baby admits to Woodruff that she disliked "the place [she] was before this last one," she also says that she "did get to church every Sunday some kind of way." Since she intends to minister to her people outside church, however, she looks up Reverend Pike primarily to co-opt his literacy in order to contact her children. Two years of messages, two years of "washing, sewing, canning, cobbling, gardening, and sitting in churches" earns her the pitiful news that the southern Whitlow place exists no longer and "[Dunn] went West," the good news that "Halle got married and had a baby coming," and the sight of "high-topped shoes that she didn't like the look of at all. At all" (146–47).

Sethe's more traditional escape route introduces her to two men: one indirectly, the other directly; one a slave driver, the other a slave savior; one white, the other black. Amy Denver's Mr. Buddy inadvertently teaches the slavewoman that not all victims of enslavement are African American. Three years younger than Sethe, lost like Sethe, more malnourished than Sethe, a "whitegirl" walks a "hundred miles. Maybe more" from Kentucky to Boston ostensibly to seek carmine velvet but actually to exchange Mr. Buddy's beatings for something softer and smoother. An indentured servant, Amy's mother "was give to Mr. Buddy." Part of her payment apparently includes sex. She becomes pregnant and dies in childbirth, after which Mr. Buddy informs his daughter that she must work off her mother's passage. She does, and he sets an ignorant, abused sixteen-year-old girl loose to fend for herself. Mr. Buddy's slave regime includes stints in the root cellar and a "right evil hand" that would throw a poker or "whip you for looking at him straight" (78–80). Her "dreamwalker's voice" and ability to re-create the mess that is Sethe's cut back into a back in bloom indicate that Amy Denver copes with the memory of Mr. Buddy's brutality by attending to pain. Despite her good hands and tenderhearted mouth, however, she retains Mr. Buddy's white male pecking-order mentality and the class consciousness that the "raggediest-looking [white] trash" often exhibit to lord it over poor blacks (31–32). His sham of a buddy system ultimately countered when Amy provides Sethe with a real, female comrade in arms, Mr. Buddy unintentionally enables another seed "in which the whole generation sleeps confident of a future" to come to fruition. Sethe names her almost lost baby after the white half of the pair of "throwaway people" who keep close to do "something together appropriately and well" (84).

Stamp Paid deliberately enables such "lawless outlaws" to cross the Ohio River to freedom (84). Reminded of her initial meeting with Stamp by the sweat she breaks into during her first visit to the clearing after Baby Suggs's death, Sethe remains certain that "the grief at 124 started when she jumped down off the wagon, her newborn tied to her chest in the underwear of a whitegirl looking for Boston" (90). Morrison relies once more on a site of memory to show how the pain of slavery creates flexible black masculinities. The exhausted mother falls into a deep sleep after the ordeal of Denver's premature birth. She wakes up in a fever-induced sweat to find Amy gone, straps her daughter to her chest, stumbles onto "three coloredpeople fishing," and waits to be spoken to. After one of the boys points her out, the elder fisherman quickly sizes up the situation and questions casually: "Headin' 'cross?" A brief but encrypted conversation results in Stamp nodding her toward a sun-baked rock where Sethe sleeps sitting up and bathes her baby in perspiration. She wakes this time to find Stamp holding out a smoking piece of fried eel, which she cannot eat. She drinks a jar of the Ohio, however, and as she begs for more, Stamp watches her streaming face and directs one of the boys to take off his coat. Ignoring the youngster who whines, "What I'm gonna wear?" the old man unties Denver and wraps her in the jacket. The complaining continuing, Stamp sighs and finally says more at one time than he has said all day long: "You want it back then go head and take it off that baby. Put the baby naked in the grass and put your coat back on. And if you can do it, then go on 'way somewhere and don't come back." Unlike schoolteacher's lessons, which methodically but rationally instruct his nephews in the ways of ownership and brutality, Stamp Paid cryptically yet passionately shows his nephews how to express compassion freely. The "boy dropped his eyes, then turned to join the other" (90–91).

Stamp's tutelage incorporates the feminine masculinity of a griot. He survives by silently reading the tiniest of signs. He observes human nature like Halle, and like Sixo he communes with nature. He knows but does not tell all the stories of his people, transmitting across generations only the ones that have evolved safely into the realm of community legend. Speaking little because, like Baby Suggs, he recognizes the dangers of saying too much, Stamp watches and waits until nightfall to take Sethe across. Contrary to her expectations, he poles his boat upriver, and just as she thinks he is returning her to Kentucky, he "turned the flatbed and crossed the Ohio like a shot." Saying, "Don't move. They'll find you," he keeps his name to himself until Sethe asks for it and bids her good-bye by warning her to "Watch out for that there baby, you hear?" Stamp can drop as well as pick up signs. He leaves open the sty that signals a crossing and puts the white rag on the post that says there's a child. Within hours Sethe stuffs swollen feet into men's shoes split by Ella to jump down off the wagon at 124. The male sky to Baby Suggs's feminine mountain, Stamp expresses his affection in his publicly private but emphatically masculine manner. If Baby bathes, strokes, and calls her children, Stamp celebrates the baby's safety not by touching Denver or telling her but by picking for her blackberries that taste like church from briar bushes that finally whip into shreds the "sly, steely old black man: agent, fisherman, boatman, tracker, savior, spy" (136). Although Stamp Paid may not talk much, he communicates volumes. Like many men, the labor of his hands represents the sign of his love.

Paul D, on the other hand, survives escape by learning to love small. Crippled by a lack of selfhood instead of physically like the special rooster he names Mister, the last of the Sweet Home men is finally forced to leave his shell along with the security of the other Pauls. Locating his pain in Alfred, Georgia, electing to beat it by way of his feet, he manages "simply to move, go, pick up one day and be somewhere else the next. Resigned to life without aunts, cousins, children. Even a woman, until Sethe" (221). "Walking off" whenever he wants to becomes the only way he can "convince himself that he would no longer have to sleep, pee, eat or swing a sledge hammer in chains" (40). After his separation from his brothers, Paul D's initial independent action involves trying to kill Brandywine, the slaver who buys him, in the names of Halle, Sixo, Paul A, Paul F, and Mister. His uprising earns him a place in a Georgia prison camp.[18] Succeeding there in shutting off his head and locking away his heart against pain or pleasure, the mover and shaker is himself subsequently moved by Beloved's presence to remember the site of his trembling. His shoes tied across his shoulder, he steps into the red wave of the "lonely and rebuked" baby ghost, and 124 Bluestone makes him tremble for the first time since the eighty-three days straight in Alfred, Georgia—albeit this time his legs instead of his hands shake from the house that he subsequently brings down (13).

Although schoolteacher moves him in the beginning, changing him into something "less than a chicken sitting in the sun on a tub," Paul starts to tremble, not so anyone would notice, only once removed from the sight of the "smiling boss of roosters" and "a last look at Brother" (72, 106). Deprived of a fair game of male challenge and the support of fraternity, he is left like Mister on his own and trembling inside. What he faces, along with forty-five other black men, proves to be a life of unfair treatment by white men in the form of chained day labor and a long night's stand trapped in a wooden box fitted into an earthen ditch. Unlike the black bodies packed below deck on the slave ships, Paul D can at least look at an aspen and swing a hammer to control claustrophobia during the day. The uncontrolled trembling of his hands occurs at night in "that grave calling itself quarters." Morrison captures the remarkable routine of prison camp life, starting with the reveille rifle shot and forced fellatio, held together by "one thousand feet of the best hand-forged chain in Georgia," and concluding with the return to the cages. Forbidden to speak anything but "Yes, sir," the prisoners carry out their commands with two shouted words: "Hiiii" at dawn and "Hoooo!" in the evening. They communicate their feelings through their eyes ("Help me this morning; 's bad") and the chain that compels "each man [to stand] in the other's place" (106–8).

Paul D exchanges his paradisiacal Sweet Home brotherhood for songs "that murdered life" and a tiny aspen "that confirmed it" within the confining community of a chain gang (221). Its griot is Hi Man, the lead chain who alone knows "what was enough, what was too much, when things were over, when the time had come" to sing out "stop." Although prison wardens view the chain as punishment, prisoners turn it into mercy. They tramp through "the astonishing beauty of feldspar" to get where they can beat to death not other lives but Life herself. Afterward they sing that flirt back to life again just to maim, mutilate, and bury her for good. Only then would they be safe. Morrison's lyrical description of prison work songs depicts the small measure of relief they offer enslaved men as well as the encoded messages their white listeners do not comprehend: "With a sledge hammer in his hands and Hi Man's lead, the men got through. They sang it out and beat it up, garbling the words so they could not be understood; tricking the words so their syllables yielded up other meanings." The passage also reveals the intimate bonds forged by the chain, completely opposite of the isolation intended by the guards. His still hands signaling to him that he has successfully "beat [Life's] butt" until she "roll[s] over dead," Paul D thinks he is safe, for "if one pitched and ran—all, all forty-six, would be yanked by the chain that bound them and no telling who or how many would be killed. A man could risk his own life, but not his brother's" (108–9).

The credo by which Morrison guides all her characters prevails, however, and once more there is no safety. It rains. Not quite forty days and forty nights but enough that the forty-six men locked in separate boxes and joined at the ankles by hand-forged iron must swim or die. Somebody yanks Paul D's chain. With no words spoken but every man aware, each prisoner jerks on the chain to his left so that "the next man would know too." Exercising the incredible self-control they have labored to master as the trench turns into a mud slide, the men wait for the signal. It comes, and one by one they dive under their cages: "For one lost, all lost. The chain that held them would save all or none, and Hi Man was the Delivery."

They trust "the rain and the dark, yes, but mostly Hi Man and each other." Morrison's black epic reads like the adventure stories it echoes but with a distinctly African American sound: "They talked through that chain like Sam Morse and, Great God, they all came up" (110). Their immersion the high point of the saga, all the prisoners emerge reborn to shuffle off through the wet night and huddle under trees in the daytime until they find shelter from a camp of sick Cherokee.

Calling their fellow outlaws "buffalo men" after the texture of their hair, these "decimated but stubborn" Indians certainly stand in their brothers' place. Morrison alludes briefly to the Trail of Tears, so named when literally thousands of Cherokee, mostly women, children, and old people, die during the ruthless drive from their mountain homes in Georgia and North Carolina to government reservations in northeastern Oklahoma. Forced to move "by the same president they fought for against the Creek," they have already lost half of their number to illness and another quarter fighting on both sides of a war that is not theirs. Now sick again and self-exiled into the woods, the group that separated from those who signed the treaty "[protect] each other as best they could" and "await the end of the world" (111–12). Sitting in a semicircle outside the encampment, the black fugitives, like Sethe, wait to be spoken to. The Cherokee provide them with small axes, mush, and stories. They point Paul D, again with no plan and the last to leave, smilingly toward springtime trees. Grasping the first of many lessons he must learn when he loosens his grip on the chain, Paul admits his ignorance, asks for direction, and sets off toward the magical North following tree flowers.

All his escape attempts prove failures. "Alone, undisguised, with visible skin, memorable hair and no whitemen to protect him," Paul D has not one permanent success in five tries (268). The twenty years during, before, and after the Civil War show him sleeping in trees, stealing from pigs, fighting owls for food, and seeing "coloredpeople . . . so stunned, or hungry, or tired or bereft it was a wonder they recalled or said anything." The benevolent, welcoming North turns out to be Wilmington, Delaware, "the meanest place for Negroes he had ever seen outside Pulaski County, Kentucky, and of course the prison camp in Georgia" (66). However, he stays almost two years with a "weaver lady" who "snap[s] him up" after she feeds him sausage (113). "Cross-eyed with hunger and loneliness," Paul asks for work at the first house he sees in the black section of Wilmington, and a woman who "look[s] him up and down" offers him sheets instead. Crying the grateful tears of "a man's first time," he crawls into bed and lets her help him pretend to enjoy sex with her instead of her white cotton sheets (131).[19]

Vowing never to leave the weaver lady's bed linens, Paul remains with her eighteen months until the Northpoint Bank and Railroad Company purchases him. Running from there, he thinks to join the Tennessee 44th Colored Regiment but arrives instead at a regiment of buffalo soldiers under a New Jersey commander. A Northpoint agent returns him to slave labor. The railroad sells his services to the Alabama Rebellers, for whom he sorts the dead and smelts iron. Ashamed of pitying what might be the sons of guards in Alfred, Georgia, the fugitive slave works both sides of a war over but not about slaves. Emancipation finds him impressed to a Selma foundry. The "walk of his life" turns out to be dangerous back roads worth all the risk, however, just to taste in Trenton the excitement of free life in the unforgettable form of his first earned purchase—a withered turnip. His form of escape becomes "Move. Walk. Run. Hide. Steal and move on" (66). Whether South or North, Paul D tries desperately not to love "the beauty of this land that was not his" or hate the sight of "more dead people than living ones" or be inspired by the freedom to "eat, walk and sleep anywhere." Nonetheless, "anything could stir him," and he "never stayed uncaught" (268–69).

From this Paul's perspective, life on the road to Bluestone/Damascus consists of "twelve dead blacks in the first eighteen miles," six of whom are men and four little boys (269). Life on the road means "five women arriving with fourteen female children" because "all their men—brothers, uncles, fathers, husbands, sons—had been picked off one by one." Paul sees young boys dazed and alone, reconfigured families of women and children, and "solitary, hunted and hunting for . . . men, men, men" (52). Prohibited public transportation, trailed by debt, preyed upon by "filthy 'talking sheets,'" the triple-K dragon that survived on black blood and "swam the Ohio at will," these men "followed secondary routes, scanned the horizon for signs and counted heavily on each other" (66, 52–53). They remained "silent, except for social courtesies." They "neither described nor asked about the sorrow that drove them from one place to another." Playing her usual name game, Morrison signals the severity of what amounts to attempted genocide with the address of a Rochester, New York, preacher to whom drifting black people are directed by a single piece of paper: DeVore (devour) Street (52–53).[20]

Paul D runs alone in no-place like this for seven years until he finds himself in southern Ohio, where "an old woman and a girl he used to know had gone" (270). The significance of 124 Bluestone Road lies in more than merely its address. In fact, initially, like Sixo and Beloved, it has no full name, or number, since in 1873 "Cincinnati didn't stretch that far." But then its story starts with its number name: "124 was spiteful" (3). Placing no lone conductor on a separate raised podium, unglamorous blues players set time and signal the commencement of their music with an unnamed somebody in the group counting off "1—2—3—4."[21] *Beloved* begins with "1—2—4." Morrison's blues technique of beginning with now, continuing with before, and ending with after, juxtaposing present with past and an (im)possible future, can be read by the numbers. The novel establishes the one maliciously lively house of blues (1), describes how its two abandoned inhabitants (2) came to be its victims, and introduces the four others (4) who at one time or another add up to make more than the sum of its original parts—Baby Suggs, Howard and Buglar, Paul D. Or, viewed in another light, the novel reduces the present of two lovers (2) to a past life for each on the left (1), and on the right considers the possibility of a doubling or a future (4). It relies on its readers' expectations about chronological order (i.e., that 3 should follow 1 and 2) to trick them into thinking pluralistically. It runs feminine circles around masculine lines to create the possibility of a postmodern African American manhood or Neal's New Black Man.

If we read between these male lines, we anticipate a future on Bluestone Road for Paul D made possible by his miserable experience from the likes of the four horsemen tempered by his education from Stamp Paid, sky to Baby Suggs's mountain, and his connection to Sethe. The renewed relationship between Paul D and Sethe begins when he asks if he can sit down on her porch and take off his shoes. Still barefoot, he allows her to lead him through the doorway to sorrow and steps "not quite in a hurry but losing no time" up the ghost-white stairs into the blues tone of 124 (20). The first black men associated with the humbling grief of the place include the dancing fools that Baby Suggs entices into its clearing out back. Before the four horsemen, 124 was a different place: a "cheerful, buzzing house where Baby Suggs, holy, loved, cautioned, fed, chastised and soothed." Out back of this 124, Baby, an "uncalled, unrobed, unanointed," unchurched, untitled preacher, who accepts only a "small caress" after her name, takes to the clearing her people and her great heart. In the heat of warm Saturday afternoons, she sits on a rock while "every black man, woman and child who could make it through" waits among trees. She calls on the children to laugh, the men to dance, and the women to cry, after which "it [gets] all mixed up." Offering her people her own heart, she shows them their salvation, saying that "the only grace they could have was the grace they could imagine. That if they could not see it, they would not have it." Allowing pain-struck men the pleasure of dancing barefoot in grass, she teaches them all how to love themselves—and one another. Then she stands up to dance "with her twisted hip the rest of what her heart had to say while the others opened their mouths and gave her the music" (88–89).

Baby's arms remain wide enough to encircle two more males with the arrival of her grandsons Howard and Buglar. However, their spiteful sister scares them off as soon as either becomes old enough to say "Gimme back my shoes" (40). The last straw for Buglar is a shattered mirror; for Howard it entails tiny handprints in a cake. Morrison elaborates on her haint's signs both to embellish her ghost story and to depict the vulnerability to suggestion of adolescent boys. Quite simply, their mother's attempt to kill them having traumatized Buglar and Howard at four and five years old, they imprint images associated with the Misery. They grow "furious at the company of the women in the house" and spend in "sullen reproach any time they had away from their odd work in town" (104). Coping involves the pleasures of supporting Denver between their knees while making up deliciously scary "die-witch! stories with proven ways of killing her dead." It also means sleeping tightly together on the bottom bunk while clutching hands to hold off the grief and fright that "drove them increasingly out of the house" (19, 120). Sethe's dreams about her lost boys flow out of 124 to portray them barely visible in beautiful trees or running down railroad tracks, always laughing and always away from her. Although Morrison is the first to insist that free adults acknowledge the absence of safety, she also understands that uninhibited children must feel safe. Howard and Buglar would rather face systematically killing men than unpredictably killing women: "Getting that close to dying made them want to fight the War" (205).

While Sethe never looks away from unsafe situations, not even from the sight of the man trampled by a mare in front of Sawyer's restaurant or the hound displaced by the baby girl ghost, she cannot completely harden herself against her guilt over the trauma to her children. She faces down the responsibility of putting Here Boy back together after grief breaks the legs and dislocates the eye even of the family dog, sending him into convulsions during which he chews up his tongue. Knocking him unconscious with a hammer, Sethe pushes in his eye and sets his bones. Nonetheless, still another domesticated male animal "gone savage with pain" refuses to remain in the house (12). Recognizing the empathy for humans noted especially in dogs, Morrison uses their house pet to signal major sorrows in the lives of the women at 124. Here Boy drinking from the puddle at her feet sends Sethe back to Sweet Home. The puppy burying bones left over from Baby Suggs's excessive giving causes her to cut a stalk of rue.

Her dog's stomach going in and out measures Denver's loneliness after the Misery. She matches her breathing to that of Here Boy to see whether or not the only presence she hears during the day is the sound of herself or someone else beside her. The sad irony of Here Boy's name is that pain finally prevents her sole substantial companion from coming when she calls him even to Denver's side.

The pain that plagues 124 comes in recurring sites of memory associated with the four horsemen. For Sethe this seems like schoolteacher's hat. For Baby it means high-topped shoes. The story of the four horsemen transposes apocalyptic visions from the Book of Revelation into the African American blues tones of *Beloved*. Before they can be judged, Morrison's people, like their Christian counterparts, must survive the tests of men who ride down the road and beings that rise out of the water. The four horsemen of Revelation can wreak their havoc because corruption and contentions divide the community. *Beloved*'s huntsmen arrive as purgation for the celebration Baby, Stamp, and Sethe give in their excess of love and pride. Baby Suggs and Stamp Paid look the wrong way when trouble appears. Because they are envious of and disgusted by the apparently special blessedness at 124, the townspeople look the other way when "some new whitefolks with the Look just rode in. The righteous Look every Negro learned to recognize along with his ma'am's tit. Like a flag hoisted, this righteousness telegraphed and announced the faggot, the whip, the fist, the lie, long before it went public" (157).

The four men bunched together and riding righteous consist of a slave catcher, schoolteacher, one nephew, and a sheriff. Morrison deflects into black humor the bloody death of the crawling-already? girl. First she presents details from the perspective of the redneck catcher, who, toughened though he is, finds astonishing the actions of these "crazy old nigger[s]." Then schoolteacher, noting that the slavewoman he bragged on for making fine ink has "gone wild," is left to criticize the nephew he left out of the hunt as punishment for overbeating the woman and causing her to cut: "Just think—what would his own horse [or hound] do if you beat it beyond the point of education"? He wishes the nephew he made stay home and feed Lillian could see the look that Sethe hands him now so Nephew could learn for sure how an animal can revert: "You just can't mishandle creatures and expect success." The nephew actually with him, the "one who had nursed her while his brother held Sethe down," certainly learns his lesson. Unaware that he shakes, warned by his uncle "against that kind of confusion," he is stunned that she would "go and do that . . . [o]n account of a beating": "Hell, he'd been beat a million times and he was white." Also amazed, the sheriff is not shaking but swallowing. Finally finding his voice, he urges the others to leave. Although schoolteacher marks his spot by spitting and "beat[ing] his hat against his thigh," nobody looks to the left or to the right as they exit because they have seen "enough nigger eyes for now." Even without looking at each other, however, everybody concedes that this is what happens when a "little so-called freedom [is] imposed on people who needed every care and guidance in the world to keep them from the cannibal life they preferred." It goes without saying that these look to be "the damnedest bunch of coons they'd ever seen" (149–51).

Truth depends on how things look. Mixing voices, tones, and points of view, Morrison individualizes and therefore humanizes the unnamed males in the horsemen collective. Generally hardened and hardening, they retain tiny glimpses of sensitivity. All except coldly rational schoolteacher appear shocked beyond belief at the sight of a mother taking a hand saw to her child; each remains convinced that "no way he could have." Even the thought makes three men back out of the woodshed while the fourth really wants to. The sheriff is particularly compassionate. Disavowing fear yet stiffening at the prospect of touch, claiming he is cold, he stands frozen until an unconscious child sighs. Then the man shifts gratefully from the shed into August sunlight. He has to force himself to carry out his duties, commandeering a wagon, which he orders Stamp to drive and places Sethe in. His touch at her elbow is gentle, and he looks away during the baby's burial when she nurses Denver. While each horseman reveals the depth or shallowness of his humanity in his response to pain, only the sheriff recognizes Sethe's agony in her unflinching stare and blinding silence. Despite their differences, however, it becomes clear to all four white men after they arrive at 124 that "there was nothing there to claim" (149–50).

Human nature will win out nonetheless, and parasites crawl out of the woodwork. Although he cannot read, Paul D understands that the sight of a black woman's picture in the newspaper spells only disaster. It has to be the kind of horrifying event "worth the breath catch of a white citizen of Cincinnati" to merit a Negro's face in the paper, and this kind of news signals carrion to scavengers (156). In Sethe's case the ghoulmongering includes polite leading questions from smiling journalists, reassurance from a jailer who confiscates her crystal earrings to protect her from herself, the ministrations of two ministers who "prayed for their souls while Sethe peeled potatoes and Grandma Baby sucked air" (12). It certainly includes stonecutters. With the help of Brother Bodwin, who speaks quietly in chambers to Sethe's judge, she is allowed to attend her baby's funeral where Reverend Pike talks loudly, though she hears no more than his first two words. When she is freed three months later, she barters herself for the letters on a grave marker, her single regret that she fails to get both words. What she does manage, pressed against pink marble and paying dearly for it, is the one that matters most to her: *Beloved*. Sethe desires to stamp her debt paid by "rutting among the headstones with the engraver, his young son looking on, the anger in his face so old; the appetite in it quite new." She thinks that ten minutes with her knees "wide open as any grave" should be enough to answer all the grave robbers. She does not account, however, for the baby's questions. Her last memories of color depict Sethe outdoing herself with the red of Beloved's blood and the pink of Beloved's headstone. Sethe's parasites, on the other hand, drain people of blood, drawing on the color in other lives to put vitality into their own. Relegated too low to their liking on the food chain, they include resentful, small-minded, self-righteous white men.

Morrison, however, always balances a schoolteacher with an Amy, a pupil with a sheriff. Sethe is not required to become a permanent Saturday girl because Mr. Sawyer is sweet enough to give an ex-convict a job fixing food during the week. But his softness remains no more impenetrable to pain than does her stiffness. The loss of his son during the Civil War renders him each year more and more "crotchety. As though Sethe's dark face was to blame." Morrison emphasizes the diminution of his kind nature when the restaurant owner begins to complain to Sethe that her potato salad, the recipe for which she has not changed, tastes too sweet. His patience and tenderness in dealing with his help succumb to shouts when Sethe comes in late, to orders to get her work done, and to threats when she "talks back." Her dulled pain limits her full awareness of his. Even a modest salary and generous benefits cannot prevent her from pilfering from her boss out of pride. She prefers the shame of stealing small items she can afford to the embarrassment of standing with the cluster of black faces "looking though a hole in [the general store's] back door" (188–91).

Morrison builds into *Beloved*'s male figures representations of cruelty coming out of childish ignorance but also the possibility, with painful experience, of grace. While Nelson Lord's naïve words stop Denver's ears, he may be partially responsible for opening her eyes. Denver experiences a brief respite from alienation when Lady Jones invites the lonely seven-year-old peeping through Miss Lady's window into her home school. So happy the child does not realize that her classmates avoid her, she is deflated not by meanness but by the curiosity in Nelson's voice when he asks if her mother cut her sister's throat: "Didn't your mother get locked away for murder? Wasn't you in there with her when she went?" The second part of Nelson's query, on the other hand, releases and so ultimately soothes "the Thing" that lies inside Denver all along.[22] The same vitality that propels her to repeat Nelson's first question prevents her from listening to Sethe and Baby Suggs's response. Her hearing "cut off by an answer she could not bear to hear," she walks for two years protected by "a silence too solid for penetration" (102–4). There is a good chance, however, after she once more musters the courage to seek communal healing, that the "beautiful boy as smart as she was with a birthmark like a nickel on his cheek" has grown into the young man whose eager welcome to her young womanhood renders Denver's face "looking like someone had turned up the gas jet" (120, 167).

Time, suffering, and association with the feminine community finally soften the stark linearity of Stamp Paid and Paul D into a flexible pluralism. Both men have known comfort, Stamp married to Vashti, Paul at Sweet Home and between sweet sheets. Bad luck, however, toughens them, sending them scampering but capable, with renewed connection to females, of tolerating multiple perspectives. Stamp initially reacts to "hand[ing] over his wife" to a seventeen-year-old boy with threatened violence and punishing withdrawal (184). Persuaded by Vashti not to kill the white boy or himself, he refuses to touch or speak to his wife. Then he slyly suggests that the slavewoman wearing a cameo on a black ribbon around her neck "owe you all some eggs" to the other person whose patience he considers tried—young master's wife. His reactions bring him little satisfaction in either revenge or remuneration so that when young master finally and abruptly releases Vashti, he considers "outhurt[ing] the hurter" by breaking her neck (233–34). He changes his name, and his attitude, instead. Converting frustrated rage into creative energy, Joshua fights the battle to help others stamp their debts paid, asks only for an open door in return, and takes pride in not having a mean bone in his body.

This pride in his charity along with unrealistic expectations of black women stamps Stamp owing yet more debt. Not once in his agony over his wife's controlled coupling does he consider her patience tried. Only after her death, his relationship with Baby Suggs, and his participation in the Misery at 124 does he acquire a measure of the painful humility required to help Paul D begin to pay off his debts. Stamp recognizes Sethe's stiff neck, which is reciprocated by the townswomen, but he "dis[believes] . . . [t]hat the door of a house with coloredpeople in it did not fly open in his presence" (184). He projects his need to outhurt the hurter, re-created as charity, onto Sethe, and he becomes angry, disillusioned, and high-toned when Baby Suggs takes to her bed to ponder color. In short, even at sixty Stamp still has a ways to go.

Too late to tell Baby, he gets most of the rest of the way by way of the blues. He does tell Paul D about the Misery and in so doing sets into motion the lovers' separation. Since, as his creator well knows, why is difficult to handle, Stamp takes refuge in how. Morrison depicts the old man doing the telling secretly in the slaughterhouse yard because sneaking has been his job, "though always for a clear and holy purpose." Balancing sexual drive against "truth and forewarning" before he shows Paul D the faded newspaper clipping, he fails to consider Sethe's feelings or Denver's needs. Belated guilt about them forces him to rethink his self-image: is he really a "high-minded Soldier of Christ" or just "an ordinary, plain meddler" (169–70)? Stamp's greatest debt, however, belongs to Baby Suggs, not so much for contributing to the grief at 124 but for idealizing her as the mountain to his sky. Believing that shame put her in the bed, he underestimates the extent to which white people coming in her yard and a contentious black community have exhausted her until a bright ribbon attached to a dark curl and a bit of scalp turns him suddenly from bone- to marrow-tired. Believing his blackberries saved Denver saves Stamp while Baby blames herself for failing to fix (on) shoes. He survives by laughing until he cries while she finally lies down, meeting his greeting "with a face knocked clean of interest." Stamp must experience his red ribbon before he can comprehend why, all her children taken from her, Baby no longer has the heart to imagine grace and wants only to "fix on something harmless in this world" (178–79). Continuing Baby's call, Morrison's word in *Beloved* explains how "information that had been in the newspaper become[s] a secret that needed to be whispered in a pig yard" (169). By speaking "unspeakable thoughts, unspoken," she purges her people of pain (199).

Stamp's ignorance, like the process by which Nelson Lord's curiosity frees Denver, releases Paul D's "Thing" so there can be healing. Healing ultimately depends on knowledge. Morrison sets two white male riders as contrast between continued innocence and the mature self-awareness acquired at 124 by Stamp Paid and Paul D. The tobacco tin in his chest burst open, Paul has been living prey to his painful thoughts in the cellar of the church where Stamp seeks him out to apologize. As Bluestone's griot promotes understanding of Sethe's story, an unnamed horseman rides up on a "high Eastern saddle" though he is obviously "Ohio Valley." Unidentified specifically as such, he is also obviously white. Stamp adroitly deflects the man's queries about "Judy. Works in the slaughterhouse." Calling him "Sir" but brushing him off like the parasite he is, the old man concentrates on comforting his half-drunk comrade as the rider remains righteous. Trotting stiffly away, returning to look down at them from his high horse, a midwestern redneck tracking a local black prostitute admonishes an ex-slave from the South for drinking at the foot of a cross. Then the white rider turns his stern back to them again while Stamp tries to divert Paul's attention from the bottle emblazoned by a golden chariot but no horse. He tells his rheumy-eyed friend a "nigger" is supposed to carry all the weight he can and begs him to take his choice of any colored house in which he wants to collapse.

Remaining more supportive than denigrating, Edward Bodwin nevertheless also rides off dumb. Morrison's attitude toward her character remains affectionately tongue-in-cheek. In spite of "prefer[ring] his figure astride Princess," seventy-year-old Bodwin will drive a cart down Bluestone Road to pick up a young black girl even though holding his own reins makes him "look the age he was." Denver waits on the porch for the lift to her new job while the old man returns to the place that continues "to surface in his dreams." Unaware of the significance of women's voices that search for "the right combination, the key, the code, the sound that broke the back of words," unaware that seeing his hat come into her yard, Sethe hears wings and grabs an ice pick, unaware that Denver runs to stop her mother from murdering, and that, alone again, Beloved sees "rising from his place with a whip in his hand, the man without skin, looking" at her, Brother Bodwin elects to notice only "some coloredwomen fighting." None of the women tells him anything else. Invigorated by yet tired out from the exciting political battles he has fought and the numbing wars he has not, a good day for him now in unbearable heat would be to "bring back the new girl and recall where his [childhood] treasures lay" (259–62).

With Stamp Paid as his mentor, Paul D both supports and stretches. He goes "all the way within his own mind" to live out a whole story to lie next to a whole woman while he still possesses, unlike Stamp, something interesting lying between his legs (Stepto 385). When he chooses to provide the bass for the blues harmonies of 124, he learns to accept the calves of his youth and to rub Sethe's feet, not count them. Confronted in the cold house by the Thing he most fears, human wildness, he struggles as well as couples with Beloved in a "brainless urge to stay alive" (264). Then he "[lays] all that mess down" (86). The biblical Paul undergoes a great conversion on the road to Damascus. Not unlike his namesake, Morrison's Paul receives his baptism of rain on the road to Bluestone and at 124 changes his tune, unlocks his head, and relocates his red heart.

His "coming is the reverse route of his going" (263). When he sits down on Sethe's porch after "never stay[ing] uncaught," Paul has learned by way of the bit how to put wildness in the eye and how to take it out and "[hasn't] figured out yet which is worse" (268, 71). Applying the violent tactics used in subduing him to beat away the vindictive baby ghost, he takes a table to the shaking 124, smashing it about and "screaming back at the screaming house: You want to fight, come on! God damn it! She got enough without you." Denver acknowledges resentfully that it "took a man" to shout off and replace the "venomous baby" (104). But Paul D rememories within the comfort of Sweet Home so that without trying he has also "become the kind of man who could walk into a house and make the women cry. Because with him, in his presence, they could" (17–18). Sethe senses in him a blessedness powerful enough to let him cradle her breasts. Paul D, always a "singing man," situates his feelings about the iron-eyed, barefoot woman in a song about chamomile sap.

More than the words, the tenor of his tunes reflects Paul's mood. Yearning "fashion[s] every note" at Sweet Home; the noises of the prison camp and the war afterward sound like "flat-headed nails for pounding." Paul D's song for Sethe contains the bittersweet ambiguity of his greeting: "Bare feet and chamomile sap / Took off my shoes; took off my hat" battles with "Gimme back my shoes; gimme back my hat" (39–40).[23] Having muffled his feelings tightly into the tin box he pictures as rusted shut in his chest, he sings them to sleep every day and dreams that a walking man can make a life with a whole woman without releasing the catch. He imagines wrong. The wildness in her terrifies the wildness in him, he tells her she has two feet, not four, and "a forest [springs] up between them; trackless and quiet." Transferring the shame of his "cold-house secret straight to her too-thick love," he deliberately replaces his hat (165). But not before the sight/site of Sethe, shoes and stockings in hand, has opened the "closed portion of his head . . . like a greased lock" (41).

A relationship with Beloved becomes responsible for the recovery of Paul's red heart. It stops when Sethe cuts and runs from Sweet Home. Its memories within are boxed away in Alfred, Georgia, where a cage "drove him crazy so he would not lose his mind" (41). By the time he arrives at 124, "nothing in this world could pry it open" (113). A suppressed spirit come back to life, however, is "wild game" and not of this world (242). Morrison places the scene where Paul D couples in the cold house with Beloved almost immediately after the girl watches two turtles mate at the edge of a stream. The language captures the longing and the conflict of passion in the tension between the clashing gravity of the turtles' plated shells and their floating heads touching. It also accepts such wildness as prerequisite for survival: "No height was beyond her yearning neck, stretched like a finger towards his, risking everything outside the bowl just to touch his face" (105). As Paul D responds to a desire for Beloved so suffocating it is not "even fun," he releases his fear of his own wildness to be comprehended and so contained (264). Repeating "red heart" loud enough to wake the dead, he touches Beloved, and himself, on the inside part and lifts the lid on a box rusted shut (117).[24]

Once he takes ownership of his head and his heart, he can slip back into Sethe's house through the back door: "His coming is the reverse route of his going" (263). Repossession of his heart permits him to take hold of his pieces: "bad whiskey, nights in the cellar, pig fever, iron bits, smiling roosters, fired feet, laughing dead men, hissing grass, rain, apple blossoms, neck jewelry, Judy in the slaughterhouse, Halle in the butter, ghost-white stairs, chokecherry trees, cameo pins, aspens, Paul A's face, sausage [and] the loss of a red, red, heart" (235). These scattered "memories within" recall not only the whole of Paul D's life; they represent the sites of most of *Beloved*'s imaginative male flooding. Without the shared history encapsulated by such images, Baby Suggs becomes an ignorant woods preacher, Denver her slow-witted granddaughter, and Stamp Paid a meddlesome old fisherman. Sethe is reduced to a helplessly resigned ex-slave and Paul D merely a burned-out black man. Recovery of his head allows Paul to put perspective on his heart and, like Stamp, to see black women more clearly for the complex human beings they are. He once perceived his Sweet Home gal as "prickly, mean-eyed . . . obedient . . . shy . . . and work-crazy." She is. He can account now, however, for the possibility of the woman who "talked about safety with a handsaw" and who "didn't know where the world stopped and she began," which she is also (164). The whole Sethe is iron-eyed, barefoot, and, at the conclusion of the novel, in pieces.

The whole man needs a whole woman to put his pieces with. Offering to bathe Sethe even while his head hurts, Paul remembers the words that Sixo used to describe his feelings for the Thirty-Mile Woman: "She is a friend of my mind. She gather me, man. The pieces I am, she gather them and give them back to me in all the right order" (272–73). Having located his specific blues place, having stopped posturing and gone inside, Paul D understands that only "this woman Sethe" can leave him "his manhood like that." Indebted to her but free, his "holding fingers . . . holding hers," he tells the friend of his mind that she is her own "best thing" (273). Morrison refers to Paul D as the last of the Sweet Home men because he is the single male left in its line, its sole homeboy soul man, and the male who circles its sorrow long enough to discover his sum while returning

Sethe her parts. He has available to him the grains of frontier manhood because Garner gathered them and told him so; Stamp Paid helps him to refine them. Schoolteacher educates him in the personality death essential for male humility, and he lights out to forge his own freedom so that he has a life to lie next to Sethe's. Theirs is neither a story to "pass *on*" nor to "*pass* on" (274; italics mine). Beloved's loneliness still roams; 124 may be sold. The site of Paul D's safe haven with Sethe remains always out there in all places and no place; it is not contained within any house but floods through the memories they make alone and coupled. *Beloved* reveals that colored men's time beats out of synch with slavery but simpatico with postmodern fluidity. It claims that the only thing flexible New Black Men have to hold their selves together is inconclusive blues stories and compassion.

CHAPTER 7

Classically Re-training Blues Boys

Morrison's *Jazz* Men

Jazz (1992) and its jazzmen merge *Beloved*'s blues with the tragicomic tradition of the nigger in the woodpile to maintain their compassion yet make a current kind of sound. Though they possess a serious, even sacred dimension, they never consider anything too holy to leave alone. They are the indirect descendants of *Beloved*'s music man Sixo, who, always off the downbeat, defends his darkly humorous originality as fiercely as his loyalty to his tribe. He dances solitary among trees to keep his bloodlines open. His name suggests the chord formed by a triad in which the fundamental tone is raised an octave, creating a new interval of a sixth. Jazzmen like Joe Trace probably descend directly from *Beloved*'s Paul D, a singing man who forges the possibility of a constructive self-identity out of a painful collective. Deborah McDowell argues in her review of *Jazz* that Joe's mother may well be Beloved: "Could she even be that 'devil child' who take[s] the shape of a pregnant woman before vanishing at *Beloved*'s end?" (1). Charmed by Beloved and under her spell, Paul D moans: "Something is happening to me, that girl is doing it, . . . she is doing it to me. Fixing me . . . she's fixed me and I can't break it" (*Beloved* 127). With assistance from Sethe and the black community, however, he finally cuts loose to make possible the swing from blues to jazz. But not before he (or one of "the lowest yet") gets Beloved into a fix, the potentially tragic outcome of which would be Joe Trace (*Beloved* 256).

Morrison's reverence for the divinity of comedy dominates her sixth novel and converts black-and-bluesmen into jazzmen. In a September

2003 interview anticipating the October release of her latest novel, *Love*, she continues to laugh off criticism of her literary somberness: "Who says I don't have a sense of humor?" (Minzesheimer 1D). When the normally subdued Alice Manfred "put[s] down her iron, hard" after demanding from Viole[n]t Trace the point of fighting some "mishandled child," then challenges her scatty-looking visitor not to take it but to make it, the seamstress burns an unseemly "black and smoking ship . . . clear through the yoke." Her unexpectedly shouted "shit" eliciting a small smile from Violet, the two "[in] no time" rock with laughter, and Violet is reminded of True Belle, who looked on the hungry, irritable destitution of her grandchildren and "laughed to beat the band." She "had to lean against the wall to keep her laughter from pulling her down to the floor with them." Feeling then and now loved, not lost, better, not beaten, Violet recalls what she has forgotten: " . . . that laughter is serious. More complicated, more serious than tears" (113).

Alice's smoking ship reminds Morrison's readers to remember once more the sixty million and more who died during the Middle Passage. The image recaptures the brutality of the black past as it suggests that, even burned out, the yoke of slavery leaves its imprint upon abused and abuser alike. Second in a trilogy on the African American experience and the excesses of love, *Jazz* traces the migration of Morrison's *Beloved* male peasants into the sphere of Harlem's 1920s speakeasies and concrete plantations. As its characters train dance on into the city, it turns the rhythms of country blues into urban jazz and transforms suffering into information. The novelist relies on various techniques of classical tragedy to relay her men's continuing pain. As blues evolves into jazz, however, the focus and tone of her writing shift from the sights and sounds of tragedy into the tragicomedy that embodies the jazz experience.

Jazz becomes Morrison's response to the call of Dante's *Purgatorio*. A classics scholar, she remains fascinated with Greek tragedy because it "makes available [the] varieties of provocative love" that she explores in her novels ("Unspeakable Things Unspoken" 3). Like the *Divine Comedy* and Aeschylus in the *Oresteia*, she questions how a cycle of tragedy can be broken to make new possibilities possible. Because jazz renders unpredictability, creativity, and change within an identifiable structure as integral to its musical process, it provides Morrison with the metaphor she seeks. Noting that the novel must now stand in place of music as cultural cement for the black community, she blends the nonhermeneutic into hermeneutics; she turns jazz into a trope that reinforces "the idea of love as a space where one could negotiate freedom" (Schappell and Lacour 365).[1] Ralph Ellison describes "true jazz" as "an act of individidual assertion within and against the group" (234). Bastien and Hostager refer to jazz's "basic turbulence" and "frictional sounds" based on the uncertainty of what will happen as the music unfolds (150). Missy Dehn Kubitschek concludes: "To prevent another disaster, [*Jazz*'s] characters must change their self-images from static, destructive blues roles to dynamic jazz roles" (153).

Music critics define American jazz as arising from a friction between two different harmonic systems: "that of the European tradition and that found in African music" (Bastien and Hostager 164). Influenced by European harmonies and African rhythms, emerging from various regional combinations of blues and ragtime, it has frequently been called America's classical music. Additionally, jazz represents one of the most abstract of musical forms, resisting either "emotional climax or denouement to experience the multiplicity of the moment" (Brown 631–32). Maintaining that African Americans have already endured the worst and prevailed, Morrison identifies black women writers along with male jazz musicians as "having a quality of hunger and disturbance that never ends. Classical music satisfies and closes. Black music does not do that. Jazz always keeps you on the edge. There is no final chord. . . . I want my books to be like that. . . . They will never fully satisfy—never fully" (McKay 411). Carolyn M. Jones believes that Morrison relies on this disruptive improvisation of black music "to deconstruct the form of tragedy, allowing a reconstruction of identity to emerge" that is not determined but fluid and creole (481). Morrison uses her jazz metaphor not only to present the possibility of breaking the tragic cycle, however. She also massages the very techniques of classical tragedy to deconstruct suffering and reconstruct joy. The *Jazz* impulse acts "to keep the painful details and episodes of a brutal experience alive in one's aching consciousness, to finger its jagged grain, and to transcend it, not by the consolation of philosophy but by squeezing from it a near-tragic, near-comic lyricism" (Ellison 78–79).

Jazz, like tragedy and jazz music, begins in medias res.[2] It pictures a fifty-three-year-old Joe crying all day, having fallen for "one of those deep-down, spooky loves that made him so sad and happy he shot [the girl] just to keep the feeling going." It focuses on Joe's wife, Violet, who, having secretly slept with a doll for years only to sit down suddenly in the middle of the street, steal a baby, and shut up, cuts her husband's eighteen-year-old lover's already dead face at the funeral. She then takes a lover of her own, whose name she cannot remember. She either sends the boyfriend away, or he leaves her out of "sympathy for the brokenhearted man in the next room" (4–5). Joe remains throughout staring out an apartment window with no view, wiping tears off his cheeks with his red engineer's handkerchief. Morrison could not have located a more apt narrative counterpart for a sad blues theme. Despite its subject, though, or its action, which begins in the middle of things, or its other tragic pointers, her slyly humorous tone signals something else. Identifiable even in the opening scene are characteristics more typical of a tragicomedy such as Shakespeare's *The Winter's Tale:* a complex, improbable plot suitable to tragedy, rapid action appearing to head for catastrophe, love as central interest, unnatural situations, significant characters, disguises, surprises, jealousy, treachery, intrigue, and external chaos enveloping the central conflict. To all this Morrison contributes male characters who take it ultimately to make it.

Having established the portrait of Violet and Joe's beleaguered relationship as its recurrent theme, presided over by a picture on their mantelpiece of the dead girl Dorcas, *Jazz* turns itself over to a chorus of related voices that collectively help it to explain how things got to be in such a sad state. With respect to jazzman Joe, this means the reader must return to Vesper County, Virginia, where the couple grew up during the backlash of Reconstruction, and listen to the stories of various blues boys. If we devoutly approach Morrison's southern rendition of classical Rome, we will hear the soft, after-supper songs about Violet's traveling father and True Belle's homebound husband.[3] Rose Dear's tale on Violet's father tells us that, "stunned by the uselessness of his back and hands . . . furious at the price of coffee and the shape of his oldest girl's legs, [he] had just quit. . . . Gone off somewhere to sit and think about it or sit and not think about it." Rose understands the wisdom of making up talk rather than telling people truth: her husband actually joins "a party that favored niggers voting," and some white landowners not-so-gently persuade him to "transfer hisself someplace" (138, 100), but not before he forfeits his property to said opposing parties.

Beaten but undaunted, Violet's father routinely resurrects himself to dispense forgetfulness like Lethe. He becomes a clandestinely defiant "birthday-every-day man who gave out gifts and stories that kept them so rapt they forgot for the while a bone-clean cupboard and exhausted soil." Like Sixo, however, the birthday boy's timing stays terribly off. Four years after True Belle returns to organize things, two weeks after Rose Dear "jumped in the well and missed all the fun," he arrives with chocolate gold ingots, too-shiny two-dollar pieces, and snake oil. Only True Belle shakes her head and laughs. Having brought his wife an embroidered cushion for their dispossessed couch, he responds "Damn. . . . Aw, damn" when he learns that the silk pillow comes too late even to line her pine box. Gone again in three weeks, the interims between his "fabulously dangerous and wonderful returns" growing longer and longer, he turns into a local legend that is "bold and secret" and as necessary as breath. Surely slower in his seventies, probably having lost the teeth that shape the smile that makes his family forgive him, he lives always out there in possibility, "the mocking, daring dollar bills sticking from his cap, jammed into the cuffs of his trousers and the tops of his shoes." Only one picture spoils the pleasure for at least the middle daughter. While the five sisters and the rest remaining in Vesper County take hope from this probably dead "phantom father," who puts by "delights to pass out among the homefolks," Violet can never forget Rose Dear in the well water (99–101).

The reverse situation exists for Violet's grandfather, a figure rendered as vague as her father's phantom is distinct. When True Belle departs Vesper County for Baltimore in 1870 because "True Belle was the one [Vera Louise] wanted and the one she took," the black woman leaves behind daughters May and Rose Dear along with a husband. The narrator speculates about the accommodations possible when a slavewoman deserts a husband that "work and distance kept her from seeing much of anyhow" (141). Morrison constructs slyly ridiculous reactions, plausible only in a slave system, which rationalize the benefits of True Belle's exit: her daughters will be more help to whoever owns them than to a mother living miles away from her husband in order to take care of a rich man's daughter. Besides, how else would she get to travel? This ironic discussion, pointless because True Belle has no choice in the matter, overshadows the plight of her equally victimized husband, who does not even corporeally appear to have any say. Whether the men respond definitely idealistically or probably realistically, the Southern Empire and its aftermath construct and then reconstruct the lives of True Belle's and Rose Dear's husbands. The final blues note played out in Rome after the fall suggests that the absent black man's legacy becomes more useful to his family than the actual man's presence.

From "the little depot called Rome," we travel to Vienna, where we receive Morrison's Freudian riff on missing fathers and motherless sons (99). She introduces us to Joe's surrogate family and highlights two male members. "Steady as a rock," Mr. Frank Williams makes no distinction among any of his six children or the baby he and Mrs. Rhoda take in and name Joseph after her father when its parents disappear without a trace (125). Central to Joseph's childhood is the youngest Williams, Victory, whose relationship with Joe remains "closer than many brothers" (123). Joe turns toward Victory to clarify, when the teacher says Joe needs two names in order to enter school, why he signs his second one Trace. Trying to pick glass from his foot to avoid looking up, he informs his brother: "Your mama ain't my mama." Unable to say who is, he declares that "another woman" and his father are coming back for him. When Victory retorts that they left him at Williams's place, which is how they know him, the way they will find him, and what he should call himself, Joe argues: "They got to pick me out. From all of you all, they got to pick me. I'm Trace, what they went off without" (123–25).[4] The boy can never find the tiny shard of glass in his foot, nor does either of his parents ever come back to claim him.

He does get picked out, however, and along with Victory trained into manhood by the "best man in Vesper County to go hunting with." For abandoned and rootless Joe, this offers a father who is not only steady but who actually selects him "to teach and hunt with. Talk about proud-making." Morrison routinely uses skill in hunting—that is, tracking (*Song of Solomon*, *Tar Baby*, *Beloved*, *Paradise*)—as a trope for the process of black male identity formation. In *Jazz*, Joe names his mentor a "hunter's hunter," the black father who, standing calmly in his earned selfhood, teaches his sons how to survive the wild and in so doing provides them with life lessons that only nature, including the human kind, can reveal. To young black Joe this means "the secret of kindness from whitepeople—they had to pity a thing before they could like it" (125). Hunters Hunter also warns his boys never to kill the tender or anything female if they can help it. Most important, "[people] ain't prey. You got to know the difference" (175). Despite disparagement by "whitefolks" who reduce his griot to a "witch doctor," the boy hunter learns at least his first lesson well. Joe understands that "they said that so they wouldn't have to say he was smart" (125).

Andrea O'Reilly argues that selfhood in *Jazz* depends less on fathers than mothers, maintaining that Joe searches for his mother's garden in lieu of looking for his father's field (375). However, the fact that Joe does not mourn the loss of a father merely reemphasizes the significance of having been selected by one. Morrison explains that the slave system caused black families to be created, destroyed, and rearranged by white people. As such, the ability to choose and be chosen by loved ones remains an important by-product of slavery for the African American community. Joe does not need to find his missing father so much as to seek a sign from his secret mother because a respected father picks him out in public. Even Mrs. Rhoda constantly reminds Joe that he seems just "like" one of her own while Mr. Frank's impartiality could be also read as indifference.

Being selected among all others by a strong, self-assured father figure can be more useful to a black son than a family name, especially when the choice is mutual.

The same may be said for brothers. While Joe has been thrown with Victory since infancy, he also chooses Victory to be the friend and brother of his youth. Victory becomes Joe's natural if not biological tracking companion. The two hunt through and work in most of Vesper County until "nine hundred Negroes, encouraged by guns and hemp, left Vienna" (173). They walk with the others "the road to Bear, then Crossland, then Goshen, then Palestine," none of which proves to be holy ground for black boys, and then at thirteen set off on their own. Only Victory neither "laughed nor slant-eyed him" when Joe confesses his search for and shame about Wild: " 'She must be tough' was Victory's reply. 'Live outside like that all year round, she must be tough' " (178–79). Lacking gentle protection, these two design their own cradle together in the arms of a giant black walnut. Once Joe falls far from the tree, however, he cannot relocate or re-create it, but he can be confident that Victory will keep clear in his mind what does not appear even on a sheriff's map. Morrison burns many of Freud's theories about male child development along with Vienna. Hunters Hunter embodies Joe's real chosen father, whom Joe has no desire to kill; Joe does away with females who represent the absence of his mother, and, since Victory, Joe never gets that close to another brother. Though the possibility exists that prison may have rattled his friend, Joe remains convinced that if Victory were alive, he could be counted on to remember precisely the direction and location of their black family tree.

Joe finds himself foggy only about what he cannot track. Because he lacks clear signs pointing out why Hunters Hunter picked him, he continues to follow Wild all the way to Dorcas, the reasons for his journey buried deep within his subconscious.[5] No one tells him outright that he has a wild mother who frightens children. Staring straight at "Joe (not Victory)," however, Hunter comments that "Crazy people got reasons" when the boys joke about killing the wildwoman. He also warns them: "That woman is *somebody's* mother and *somebody* ought to take care" (175). Morrison reminds us that locating a (family) tree becomes difficult when "you're lost. Or if you do find it, it won't be the same. Maybe it cracked from the inside, bored through by crawling life that had to have its own way too, and just crept and bunched and gnawed and burrowed until the whole thing was pitted through with the service it rendered to others. Or maybe they cut it down before it crashed in on itself" (173).

Jazz's ruminations on the desecration of black families before and after Vienna burns take us into the central break of the novel: the story of Golden Gray.

In terms of a tragic five-act structure, the Golden Gray segment conveys the voices of fate and hamartia, which result in rising action and culminate in climax. In the case of *Jazz*, this means that the shaping hand of slavery leaves its print on Harlem's jazz generation. However, Morrison tweaks the classical form into a jazz break.[6] Critics have noted Golden Gray's nod in the direction of Charles Bon. Certainly Morrison, like Faulkner, uses her fictional county to depict the tragedy of miscegenation and incest in the Old South. In addition, the names of its people and places suggest a romantically classic South. News that his beautiful daughter Vera Louise is with child by a "Negro boy from out Vienna way" renders wordless Colonel Wordsworth Gray, patriarch of Vesper County's county seat, Wordsworth, and his own Big House. Her allusions to the neoclassical poet responsible for England's most famous elegy and the poet who ushered in its romantic movement help Morrison exaggerate and then comically deflate a romantic Faulknerian theme. Standing up, sitting down, standing again, left hand frantically patting the air, the colonel looks deeply hurt for a few seconds, after which his rage "swamped and flooded the room." Sweating out "the terrible thing that had happened to his daughter . . . for there were seven mulatto children on his land," he takes the only appropriate action. After slapping Vera Louise into the serving table, he lays a lingerie case on her pillow full of so much money "the message was indisputable: die, or live if you like, elsewhere" (140–41). Vera (Louis)e, like Henry (Sutpen) and Charles (Bon) in *Absalom, Absalom!*, derives her name from the traditional epithets of serious French royalty. While pampered Vera's name also means "true," it is True Belle and Henry LesTroy, continuing to serve their people despite their laughter, who turn out to be the real thing.

Vesper County's star-crossed union produces a beautiful boy child of golden skin, gray eyes, and champagne-colored curls. Born into Baltimore luxury, spoiled fussy by the nouvelle suffragette Vera Louise, and indulged by a "laughing, laughing" True Belle, Golden Gray grows up believing himself to be the Fauntleroy figure that Vera Louise dresses him as and reads him romantic stories about. The "out-of-state newcomer, rich and headstrong," finds nothing to do with her life but read, write renegade pamphlets, and adore the so-called "orphaned baby she fancied." Bereft of other family, True Belle feeds Golden her "test cakes" and picks the seeds from his melon (139–40). Thus, two variations on the myth of southern womanhood, a fallen pedestal lady and a mocking rescuing mammy, focus all their maternal energy onto an only child and a son at that. True Belle, however, at least attempts to stay real through the release of laughter, though she sends the Golden boy food baskets every week he remains at boarding school, gives away frayed shirts rather than let him wear them, and then toasts his majority by mapping out the location of his father. These actions require the tough love of a true woman, not the faux lady who "lied to him about practically everything including the question of whether she was his owner, his mother or a kindly neighbor," except after eighteen years the fact that "his father was a black-skinned nigger" (143).

Jazz offers two possible takes on Charles Bon's "expression you might call smiling but which was not" (*Absalom, Absalom!* 319) when it becomes Golden Gray's "smileless smile" (*Jazz* 156). Is this young man whose "yellow curls covered his coat like a farmer's" what "True Belle loved and Violet too. Or the vain and hincty pinchnose worrying about his coat and the ivory buttons on his waistcoat? Come all that way to insult not his father but his race" (143)? Morrison's deliberate ambiguity with respect to Golden Gray may be a response to the shot she takes at a previous "high-yellow dream child" in *The Bluest Eye* (62). During a conversation with Gloria Naylor, she admits to showing unfairly only a "façade" of the Maureen Peal that "everybody has . . . in his or her life": "I never got in her because I didn't want to go there. I didn't like her. I never have done that since. I've always regretted the speed with which I executed that girl. She worked well structurally for [Claudia and Frieda] and this and that, but if I were doing that book now, I would write her section or talk about her that way plus from inside" (581).

Like Maureen, who "suffered as much as a Pecola Breedlove did in this society," Golden Gray aches just like Joe Trace (Naylor and Morrison 581). The narrator notes that it "had rocked [Golden] when he heard who and what his father was. Made him loose, lost." He fingers then tears his mother's clothes, sits pondering things scattered in the grass as well as images messing up his mind, and breathes in the sour smell of despair. His True Belle helps him up from the lawn, washes his hair, and tells him how to find what is left of his father: "It don't matter if you do find him or not; it's the going that counts" (159). We go with him to discover the Golden Gray who, despite potential ruin to his beautiful linen, cannot shake the sight of a naked, muddy, berry-black woman alone and wounded in the woods. Starting to drive off, he stops when he cannot reconcile the "pride he takes in his [shiny black] horse, the nausea the woman provoked" and goes back to see about his vision. He spots her pregnant but unconscious body, and, uneasy at the prospect of remembering the picture of himself walking away a second time, he carries her to his carriage in a burst of recklessness calculated to "defend himself against patricide. Maybe" (144–45).

This is the Golden Gray who "scrapes the mud from his Baltimore soles before he enters a cabin with a dirt floor." Reining in his horse as the rain stops and the road dips down into a valley, he begins to "hear things outside himself," to pity the sight of a rocker without arms that lies on its side in a fenced-in dirt yard (150–51). Wondering whether or not to retrieve the broken rocker and rearranging his clothes on the cot in Hunter's cabin move him to tears. In essence, Golden's awareness of his newfound pain presents him with the possibility of understanding somebody else's. His elaborate clothing now reminds him of "an empty man with one arm folded under." Before he hears about his father, he thinks callously that everyone lives "one-armed like [him]. Now [he feels] the surgery." He recognizes his father's "absence: the place where he should have been and was not" and realizes there is no remedy for it but to "go away from where he is not to where he used to be and might be still." He denies feeling anger. He intends, however, not to be healed but to "freshen the pain" so that they "both know what it is for." Refusing his need for the arm, Golden does want "to know what it could have been like to have had it," to behold the phantom father: "I will locate it so the severed part can remember the snatch, the slice of its disfigurement" (158–59). The boy who locates his blues can now "finger its jagged grain" (Ellison 78–79).

But because his pain does not feel color-coded or connected to blood, he can ask himself: "What do I care what the color of his skin is, or his contact with my mother?" Because he understands the longing for authenticity, for "a right to be in this place, effortlessly without needing to acquire a false face, a laughless grin, a talking posture," he can hope to tell his father "all about the missing part of [himself] and listen for his [father's] crying shame," saying: "I will exchange then; let him have mine and take his as my own and we will both be free, arm-tangled and whole." The young man who musters the strength to look into Wild's doe eyes with the "dawning gray of his own" may also find "the courage to do what Duchesses of Marlborough do all the time: relinquish being an adored bud clasping its future, and dare to open wide, to let the layers of its petals go flat, show the cluster of stamens dead center for all to see" (159–60). Morrison does yeoman service during Golden's break of repairing her mistake with Maureen Peal. Despite his self-deception and his "grand fake gestures," this Golden Boy, like the high-yellow dream girl, is still a child in pain (155). By sympathizing with Golden Gray's missing arm, we come to realize the significance for Joe Trace of just seeing his mother's hand.

Because his adopted family accepts him for who he is and is not, even an unmothered Joe becomes capable of caring for that family and himself. Rejection by her family causes Vera Louise to experience ambivalence toward the boy, possibly even brother, with whom she rides in the woods.[7] Delivering his child, she neither sees nor names him again, which creates not only hatred but self-hatred in their son. Likewise, Wild's sexuality both attracts and repulses Golden. He attempts to avoid her by "not looking to see what he could see of her private parts, the shock of knowing the hair there, once it was dry, was thick enough to part with a fingernail." He tries to hide her under his coat, to drape over her the shiny green dress he does not realize belongs to his mother, but the girl appears more naked under both than before he covers her. She also looks violent, but "that is because she is exposed under that long coat, and there is nothing to prevent Golden Gray from believing that an exposed woman will explode in his arms, or worse, that he will in hers" (153). The boy shapes a chivalric white Western story that will impress his honor and restraint upon his biracial father and claims simultaneously his bragging rights as the cool black knight errant, who blows apart its conventional ending by rescuing the fiery dragon: "Except this monster without scales or flaming breath is more dangerous for she is a bloody-faced girl of moving parts, of luminous eyes and lips to break your heart" (154–55).

Thus, despite her sympathy for his suffering, Morrison also responds to her golden boy like Golden does to Wild: as if she "didn't want to go there" (Naylor and Morrison 581). Then he turns into the lying hypocrite, the Golden Gray who seriously considers passing. While Vera Louise looks anxiously and True Belle shakes her head in amusement at the palms of his hands and the texture of his hair, he thinks naïvely that there is only one kind of nigger: "True Belle's kind. Black and nothing. Like Henry LesTroy. Like the filthy woman snoring on the cot." He is, however, too abruptly introduced to "another kind—like himself" (149). Like Marie Cardinal's "first encounter with the Thing" (*Playing in the Dark* vi), Golden's torn reaction to the "awful-looking thing lying in wet weeds" occurs because it represents "a thing that touched him before its fall," the thing in the averted glances of the servants at boarding school or in True Belle's smile, a thing that comforts as much as it frightens. Morrison attributes the collapse of the delicate, Algerian-born French girl to the fact that a black woman has been the child's "first and major love, which may be why two gallops beyond that hair, that skin, their absence was unthinkable." On the other hand, Cardinal's vision prefigures that of Golden as "everything he was not as well as a proper protection against and anodyne to what he believed his father to be, and therefore (if it could just be contained, identified)—himself."[8] Although Golden Gray shudders at the thought that Wild might touch him, "it is also true that he [as Morrison overcame hers about him] overcame the shudder" (149–50).

Furthermore, he survives a touchy introduction to his father. The world of Wordsworth knows the virile black man, who has located his identity, assumed his role as griot, and been dubbed a hunter's hunter by the men in his community, as Henry LesTroy or Lestory or "something like that" (148). Although Henry's unpolished appearance and primitive surroundings suggest fallen Troys, Philip Page describes him as "the story" in the sense that Hunters Hunter has "perfected the story's principal metaphor, tracking" (164). Because, however, he "never knew [Golden Gray] was in the world," his own son unexpectedly traps him when Golden hunts him down (171).

Patty's boy Honor witnesses their encounter. Instructed by Mr. Henry to "see bout the stock," the thirteen-year-old black boy who first faces Golden Gray from the back of a mule is already incredibly well trained in the art of tracking. He notes at once the intoxication of the creamy-skinned man lurching down the steps of Hunter's cabin and assumes he has come to collect pelts or wild turkeys.[9] He determines the man to be white from his "smileless smile," even though he "saw Mr. Henry's face when the whiteman told him he was his son," and infers his social status from the clothes of a "gent who sleeps in his own yard after a big party rather than in his wife's bed" (155–56, 168). Sensing that he should wait to be spoken to and glad for the questions that follow instead of statements "nobody wanted to hear," he concludes from Golden's queries that a drunk white gentleman seeks but does not know Mr. Henry (156). Honor goes immediately on his guard and remains deliberately vague with his answers. The only emotion he reveals, which Golden's terror prohibits perception of, is pride in responsibility. Morrison's version of Honor inverts romantic suppositions. While Golden might assess him as boorish and recalcitrant, the boy willingly but cagily carries out his duties to his mentor and his people with pride and honor.

Anticipating Hunter's instructions to Joe and Victory about protecting the young and, when possible, the female, Honor also treats Wild with skill and compassion. Even at his tender age, he has seen enough men slumped over a plow, women worn out from childbirth, and children stillborn to "know the difference between the quick and the dead." He detects life in the body lying naked under Vera Louise's gown. Never lifting his eyes from the girl's face, except to glance briefly at the man who rummaged through Mr. Henry's rooms to find the dress to lay on her, he pats the slash on her forehead with its sleeve and finds her face "fire hot," the blood "dry as skin." He says one word, "Water," and abruptly leaves the cabin (162). Golden Gray remains rooted. Although the biracial man-boy can go neither forward nor back, the black boy returns with well water, which he dribbles into the black girl's mouth, and then removes large patches of blood from her face with a clean burlap sack. Kneeling by the cot while Golden towers above, Honor continues his care as the rough-hewn manor lord enters, succinctly encapsulating for Mr. Henry the problem and its probable cause in the same breath he relays the status of his farm chores. Honor and Henry pull a reluctant baby from the womb of a hostile Wild while "the city man looked faint" (170). Honor also goes to fetch his mother and more cane liquor when the new mother refuses to nurse her newborn. Answering all of Mr. Henry's commands with a crisp "Yes sir!" his actions are worlds away from those of the man's son, who rudely violates his father's house and all its rules of hospitality as he runs cold eyes arrogantly up Hunter's body like a scathing hot tongue.

Morrison depicts their confrontation by inverting the terms of a Western/western shoot-out, revealing how race confuses expected signs and preconceived notions. Quickly sizing up indications of Golden's ineffectual masculinity in his thin boots, elegant clothes, soft hands, and absent pistol, Hunter tosses his woodcock in the corner but keeps his rifle in his arm and his hat on his head. He checks the level of his uncapped liquor bottle and, wondering at his visitor's insolence or carelessness, asks directly if they know each other, the bang in his question its omission of "sir." However, the boy "didn't hear it because he had a bang of his own. 'No. Daddy. We don't' " (170). Their conversation then becomes a semicomic showdown of cultures, the pale son's oblique challenges countered levelly by his perception of the "blackest man in the world" (157). The attitude of the smart-mouthed squire toward his war-weary knight is haughty and disrespectful.[10] Despite his initial shock, Hunter maintains a patiently cautious distance until the son questions whether or not his father ever thought "about her? Wonder where she was?" Hunter immediately supposes the reference to be True Belle and smiles when he asks about her. His response when Golden's subject turns out to be Vera Louise points up the gulf between their perspectives toward "my mother!" and "yo' mama!": "Aw, man. What I look like wondering where a whitegirl went?" Dark-skinned son, probably of a white man and a black woman, Hunter assumes his mother's race but rides with a girl of his father's; light-skinned son of a black man and a white woman, Golden takes his mother's race but carries on with a girl of his father's. Refusing to bite at his boy's bitter sarcasm by saying calmly that the name Golden Lestory simply wouldn't suit well "in these [Western] parts," the older man turns to baby Joe, who needs more immediate attention. Golden's reaction: "How touching" (171–72).

At this juncture the father talks man-to-man with his son. Hunter informs Golden that he is welcome to stay but not to criticize and that he must act like a civilized adult: "Get a hold of yourself. A son ain't what a woman say. A son is what a man do. You want to act like you mine, then do it, else get the devil out my house!" When the boy complains that he does not want to be a "free nigger" but a "free man," Hunter retorts: "Don't we all. Look. Be what you want—white or black. Choose. But if you choose black, you got to act black, meaning draw your manhood up—quicklike, and don't bring me no whiteboy sass" (172–73). Although a suddenly sober Golden Gray entertains notions of blowing Hunters Hunter's head off—tomorrow—the Gray boy's romantic white illusions are blasted sky high by the Hunter man's shrewd black realism. Or perhaps by the girl.

The "sweet but abused" young thing that Hunter names Wild because she bites his face when he turns his cheek to tend her becomes the constant companion of Golden Gray and a memory precious to her caregiver. Because a hunter's hunter is "more used to wood life than tame," he identifies the new mother immediately as "touchy": "Oh, she's wild. Thinking, some things are like that. There's no gain fathoming more." Thirteen years later the by-then old man senses again the eyes watching him as Wild when he sights them in the cane field level with his feet, her touch at his shoulder.[11] Unafraid but sad, he thinks maybe if he "had handled it right," she (and, earlier, Vera) would have remained in the house, rested, and perhaps not craved "hair the color of a young man's name." Those who spot her and "that queer boy she set so much store by" have a "regular jolt: the young man's head of yellow hair long as a dog's tail next to her skein of black wool." The two of them take their place in community myth. Wild comes to be the sweet disruption that can especially overwhelm pregnant girls, young men, and even unprepared grandfathers like Hunters Hunter when they start dreaming about her low "babygirl laugh" (166–67). Golden Gray becomes both the thing to fear that makes him beautiful (but not her) and the cocky rooster she holes up with "like a dog in a cave," his clothes "all mixed up with hers." Together they inhabit a cavern of sun, a "private place, with an opening closed to the public," where "once inside you could do what you pleased:

disrupt things, rummage, touch and move. Change it all to a way it was never meant to be" (182–84).

The possibilities open to a boy who walks on Wild's side are myriad, seductive, and dangerous. However, masculine self-development requires exploring Mother Nature and assimilating the primitive. Wild's son remains aware of three solitary journeys he makes looking for this brain-blasting witch woman who is "everywhere and nowhere" but "still out there—and real" (179, 167). In Vienna, Joe lives through fearing her, then joking about, obsessing over, and finally rejecting her. Hunter's fallen Troy teaches him to appreciate her and to spot her presence by the blue-black male redwings that flock to her side and the stolen honey she likes to eat. His initial, halfhearted search occurs after a dawn of spectacular fishing when he hears with pleasure what he thinks to be "music the world makes." However, he identifies the sounds as a woman's voice when he detects words, since he knows that woods music makes no sense. Finding traces of Wild that track to the entrance of her "hide," he calls out to her but declines to enter when its fragrance of mixed "honey and shit" leaves him "disgusted and not a little afraid" (175–77). Joe's first taste of sex is sour.

He worries when Freud's Vienna burns that his Wild had confused fire with "flowers moving toward her, or flying golden hair" and "lost her breath to it" (174–75). To reassure himself that she remains alive, he returns to the fertile fishing hole and drops to his haunches. Climbing above the opening to slide inside, he perceives cold signs of human life and "nothing a woman could use." He drowses briefly while he waits for her, finally hauling himself out, but as he turns to go, four redwing blackbirds "shoot up from the lower limbs of a white-oak tree" (178). This white matriarch is huge, isolated, on thin soil, and entwined in its own roots. On hands and knees before it, Joe hears the breathing of someone who refuses him the slightest sign of presence. Bowing, like Lady Chatterley, to Westernized shame about sex with a primitive lover, Joe suddenly views Wild as indecent and himself as ridiculous. His beloved woods, full of her, become tainted; angry at himself, he fires his rifle at the tree. He does no harm only because the shells are still in his pocket.

He does do himself damage by giving up on an inside bed-life for work. Sleeping little or outside, Joe falls on Violet asleep beneath the broken sleeping tarp in his black walnut tree and labors even harder after she claims him. But he attempts one more time to locate Wild. He goes down to the river white people call Treason after the treachery of the "very ground you walked on" and finds the white tree whose roots retreat to its trunk for "what was needed." Morrison's description of Joe trying to give birth to himself, or make passionate love to the forbidden white lady, or Wild, or Violet, is comically lyrical. Risking a path that could swallow "[his] whole self," sticking his head in the invitingly hidden hole to discover "pitch dark" and a "domestic smell" that leads him on, Joe almost backs out until light "hit him so hard he flinched." Driven to burrow but going nowhere, "Treason River glistening below," he spots the crevice. Entry on his behind feels like "falling into the sun. Noon light followed him like lava into a stone room where somebody cooked in oil." As he floats in an orgasm of tranquil watchfulness, the color of the cave walls changes from gold to blue, and he sees what there is to see.[12] The sights include a "green dress. A rocking chair without an arm. . . . But where is *she*?" (182–84). As she mixes metaphors of sex and birth, dark and light, black and white, wild and tame, male and female, young and old, poor and rich, Morrison changes it all to a way it was never meant to be. As long as Wild, repressed or unleashed, remains Joe's sweet "Thing," however, he cannot hope to inhabit freely an undercover world with Violet. As a result, he must take a fourth solitary journey during which he confuses his clothes all up with hers. Until he is able to sort it out, though, the "hers" also stay mixed up in his head: mother, Wild, lady, lover, Dorcas, daughter, wife, Violet, woman.

We have traveled along country roads with Morrison's black Joe to see how darkness in America plays out as blues tragedy. We then track him into the city where he penetrates Wild/Dorcas's chamber of light and becomes reborn once more to walk with Violet into a tragicomic jazz place "both snug and wide open" (221). Joe leaves the woods for the wrong reasons. Encouraged by Hunter to love women, he runs from the Wild he can neither find nor control; accustomed to the woodsman's solitude, he does not fear urban loneliness. Here Morrison inverts the Shakespearean technique of shifting from court to green world and back again. While the playwright's characters get in touch with the wild in their nature by retiring to woods, islands, forests, or taverns, the novelist's people simply relocate Wild in the city. However, Morrison notes that urban values conflict with those of the tribe, and therein lies the function of her novels:

> I agree with John Berger that peasants don't write novels because they don't need them. They have a portrait of themselves from gossip, tales, music, and some celebrations. That is enough. The middle class at the beginning of the industrial revolution needed a portrait of itself because the old portrait didn't work for this new class. Their roles were different; their lives in the city were

> new. The novel served this function then, and it still does. It tells about the city values, the urban values. Now my people, we "peasants," have come to the city, that is to say, we live with its values. There is a confrontation between old values of the tribes and new urban values. It's confusing. There has to be a mode to do what the music did for blacks, what we used to be able to do with each other in private and in that civilization that existed underneath the white civilization. I think this accounts for the address of my books. (LeClair 371)

Thus, even reestablished in the city, Morrison's peasant men remember the black and white blues voices left behind. Though they have to rent rooms "smaller than the heifer's stall and darker than a morning privy," they stay to stroll along the street among multitudes who "moved the way they did, and who, when they spoke, regardless of the accent, treated language like the same intricate, malleable toy designed for their play" (33). Part of what they love is the apparition they abandon. This includes veterans betrayed by commanders for whom they fought fiercely, longshoremen paid far less than comparable white laborers, strike breakers hired by Mr. Armour, Mr. Swift, or Mr. Montgomery Ward and then fired for being successful. They follow the "four-day hangings in Rocky Mount: the men on Tuesday" and the young church tenor "mutilated and tied to a log" (101). For Joe, the specter involves Harlan Ricks and Clayton Bede, who successively own the poorest soil in Vesper County. He and Violet work together to turn white men's rocks into crops; they accrue only debt that, what with interest and items from the company store, quadruples. It takes them five years to pay it off. On the other hand, city peasants like to recollect the vision of men "who wore hats to plow and to eat supper in; who blew into saucers of coffee, and held knives in their fists when they ate" (71). The sight of tall Joe with his country smile and sad eyes touches city women, moved even more by the blues note in his voice.

It takes the city to remove the steady blues pitch of Joe's voice and transform it into the unpredictable jazz tones of possibility. Jazz has been called both "the music of the collective" and "the music of boundless individualism" and so supports Morrison's view that others help shape subjectivity (Berendt 161). The city also rebuilds the structure of blues tragedy into jazz tragicomedy. Grewal defines Morrison's city as "a place of deliverance, the northern city being what the southern town of Palestine was not: the promised land" (125). This explains why "the main tradition of black American literature has been persistently pro-urban in vision" (Butler 9). The city dances with Morrison's peasants even before they put shoe leather to pavement. It says in the speech of some "hometown buddy," "Man, you best . . . pack your suitcase and don't bring no high-top shoes," seduces them to be their "stronger, riskier selves," and thus makes them vulnerable to the hubris that precedes a tragic fall—or makes possible comic fulfillment (32–33).

The *Jazz* city suggests Morrison's place of contradiction. Slanting daylight slices the buildings in half, leaving cold-looking white faces at the top and a civilization of shadow below where "any blasé thing takes place: clarinets and lovemaking, fists and the voices of sorrowful women" (7). The same streets that arouse jealousy "too late for anything but foolishness" can produce a "crooked kind of mourning for a rival young enough to be a daughter" (111). The people down there in the shade feel "top-notch and indestructible," happy and looking up. Morrison does a marvelous job of lyrically re-creating the hep hope that created New York's "New Negro" Renaissance: "Hoodlums hand out goodies, do their best to stay interesting, and since they are being watched for excitement, they pay attention to their clothes and the carving out of insults." Her narrator admits that "Nobody says it's pretty here; nobody says it's easy either. What it is is decisive, and if you pay attention to the street plans, all laid out, the City can't hurt you." Being street-smart means wearing your best poker face while you watch everybody else closely to figure out what they will do before they do it. It means being "welcoming and defensive at the same time," aware that the city encourages people to "think they can do what they want and get away with it." Without this road skill, folks end up like Joe and Violet: "out of control or controlled by some outside thing" (7–9).

The possibilities for tragedy, then, become paramount at this time in the city. Its black people are susceptible to hubris, and here the peasant is allowed his tragic fall. Classical tragedy typically presents the downfall of a person of significance. However, in American culture, unlike European, the protagonist may be even a slave of noble spirit, who faces fate with dignity and courage. Similarly, jazz history and criticism traditionally concentrate on the big names, but, in fact, "perhaps ninety percent of the music has always been made by unknown players" (Collier 263–64). In her *Jazz*, Morrison moves away from the "glamorous class of writers and musicians patronized by whites" to reclaim marginalized "foot soldiers": the local players, the door-to-door salesmen, hairdressers, office cleaners, and factory workers (Grewal 123–34).

Because the city can perform its riff on an expansive country night sky, these rooftop jazzmen get pumped not so much by love as desire. As they and the city grow up together, they come to love the way they seem in the city so much they "forget what loving other people was like—if they ever knew, that is." They brighten themselves by taking in city breath like laughing gas every morning and forget about stars "made irrelevant by the light of thrilling, wasteful street lamps." When the city does its unbelievable sky, they can be diverted from dreaming about the trash, and flowers, buried deep down in the ocean or the maggots, and mushrooms, thriving under a rock. When this sky "go[es] purple but keep[s] an orange heart," redcaps reminiscing about country skies glimpsed from train cars as well as "sweethearts, free and illegal, tell[ing] each other things" can completely miss it drifting "beautiful as an Iroquois" past their windows (35–36). As here, Morrison's rendition of the erotic results "less from a particular carnal web [and more from] emotional longings, buried histories, a suppressed past haunting the present" (Brown 632).

Such unsatisfied desire causes city men to stay armed. Morrison depicts city hunters who keep their hats on their heads and their weapons at hand, "men of every description" who remain on the defensive (35). Some appear overtly angry. Like Joe, or Felice's mother, they resent white men who loud- or soft-talk them out of a piece of the rock in Inwood or Tiffany's. They see red at thousands of whites who accept an invitation to "come see a colored man burn alive" (128). Even when Armistice is seven years old, veterans on Seventh Avenue wear "their army-issue greatcoats," partly because "nothing they can pay for is as sturdy or hides so well what they had boasted of in 1919" and partly because they are still not safe from "fays and the things they think up" (9–10). It turns into a cold day in July 1917 when Alice Manfred stands for three hours on Fifth Avenue to watch beautiful men march in protest of the St. Louis race riots and listens to them heat up drums that communicate what their frozen faces cannot. Even when they meet openly, they express covertly things they think but do not trust themselves to speak.[13]

Hurt by the cold faces and the hot drums, Alice becomes afraid of the men's music. While she senses that its tone has something to do with silent African American males dancing down streets to profess or contain their rage over two hundred dead, she judges jazz as that "lowdown stuff" signaling "Imminent Demise" (56). Despite her reservation, the seamstress inadvertently makes what may be the most lyrical address ever for the "complicated anger" that defines jazz. A combination of hostility and appetite, it longs "for the bash, the slit"; it reflects "a kind of careless hunger for a fight or a ruby red stickpin for a tie—either would do." It "faked happiness, faked welcome, but it did not make her feel generous, this juke joint, barrel hooch, tonk house, music. It made her hold her hand in the pocket of her apron to keep from smashing it through the glass pane to snatch the world in her fist and squeeze the life out of it for doing what it did and did and did to her and everybody else she knew or knew about" (59).

Music represents merely one of the ways men in the city discover to "accommodate themselves to tall buildings and wee porches" (34). Some turn out to be just the average black Joe on the street. Morrison's narrator frowns at Alice for reading too many newspapers that tell her "too little about too much" and not spending enough time watching how individuals maneuver themselves on streets that will "confuse you, teach you, or break your head" (72). The seamstress misses blind men who see clearly enough not to compete with the old uncles playing six-string guitars on sidewalks, the "blacktherefore" bluesmen well positioned on crates to indulge peg legs while their real ones carry "the beat and the guitar's weight" (119). She skips over the colored saxophonist who floats placidly down from sky high and the young trumpeters on top of roofs who play so sacred people would think things had been forgiven, their maple-sugar runs "pure and steady and kind of kind." Only brass cut as fine as a "young girl singing by the side of a creek, passing the time" can outdo the lowdown clarinets (196). Never having seen her, the young men make her up on rooftops without protective railings, rooftops with sleeping pallets and tomatoes planted in lard cans.

Though it is mostly the women who wonder "how long, how long," men, too, find alternative means to sing out time and space (56). Alice avoids hearing sidewalk preachers with "long-distance eyes" perched precariously on wooden boxes or broken chairs while listeners crowd close to shout insults or chime in with the right word at the right time (223). She does not see the men who dig deep holes in the streets to make room for more high buildings. She most certainly shies away from the birds.[14] These include the man in the straw hat who tilts the earnest girl's face toward his to remove a speck from her lip. His hand on the wall over her head and the turn of his jaw signal his silver tongue. Alice goes nowhere near the singing men in spats that Joe calls "sweetbacks." These are the twenty-year-olds who shine "like patent leather," lean their heads in together to croon, fingers snapping, coats arranged artfully across shoulders, closed off from him by something they have that he wants (132). These wise young roosters with silk handkerchiefs instead of gun handles sticking out of belted jacket pockets need not track anybody because the chicks trail them.

The chicks even find the place. Morrison takes some of her roosters off the street to touch their inside part. These indoor birds range from Malvonne's nephew Sweetness, who steals stuff out of a local mailbox after which he alters his name from William Younger and becomes Little Caesar, to Dorcas's first dancing partner, Martin, who "had been in her elocution class for a hot minute." Martin's teacher gives up on him when she realizes that "he would never relinquish 'ax' for 'ask'" (66). Malvonne does not realize until too late that the good behavior of the nephew she has reared since he was seven is restricted to daytime hours and does not extend into her nighttime office shift. Sweetness has long since left to wreak havoc as emperor of some "city ending with O" (41). Sixteen-year-old Dorcas does not get to step out with either of the short brothers to whom she offers up her tall body in exchange for a dance. Such easy movers that they resort to each other for partners when competition gets tough, the boys turn on their smiles when Dorcas moves toward them out of the shadows. Sustaining eye contact while they look her over, one brother whispers to the other who immediately wrinkles his nose, his "smile bright as ever," and the smooth-as-steel high-steppers turn her away as they turn away from her. Dorcas becomes "acknowledged, appraised and dismissed in the time it takes for a needle to find its opening groove." The brothers deem her body, although "young and all she has," as unworthy as a bud bitten on the vine. The city beckons her to "Come and do wrong," but Dorcas is not able to give herself away to boys that she cannot possibly realize are in all likelihood homosexual (67).

Such humiliation makes it doubly important to her that she capture the cock of the walk. While, even because, Joe allows her to work the "stick of the world, the power in [her] hand," she rejects the old rooster for a new hawkeyed lover (191). Acton represents Dorcas's ticket to an adult bash where a small charge covers openly illegal liquor, unforbidden secrets, and "dressed-up nakedness." Morrison reenvisions the self-centered callousness of Faulkner's college crew when satisfaction for Dorcas becomes "Two arms [that] clasp her" and the ability to "rest her cheek on her own shoulder while her wrists cross behind his neck." No white in his mustache, Acton is "up-and-coming . . . tireless and a little cruel," gifted with touching without feeling. Unlike attentive Joe, he is selective, unreliable, and plies her with no presents. His "savvy self" incorporates his greatest not-free prize, which any self-less girl would feel lucky to get. Her catch traps Dorcas, who feels "as happy as she has ever been anytime" (188).

Morrison writes as savagely as Faulkner about the predatory tendencies of the young, especially when they smell blood. When the red wash spills over onto them, however, they find it distasteful. Acton acts embarrassed when he has to hold Dorcas up after Joe shoots her shoulder at the party and annoyed that her blood has stained his shirt right through his best jacket. Although Joe remains ecstatic about whatever kind of woman Dorcas wants to be, "Something about that made [her] mad." Dorcas declines the responsibility, and the messiness, of slowly making her own self and substitutes instead the fast personality that she acquires from Acton. Her friend Felice describes the attitude of males when love becomes possession as "treat[ing] her bad" and the female position as "having friends who want you to have him, and enemies who don't" (216). The very language of power reduces love to war. It also shoves the self way off balance.

Alice is partly right to fear that the crows of young roosters and the coos of baby chicks signal Imminent Demise. Black men and women in the city wound each other constantly. However, it is not the music that kills them but something unwell in the cultural water. Emasculated by white men, who fondle black men's women in kitchens and bargain basements, call their wives "out of their names every single day of their lives," and put "fists in women's faces so the husbands' spirits would break along with the women's jaws," some sweet black men exchange soft bed pillows for night-walking the hard streets (78). Smothered by black women, who become enchanted by the possibility of a romantic paradise and the "frail, melty tendency of the flesh," some, such as Neola Miller's fiancé, flee the state (63). Others hurt their women. Headlines scream: "Man kills wife. Eight accused of rape dismissed. Woman and girl victims of. Woman commits suicide. . . . Woman says man beat. In jealous rage man" (74). Still others, like the frowning men and the white-gloved but hard-handed usher boys at Dorcas's funeral, throw women out of the church.

Black women, however, have learned to fight back. Armed and dangerous, those with the least money choose the deadliest weapons. Morrison's lethal humor underscores the Swedish tailor smiling his wonder at the "Negress" who cuts him from earlobe to teeth and renders ironic the iceman whose neck reveals four evenly spaced ice-pick, or meat-fork, holes. Black men run through the streets "holding one red wet hand in the other, a flap of skin on the face," arriving alive at hospitals sometimes only because "they left the razor where it lodged" (77). The women who shun blades, lye, or glass take up God, church, money, clubs, or armed men: "Any other kind of unarmed black woman in 1926 was silent or crazy or dead" (78).

Silent and crazy but not yet dead, *that* (Wild) Violet defends herself on the day of Dorcas's funeral by releasing her parrot. This unnamed exotic, unanswered except for "Go on off somewhere" as it squawks "Love you" weakly on the frozen windowsill, receives the complicated anger Violet puts aside when "mother-hunger had hit her like a hammer" (93, 108). Her treatment of her imported substitute father/husband/son also shows the indirect abuse suffered by domesticated "birds" at the hands of unsatisfied women. Violet has not yet learned how to love. Her need to possess, indicated at seventeen when she tells Joe to "find somebody else's tree," continues into their marriage as she calls a cherished pet merely "My parrot" (104, 93). Challenging out of desperation bird and man to "freeze or fly," Violet confronts simultaneously the knife lost for weeks, found finally in the parrot's cage and used to cut its beak as well as Dorcas's face, and the habit her husband has become, one of those routine "necessary things for the night" (3, 27). She deals with her responsibility for violating the parrot's nails and ignoring Joe's needs by letting both go. Recognizing from her own hurt that wounded males tremble and forget how to fly, she makes her two "manage somehow to fly away on wings that had not soared for six years. Wings grown stiff from disuse and dull in the bulb light of an apartment with no view to speak of" (93). Morrison refers to the something in the not-so-well water that causes black men and women to attack one another as the master narrative and the white gaze: the ill effects of certain American attitudes on African immigrants.[15] African Americans make love, music, or war with one another to counteract being controlled by some outside thing.

Jazz suggests that this keen aversion to cages appears even in males with an inside track. Powerful white men confined in 40th Street offices cannot spot the cleaning lady clearly enough to conceal their indiscretions. Invisible to them, Malvonne looks at desk photographs, examines wastebaskets, or listens to "hallway conversation" and "bathroom laughter." As a result, she understands who "had a passion for justice as well as ladies' undergarments, who loved his wife and who shared one. The one who fought with his son and would not speak to his father" (41). However, she is more interested in watching the neighborhood people. She knows that pride "cuts down the pain" of being sliced in the Harlem Hospital emergency room if the Negro surgeon wields the scalpel (7). She observes Duggie the druggist hiding little tables behind a rickety magazine rack "against the law that said if he did it, it made the place a restaurant" (93). While the weapons of assimilated front men appear generally less obvious than those of black Joes on the street, they aim no less precisely to break down barriers.

Old cocks, who accommodate to tall buildings and wee porches by losing touch with Wild, exist no less subject to violence. Their deaths are simply slower. If the "young are not so young" in the city, the men who manage to reach forty frequently turn into husbands "hunting an open market" or uncles who sit around reviewing or butting into other people's business.[16] Some, such as those in attendance at Violet's baby stealing, "slap the children for being slappable" (11). When Violet lifts baby brother Philly from his carriage and laughs to beat the band, the disgust in a man's voice, "You left a whole live baby with a stranger to go get a record?" reduces big sister to tears and adds years to the man's age. Others become long-distance parents. Felice's cold-eyed father has seen his daughter "less than two years out of seventeen." Frustrated by secondhand political periodicals that he will not forego though they "worr[y] his blood," Walter wants either to sleep when he comes home from Tuxedo Junction where he works or to be waited on by somebody else (199–200). After he gives up living in the country to go out on the road, he remains equally argumentative but far more arrogant as a "proud Pullman porter." He gets to confirm that the world contains two kinds of whitepeople, the "ones that feel sorry for you and the ones that don't." He also gets to be tickled that both are scared to compete with Negroes who "play baseball 'in the flesh and on the lot, goddamnit' " (204). Reading a letter addressed to Panama stolen by Sweetness, Malvonne learns about Winsome Clark's husband, who does not make enough money doing a dangerous job in the Canal Zone to keep his wife and children afloat. Winsome's husband loses them all when his "dearest wife," wishing that he not worry "except to stay among the quick," has to take a slow boat back to both their mothers in Barbados (43).

Malvonne also discovers that some old cocks use home as headquarters to raid the henhouse next door. "Perspiring and breathing lightly," she worries over what to do with a steamy letter stamped to Mr. M. Sage by his lover in the same building and finally decides to mail it together with a cautionary note and subtle instructions that "daddy" read *Opportunity Magazine* (44). Alice's husband turns into another such sly cock bitten by Wild late in life. Gone to his grave are the lips and hands with which he had kissed and lifted Alice, and another, but the smile that forces her to force him to choose still has teeth in it. Her access to the invisible stitches that help heal Violet comes from Alice's realization that for seven solid months she thirsted for the blood of a woman "with a taste for brightly colored dresses" (222). Her plans for her wayward husband unfold vicious but vacant, aimed only at his stuff: "sugar in his motor, scissors to his tie, burned suits, slashed shoes, ripped socks." For the woman who wears a red dress to his funeral, however, nothing would do but the dream of pulping her to death underneath the shoes of a horse Alice neither "owned nor knew how to ride" (86). Diverted by her husband's death from actually doing something wild, she is left for thirty years with nothing but anxiety.

Alice's reaction projects her rage at dispossession onto the other woman. Violet's last-ditch boyfriend, on the other hand, feels sorry for the other man crying in the next room and disgusted with Violet when she tries to do Dorcas's dance steps. Violet can no longer remember the name of the man she stepped out with if "[her] life depended on it" (111). Such comically crazy behavior by old cocks and aging chicks suggests that Wild can never be tamed and that the concept of one person owning another is best left alone.

Joe's new best friends, now also old cocks in the city, cope with husband- and fatherhood by staying in touch with the wild child inside. Bud and C.T. play checkers on the stoop and compete with each other at tall-tale-telling. Stuck, who won't stick to one wife, and Gistan, the jocular father of sons who clown on the curb, play cards with Joe on Fridays. The attitudes of these men reflect Gurian's view that masculine autonomy requires male support and that men communicate by working or playing together. Gurian argues that male friendship becomes harder to sustain than female relationships as it is "often not talk-dependent" but "proximity- and activity-dependent" (53). Morrison admits to having assumed that "all men ever learn about being men they get from other men" but being "amazed at how little men taught one another" (McKay 410). Her *Jazz* narrator insists that things would have concluded differently if Joe had confided in Gistan or Stuck. Instead of helping him confront his confusion, however, his friends censor news of Violet's public craziness, which carries through the community like wildfire, and stand awkwardly out in the hall on New Year's Day when they come to check if he has come home. Joe describes his affair as "not a thing you tell to another man" because men who put "all their business in the street" deny such a woman as important. He is not sure he could make clear even to Victory his feelings about Dorcas, much less to Gistan who "would just laugh and try to get out of hearing it" and Stuck who "would look at his feet, swear [Joe has been] fixed and tell [him] how much high john [he needs] to remedy [himself]" (121). Joe does tell Dorcas he sees her as his deliverance, but not adequately, since he does not completely understand it himself. It takes Violet who, "meaning to or not meaning to . . . got him to go through it again" (119).

Joe is an old cock made New Negro seven times to survive. The first time he names his "own self" since nobody else knows "what it could or should have been" (123). The second change happens when his woodsman's gift appears powerful enough to impress even a hunter's hunter, who chooses him to mentor into manhood and teaches him to "live independent and feed [himself] no matter what" (125). The third occurs when Vienna burns and he is dispossessed, the fourth when he takes his wife to board a train for the city, and the fifth when they move from the stink of Little Africa on uptown. The sixth time he survives being almost killed by white men when he goes to help a little boy who falls during the 1917 riots. The seventh change comes two years later when he marches down city streets with the colored troops of the three six nine, his heart so proud it almost splits in half. Then, if his female counterpart hits upon the "one and final thing she had not been able to endure or repeat" (101), the black male changes "once too often." Makes himself "new one time too many." None of his metamorphoses can possibly prepare him for "what an eighteen-year-old girl might instigate in a grown man whose wife is sleeping with a doll" (129).

Morrison articulates the climax of Joe's blues tragedy in primordial as well as Oedipal terms: "Snakes go blind before they shed skin for the last time" (129). Nonetheless, *Jazz* downplays both climax and dénouement in favor of possibility. Trained to track by the best hunter ever, Joe accepts instinctively that if "the trail speaks, no matter what is in the way, you can find yourself in a crowded room aiming a bullet at her heart, never mind it's the heart you can't live without" (130). Hamartia for him becomes a primal re-action: "I wasn't looking for the trail. It was looking for me" (130). He also affirms that despite the pain he would "strut out the Garden, strut!" to make up his mind to choose for the first time not to fall but to rise in and follow love (134). Thus, for Joe, Dorcas represents "the reason Adam ate the apple and its core. . . . [W]hen he left Eden, he left a rich man. Not only did he have Eve, but he had the taste of the first apple in the world in his mouth for the rest of his life. The very first to know what it was like. To bite it, bite it down. Hear the crunch and let the red peeling break his heart" (133). Similar to Early Modern Jacques's description of the seven ages of man, modern Joe expresses the cycle of experience metaphorically through the fixed number seven. However, American survival for the African American male means he must make himself over at the drop of a hat. Joe knows firsthand that being new in his day involves more than a state of mind. To stay wholly new, a man has to remain half wild.

Sometimes the threat to black male endurance can be sighted in the form of specific white men; sometimes it appears ubiquitous or subconscious. It is always armed, however, and frequently forbidden. But though the inevitable conflict proves cathartic, it does not have to end in a classical catastrophe. In Joe's case, the old rooster locates redemption by relying on his warm, wide, watching two-color eyes, a "sad one that lets you look inside him, and a clear one that looks inside you" (207). Page declares that Joe errs by egotistically assuming he has a "unitary self, that he can create and recreate that self, and do so by possessing others," reclaiming his past, and reifying Dorcas as Wild (162). Morrison, however, defends her character as she defines the inception of jazz: exslaves are "talking about love, about loss. But there is such grandeur, such satisfaction in those lyrics. . . . It's as though the whole tragedy of choosing somebody, risking love, risking emotion, risking sensuality, and then losing it all didn't matter, since it was their choice. . . . [J]azz represented ownership of one's own [body and] emotions" (Schappell and Lacour 365). Furman adds that "Morrison implicates the city in Joe and Violet's failings." In essence, they are "betrayed by the city's wonderful promise of perfection" (95). While the upshot results in the two getting totally out of control, partly because of outside things, Morrison maintains that if these things are tested, confronted, and understood, "freedom that is more than license" and thus "true, adult agency" become possible (Schappell and Lacour 366).

Morrison signals her characters' adult recovery as "a new affection for each other and for the city" (Furman 95). In classical terms, this would constitute the entrance of the deus ex machina. Morrison expresses the god from the machine metaphorically as sweetheart weather or spring in the city, narratively as the character Felice, and structurally in the form of the Talking Book.[17] Modern tragedy already allows for a mixture of sadness and mirth. *Jazz*'s plot, however, summarized up front as the plight of a woman's husband who "fell for an eighteen-year-old girl with one of those deepdown, spooky loves that made him so sad and happy he shot her just to keep the feeling going" (after which the woman cuts the dead girl's face to be thrown out of the church and forced to run through the snow to free her parrot to "freeze or fly"), looks calculated for tragedy but concludes in felicity. Like a black phoenix, the bird returns to rise again.

Spring in the city appears as the time when "people notice one another in the road; notice the strangers with whom they share aisles and tables and the space where intimate garments are laundered." During this season the city seems to urge "contradiction most," though "really there is no contradiction—rather it's a condition: the range of what an artful City can do." Morrison's description highlights figures of blackness (tar, darkness, gloom, shade, woolly green hair, jet-black boxes) along with angles, indirection, and change. In so doing, she suggests that the scope, variation, and arrangement of space available indirectly to individuals cooperating within a group, specifically the urban black community, become infinite. A fine example of one such "strange sight" is Joe crying openly: "It's not a thing [men] do" (117–18).

Felice arrives to set things straight for Joe during sweetheart weather, "the prettiest day of the year," a day so "pure and steady" that, "standing in the middle of a concrete slab, scared for their lives, [trees] preened" (195). Carrying an Okeh record under her arm and stewmeat in her hand, this flexibly solid, mature young black woman fills the space first Dorcas and then Dorcas's photograph formerly held. Felice's song offers Joe a fresh perspective. She sees nothing crazy about straight-talking Violet, and she appreciates Joe's genuine interest in women. Although her anger at her friend for deliberately dying colors her memory of Dorcas, her very skepticism provides Joe with a way to view Dorcas sympathetically, as the sorrow that connects his tracks to Violet's. The savvy seventeen-year-old describes Dorcas as having "all the ingredients of pretty" but simply not getting it together. Men flock to her at first but then run scared because she pushes them to risk while she plays the damsel in distress. Their deus ex machina visits the Traces ostensibly to ask for her ring but actually to let the "old man" off the hook for outright murder. Joe must accept that his condition combines innocence with guilt. By doing so, he discovers forgiveness and peace through the communal bonds of suffering. In the process Felice, too, is transformed. From Violet she finds that if "you don't [change the world], it will change you"; from Joe she learns to love soft and to laugh because people are not really mean, merely comic. Morrison compares Felice to the semiprecious black opal, which both refracts and reflects light to produce a myriad of colors. Named "right," she refuses to equate happiness with possession and responds to fighting over love: "But what if I don't want to?" (201–16).

"Sauntering through the sunshafts like that," Felice becomes potent enough to make even Morrison's know-it-all narrator "doubt [her] own self" (198). Like an artful jazz performance, the voice of *Jazz* admits that its vision is faulty, that it does not imagine its characters well enough, that it is willing to fail. Its players talk back to it the way jazz musicians do. It must listen and learn from them. It cannot, however, allow them to "write [its] book" because, like human self-development, writing signals an individual's complicity with the community. The text signifies a bridge between author and audience (Schappell and Lacour 116–17, 106). Thus, Morrison's conception of a Talking Book, a story in a sense writing itself, acts as both deus ex machina and chorus. A personification of the impersonal authorial voice, the narrator embodies the "author incarnating—as a God might take on human form—as fictional muscle and bone, giving herself a consciousness and presence in the text." When s/he renounces authorial powers for personal identity, the narrator is "subject to the aspirations and urges of humankind" (Furman 100–101). Most critics agree that, similar to the unknown revelator in "The Thunder, Perfect Mind," the name of *Jazz*'s sound sounds feminine; some, however, like Paquet-Deyris, refer to the narrator as "he" (229). This discrepancy suggests the androgynous quality of the griot. The book's final plea for its readers to "Make me, remake me" recalls the blind griot's comment to his/her youthful listeners in Morrison's Nobel Prize lecture: "I trust you now. I trust you with the bird that is not in your hands because you have truly caught it. Look. How lovely it is, this thing we have done—together" (474). Although the narrator alone cannot completely grasp Joe and Violet's story, her/his people together are able to integrate it in order to elude the suffocating yoke of history.

The Talking Book also captures the erotic, creative intimacy Morrison claims is the secular revelation of "reading, holding, surrendering to the book": "When it's tactile, your emotions are deeply involved" (Carabi 43).[18] This theory helps explain her book's epigraph from the ancient Egyptian *Nag Hammadi*:

> I am the name of the sound
> and the sound of the name.
> I am the sign of the letter
> and the designation of the division.

Jazz/*Jazz* absorbs sound and sense, chaos and order to make "change, originality, and unpredictability within a recognized structure into central parts of musical process." Thus, it provides "an apt metaphor" for social, and personal, change (Kubitschek 142). Morrison expresses Joe's revelation as he descends the steps of the Elevated to buy milk to take home from the second-day crate and his redemption when he tells Violet: "This place needs birds" (214). Violet buys one that is not well. When "neither food nor company nor its own shelter was important to it," they agree that "nothing was left to love or need but music." Free access to the rooftop "where the wind blew and so did musicians in shirts billowing out behind them" renders the new bird, as well as the now comfortably middle-aged one, "a pleasure to itself and to them" (224).

Jazz reenvisions the old chicken-or-egg question in terms of masks and drums. Morrison questions those who tout the superiority of Western culture until they measure its civilization thoroughly against others, and find it not wanting, and until "Western civilization owns up to its own sources in the cultures that preceded it." Much of the satisfaction she derives from reading Greek tragedy lies in "its similarity to Afro-American communal structures (the function of song and chorus, the heroic struggle between the claims of community and individual hubris) and African religion and philosophy." While she feels "intellectually at home there," however, it is not the culture that has quality for her but the work ("Unspeakable Things Unspoken" 2–3). So which comes first for Western civilization: cold-faced male figures wearing (Greek) masks or masked men beating (African) drums? Does the drum encourage the mask or does the mask endorse the drum? Did Morrison's study of classical literature at Cornell arise from its similarity to African (American) rhythms, or did Greek culture affect her approach to *Jazz*? Did African art influence classical responses to suffering, as many anthropologists now speculate (and thus Morrison's interest in the connections between the drum and the mask), or is it the other way around? Although the site of blues trauma represents the place of such stuck records, the postmodern tendencies in *Jazz* reverberate strong enough to get its men out of the groove. Morrison's postmodern masculinity becomes a tragicomic jazz performance, pondering certainly the depths of all these possibilities but rising above them by endlessly improvising.

CHAPTER 8

Putting down Parking Lots out There

Morrison's Unpaved Male *Paradise*

Morrison's seventh novel, *Paradise* (1997), lives up to its mystical number in her cosmos; it also figures as an inversion of its creator's original handiwork, *The Bluest* become blackest *Eye*. The book represents in more ways than one a culmination. Third in a trilogy on the African American experience, its chronology encompasses the failed Reconstruction of the 1880s as well as the almost as unsuccessful second Reconstruction of the 1960s, marking with savagely ironic sexism and racism the date of the American bicentennial, July 1976. Signifying on Dante's three-part *Divine Comedy*, *Paradise* discounts the American Dream. It insists on the impossibility, even the danger, of earthly perfection.[1] If Dante's *Paradiso* transcends earth, Morrison's embraces the inextricability of the heavenly and the not-so-divine. While *Il Paradiso* confines itself to Catholic cosmology, *Paradise* articulates then extends Africanist, European, African American, and womanist spiritual and artistic sensibilities.

Like Dante and Virgil, *Paradise*'s male characters are determined by what is "Out There." The frontier myth continues to inform American masculinity. Michael K. Johnson finds contained within the frontier narrative's chronicle of conquest a plot of male identity formation, which rests upon the belief that an encounter with otherness transforms the subjectivity of the hero.[2] The hero thus becomes a new man and the representative of a new manhood. His masculinity ranks superior to both the savagery of the American Indian and the ultracivilized maleness of the European because American manhood combines the best elements of both. If the white frontier master narrative accounts, then, for the achievement of an American masculinity, the black man has been denied his manhood. Johnson contends that African American male writers have, in fact, engaged the mythic narrative of the frontier, altering and extending its tradition in ways that transform the experience of journey into a black one. Like her colleagues, Morrison envisions the frontier allegorically as the imaginative realm of "what if," an American place where black community thrives. However, unlike the exclusionist thinking of many black male writers, Morrison's position remains antiutopian.

Emblematic of the mass exodus of blacks from southern and eastern states into freshly settled frontier territory, the male founders of Haven and of the new haven called Ruby represent what William Loren Katz refers to as *Black People Who Made the Old West*. Peter R. Kearly summarizes the work of recent frontier historians who collectively acknowledge that "the American West was not just populated by heroic cowboys and gun-slinging desperados, nor white homesteaders threatened by tommy-hawk wielding Indians, nor macho hard-drinking and gambling bachelors with the only women being whores and mothers of too many children" (10). Frontier scholar Patricia Limerick suggests that the popular conception of the word *westerner* presents "an image of a handsome white man on a handsome horse" even though white males made up a minority of the western population (94). The concept of "the West" has been conflated with white migration westward so that "whites are given homogeneous authority over the history of the settlement of the West despite the fact that multitudes of African Americans and immigrating people from Asia were among the thousands who migrated to the territories west of the Mississippi" (Kearly 10). Historian John Ravage confirms that, since Spanish settlers arrived with over forty thousand blacks along with undetermined numbers of mulattos and mestizos, black people were already occupying land acquired later by the U.S. government in the Louisiana Purchase of 1803. In addition, the French came accompanied by domestic servants from colonies in Jamaica, Haiti, and the West Indies. The great Indian peacekeeping purge of 1817 saw Cherokee, Choctaw, Seminole, Creek, and Chickasaw tribes segregated from their black family members. Ex-Union buffalo soldiers, assigned to keep frontier peace after the Civil War, occasionally accompanied black homesteaders. Land promoters encouraged former slaves to become future squatters. Railroad, mining, and hotel entrepreneurs along with cattle ranchers hired black migrants.

The setting of *Paradise* could be construed, then, as "part of a long suppressed and unrecorded history of black settlement and stories of self-made communities . . . built around one or two churches and around a code of ethics, supreme among which was to protect and respect the women" (Kearly 11). Morrison counts such romantically rigid paternalism as ultimately destructive to the women and to the men. She nonetheless refuses to blame black men whose masculinity becomes fixed by Western concepts of physical beauty and romantic love, both of which are "Out There" in their association with American cowboy culture and "out there" in their unreal impossibility.[3] Her not-so-bad guys have collectively lost their sense of black humor and the humility that goes with it.[4] When Morrison names a child bride in her grimly comic *Love* "Heed the Night Johnson," she calls upon the healing power of laughter that time and again has saved her people. Conversely, the defenders of New Haven try to expunge the comic gods because dancing for Dionysus at night or any other time can be dangerous. Their actions illustrate the certain violence that occurs, however, when a community fails to understand the tragic nature of laughter: that welcoming joy in the morning instead of dreading Righteous Spirit's arrival always comes accompanied by pain.[5]

Although a number of critics identify *Paradise* as Morrison's most antimale work, it consistently relies on bleak contrast to spotlight what masculine potential can be.[6] Her novel inverts what Melville termed the power of blackness as well as the power of men. It highlights a brightly, androgynously multicolored convent world against a dark backdrop provided by a seen black male presence and a less visible but paramount white male presence within Ruby. The negative male characters fall into opposing binary radicals, either extremely disrespectful to or overly protective toward females. Violating the cardinal rule of a hunter's hunter, they perceive women as prey or on pedestals. With her first sentence, "They shoot the white girl first" (that is to say, other females will follow), Morrison signals gender to be as serious a problem in Ruby as race: the women leap, the men take aim, and the writer freezes her frame. The black men who wash out of the negative to emerge in living color manage between past and present reconstructions to find their balance connected to a feminine flexibility, to retain or regain their sense of humor, and to unsettle the frontier.[7] Such a double take on American frontier legend, slyly underscored by the very language of *Paradise*, will—hopefully somewhat as subtly—be attempted in the text of this analysis.

Urban Cowboys and Horse Whisperers

The men who sight women as prey run the gamut from abusive husbands, absent fathers, and untrue lovers to stalkers, rapists, manipulators, and molesters. However, Morrison leaves none named totally defenseless. She almost always lets the reader in on why as well as how her frontiersmen come to act the way they do. While the convent women drift one by one into the embezzler's cartridge-shaped sanctuary to dodge the predators in their lives, the male drifters who drive these women to the edge do so by imprinting their brand of pain onto their cows. First to saddle up are urban cowboys who brave mechanical bulls and use women for target practice unlike the more mystical and increasingly rarer horse whisperers.[8] Mavis Albright's neighbors have been annoyed for years by the foolish ostentation of the mint-green Cadillac her husband cannot afford to maintain. Reminiscent of the way Macon Dead waxes his shiny green Packard, Frank treats his car far better than his wife. Fond of drinking Seagram's without a glass, he exemplifies the suburban flop whose idea of bringing home the bacon excludes Spam. Leftovers from his working-class paycheck, after taxes, car support, and drink, render even refrigeration impossible and Mavis compelled to purchase weenies from the Higgledy Piggledy on a daily basis: she "had a whole chuck steak go green on [her] once" (22). She looks forward to the luxurious freedom of driving the gas-guzzling Cadillac to the store but has to take her twins along after making excuses for Frank's hangover: "You can't expect a man to come home from that kind of work and have to watch over babies while I go get something decent to put in front of him. I know that ain't right" (23).

Morrison depicts the Albrights as the stereotypical flat welfare family. Black or white, they become "Grayed in, and gray."[9] Shabby surroundings, sullen kids, hostile husband, colorless wife, and far flashier car (or horse) taking up half the front yard, these details capture such a clan today or in Faulkner's *Spotted Horses*. Untrained to cope with work, money, or childcare, the downtrodden parents of too many children find themselves trapped in a vicious cycle of self-destruction, which finally smothers their newborns. Since unreliable Frank relies on his offspring to enable him to unemasculate himself upon his sink of a wife, the scapegoat in his family of dependents is not Sal but Mavis. *Paradise* inverts *Tar Baby*'s tale of an abusive mother as Frank's mishandling of male power causes a daughter to dig her nails into her mother's side until they draw blood.

If the "familiar fright" of the husband she lumps with the "other children" almost numbs Mavis, her children terrify her. Frank erupts like Macon Dead's smoldering volcano. A blankness or even periods of playfulness when enough alcohol is in or at hand vie with explosions of physical or psychological violence. His idea of lovemaking is to throw his wife's nightgown over her head and, riding her trussed like a roped calf or a limp Raggedy Ann doll, rubbing "himself to climax while chewing a clump of her hair through the nightgown that covered her face." If he becomes bored by or lacks the energy to put on his own rodeo show, he forces his children to rope and ride their mother. Dinner-table conversations, such as the one that follows the deaths of Merle and Pearl, engage the children in not-so-subtle threats against Mavis. Frank elicits peals of laughter from his eldest daughter when he characterizes the edge of his old shaving razor, placed ominously by Sal next to her plate, as sharp enough to "Cut the eyelashes off a bedbug." After Billy James spits Kool-Aid into Mavis's plate, Frank merely suggests that he stop playing in his mother's food in the same breath that he asks Frankie to pass the catsup (25–26).

This erratic suburban wrangler has corralled his calves. He keeps his cow in line by deliberately leaving her in the cold outside the family circle yet also isolated from friends. Mavis becomes so frightened that she hears the voices of her children snickering behind the door as their father rapes their mother and envisions Sal's eyes as "cold and unforgiving as they were when she was told of the accident." Like many practiced sadists, Frank employs uncertainty as the most sophisticated weapon in his torture chamber. The accuracy of his arsenal results from indirect as much as direct action, from what he implies along with what he says or does. The final straw for Mavis, and the signal she interprets to be her husband's nod for her children to knock her off, is Frank's carefully vague comment: "I don't know, Mave. I just don't know. . . . Maybe we can fix it. Maybe not. . . . Don't see how, though" (26).

The cocky vulgarity sported so casually by the urban cowboy registers in the offhand way Frank handles his wife and kids set against his heavy-handed display of his gaudy car. Despite its superior rating among her husband's valuables, however, Mavis appraises the Cadillac equally as important. The machine represents for both, albeit in contrasting manifestations, harbor and ship. While it "wasn't hers; it was his," Frank's wife loves it "maybe more than he did" because it marks the spot "where the twins had been, the only ones who enjoyed her company and weren't a trial" at the same time it allows her to leave (25). When she takes the car, she steals Frank's heart. Even on the road her city cowpuncher haunts her, reincarnated as a black-jacketed, gold-chained, open-shirted motorcycle maniac, whose hairy torso appears at gasoline stations and in side-view mirrors. As the car grows dustier under Mavis's rough care, however, the image of its stalker becomes fainter until it is finally left in the dust.

The outside of the Caddy remains permanently scarred from constant abuse but the inside comfortably worn with fistfights and fun, signs of a fully lived life. Its new driver changes its color from the green that Morrison associates with order and ownership to the red that signals dangerous freedom. Coping less than serenely with the "stable excitement of facing danger while safely strapped in strong metal," the woman whom Frank calls the dumbest bitch on earth does not lean on her husband to execute her escape or to enable other girls to get farther Out There (33). With a little help from her car and her outlaw girlfriends, she heals herself. The Cadillac's loud magenta color gradually fades along with the lipstick belonging to one of Frank's lovers, which Mavis locates in its glove compartment and smears on her mouth. Such slight alterations correspond to the imperceptible personality death of the twenty-seven-year-old girl, who finds it impossible to defend herself from her eleven-year-old daughter and relies on drive-throughs to feed her family, and the birth of the woman who finds fighting exhilarating and can create "crepe-like delicacies without shopping every day" (171).

If Morrison attributes a house free of hunters to Mavis's transformation, she places the blame for Mavis's dysfunctions and the mutually destructive marriage firmly not on the cowboy but on cowboy culture. Frank simply cannot bear to grin and leave off clinging to his mechanical bull, symbol of male potency in frontier towns. He cannot get away from men on the street, who slap the hood and smile when he drives it home, who lean in to sniff its odor, hit its horn, and laugh. He fails to understand that they laugh and laugh "some more because its owner had to borrow a lawn mower every couple of weeks; because its owner had no screens in his windows and no working television; because two of his six porch posts had been painted white three months earlier, the rest still flaking yellow; because its owner sometimes slept behind the wheel of the car he'd traded in—all night—in front of his own house." While the town women manage to refrain from laughing, even they fail to interfere at the sight of Mavis wearing sunglasses on cloudy days, "flat-out star[ing]" instead, and "shak[ing] their heads" (28). Although Frank shoots himself in the foot on a daily basis, Morrison asserts that failing to offer him a hand up is commensurate with blaming a victim.

If Frank's stupid mishandling helps render Mavis repressed and defeated, Gigi's experiences with men do not make her volatile and sexually promiscuous. This behavior results primarily from inherited idealism. Gigi is, in fact, graced by the presence then thrown by the absence of several generous but restricted horse whisperers. A fifty-two-year-old death-row inmate, her father receives a life-sentence reprieve at the end of the novel. Morrison deliberately omits any knowledge of Manley Gibson's crimes. We come to respect him, however, as a man who appreciates the outdoors and Kentucky Fried Chicken, who treasures the only photograph he has of the child he has neither seen nor heard from since she was eleven, and who would and does from the features of a thirteen-year-old recognize her adult face anywhere. Despite, perhaps because of his fifteen years in a gray penitentiary, this man loves working beside the blue of a lake, remains nonplussed at his daughter's army fatigues and the fact that she may be "packing," and wonders if she still carries the locket he gave her. He must stop himself from touching her for fear of demerits from the guards, saying merely, "Ooh, honey, oh, honey, my little girl," and later, on the bus back to prison, reviews every detail of their meeting (310). The felon Gigi calls Daddy Man does not fail to ask about her mother and grandfather, and his last request is that she write.

Gigi's grandfather acts equally unsuccessfully supportive. When she calls him crying from a phone booth in Mexico, having fled the sight of the "map of red" spreading across a "neat little colored boy's" white shirt during race riots in Oakland, California, he accepts her collect charges and orders: "Bring your butt home, girl. World change enough to suit you? Everybody dead anyway. King, another one of them Kennedys, Medgar Evers, a nigger name of X, Lord I can't think who all since you left not to speak of right here remember L.J. used to work down at the route two mall somebody walked in there broad daylight with a pistol shaped like nothing nobody ever seen before" (65). In spite of his limited range and small-town status in Alcorn, Mississippi, this socially conscious citizen becomes a major source of Gigi's broad political activism. Though he stands staunchly for the power of place to heal its wounded soldiers, telling his granddaughter to return at once to Alcorn, Grace, like shell-shocked Shadrack, has misplaced her sense of direction with the loss of her Daddy Man. She responds, "I'm coming, Granddaddy. I'm heading home right now." However, letting "her head fall back on the plaster wall near the telephone," she sets out for Out There (65).

Mikey Rood embodies Gigi's comrade in arms. He holds her hand as the wall of advancing police, men in "fight-face," cut off escape from the roar and blood that result in over a hundred dead on Oakland streets; he bequeaths to Gigi his vision of a "man and a woman fucking forever" in Wish, Arizona. Giving his girlfriend careful directions to meet him at his hometown where they will find "loving to beat the sky" after he is released from jail, the man Morrison associates with crudeness or a medieval cross reveals more of the lover and storyteller than fighter. He describes repeatedly and in lavish detail the desert shapes that suggest a dark couple moving constantly and rhythmically in changing light. He maintains that the formation would constitute a widespread attraction were it not for its inaccessibility and the concerns of local Methodists. Those "repressed rednecks," incensed less about the prospect of sex than about same-sex since the shapes must be, for some, two females, for others, two males, live themselves "too scared to have wet dreams," much less blow off their rocks. Nonetheless, they know they need the couple. "Even if they never went near them," Mikey explains, "they needed to know they were out there." It takes a man born to die nailed to a tree to understand intimately the desire to mount a scapegoat, whether sinner or saint, even one that lies "moving, all the time moving" in the shape of a dangerous stone (63).

When rude Mikey fails to make a nonexistent Wish by Easter, Gigi realizes "There was no Mikey, there was no Wish, there was no I-3 [trinity] and nobody was fucking in the desert." She reluctantly gives up the man but, seated precariously astride a more refined but no less mean breed of Frank's mechanical bull, clings "for dear and precious life" to a vision of "eternal desert coupling." Romantic idealism becomes as destructive to Gigi as it does to Pauline in *The Bluest Eye*. It is not dreams of social justice or nightmares of broken children that break her heart but the loss of desert lovers. Mikey "did not invent them," however. He "may have put them in the wrong place, but he had only summoned to the surface what she had known all her life existed . . . somewhere." Like Pauline, Gigi's search for romantic love leaves her bereft. Instead of the church, she finds release where the "dope was heavy, the men always ready" or in a losing battle until she locates the convent. Her introduction to Dice, Mikey re-formed into the dwarflike man she meets on board the MKT and stands toe to toe with, inadvertently gives her the knowledge required to complete her quest outside Ruby (64–65).

A heroine seeking felicity, obstacles pitched in her path to test her resolve, allegorical messages secreted within natural or manmade events, shapes that shift, a dwarf named for fate: these reconstitute a comically updated, upside-down *Faerie Queene*. Dice certainly throws Gigi something besides a chance at the brass ring of holy matrimony. Although she seeks him out so as to "talk to somebody who wasn't encased in polyester and who looked like he might smoke something other than Chesterfields," the ice-crunching man with the gold stud in his ear turns out to be even more hip than his East Coast clothes. To their encounter with the dining car counterman, Gigi goes loaded for polar bear. The attendant charges Dice for a cup of ice; she counterattacks the iceman heatedly. The counterman dodges behind rules and the threat of a conductor; Dice smiles coolly and tosses him twice the cost of a cup. Gigi argues principle; Dice, "A five-cent principle ain't no principle at all" (65–66).

What could have been friction between hot and cool heads melds into a contest of stories. Shoving everything she has stashed away into the pot means that Gigi must gamble on her vision of the desert couple, which Dice has not seen but raises with a pair of trees entwined near a lake in a wheat field outside Ruby, Oklahoma. Squeezing "in between them in just the right way" supposedly produces unduplicated ecstasy, perpetual bliss, and "can't nobody turn you down." To get way "out in the middle of nowhere," she need only check out "the best rhubarb pie in the nation" (66). Though their wordplay battle appears to unfold in a draw, the tiny but virile horse whisperer wins the war, leaving a lingering impression on Gigi's life. He knows why but says nothing when she lies about going home. Standing on tiptoe, he does not take offense when she helps him collect his baggage. This gentle dwarf may be short, but his grace extends long. Unlike metaphorically challenged Gigi, he understands the difference between the literal and the figurative. Thus, he can distinguish between a winning and losing fight and one worth fighting for. Warned not to get wet by what proves to be far more than a lying freak, Morrison's Red Cross Lady finds herself mincing not much later alongside a field of wheat that could pass for Al(l)corn, Mississippi, asking about rhubarb she claims to hate.

Roger Best provides her ride to the convent's down-home barbs and rue. As the less-than-Lady welcomes "waves of raw horniness," provoked by her tight pants and screaming tits, and clicks towering, un-Dorothy-like block heels on the edge of Central Avenue, a sudden absence of wind brings the sound of his engine, the brand-new van that serves as ambulance and hearse in a town known for its not-sick-and-dying (67). Gigi scoffs at Roger's assumption that she heads for the convent, taking him up on his offer of a free trip straight to the track. Nonetheless, she becomes the first live body saved by the ambulance. A short stopover transforms Mother's dead body into what proves to be the last paying passenger in the hearse, which transfers a nun, not the non-Lady, to her train home. Insisting that he be on instead of in time at the station, Roger's cautionary voice sounds inept over the throb of his engine. He leaves Gigi stranded and not at all at home in the strange-looking convent to act as Connie's temporary watcher or second-best sight and her own best savior. For Morrison, home lies not only where the heart is but also where the heat is. Famous for its hell-fire peppers as well as its rhubarb pie, the convent requires its occupants to provide one another with love along with a hard time. For the most part imperfect, earthly paradise offers individuals momentary glimpses of harmony. The living must seek temporal homes wherever they travel. Permanent home may be found only in death.

Roger's "overpriced buggy" signals him as another horse whisperer who thrives and fails on too much flexibility (106).[10] Dice rides the rails, Mikey is on the lam, Manley cops the bus, and Granddaddy stays home but travels miles in his mind. While Roger's van costs as much as Frank's Cadillac, it does not merely sit in the yard like a scared stiff but, doing double duty, serves both the living and the dead. The lack of hospital or mortuary business in rigid Ruby, however, prevents even a good driver from making his car payments on time. His head full of promising plans, Roger has a history of making do. All his projects are adjustable. His veterinary practice might be illegal, but no one else knows or cares enough to drive the long distances to help black ranchers yank stuck foals from the wombs of mares. Although Roger refuses to slaughter anything, his butcher business includes skinning, carving, and refrigerating. He always intended to study medicine, but fate in the form of an only surviving child's sorrowful parents flips this dream over into mortuary science. Not exactly brain surgery, his latest proposal for a gasoline station would still allow him to dismember and repair—the engines of cars.

Able to go without the wind, Roger reworks the possibility of his garage around unpaved roads, unhappy competitors, and the objections of local churches. He is willing to locate it away from Holy Redeemer, find a way to make it accessible to locals as well as those who never pass through, and fill it with "something Anna don't stock. No point in getting her riled up" (186). The failure of his ideas results not from his lack of creative enterprise but from acute flexibility, and the fact that the deck remains stacked against him. Roger will no more be invited by the overbearing Morgans to "make out" in rent-controlled Ruby than he was encouraged by his undermined parents to matriculate in white-dominated medical schools or at Meharry (106). His personal life also continues daring but defeated by things without and within his reach. The first to violate, by marrying a light-skinned woman, what his daughter calls Ruby's 8-rock rule, he exists caught forever between a rock and a hard place. His time in paradise, however, is fortunately damned for it.

Pat Best calls the town's tall, graceful blue-black males, "whose clear, wide eyes gave no sign of what they really felt about those who weren't 8-rock like them," not the talented tenth or the Nation of Islam but eight-rock, after "a deep deep level in the coal mines" (193).[11] One of Ruby's founding fathers among eight other ebony families that seek refuge there, agreeable Roger Best marries Delia of "sunlight skin" and "no last name" (197). Even as a young soldier on leave speaking Louisiana to a Tennessee girl, the love in his voice lay unmistakable in his eyes. It endures shrouded beneath the desperation of his business ventures, not to speak of his need to please and appease. His chosen cracker wife lives and dies an outcast, described by Steward Morgan before they abandon Haven as "the dung we leaving behind" (201). She suffers from a baby who "was coming too soon, legs folded underneath" and arrogant 8-rock men who ignore their wives begging them to drive for help from the white nuns out at the convent because they look down on Delia. Delia's husband arrives from his mortuary graduation too late to do anything but a beautiful job of making his dead newborn and wife his first success. While this easygoing 8-rock may not be great at coming or going anywhere on time, he remains the very best at being at his station in time, operating on the in-need or even dead.

Roger, however, is not the only other-oriented man that Gigi encounters at one end of Ruby's "straight as a die" main street (10). At the opposite stands Coffee (K.D.) Smith, also overly attached to a woman buried before and after childbirth but without benefit of a mortuary. Coffee Smith, nephew to the powerful 8-rock Morgan twins, becomes Kentucky Derby Smith when Ossie Beauchamp organizes a comically outlandish horse race to celebrate the christening of Central Avenue. Its seven-year-old winner, grinning as though he had finished first at the greatest flat race in the land, takes Ossie's Purple Heart as his prize. His mother hangs on long enough to watch him ride. Her brothers gave this "sweet, modest laughing girl whom [they] had protected all their lives" to K.D.'s father, also Coffee Smith, an army buddy who dies during World War II (113). Transferring their sister, still worn out from pregnancy, to the New Haven site after their soldier's welcome home to Haven turns out disappointing, they cannot arrange that she live out her widowhood. These 8-rock bluebloods fail to provide Ruby with serious medical attention because hospital wards ban colored people and the on-duty nurse cannot contact a veterinarian to examine her in time.

The sister's death on the waiting room bench inspires her brothers' deal with God. Ruby, the town named after Ruby, the girl who lacks the strength to care about its name, becomes the perfect site for the men's anger and grief: "It was the shame of seeing one's pregnant wife or sister or daughter refused shelter that had rocked them, and changed them for all time. The humiliation did more than rankle; it threatened to crack open their bones" (95). The brothers create Ruby to "mourn the sister and honor the friend and brother-in-law who didn't make it back." The sister's son, on the other hand, "heir to his father's dog tags, witness to his mother's name painted on signs and written on envelopes for the rest of his life, was displaced by these sad markings" (17). His time in a too-perfect town dedicated to his idealized dead mother wears away at his courage, his humility, and what used to be a joyous sense of humor. K.D. grows up diminished by his surroundings, spoiled by the women who tended his mother, favored by the men who enlisted with his father, and overlooked by uncles who come to love the town more than the woman's son.

If Roger Best's learned other-hood leads him to reach excessively outward, trying to make up, K.D.'s causes him to focus incessantly inward, trying to make out. Named after a horse race but inheritor of dog tags, he does better with dogs than with horses, towns, or women. Accorded such easy access to the "free wind blowing Night's mane" and his Uncle Steward's fast truck or Impala cruiser as well as the fine black Oldsmobile polished to perfection by his Uncle Deacon, K.D. is left to go to the dogs (96). The collies confined to the shed in town act so "thrilled to see him" that he has to "straddle Good to keep her down." But when he sings in a soft Motown falsetto the song he made up for her when she was a pup, she lets him comb the "mess" out of her silky hair and soft ears, which comes from running wild on Steward's ranch: "Everybody needs a good good good dog." His hands deep in her hair, palm under her jaw, she licks his chin and stretches her pleasure. Finished with her, he curries Ben's coat with the same steady hand and gentle bristle-brush touch. K.D. has been good to the dogs as long as he can, however. The combination of sensual grooming and simultaneously attempting to think like his uncles proves "too hard" for him, so he simply stops trying and slips off into his dream of choice, which includes Gigi and her baked-Alaska breasts (53–55).

His uncles' way of thinking sends him straight to the dream that leads to fast women. Taking the MKT once with Steward and Deacon into an Oklahoma city, K.D. waits on the curb while the Morgans talk important business inside a nearby building. When he hears excited voices and wanders over to watch, he looks with the wide eyes of a child: "June voices are doubled by the sunlit water of a swimming pool," which, actually average in size, appears to fill his horizon. What must be hundreds of white children play in the pool, "their voices a cascade of the world's purest happiness, a glee so sharply felt it had brought tears." The pop of Gigi's gum triggers again the "yearning excitement of sparkly water and the June voices of swimmers" (57). Chastisement then or now from his elders is a small price to pay when K.D. sets flashily sumptuous possibilities against an expectant Arnette's cropped bangs, "neat shirtwaist dress," and nagging, accusatory face. So when she says upon seeing Gigi,

"If that's the kind of tramp you want, hop to it, nigger," he slaps her mouth and fawns all over Gigi, trying to get a muzzle on the girl (54).

It becomes his dream, not his behavior, that K.D. reviews in Deacon's car en route to a family conference with Arnette's father and brother about the slap, not the pregnancy. Morrison juxtaposes K.D.'s cavalier attitude toward an absent Arnette against glimpses of himself and Gigi riding as hard and fast as an Impala will allow. All the men gathered at the Fleetwoods' except Richard Misner, new minister elected blind arbitrator, consider the fifteen-year-old girl's situation less significant than the flexing of male egos or the marking of territory. They include no women. They cut Misner out of the complete picture. Thus, K.D. feels justified in ignoring his paternal responsibilities, thinking: "You cornered me at more socials than I can remember and when I finally agreed I didn't have to take your drawers down you beat me to it so this ain't my problem" (54). Gigi, on the other hand, entices K.D. to do all the driving by saying: " 'Listen, you want to argue, take me back.' 'No. No, I don't want to argue; I just want to . . . ride.' 'Yeah? How fast?' 'Told you. Fast as I can.' 'How long?' 'Long as you want.' 'How far?' 'All the way' " (75).

Misner's irritation with K.D.'s "devious smile" and "oily apology," signs of a male "too quick to please," is justifiable enough from the outside. Reducing him simply as "servile to his uncles," "brutal with females" does not take into account the inside story of why or to what end a good boy with a lovely smile lets a girl dog him (62): "Like sugar turning from unreasonable delight to the body's mortal enemy, his craving for [Gigi] had poisoned him, rendered him diabetic, stupid, helpless." The romantic yearning he has stroked for years, "an aching, humiliating, self-loathing love that drifted from pining to stealth," drives him to treat like a dog the woman who will become his wife (147). That wife's best friend, Billie Delia, however, cuts to the chase: "The real battle was not about infant life or a bride's reputation but about disobedience, which meant, of course, the stallions were fighting about who controlled the mares and their foals" (150). Although the studs allow Misner to see him only as a slick self-seeker, K.D. is actually a dog whisperer spoiled by poor handling into a bad bad bad dog.

By contrast, a stay at the convent inspires the other dog in question to bay at a big sky rather than eyeball "a woman with her breasts on a tray" (75). If Mavis is a one-man battered wife who fights free of her husband finally to make her peace with her children, Gigi represents everyman's exhibitionist who ultimately embraces one person in private to make peace with nobody. She does, however, offer everybody a cockeyed sense of humor as she gets back into the fray. Billie Delia refers to Mavis as the nice one and Gigi as the funny one, for whom Billie overcomes an instant antipathy and comes to appreciate. As Baby Suggs observes in *Beloved*, Gigi must first imagine Grace before she can find Grace. Still in prison at the book's end but on his lunch break, her father witnesses his daughter but not her companion (probably still Seneca) dressed in camouflage, still playing her radio. Grace's stillness, however, nudged into action by horse whisperers, belies a newfound but calmer commitment to bathing nude only in a private part of the lake and an ongoing battle for public human rights.

Toontown Banderilleros and Gold Rush Agents

Male lovers serve as seasoned irons for Mavis and Gigi's most searing brand of pain—and a major reason they irritate each other. The presence or absence of sons and fathers is prime cause for Seneca and Pallas to hurt themselves and huddle together. Eddie Turtle displays a variation on Frank Albright's type of abuse toward childlike Seneca: "She had known him for only six months, but already he knew how hopeless she was." While this first-timer may be "guilty as charged" concerning his treatment of children, his own innocence becomes manifest in his role as son, not husband. Eddie represents another naïve dog lover, more concerned with their diets and exercise than his girlfriend's survival. He inherits his perfectionist behavior, however, from an obsessive-compulsive mother who makes him jumpy as a rabbit. Locked up for a hit-and-run accident that hurts a child, he tells Seneca to bring him some shoes and a Bible, like "all first offenders," straightaway. Too eager to please because otherwise people "might not like her. Might cry. Might leave," Seneca does her best but, as usual, bungles the job. Eddie's pleasure in the extravagant, size eleven, black-and-white running shoes is diminished by the oversize *Living Bible* without color pictures she travels to Preston, then Bloomington, Indiana, to buy because it has "lots of lined pages for recording . . . whole families' activities over the years" (131). For impatient, conflicted, godforsaken Eddie, the book accommodates way too much.

Both young people have been scarred by discontented mothers and the lack of other family. Seneca's nineteen-year-old "sister," Jean, leaves Seneca, at five, home alone to forage for herself for good. Mrs. Turtle refuses after her husband dies to budge from her shell at all for anybody, "even if that somebody was her only son." A strict vegetarian, she vows to live forever by eating one "(and only one)" each of seven greens and seven grains a day. She rejects anything with "hooves, feathers, shell or scales" at her table along with Eddie's proposal, conveyed by Seneca, to cash in his dead father's savings bonds to get him out of a mess. In the meantime, Eddie, "too nervous and irritated to eat" the ham sandwich Seneca brings him, sits in his cell "Whining. Blaming." The behavior of this effusive victim contrasts sharply with that of the involuntary male inmates. Unlike Eddie, these men seem happy with their visitors. Eyes soft with pleasure, they notice everything, listen carefully, offer domestic advice, and hold their children. Holding back the inside part and vigorously ignoring the guards become integral to their management of masculinity behind bars. Eddie, on the other hand, is embarrassed by the size of his Bible, wants mustard instead of mayonnaise on his sandwich, and makes Seneca promise to carry out his command that she at least do four things right. The cryptic shorthand of an obviously angry boy can be reduced to: "Send, sell, get, call" (132–33).

Eddie's agent finds his mother in Wichita, obsessed by "grave-faced men [lying] softly, courteously to each other" on television. If a compliant Seneca cannot say one way or another whether she has watched the Watergate trials, Mrs. Turtle has emerged so publicly hardened from her private anxieties that she can declare having absolutely no intention of allowing her son to put her "in the poorhouse so a slick lawyer can stay rich." She offers Seneca a sparse, vegetarian supper but no bed for the night. When her visitor retraces her steps, however, to observe through a window the woman alone, Mrs. Turtle is shrieking "for all the world like the feathered, finned and hoofed whose flesh she never ate," sobbing into thin air a "flat-out helpless mothercry" (134). The girl is stunned to see that the woman, like herself, stays intensely private about indulging her pain. Alone in her arena, provoked by her own banderillero, Seneca attacks herself by marking a razorblade roadmap across her arms for relief and thrill. Resistant to his mother's barrage of banderillas, but not her mixed signals, Eddie goes public with his barbs. Anxiety about whether his childhood home will offer shelter to either tortoises or hares finds him bullying people, especially children, from whom he then flees or about whom he complains because they make him so nervous.

Sitting "frogged-legged" on a plastic bench in the bus station, Seneca recuperates from her panic and repulsion to Mrs. Turtle's wet heaves by sipping ginger ale, not eating peanuts, and not crying. Ankles crossed, knees spread, the young bull(turned)frog makes an easy target for Mrs. Fox's gig. Morrison peoples her dark Toontown midwestern with comic animal-like copies of human predators and prey.[12] Norma Keene Fox merges a Marilyn Monroesque cartoon villain with a character from an African (American) folktale or Aesop's fables to illustrate that a victimized woman becomes especially capable of preying on children.[13] She assesses Seneca, with her long lashes, wide clogs, and webbed bag, as a not-to-be-missed, garden-variety pet. Her chauffeur David, acting more like Goliath, serves as her surrogate sharp eyes and go-between bodyguard but nobody's giant slayer. Merging unobtrusively into the background among the motley array of bus station inhabitants, this gray-eyed, gold-buttoned man "in a gray chauffeur's uniform stroll[s] the floor as though looking for his passenger" (134–35). In other words, he cases the joint.

David appraises Seneca to be a docile, clueless, penniless runaway. He approaches her politely, "authorized to offer [her] five hundred dollars for some complicated but quite easy work." Ushering her effortlessly outside the station into a quietly throbbing limousine, the silver fox hands her without speaking into the clutches of a pretty, animated champagne-haired woman. Before Seneca can collect her wits, gorgeous surroundings and food "too pretty to eat" seduce her into doing unspeakable things. Neither wealthy, absent Leon Fox nor Norma's son, away matriculating at Rice, notices why this bored wife and mother prefers midwestern isolation to carry out dark, undercover activities. Always free to leave, Seneca moves from "peacock feathers to abject humiliation," from "caviar tartlets to filth. But the pain framed the pleasure, gave it edge. The humiliation made surrender deep, tender. Long-lasting." Mrs. Fox calls her "many sweet things" but never once asks her name, handing over the money and a cashmere serape when Mr. Fox telephones his imminent return and returning increasingly squirrelly Seneca to David. David, gold buttons "extra gleamy in the sunlight," drives her back to her bus station habitat without ever saying a word (135–38).

Vulnerable to attack by large perverts of either sex, tiny mousy Seneca learns to travel "resolutely nowhere, closed off from society, hidden among quiet cargo—no one knowing she was there" (138). A stay at the convent, however, gives the mole means to live in the light of day. Her eyes looking directly into those of the other, she can by the end of the novel refuse a woman who attempts to make contact. Haunted by the huge chocolate eyes of the child she had at fourteen, Seneca's mother finally locates the steady gaze of a girl who can now smile and say no: "That's okay. Everybody makes mistakes" (317). Jean is enabled not by David but by Jack, husband and father become, unbeknownst to him, both giant killer and seed planter. It is Jack who, again inadvertently, makes sure Jean understands that the grown woman who can forgive her and so finally go easy on herself has to be Jean's daughter Seneca.

The picadors who stick it to Pallas get caught up in the paltry glitter of the contemporary California gold rush. Unlike Seneca, who represents the poor little poor girl, Pallas suggests the poor little rich girl. Her father, Milton Truelove, does not stick "around enough to notice anything" because he is a big-time entertainment attorney "with a small client list." His agency, however, expands more than sufficiently because it includes two "crossover black entertainers," young performers who "hit the charts and stay there." Like Milton, Pallas's careful caballero lives by applying the adage that, used smartly, less is more. A struggling (con) artist/school janitor, Carlos enables his protégé, who eludes her brother Jerome's notice and that of the sharp-eyed housekeeper, to garner short-term glamour. She manages to mix running away from her father with a holiday jaunt to impress her mother topped off by elopement with the "coolest, most gorgeous man in the world." Only her address and red Toyota prevent plump sixteen-year-old Pallas from outright torture by juvenile predators at her high-toned high school. For the most part, they ignore her. Excluded from her father's agency, she substitutes food and then life with Carlos for diversion and pleasure. He helps her to start her stalled engine by pressing her pedal to the floor. He follows her home in his Ford. He accepts her gift of a record album only if he can reciprocate with a chili dog. Carlos always holds back on her eagerly proffered presents, holding out, with respect to favors or sex, for more. His deprivation overstimulates Pallas's performance. Although she does everything in her power to inspire him to make love to her and he appears to respond passionately to their necking, for weeks he defers going all the way until "[they] are married." However, the sculptor gets hugely excited by the idea of painter Divine (Dee Dee) Truelove's "perfect place for an artist" (166–67).

While her father hustles about procuring for young, vocal self-starters, Carlos acts as Pallas's listless gigolo and ardent escort out of Milton's unsatisfying California scene. Molded by a languid Latin lover to make most of the sweet music herself, Pallas provides Carlos's entrée into the self-indulgent New Mexico art world of her mother. Her last day at home includes a busy spree of check cashing and shopping, acquiring gifts that Carlos reluctantly (but Dee Dee eagerly) accepts. The girl stocks up on things "anybody's mother would like, but in a variety of colors and styles because she couldn't take a chance on having nothing that would please a woman she had not seen in thirteen years." If she thinks she has bought the whole package in the form of a "movie-star-looking maintenance man," she does not plan to turn her treat wholesale over to the other woman. Life with mother includes spectacular scenery, marvelous food, and artistic intercourse among the three of them late at night under the stars. The climax leaves Pallas cold. When Carlos's final weary words sigh, "This is the home I've been looking for," and Dee Dee's yawning "Of course it is" elicits his responsive yawn, Pallas fails to read the signs. Had she calculated "the simultaneous yawns, the settling-in voices," though, coupled with their closeness in age, she still could not have prevented "the grappling bodies exchanging moans in the grass, unmindful of any watcher." But the deficient arithmetic of a high-school dropout does not prepare her for this double-cross nor for boys who will sideswipe a girl's red Toyota to score a bull's-eye on the bottom of a lake (166–69).

Like a parody on the birth of an underage Pallas Athena, virgin goddess of art, war, fertility, water, and wisdom, who springs fully formed from her father's head, Pallas's ideas about such topics jump uninformed out of (John?) Milton Truelove's brain. His cynical Hollywood school of thought suggests that, far from lost, paradise comes up for auction and gifted young people represent commodities to argue over. He sticks his daughter with his catch-as-catch-can philosophy. On what she thinks is the "happiest day of her life," however, as she does last-minute Christmas shopping in preparation for her grand tour, the behavior of a "crazy woman" on the escalator halts Pallas's step. A combination of Hagar's bizarre last scene in *Song of Solomon* and *Tar Baby*'s woman in yellow, this figure marks a disturbing cross between a child playing at dress-up and a heavily done-up prostitute. As she dances up the steps, rolling her hips and swaying her head, the woman recalls "a bygone era of slow grind in a badly lit room of couples. Not the electric go-go pace of 1974." Her eyes lock with those of the girl in designer clothes. Piped-in carols play backup for her singsong: "Here's pussy. Want some pussy, pussy." Although a combination of fascination and panic confuses Pallas at the time, subsequent experience, including gang rape and a stint at the convent, allow her to perceive the figure "in greater detail than when first sighted." Far from having "nothing in common," she and the "revolting" woman are two sides of the same coin (163–64).

Her father, on the other hand, pays no closer attention to the daughter he named when she calls him from Oklahoma than while she lives at home. Calling her "kitty," unchaperoned boys in a truck force Pallas's car off the road after which they abuse her physically and psychologically. She stands hidden up to her neck in a lake, afraid to speak lest she choke on black seepage. The consummate sexual performer comes to be terrified of the horrible things that could touch her below the surface as she keeps her head barely above water. Morrison deliberately counters the effect of the white drivers' brutality with the restrained behavior of Indian boys who ride alongside the girl in the back of an oncoming truck. Despite her recent baptism, Pallas blames the lack of proposals to pick her up on the loss of her expensive huaraches—until a "truckful of Indians" stops. She connects the woman in a fedora in front, along with the child on her lap, to a civilizing presence among the men, making it "possible to accept the offer of a lift" (173). In the same boat with bedraggled Pallas, monitored by a female with a child, the six young Indian men stare at her hot pink shorts without smiling but hand her an onion and a baloney sandwich out of their paper sacks. They also help her step down from the truck.

Milton responds to Pallas's phone call by doing nothing and saying, "We'll talk." Speaking rapidly over and through her halting appeal, he vents his frustration onto her, threatens to sue Carlos and the school, blames her "bitch" mother and their mixed marriage, places his aides on alert, tells Pallas to get herself to the police, who will take her to an airport, and avoids attending to her himself. Although Milton signs off, like Manley Gibson, with a "Love you, baby," the prisoner is serving time and unable to come while the advocate will not take time off from overseeing his own California agency (253). Gigi must learn to let her father off the hook. Pallas has to ignore her father and let her mother go. Neglected and not held at home, she finds time to heal at the convent, putting her head on Seneca's tiny bosom, sitting on Connie's lap, or sleeping in Mavis's room. Such attention enables Pallas to reject fool's gold and give birth the human way to something real—her son Divine. Morrison's conclusion pictures the girl returning to her mother's place where Dee Dee, obsessed with painting her daughter's portrait, attempts to get the child's face straight in her head. Unable to get out the right words to draw the attention of the girl passing by with a sword in her hand and a baby strapped to her chest, Divine Dee Dee is left holding her fifteenth canvas and shouting "Urg. Urg. Neh!" (311). She catches sight of but cannot hold her daughter one last time as the girl rummages under the guestroom bed "(where Carlos—the motherfucker—used to sleep)" (311–12). With a "satisfied grunt," Pallas holds aloft her good leather sandals and climbs back into a beat-up car containing either women or men. Milton never notices she had been pregnant.

The Good, the Bad, and the Ugly

Divine's unspecified father falls among the various unnamed and nameless good, bad, and ugly hombres that Morrison disperses throughout *Paradise*.[14] Whether he be apathetic user Carlos or a member of Pallas's avid "dickface" gang-rapists, he fits together with Ruby's white bullies and Seneca's variegated pedophiles into the category of one bad dude (163). Ensconced safely within what she perceives as the "blessed malelessness" of the convent, Seneca can speculate about the variety of males who find her attractive (177). Starting with a foster brother who jerks off the safety pin "holding the waist of her jeans together," a bevy of boys abound who "snatch her" as well as men who "flash her." She always winds up the one whose nipple is "tweaked by a boy on a dare from his sniggering friends." It is she whom "the man sitting with his baby daughter on a park bench" picks to lift "his penis out and [make] kissing noises." Far from providing refuge, her boyfriends redirect toward Seneca their fury at her complaints of fondling by "friends or strangers." Thus, Seneca learns to blame herself for attacks against her. The convent teaches her, however, that the "something inside that was the matter" is, on the contrary, an outside, refreshingly childlike freshness, which unconcealed serves as a lure for pedophiles (260–61). She also comes to realize that, when she freeloads, one truck driver, "splicing his questions, curses and threats with mild flirtations," will hold her against a tire while another, usually accompanied by his wife, will willingly or not offer her a free ride. She learns to navigate both.

Isolated Ruby also draws unidentified boys who bully on a dare. They reaffirm for her fathers that "men strong and willing were needed when lost and aimless strangers did not just drive through." Easily tagged by their cars and license plates, these strangers, "young and drunk or old and sober," spot several colored girls, and the race is on: "The drivers slow down, put their heads out the windows and holler. Their eyes crinkled in mischief they drive around the girls, making U-turns and K's, churning up grass seed in front of the houses, flushing cats in front of Ace's Grocery Store. Circling. . . . One of the passengers has opened the front of his trousers and hung himself out the window to scare the girls." Emerging one by one from their various outlooks, the townsmen "see the wish in this most militant of gestures, and smile. Smile reluctantly and in spite of themselves because they know that from this moment on, if not before, this man, till his final illness, will do as much serious damage to colored folks as he can." Guns not pointed but held slackly at sides, the fathers circle the circling cars and intimidate the boys out of town, their tires spinning, dust spuming "in the tread they left behind" (12–13).

Another white stranger, however, passing through Ruby with his wife and child, might be excessively benign. Morrison signals the parents' race by noting their child's feverish blue eyes and bright-yellow hair. The stranger's car, a station wagon, suggests his harmlessness despite its Arkansas plates. When he enters Ace's Grocery, this "city-dressed man in his forties" smiles his greeting and grins his apology to Richard Misner "for having violated the male rule of never asking for directions. 'Wife made me stop. Said she's had it.' " Connections established, he wonders about a doctor for his child and expresses gratitude when Misner offers to fetch medicine while the wife and baby come in out of the cold. Anna Flood suggests that the baby's condition may require more than mere cough syrup. The man goes to get his wife. As Anna mulls over making cinnamon toast for the beleaguered adults and mashed bananas for the constipated baby, the wife elects to "stay put," and her husband is obliged to "keep the motor running." As he drinks the hot coffee handed him, she sounds the horn for him to buy her snacks and cola. Laughing off the idea of a blizzard in Oklahoma, apparently ignoring Anna's advice to "gas up" as well as Steward's to "ride it out somewhere," the good-natured stranger will be recognized by the bottle of cough medicine inside a snow-covered station wagon found not far from the convent. The car goes unnoticed until flesh falls off skeletons. Driven this time by a female, too good or too afraid to accept hospitality from black people, a clueless male in light clothing and thin shoes along with his sick child are given no second chance. Together but alone, the white family, despite their obvious love for one another, becomes "Just some lost folks" (121–23).

The inelegant efforts of a long-gone, unnamed embezzler represent *Paradise*'s ugly side. Morrison constructs her illicit mansion turned convent school to reflect her denial of dualism. Shaped "like a live cartridge," built with its windows facing north like lookouts, this "embezzler's folly" screams "fright, not triumph." It also shouts contradiction. While the north end curves to a "deadly point" containing the living and dining areas, the broad southern back-end shelters "signs of his desire in two rooms: an outsize kitchen and a room where he could play rich men's games." Because the house offers no egress from which to see the sun either rise or set except through bedroom blinds, interior light remains "always misleading." The embezzler's idea of good-time entertaining in an isolated fortress appears "no more sophisticated or interesting" than he, involving mostly "food, sex and toys." Arrested by northern lawmen after his one and only voluptuous affair, he is replaced for a pittance by "four teaching sisters" who "diligently canceled the obvious echoes of his delight but could do nothing to hide his terror" (71). Incredibly crude before, with its brass bathroom male genitalia/paraphernalia and alabaster vagina ashtrays, the school becomes even uglier when nuns attempt to erase sexual evidence as they encourage stilled Arapaho girls to sit and forget. Morrison begins her book with armed hunters out of place among rooms "where macramé baskets float next to Flemish candelabra; where Christ and His mother glow in niches trimmed in grapevines. The Sisters of the Sacred Cross chipped away all the nymphs, but curves of their marble hair still strangle grape leaves and tease the fruit" (4). The very dissonance of this awkward attempt to reinstate decorum encourages the outlaw women inside to understand: "Never break [body and spirit] in two. Never put one over the other. Eve is Mary's mother. Mary is the daughter of Eve" (263).

Like the wildly practical house in *Sula* belonging to women who love men, the remade mansion/convent reflects not so much femininity, or malelessness, as it does androgyny, flexibility, and a sense of timelessness apparent in its architecture and furnishings. On the other hand, the male-driven world of Ruby, rigid and linear, dates itself by the year and make of its cars. Morrison places her riotous embezzler alongside her sedate nuns to illustrate that earthly paradise is neither perfect nor clearly visible. What looks bad or even ugly from one direction can turn out to be good when viewed from its opposite. Unidentified males in trucks and cars can rape, bully, or, without much help from their female counterparts, share their food. They can also, under a little pressure from women, get everybody lost. Or they can hide out to save their own skins and inadvertently offer sanctuary to various very different others. One woman's bad or ugly dude, then, can be good for another.

Have Gun, Will Travel

The unnamed hombres, along with the banderilleros and picadors who provoke Seneca and Pallas, operate primarily as agents. Thus, they are harder to separate from the specific women with whom Morrison associates them. Ruby's paladins, on the other hand, constitute more distinct, individualized portraits of her Old and New Fathers.[15] Conversely, Morrison deliberately limits overt signs of the founding mothers to a single name and, as town historian Pat Best notes, generally connects them to their men. Morrison frequently expresses the contrast between Old and New World black women in terms of harbor and ship. Depicting their male counterparts, particularly in *Paradise*, as Old World walking or running men and New World riding or driving men, she affirms, as with the women, the need for a balance between extremes. The Old Fathers who found Haven have to outfox the world as they wander through it on foot. In addition to their nine large intact families, they become responsible for some fifty fragments of others, six adolescent orphans, and two stolen children, "snatched up because the circumstances in which the children were found wouldn't let them do otherwise," for a total of one hundred and fifty-eight people who make the original journey from Mississippi and Louisiana to Oklahoma (189). Morrison lists as "legend" the roll call of the first families; it resounds like a biblical, epic, or Faulknerian catalog of names: "Blackhorse, Morgan, Poole, Fleetwood, Beauchamp, Cato, Flood, and both DuPres" clans (188). Individually and collectively, the names of these men communicate a sense of history that encompasses the descendants of "those whose worthiness was so endemic it got three of their children elected to rule in state legislatures and county offices" and one viable run for governor (193).

Morrison describes what drives these men to run as the "Disallowing." Initially they deny what should have been obvious: while most of the "Negro men chased or invited out of office (in Mississippi, in Louisiana, in Georgia) got less influential but still white-collar work following the purges of 1875 . . . they alone . . . were reduced to penury and/or field labor." The sole feature that "distinguished them from their Negro peers" was the 8-rock midnight of their skins. Attributing their treatment to the divisions between free and slave, rich and poor, and "usually but not always, white against black," they take their "history, those years, each other and their uncorruptible worthiness and walked to the 'Run.' " Here Morrison alludes to the all-black frontier towns that spring up after the 1889 land run in Oklahoma Territory. Her 8-rock characters find their worthiness Out There disdained not only by arrogant easterners; their lighter-skinned brethren in Fairly, Oklahoma, also reject the men and, in so doing, their wives and daughters: "The sign of racial purity they had taken for granted had become a stain" (193–94). Afterward they no longer consist of "nine families and some more." They transform into a "tight band of wayfarers bound by the enormity of what happened to them." Their abstract horror of whites becomes clarified by hatred for men like themselves in "all ways but one," men who exclude them and then offer them means to subsist within that exclusion (189). Led by hurt pride and Zechariah Morgan, the Old Fathers proceed to make a pact with God promising an "unadulterated and unadulteried" bloodline in exchange for their survival. The "magic" holds, however, only so long as it resides in Haven, then Ruby (217). Thus, that which worries the men, Old and New Fathers alike, emanates from a worship of the purity of the women.

Morrison continues to question the romantic ideals and rigid, self-righteous patriarchy that her western paladins imitate—but derive disparately from that of European chivalric knights—in the rift between Coffee and Tea Morgan. Strong, raggedy, shot at, "robbed of their rifles by two cowboys," afraid of nothing save the condition of the children's feet, the Fathers shooed away from Fairly, OK, by some "highfalutin men in collars and good shoes" find themselves lost and angry yet far from finished (98, 96). Because he limps, Zechariah (a.k.a. Big Papa, né Coffee)

Morgan rides sitting stiffly erect on a plank board. Patricia Best, Morrison's spoof on feminist historians, speculates in her study of Ruby's patrician fathers that Black Coffee Morgan must be a variant combination of the African Kofi and the French Le Moyne, and that Kofi renames himself Zechariah after the Old Testament visionary who anticipates the results of disobedience: "The punishment for not showing mercy or compassion was a scattering among all nations, and pleasant land made desolate" (192). His own slave history rendering him terrified of divisions among families, he allows his fear to separate him from his brother.

Taunted personally and professionally while Louisiana's lieutenant governor, touted as an embarrassment to blacks and a threat to whites, refused even menial labor, misinterpreted as cold and distant, Zechariah is reduced in 1873 to boarding his family with that of a sister. Before he turns into Zechariah-on-the-run, however, he resides quietly as domestic Coffee to his close twin Tea. His brother's public rejection offends Tea equally, but he handles humiliation differently. White men "amused by the double faces" accost the two outside a saloon and instruct them at gunpoint to dance. Unlike Tea, who "accommodated the whites, even though he was a grown man, older than they were," Coffee "neither cried out nor limped away" when he takes a bullet in his foot: "From that moment they weren't brothers anymore" (302, 189). Taking up with other like-minded men, former legislators whose misfortunes resembled his, newly named Zechariah forms the core of the Old Fathers: "Needless to say, Coffee didn't ask Tea to join them on their journey to Oklahoma" (302). Afraid of shame for his brother that could more accurately be called shame of himself, Zechariah becomes that which he fears. He never acknowledges his other half again and starts a new life for himself on the lam. Old, lame, carried at the tail of a line of those like him, he renews the destructive cycle at Fairly, reelects to follow a god of separatism, and when he locates the perfect home site to do so, calls upon his son to "'Run!' And Rector [a.k.a. Big Daddy] did" (97).

The sins of the Fathers in *Paradise* are certainly visited on their sons. All fourteen New Fathers follow the path established by their forebears but with a twist. Having fought, rather than outfoxed, the world during World War II, they withdraw from the world after the second Disallowing. The promised scattering occurs with the enlistment of 8-rock males. Those "that survived that particular war came right back home, saw what had become of Haven, heard about the missing testicles of other colored soldiers; about medals being torn off by gangs of rednecks and Sons of the Confederacy—and recognized the Disallowing, Part Two. . . . So they did it again" (194). Arrogant as ever about the purity of their blood, they abandon the desolation that suffocates post-Depression all-black towns and move further west. The New Fathers constitute yet another catalog of names: "Deacon Morgan, Steward Morgan, William Cato, Ace Flood, Aaron Poole, Nathan DuPres, Moss DuPres, Arnold Fleetwood, Ossie Beauchamp, Harper Jury, Sargeant Person, John Seawright, Edward Sands and . . . Roger Best" (194–95). With the advent of modernization, however, and the availability of the automobile, these men ride or drive through Ruby rather than walk around Haven.

Although Drum Blackhorse, former state officeholder and of African and Native American mixed blood, and his son Thomas walk at the head of the line of Old Fathers heading west, the car tracks of the New Fathers following them erase their footprints. Hunt contends that as Haven and Ruby drift farther away from African and Arapaho values to embrace the traditional Euro-American model, they creep closer to self-destruction. The founders' patrician mentality creates barriers and prohibits a peaceful bond between the townspeople and the land (121–22). In *Sisters of the Yam*, bell hooks suggests that restoring a harmonious connection to the land would encourage a rejuvenation of the African American community.[16] Morrison illustrates the more urban male thinking of her New Fathers at its most extreme in the inflexible attitude of Elder Morgan, Steward and Deacon's oldest brother, whose striking return from World War I snaps shut the gap between Reconstruction and World War II.

When Elder disembarks from Liverpool to Hoboken in 1919, he strolls the streets of New York City before boarding his train home. He notices two men gesticulating at what he takes to be a streetwalker and, "registering contempt for her trade," assumes an immediate affinity with the shouters. As one of the men smashes his fist into the face of the woman, however, the scene slides "just as suddenly . . . from everyday color to black and white." Spontaneous violence having been integral to his life for the last ten months, he runs toward the white men as they turn to kick the now unconscious black woman and continues to hit one until the second attacks him. All are hurt. No one wins. A frightened Elder flees from the police, concealing his torn uniform under his overcoat. He displays the memory of "that whiteman's fist in that colored woman's face" for the rest of his life. The replayed shame of running off and leaving her becomes his rendition of the place of the stuck record. It remains immortalized with him when the Morgan men see to it over his wife's protests and his dead body that he is "buried as he demanded to be: in the uniform with its rips on display" (94–95). Like his old father, the eldest son continues to indulge blues pain. Like their older brothers, the New Fathers ritualistically re-create scenes of rejection. Reproduced every Christmas, the Disallowing pageant substitutes for Nativity as the children take the parts of their abused parents and grandparents.[17]

With the support of Richard Misner, however, some of the Sons and Daughters of the New Fathers attempt to find a different groove. While they continue to "finger the jagged grain," they seek new ways to transcend old hurts.[18] Scattered sporadically throughout the text, many not specifically identified, their names read less like a catalog than a cacophony: Royal, Destry, and Vane Beauchamp; Wisdom Poole's brothers Apollo, Brood, and Hurston and his sister Caline; Timothy Jr. and Spider Seawright; two Person boys, a couple of DuPres children, Lorcas and Linda Sands. Not one local church, Methodist, Pentecostal, or Baptist, is safe from "the sass, the pout, the outright defiance of . . . the ones who wanted to name the Oven 'such and such place.' " Emerging from a variety of perspectives, the Children come together at a town meeting in Calvary Church to voice their right to disagree about an interpretation of the saying on a community icon. The Fathers state that the letters, embossed originally on the communal Oven by ironmonger Zechariah Morgan, command: "Beware the Furrow of His Brow." Since the symbols have faded now and become difficult to discern, the Children declare that no "ex-slave would tell us to be scared all the time" and insist that the motto urges action: "Be the Furrow of His Brow." The Fathers call on the then five-year-old Miss Ester's "finger memory." The Children howl "at the notion of remembering invisible words you couldn't even read by tracing letters you couldn't pronounce." Differences between fathers and offspring grow deeper than generational. They again involve issues of obedience: the fathers' faith in a fixed past and that "you say sir when you speak to men" counters the sons' and daughters' conviction that they have an obligation to question and participate in their own history (83–84).

Morrison takes her stand about reevaluating reality in her 1993 Nobel Prize lecture. Depicting insight in the form of an aged blind griot, either female or male, she affirms the significance of language as agency and the importance of generations and genders listening carefully to one another. So when a Morgan twin attempts to close communication at Calvary by announcing to the Children: "Act short with me all you want, you in long trouble if you think you can disrespect a row you never hoed," Misner retorts: "Seems to me, Deek, they are respecting it. It's because they do know the Oven's value that they want to give it new life." In modern culture, language represents power as well as connection. Because Ruby is modernized, communal space has been lost, and the Oven is no longer literally functional. Thus, as Morrison predicts with the humorous linguistic battle over Not Doctor Street in *Song of Solomon*, its meaning must become metaphorical. Controversy occurs, as she illustrates by outlining arguments prior to actual Oven letters, about who controls interpretation and the application of history. Problems also arise concerning attitudes of address. Although some of the Sons, "strained and close to tears," vehemently stand their ground, others like K.D. and Jeff Fleetwood go not-so-placidly the way of their fathers. Some, like Menus Jury, go way awry. The New Fathers, however, perceive all as "in trouble or acting up behind every door." While one unidentified older male voice proclaims, "That boy needs a strap. Blasphemy!" Steward Morgan shuts down passionate debate by promising frontier violence: "If you, any one of you, ignore, change, take away, or add to the words in the mouth of that Oven, I will blow your head off just like you was a hood-eye snake" (83–87).

Sounding on a lower frequency as strident as some of the Sons, those New Fathers bound for trouble include the ones least pliant, those trapped in the place of the stuck record. The Fathers who refuse to enlist in a war upon women have sons and daughters who stand up at Calvary. Two New Fathers die outside Ruby. Beautiful Billy Cato, preferring to make people laugh, loses his life on the battlefield, his recovered wedding band "too twisted to poke a finger through" (199). Because nothing remains to bury except some worthless effects, his father-in-law and fellow New Father, Roger Best, exists in limbo, out of work for either his ambulance or his hearse. Had Ace Flood not previously cashed it in at a hospital in Demby, he would quite probably have gambled on the hunters. His appetite for immutability apparent in the tough construction and management of his grocery, he lives long enough to see the store "change from a necessary service in Ruby to a business patronized by the loyal for certain items, though they balked at his prices and more and more drove their trucks to Demby for cheaper and better supplies" (120). After his death and under the more flexible stewardship of his daughter Anna, the store reduces the size of its inventory but blossoms through variety, style, and comfort.

The DuPres family possesses a long line of successful shopkeepers and skilled laborers. Proud of their statehouse heritage, Nathan and Moss are even more pleased to be descended from artisans, whose "serious work" was eliminated by white immigrants resistant to fair competition. If they take their craft seriously, the DuPres play and pray easily: "Virtue, unexpected goodness, made them smile." In addition, they talk seriously to each other and seek answers from one another. Supper-table conversations focus on "the problems each member was having, how each and all could handle or help," how a behavior measures up ethically. Their dislike or disapproval of the convent crew thus becomes moot. Confronted with the prospect of a witch-hunt, Pious DuPres calls on Deed Sands, Aaron Poole, and the Beauchamps, famous since Ossie's horse race for upholding the values of moral courage and serious play, to defend the women. Pious knows that, although and even because these men live on the outskirts of Ruby, they will quickly respond in his favor.

Paradise never directly addresses John Seawright's ethical stance. His name, however, and the fact that he says nothing when two of his sons speak out at Calvary suggest a certain mystical fluidity. Sargeant Person, Wisdom Poole, Harper Jury, and Arnold Fleetwood, together with the Morgans, represent the most rigid of the New Fathers. While they view themselves as paladins, they prey upon women in order to protect them from themselves. Morrison underscores the limitations of these men's self-awareness by their location within Ruby proper and in their names. Owner of Sargeant's Feed and Seed, Sargeant Person can spell neither of his. His misspelled given name suggesting a misplaced affinity for military order, his surname, as Pat Best sarcastically observes, reads equally inaccurately: "How come that ignorant Negro doesn't know his name is Pierson?" (197). Sargeant snaps to it, however, when it comes to doing business. Aware of "how much less his outlay would be if he owned the Convent land" and how his chances of obtaining it improve with all the women gone, he reveals his hypocritical duplicity in his actual motives. The irony of his name needing no comment, Wisdom Poole is not a legitimate New Father. He joins the hunt merely because he needs "a reason to explain why he had no control anymore over his brothers and sisters," to clarify why "those who used to worship him, listen to him, were now strays trying to be on their own" or fighting over a woman (277).

Her midwife's experience endows snatched-up orphan Lone DuPres with the insight to see into the men behind the paladin mask. She knows that New Fathers with guns and a willingness to "go gallivanting off" merely shift the "fangs and tail . . . somewhere else. Out yonder all slithery in a house full of women" not "locked safely away from men; but worse, women who chose themselves for company, which is to say not a convent but a coven" (276–77). Morrison withholds Lone's divinations until just before the massacre so that, almost too late, readers learn that Harper Jury's motives really weigh on his wife and children. Harper never allows his only son, Menus, to forget the betrayal of Menus's mother, Martha. He worries his second wife, Catherine, into a "nervous digestion carrying on about what she was doing and who she was seeing." His time at church to testify about his sins always turns into a diatribe about "loose women who could keep you from knowing who, what and where your children are." Harper harps on as judge and jury at his son's trials, too, forbidding Menus to marry the "pretty redbone girl" he brings home because she is "more like a fast woman than a bride." Lacking the courage to stand up to Harper and live with the woman elsewhere, Menus lets her go, blames his alcoholic failures on a stint in Vietnam instead of his own cowardice, and exacts as his price of submission his father's "undisturbed acceptance of his affliction." The convent women who witness the pain and wipe up the vomit of this defensive, manipulative male merely render him "ripe for a raid on anybody" (277–78).

Morrison concludes her lineup of paladins who scapegoat women with Arnold and Jefferson Fleetwood and a regenerated K.D.: "As for the Fleetwoods, . . . well, they'd been wanting to blame somebody for Sweetie's children for a long time" (277). Making use of the adage that the children who go bad are always somebody else's, perfectionist father and imperfect son attribute the disabilities of incestuously overbred offspring to inept midwifery or the United States government. Lone is well aware that, because "Men scared of us, always will be," she cannot expect the Fathers' thanks. Her mentor, Fairy DuPres, tells her that midwives represent "death's handmaiden standing as between them and the children their wives carry." As such, males become reliant on the interference, the "secret skill," and the orders of females, and the dependency annoys them—not to speak of a woman's ability to read their thoughts (272). Although they can eliminate Lone's livelihood in exchange for the rare doctor who consents to treat black patients, fathers and grandfathers must still cope with shame about sick progeny. In addition, Fleetwood husbands stay grateful but infuriated at their wives' devotion to their children. Jeff's association with Agent Orange becomes the likely next villain. However, black former soldiers cannot shoot the Veterans Administration, and the convent women—despite the fact that Lone delivers some of the unpromising children long before the first female arrives—begin to look good.

As usual, K.D. crusades under his uncles' flag, but his current battle aims to eradicate embarrassment over being rebuffed by a female who once looked good to him. Now a family man, who tops Jeff's dysfunctional children with a son possessing an intact brain and all his fingers and toes, he can afford to reject as strange the woman he stalked for years. Such adroit projection segues beautifully into an attack on all the women in the name of an attempted abortion by his pregnant (but unloved) past lover and present (bitter) wife and their violently revolting preemie, called Che (as in Guevara) by Gigi. The Paladins perceive the problem as anything but their own blood. The women carry the praise and the blame.

The Lone Ranger and Tonto

What finally saves one of the Morgans is riding together. Rob Davidson identifies the protagonist of *Paradise* as Ruby (356). Geoffrey Bent agrees and maintains that Morrison undermines her talent for characterization by making her protagonist a town. Bent further argues that, because virtue and vice are connected to place and "rigorously sorted along the convenient divide of gender," the novel falls prey to exclusivity: "All the women are good, all the men bad" (148–49). If readers consider the protagonist as male and twinned, however, something quite the contrary occurs. The Morgans certainly function as Morrison's metaphor for their inner circle's "narcissistic claims to perfection," but their relationship also reveals an underlying disunity that counteracts the same (Dalsgard 242). Morrison, fortunately, refuses access to paradise anywhere in her textual geography.

While the Morgan set fathers no living offspring, they remain blessed with inexact replication. Steward and Dovey are sterile. Deacon's sons Scout and Easter die in Vietnam at the ages of nineteen and twenty-one.[19] Disenchanted about their safety, Soane believes her cynical self-righteousness prevented other pregnancies to produce "an absence too heavy to carry" (102). Seeking safety amid hard times also distorts her husband and brother-in-law. Morrison describes the brothers who savage the convent as "once identical: Although they are twins, their wives look more alike than they do. One is smooth, agile and smokes Te Amo cigars. The other is tougher, meaner, but hides his face when he prays. But both have wide innocent eyes." Single-minded when they "had nothing to lose," they find that with success "everything requires their protection" (12). The pair naïvely assume they have made manifest the American Dream. Loners, except for each other and the sisters they marry, they range their territory on Night instead of hi yo Silver, or in a truck or an Impala or a shiny black Oldsmobile. If they "performed as one man," however, they "always seemed to be having a second conversation—an unheard dialogue right next to the one they spoke aloud" (62).

This unspoken affinity for disruption as they pull together distinguishes the black Morgan "hosses" from the rest of the New Father paladins turned predators.[20] That which separates them from each other lies in the nature of their dreams. Morrison comments in *Love* that a dream is merely a "nightmare with lipstick" (201). Both suggest an individual's inner self, the hunted along with the haunting. Descended from males who have not "forgotten a thing since 1755," neither Steward nor Deacon can "put up with what he couldn't control," and both can hold a grudge indefinitely. The combination proves mighty deadly. Lone recognizes immediately upon overhearing the conspirators' pre-attack plans that "the only voice not singing belonged to the one conducting the choir" (278–80). This voice performs in two-part harmony.

She does not realize, however, the focus or the impact of the twins' visions. The Old Fathers' unhappy oral history drives Steward. Although he is immensely fond of Elder's story about his battle in Hoboken, it "unnerved him to know it was based on the defense of and prayers for a whore." His favorite tales involve Big Papa's suffering and subsequent engagement with a small, walking man. When the Old Fathers, eating trash, "raggedy as sauerkraut," dreaming of "shirts with both sleeves," find themselves pushed to the edge, lame Zechariah limps apart from the line, his son Rector as witness. He drops, groaning, to his knees and hums fervently to his Father his prayer for guidance. Overcome by the "sweetest, saddest sounds" he had ever heard, Rector is swallowed by the "heartbreaking music" and, "floating inches aboveground," hears thundering footsteps. These give way to the appearance of a "small man, seemlike, too small for the sound of his steps." The Old Fathers, led by a suddenly erect Zechariah, follow the walking man to the place they believe is theirs. Their tale suggests miraculous faith, renewed purpose, and, most important, being specially selected; it becomes an American adaptation of African lore and Old Testament theology. In "God's time" the chosen find the Promised Land and the American Dream. Steward interprets their saga to mean that success follows sacrifice (95–98).

This half of the Morgan duet believes devoutly that the "young simpletons" who want to desecrate the Oven have "no notion of what it took to build [Ruby]. What they were protected from. What humiliations they did not have to face" (93). He stands convinced that "Had he any sons, they would have been sterling examples of rectitude, laughing at Misner's notions of manhood: backtalk, name changes—as if word magic had anything to do with the courage it took to be a man" (95). Steward has been faithful steward to the law of the Old Fathers' letters but has neglected their intuitive spirit. He fails to recognize the deliberate slyness inspiring the words Zechariah forges onto the Oven, the way multiple meanings disguise warning behind obedience: " 'You' (understood), vocative case, was not a command to the believers but a threat to those who had disallowed them" (195). He overlooks that, when his grandfather of more than one name finds himself in a conundrum, he locates direction not out of words but from sound. Oblivious to such nuances, wide-eyed, thick-skinned Steward ultimately does not care. The essential for him lies not in meaning but in gain or loss: "Personally he didn't give a damn. The point was not why it should or should not be changed, but what Reverend Misner gained by instigating the idea." Grown increasingly literal, terrified of being lost, on foot, and unable to protect his good women, he reacts to the mere "thought of that level of helplessness" by wanting "to shoot somebody." As Dovey laments, however, the more Steward acquires to ensure his safety and that of Ruby's women, the more he visibly loses. Having already forfeited his hairline, taste buds, and ability to father children, he will now sacrifice the present generation "to get to the next one" (94–96). The more he gains by following in the frontier footsteps of his fathers, the less he becomes.[21]

Deacon's dream connects him closer to the feminine than the masculine. As incensed as Steward at the audacity of the young, driven on a weekday to blow out the brains of quail to keep his own from exploding, the shooting settles Deacon and provokes his most powerful memory. He "remembers everything" about accompanying the men in his family on a grand tour to "examine, review and judge other Colored towns." While the Old Fathers, "having been refused by the world in 1890 on their journey to Oklahoma," learn to deny one another nothing, the Morgans carry their rejection "like a bullet in the brain" (109). Thus, they will admit to no satisfaction at the dissolution of some all-black towns, remarking merely on the "mystery of God's justice," but they take the twins to see for themselves. The vision Deacon recalls most vividly in one of the "towns intoxicated with wealth" involves watching "nineteen Negro ladies arrange themselves on the steps of the town hall." The delicacy of their summer dresses overwhelms him. He recollects every detail of the material as well as the hats "that called attention to the wide, sparkly eyes of the wearers," the small waists, slender feet, creamy skin. Morrison calls attention to the romantic excitement provoked by a scene as potentially fatal as Faulkner's "An Odor of Verbena."[22] At a vulnerable age the twins feel that if they "had not thrown themselves off the railing they would have burst into tears." Like his nephew will later, Deacon is more than willing to endure the public humiliation of "crack[ed] butt" for the sake of those glamorous women's smiles (109–10).

Deacon's romantic dream incorporates "Quiet white and yellow houses full of industry; and in them . . . elegant black women at useful tasks" into Steward's miscalculations about loss and gain and the 8-rock ideal of blue-black blood (111). The convent draws to a head threats to it all. This place suggests the possibility that a grandnephew may have been destroyed there. It serves as a reminder of the desecration of Deacon's marriage and the potential of a "mixed-up child" from his relationship with Connie. It symbolizes the "degradation" of the nineteen Negro ladies, that moment the brothers share of "sunlit skin and verbena." The convent dooms the twins' personal history, which has carried them through war and conquest, to probable extinction, a deprivation unforgivable and even more intolerable in its "loss of charity" (279).

Separation from his other half, the result of his brother's affair with Connie, causes Steward's bitter rancor toward the convent. Deacon's glacial pride leads him to attack the women. He becomes driven to erase the shame of his fatal attraction and "the kind of woman he believed was its source: An uncontrollable, gnawing woman who had bitten his lip just to lap the blood it shed; a beautiful, golden-skinned, outside woman with moss-green eyes that tried to trap a man . . . to enfeeble him so they could do carnal things, unnatural things in the dark." He blames Connie for the adultery that costs his family its place among Ruby's pure originals. The Disallowing pageant now represents only seven holy families out of the nine original founders. The Cato line having been cut with the last of its males, the only explanation for the loss of the other is Deacon's impurity. His guilt over his betrayal and the death of his sons wears away at his marriage. However, Deacon manages to convince himself that the "ravenous ground-fucking woman" weasels her way into his wife's affections and wields potions that render Soane "less loving than she used to be" (279–80). Faced, though, with an underhanded duel to the death involving his former lover's physical presence, seeing "in her eyes what has been drained from them and from himself as well," breathless from the blood near her lips, he "lifts his hand to halt his brother's." The bullet that enters Consolata's forehead tells him who, between the twins, is physically superior. The confession that "This is our doing. Ours alone. And we bear the responsibility" makes Deacon the spiritually "stronger man" (291, 289).

In essence, the Lone Ranger becomes lost when parted from Tonto. The situation can also be reversed. A strange, green-eyed cowboy saves Connie. Her own green eyes, smoky skin, and tea-colored hair betraying her mixed Portuguese Gypsy heritage, Connie is snatched as a nine-year-old sitting in street garbage by her first and last love, Mother Mary Magna. Raised up to worship the spirit, she grows so hungry for her own flesh that she eats "the man's," quailing the hunter who blows out without blinking the brains of quail.[23] Deprived again of physical pleasure with Deacon's desertion, Connie learns "in sight" from Lone, steps into Scout, acquires the respect and gratitude of his mother but shrinks spiritually on the death of Mother. She is orphaned more intensely at fifty-four than when she was abandoned as a street baby; her "rope to the world had slid from her fingers." Until the arrival of her lone stranger, she drinks "prisoner wine" seriously to escape from depression and merely goes through the motions of caring for freeloaders, wishing she could muster the strength to "beat the life" out of them all (247–48).

While Dovey's smooth-muscled, shaggy-haired young "Friend" still drops by to comfort her "on and off every month or two," originally in a flurry of orange-red butterflies, Connie's visitor comes after menopause. Despairing that God has given "satanic gifts" to "a drunken, ignorant, penniless woman living in darkness unable to rise from a cot to do something useful or die on it," middle-aged Connie is reduced to seeing herself as a grayed-in and gray nobody: "Her colorless eyes saw nothing clearly except what took place in the minds of others." She has turned into the opposite of the person who rolled in the dirt so as to taste the flesh and "thought she was seeing for the first time because she was looking so hard." Convinced that God rightly punishes her for converting a living man into a deity, she believes that he "burned the green away and replaced it with pure sight that damned her if she used it" (248).

And then "A man approached" of light step and medium stature. Sporting a cowboy hat that disguises features Connie cannot see anyway, he sits on the kitchen steps in "shiny black work shoes" and mirrored sunglasses that glitter.[24] He answers Connie's inquiry with "Come on, girl. You know me" and tells her he is "traveling here" in soft tones that span the ten yards between them. His presence all the way from "far country" inspires her "slide toward his language" and makes her feel weightless, like Rector's response to the small, walking man. Suddenly beside her without having moved, he removes his hat "not six inches from her face" to reveal a cascade of "tea-colored hair" and eyes "as round and green as new apples" (251–52). His smile and slight, seductive wink provoke her laughter along with a redeemed identity and sense of purpose. After his visit Connie becomes Consolata Sosa, suggestive of the Spanish *consolador* and the English *consolation.* This soothing new woman creates rituals that enable others to heal themselves if they will act on her say-so. Her followers learn to "loud dream." They lose count of their days but are no longer haunted. The arrival of a complex, androgynous Lone Ranger, who combines characteristics of both Connie and Deacon, indicates that Connie has reached a serene equilibrium between male and female, flesh and spirit, and can now show others how to appear "calmly themselves" (266).

Morrison's earthly paradise exists perpetually all mixed up. In it unvirginal Connie puts on Mother's "shiny nun shoes" to go to work, but then so does Connie's rendition of Dovey's male Friend as well as Deacon Morgan, until he can no longer bear to wear them (259). Changed forever by the shootings, Deek forbears to say a word in public but walks well dressed and barefoot within Ruby instead of waxing and driving his car through by himself. He gives his bank as he passes it by not a second glance. Feeling an incompleteness exotic to a twin, he finds a friend in Richard Misner as Steward takes on K.D., concentrating on making his nephew rich while "waiting on Dovey to come round, which she seemed to be doing, because there was an obvious coolness between her and Soane" (300). A proudly humbled Deacon rejects Steward's materialistic ways, but unlike Soane, unlike Coffee, and with Misner's support, refuses to renounce Tea. He continues to be his brother's keeper while Ruby's world turns round and upside down.

In this dynamic version of paradise, blind Connie removes mirrored sunglasses like the ones Deacon carries in his pocket to wear when he comes to kill her and looks beyond his innocent eyes with her own bereft of green to welcome his second self with a warm "You're back" (289). Here a betrayed wife learns to love the other woman. Combative Gigi appeases her hunger for overly idealistic men with a real childlike Seneca woman. Inept Mother Mavis comforts her no-longer difficult daughter, Sal; abandoned daughter Seneca smiles at her grown child mother, Jean; betrayed daughter Pallas ignores her disloyal mother, Dee Dee, to name her son for his grandmother Divine. Connie's solace comes to her in the songs of Piedade, a wordless nurturing figure with a name that combines the pious Pieta with a hip daddy and brings with it the sights and sounds of the loud city and the hushed sea of her lost childhood. Like Ruby, the convent provides an ambiguously precious haven. The Lone Ranger is never left alone there. Even if he temporarily leaves Tonto, as Deacon does Connie or Coffee does Tea, if she possesses enough insight, the loss can teach him/her ultimately to say with reckless joy: "Sha sha sha," an acronym for she/he/all, "meaning, he and I are the same" (241).[25]

Morrison's redemptive not-a-Lone Ranger merges the Lone Ranger *and* Tonto. She accords final frontier status only to those who fold at least two into one. Although three ministers attend to Ruby, Reverend Misner alone incorporates Morrison's vision of the modern double-voiced griot, the dedicated outlander who, like the writer and her ideal reader, seeks enlightenment in order to locate consolation.[26] Associated with apocalyptic passivity, Pastor Simon Cary carries on at the Church of the Holy Redeemer, accepting outbursts over Oven words as a prediction of "Last Days" (102). Personally "soothing and jovial," he and his wife, Lily, remain "treasured for their duets." Pastor Cary deals with human difficulties such as the "malice set roaming" at K.D. and Arnette's marriage with a smiling nod and a reassuring pat on the shoulder while folks ask the

"Precious Lord [to] take [their] hand" and wait patiently for Armageddon (155–56). Reverend Senior "Take No Prisoners" Pulliam opts for a much more proactive approach to pain (143). Viewing the Oven problem as evidence of "Evil Times," he stands behind New Zion's pulpit and tries to scare people to death into being good (102). Dark, wiry, elegant, narrow-eyed, "white-haired and impressive," he loathes "backtalk" from anybody, but especially the young, and defines such conversation as anything contrary to his party line: Old Testament literalism and puritanical hellfire-and-damnation (85). He dampens wedding bliss by delivering a sermon on love as "divine only and difficult always" (141). He blasts the guests at the ceremony: "You can only earn—by practice and careful contemplation—the right to express [love] and you have to learn how to accept it," in essence to be "pure and holy" and place sinners in the hands of Pulliam's angry God (141–42).

Misner responds to this Old Testament pull-'em-downer and what he views as a personal affront by "holding holding holding" up his comforting New Testament cross (147). So furious he cannot speak, he lets his cross do the talking while K.D. and Arnette stand separately, each uncomfortably humiliated under it, comprehending his implications no more than they take in the weight of Pulliam's "long Methodist education" (142). Conflict, again, arises over interpretation. Each Rubyite can apply the symbol only to the specifics of his or her life. On his knees afterward, Misner is "angry at his anger, and at his mishandling of it. Used to obstacles, adept at disagreement," he "loved God so much it hurt, although that same love sometimes made him laugh out loud. And he deeply respected his colleagues" (159). Because he knows that he is far from perfect, this man seeks to understand exactly what in Pulliam's speech would cause a messenger of consolation from Mount Calvary Church to disrupt a wedding party. Morrison lets us know through her disciple that we will never get it right and that, without insight into ourselves and the gift of sympathy for others, our young people will always be caught in the middle.

If Lone DuPres acts as Old World midwife to Morrison's community, Richard Misner represents her New World minister. Manifesting griot androgyny, he embraces duality and allows disagreement, including that between spirit and science. A virile "milkman," he attracts among others the lovely, flexible Anna, stimulates the youth to productive political activism, and tolerates the stiff-necked New Fathers so that he can show them the quality of unstrained mercy. If Lone calls her gift of sympathy "stepping in" while Consolata prefers "seeing in" or "in sight," Misner learns to see through a glass darkly when the door looks shut. As Morrison notes, acceptance of alternative possibilities often becomes merely "a question of language" (247). Lone calls Connie a foolish "hardhead" to be so skeptical of earthly "magic" and instructs her not to "separate God from his elements. He created it all. . . . Don't unbalance His world" (244). Lone explains the absence of victims at the convent massacre as God stepping in to give Ruby a second chance. Misner doubts the mystery of such a "convenient mass disappearance" and, upon returning from out of town, goes with Anna to see for himself. Telling her that his "tight fire" burns hot "when it counts," he gathers convent peppers after which he senses the presence of a window while Anna, balancing brown chicken eggs in his white handkerchief, perceives a door (115, 304). Subsequently, both focus "on the sign rather than the event" and avoid saying out loud what each secretly wonders: "What would happen if you entered? What would be on the other side? What on earth would it be? What on earth?" (305).

Misner responds to this challenge with one of his own. Reverends Cary and Pulliam remain unchanged by the convent deaths; the first continues to corral his flock as the second scares them into stampeding. Trying as usual to piece things together, Misner finds inspiration from the death of Jeff and Sweetie's youngest, poignantly called Save-Marie, sounding like "Save me." He asks those congregated at Ruby's first funeral: "Who could do this to a child? Who could permit this for a child? And why?" Attempting to comfort the gathered mourners, explaining that moments of "aching sadness" lead us to reenact the Fall and thus to "confirm, defer or lose our faith," he answers his own call by suddenly deciding to stay in Ruby (295). Misner's epiphany about the dream we call American reveals "no better battle to fight, no better place to be than among these outrageously beautiful, flawed and proud people. Besides, mortality may be new to them but birth was not. The future panted at the gate." Though messages concealed in words may never be satisfactorily deciphered, this moment makes clear to Misner that salvation is "lying in wait for us to know the splendor" (306–7).

Space (Grace): The Final Frontier

Morrison reinforces the possibility of redemption by supplying *Paradise* with inconclusive conclusions that require her readers to confirm, defer, or lose their faith. Peter Widdowson suggests that either the community closes ranks in a bleak assessment of modern America, namely *status quo redivivus;* or, young people like Billie Delia prevail by following *Beloved*'s Denver on out the yard; or, less realistically, the convent women as well as their Cadillac magically disappear and marvelously reappear in the coda, resting before they shoulder "the endless work they were created to do down here in Paradise" (332–33). An alternative analysis, as in *Jazz*, may be found by embracing the text itself. Through it Morrison affirms the ritual of interpretive reading, the delicate and complicated dance between writer and reader, as a sacred one. In essence, *Paradise* allows us a glimpse of paradise. As we simultaneously possess, surrender ourselves to, and turn its pages, "Out There" (fear or awe of the frontier) and "Out There" (fear or awe of difference) become transformed into a lowercase, less intimidating "out there" (welcoming new frontiers, difference, and individuality within community).[27]

Ultimately, Morrison re-envisions an American paradise that allows Tom or Jim to stay home with his "bullet around his neck on a watch-guard for a watch" while Huck or Becky "light[s] out for the Territory ahead of the rest" (Twain, *Huckleberry Finn* 362). As one individual seeks solace in the absence of order, another avoids chaos. The real key to the kingdom, however, is to locate the balance between within a single psyche. *Paradise* confirms Milkman's previous leap of faith: Deacon Morgan breaks from but does not give up on his brother, Richard Misner criticizes but chooses to stay with Ruby, and Billie Delia—her very name integrating male with female, black with white, youth with age, past with present—leaves Ruby but refuses to choose between Brood (dark) and Apollo (light). She hopes "with all her heart" that the "women she had liked" are still "out there, waiting and darkly burnished with pointy teeth" (308). An equally triumphant European Catholic touch, however, disrupts Billie's Africanist-sounding assertion, as those women continue cradled in visionary bliss by Connie's mysterious dream-figure, Piedade. Morrison locates peace in the ongoing search for possibility. She defends the pathway to life through death's door. Whether her American cowboys drive cars, trucks, or motorcycles; ride horses, on trains, or in busses; walk or run, they find no parking lots, paved or otherwise, Out There in paradise. Glimpses of the divine are fleeting and always within. As Consolata says to her first neophyte: "Scary things not always outside. Most scary things is inside" (39). This holds equally true for the serene. Especially for men at home on the range, out there rests in here.

CHAPTER 9

Laying down the Law of the Father

Men in *Love*

"For and with" her beloved maternal grandmother Ardelia Willis, Morrison's eighth novel explores looking for [L]ove in all the wrong places. It also re-locates [L]acan's Other.[1] Since Morrison maintains that Old World black women like Willis constitute the essence of love, *Love*'s Up Beach L could be considered the swamp women of *Tar Baby* or Ardelia reincarnated—enduring, nurturing females out of the house of Chloe who embrace and transfer their ancient, sacred properties (Moyers). The "sign of [L's] letter" might also represent the healing language of laughter, in this case a comic inversion of French psychoanalyst Jacques Lacan's singularly serious theories about Sex and the Word (*Jazz* epigraph). While all of Morrison's novels slyly undercut white male authority, *Love* (2003) takes a direct stab via the black vernacular; it reduces the mighty Law of the Father to pesky Police-heads. Suggesting that white masculinity assumes the rules of patriarchy, Police-heads establish a frame of empowered masculinity against which *Love*'s feisty black male characters can be considered. Whatever the sound of her name, L reveals that when African American women search for "Big Daddy everywhere," they lay down (to) the Law of the Father instead of "living [their] lives hand in hand" (*Love* 189).[2]

Morrison confesses to an obsession with love and its excesses: *Beloved* and a mother's love for her children; *Jazz* and romantic love; *Paradise* and the love of God (Rose). *Love* widens this net to examine, literally and figuratively, love of (the) Man. It illustrates that even the limited institutions ostensibly structured to profit black women—a few female academies and honeymoon resorts, the many brothels—have actually benefited and are ultimately controlled by white men. Christine Cosey comes to learn that "Maple Valley, Cosey's Hotel, Manila's whorehouse—all three floated in sexual tension and resentment; all three insisted on confinement; in all three status was money. And all were organized around the pressing needs of men" (92). These repressed states operate on the psyche as does Lacan's Other, which he describes, loosely speaking, as a vast, tangled network of the unconscious, a process of desire set in motion by difference and associated with parents, language, and the symbolic order. Unlike this Western white male definition of desire, imitated in *Love* by Dr. Rio among others, Morrison transforms the L of Lacan into the L of Love. L's domain is the kitchen, formerly at Cosey's Hotel, currently at Café Ria.[3] Her take on her humble hot spot is that "Girls like the place a lot. Over iced tea with a clove in it, they join their friends to repeat what *he* said, describe what *he* did, and guess what *he* meant by any of it" (65).

She also defines this attitude as "Foolish," though the girls "spice the lunch hour and lift the spirits of brokenhearted men eavesdropping at nearby tables," and asserts that when the "women's legs are spread wide open . . . [m]en grow irritable, but they know it's all for them" (66, 3). In essence, *Love*'s L warns women that men don't like to buy the cow if they can get the milk for free. In addition, she rejects parapraxis for Freudian slips of the tongue and would certainly insist that Lacan's phallogocentric opinions are merely cocksure. As Terry Eagleton quips, it is this "cocksureness, by which those who wield sexual and social power maintain their grip," that semiotic fiction seeks to challenge (189). Morrison's fiction now includes books for children as well as novels for adults. Style and purpose, however, remain similar. The hip language of *Who's Got Game?*, which fools around with traditional fables like *The Ant and the Grasshopper*, reflects the irreverent wordplay and inversions found in *Love*. Thus, the writer clearly intends her semiotic fiction to replace the loss of music as her community's source of lesson and laughter. *Love* especially questions some of Lacan's more arrogant, contemptuous attitudes toward women, comically converting his patriarchal Law of the Father into troublesome Police-heads.

Those theories of Lacan particularly relevant to men in *Love* involve the question of the human subject, its place in society, its relationship to language; his reinterpretation of Freud's Oedipus complex as precursor to subjectivity; and the birth of desire. Lacan agrees with Freud that, during an early stage of development, the infant makes no clear distinction between subject and object, itself and the external world. He calls this state of being the "imaginary," a condition lacking any defined center of self in which what "self" there is seems to pass into objects, and objects into it. Here the child resides in a symbiotic relationship with its mother's body. Difference blurs, although the child experiences what it knows of the external world as dependent on itself. From this pre-Oedipal state the infant moves into Lacan's "mirror stage," where it begins to develop an integrated self-image or ego. Still physically uncoordinated, it sees reflected in the mirror a "gratifyingly unified image of itself," one that is basically narcissistic, one that both is and is not itself. Because this reflected object becomes at once part of and yet not itself, the child responds to an essentially alienated image. For Lacan the imaginary exists as this ongoing "realm of *images* in which we make identifications, but in the very act of doing so are led to misperceive and misrecognize ourselves" (Eagleton 164–65).

The " 'dyadic' structure gives way to a 'triadic' one," occurring when the father enters to interrupt a not always blissful harmony. Lacan calls this disruption the Law of the Father. Because the father disturbs the infant's libidinal relationship with its mother so that it must accept the broader familial and social network, the Law signifies the social taboo on incest. It also indicates that the child represents merely part of a structure already predetermined by the practices of the culture into which it is born. The appearance of the father figure therefore not only drives the child from its mother's body; the father drives its desire into its unconscious. That moment when the child recognizes the prohibition symbolized by the father segues into its repression of guilty desire and the birth of its unconscious. The unconscious *is* desire (Eagleton 165).

For the Oedipal drama to play out, the child must have a vague notion of sexual difference. Only by acknowledging the necessity of distinct gender roles can it become properly "socialized." The father's entry serves to confirm this difference. Signified in Lacanian vocabulary by the phallus, the term, as Jane Gallop emphasizes, should not be limited to the masculine but designates "as a whole the effects of signification" (Gallop 112; Lacan 285). Lacan contributes to Freudian theories about human development by rewriting the account of the Oedipus complex in terms of language. The child becomes the signifier, its image in the mirror the signified. The mirror scenario can also be interpreted as a kind of metaphor for infantile plentitude: thus far unplagued by gaps between signifier and signified, subject and world, the infant finds in its reflection an unblemished identity, which the relationship between language and reality will not support.

The entrance of the father in effect plunges the child into poststructuralist anxiety. It must grasp that identity comes about only when one subject excludes another; it discovers sexual difference about the same time that it decodes language. In terms essential to Morrison's fiction in general and to *Love* in particular, human access to language and understanding of sexuality mean that the individual "unconsciously learns that a sign has meaning only by dint of its difference from other signs, and learns also that a sign presupposes the *absence* of the object it signifies." When we accept that the presence of the father, symbolized by the phallus, indicates that we have to assume "a place in the family which is defined by sexual difference, by exclusion ([the child] cannot be its parent's lover) and by absence (it must relinquish its earlier bonds to the mother's body)," we have successfully negotiated the difficult passage through the Oedipus complex and have arrived at Lacan's symbolic order: the preordained social rules and sexual roles that constitute family and society (Eagleton 165–67).

The subject that emerges from this painful process, however, is split, divided now between the conscious life of the ego and the unconscious or repressed desire. The child has been banished from the full life of the imaginary to the indirect world of language, empty because merely an endless progression of difference and absence. The metaphorical realm of the mirror yields to the metonymic arena of language. The child becomes resigned to moving along a potentially infinite linguistic chain of signifiers, which Lacan names desire. For this psychoanalyst, human desire arises from the continual striving to satisfy a lack; human language works from the absence of the real objects that signs come to designate. To enter language, then, means to be severed from the "real" and reduced to a search for substitutes.[4] As Lacan remarks and *Love* reconstructs, language is " 'what hollows being into desire' " (Eagleton 167–68).

Several initial reviewers criticized what they perceive as Morrison's heavy-handed treatment of the "L word." Grossman describes the book as a "maudlin, mixed-up story with some assembly required" and accuses L's opening exposition of coming at us "in the foreboding tones of Rod Serling introducing a *Twilight Zone* episode" (75). Miller agrees that *Love*'s title bespeaks a Nobel Prize winner in danger of bowing under the "leaden mantle of Greatness" (10) while Kakutani calls the novel "one of her slighter efforts" (35). Campbell maintains that Morrison's response to the consciousness of living in a "wholly racialized world" rides the current wave of multiculturalism yet essentially creates a "world which is almost wholly African-Americanized, in which separate existence is presented as not only inevitable but good" (21). Although Morrison's passion for the village and faith in the possibility of redemption for all can occasionally collapse into pontifical purple prose, she obviously rejects segregation of any kind and usually remains lyrically in control. Many of *Love*'s more intense reflections about love may actually be one of its strengths and part of its point about the magic of black men. Bill Cosey overreacts to too much Dark, who was his father and is Lacan's interpretation of desire or the Law of the Father.

What Dark gains as he snitches on others to satisfy his lack of middle-class "order, stability and mutual support—no small blessing in a hostile, white-run world"—he loses in "vitality, in wildness and . . . in truth" (Miller 10). L, on the other hand, who hums more than she speaks, knows that her people, black men especially, need to love themselves anew. She treats love as something we do neither for safety nor for others but for ourselves.[5] Unlike Lacan's haunting unconscious desire, or Other, which appears as *Love*'s repressed Dark, Morrison's concept of love, while equally primal, is expanded and expansive and "nearly classical" (Miller 10). It remains "rooted in a tradition of a people who, from their beginnings in this country, had been denied the right to express love, and thus have invented their particular strategies to hold onto it" (Christian 34). If it can ransack the lives of her characters, "leaving them dazed and bereft, with blood on their hands" (Miller 10), it also represents " 'risk' and 'freedom,' incapable of being completely contained" (Christian 34).

Morrison calls the Thing, which tries to contain black men and explains "the craziness heaping up, holding down, and making women hate one another and ruin their children," Police-heads. A village term comically fusing Lacan's Law of the Father with his symbolic phallus, this exists as an "outside evil," "dirty things with big hats who shoot up out of the ocean to harm loose women and eat disobedient children." Morrison has long identified large hats with small-minded, sexually perverted white slavers such as *Beloved*'s schoolteacher. Although L acknowledges that sad personal stories about "dragon daddies and false-hearted men or mean mamas and friends who did them wrong" account for the way many black women "open their legs rather than their hearts," she also knows that sometimes "the cut is so deep no woe-is-me tale is enough." Then we have to take on the Other—or Police-heads (4–5).

Police-head masculinity takes the form of white rules of patriarchy. As Bill Cosey informs Sandler Gibbons, "Every law in this country is made to keep us back" (44). The novel starts with Bill's birth in 1890. Although Police-heads disappear for a time, during Reconstruction and the world wars afterward, they return afresh in the 1940s "with new and bigger hats." Identified as loitering like wide-mouthed thunderclouds over the wild surf or rumbling bass whoops of joy above the beach at sunset "when lust is keenest," their profiles are male, and they hang heavily over the sea L calls her sweet tenor man. These dark images represent white male law, which takes its pleasure in raining on black male parades or takes advantage of black female sexuality. While such sea demons prey on black people mainly at night, they so relish particularly self-destructive African American community or family events that for those they will show up in bright morning, "bold as a posse" (5–6). Only when black men fail to imitate or usurp their magisterial control do they "sneak off like pickpockets from a breadline" (5–6). After Cosey's Hotel and Resort closes down and folks travel back and forth from cheap government housing to malls and movieplexes, no one has a "cloudy thought, let alone a memory of Police-heads" (9). L's thoughts, however, warn her people to be aware of the Law of the Father, especially in an ocean of calm. White law has changed little from 1890 to *Love*'s 1990s present.

The hardest-playing Police-head is Chief Buddy Silk. When William Cosey takes his father's dearly bought money and scoops up beach land close to a cannery to build the "best and best-known vacation spot for colored folk on the East Coast," he also indulges his fondness for fishing (6). He shares his boat most often with Sheriff Silk, smoothest member of a white family "that had named a whole town after itself and gave epic-movie names to its streets" (40). Bill can temporarily bend back Buddy Silk's long and long-lived Dixie Law arm with bribes of boat bashes, where a rod catches more than mere fish. Sandler, however, recoils when he goes along on one of these infamous parties. He does not mind the middle-aged white men or the well-off black men or the laughter or even the black women provoking it. It is "the talk, its tone, its lie that he couldn't take." Like the empty separation of language from reality in Lacan's symbolic order, conversation at sea operates "as fuel to feed the main delusion: the counterfeit world invented on the boat; the real one set aside for a few hours so women could dominate, men would crawl, blacks could insult whites. Until they docked. Then the sheriff could put his badge back on and call the colored physician a boy. Then the women took their shoes off because they had to walk home alone" (111).

Boss Silk, Buddy's son, represents a different kettle of fish. Unlike his good-old-boy predecessor, he never smokes and refuses May Cosey the gun that Chief Buddy would have offered for sport when she starts wearing an army helmet. A "poor, hungry preacher's child," product of a continually crumbling world, May believes her survival depends on "colored people who rocked boats only at sea" and takes increasingly comic precautions against those who would threaten it (96). In the same way that Faulkner's modern wave of town fathers retracts Miss Emily's rose, Boss

Silk takes a narrower view than that of the more laid-back first generation toward "Negroes with guns, even though they both wanted to shoot the same people" (97). Boss, not Buddy, chooses money over sex as he increases Bill's police fee to stay open and sell liquor. Boss desires shame "for sure, but [Heed] didn't know it if included her tits." And persnickety Boss makes a prime candidate for blackmail when Heed baits him with provocative fishing pictures of his father "addressed to [his] mother care of the *Harbor Journal*" (187).

Morrison calls her 1990s rendition of perverse white law Administrators, who shall remain nameless. Junior Viviane encounters one at Correctional; like Heed, stopping him stays forefront on Junior's mind. The focus of this fatherly legal system includes "Conferences" and "Office Duty" to be exchanged by incarcerated female minors for "sexy underwear" and "trips off campus." Junior, however, sexually innovative and already valued for her typing skills, does not require the favors of an old man nearly thirty with a penis that "couldn't compete with raw vegetables, bars of soap, kitchen utensils, lollipops, or anything else inventive girls could conjure." An early Exit Conference, cowardly Guidance Counselor, and embarrassed prison Committee hone her blossoming expertise. When the Administrator, jovial and relaxed perched atop his balcony railing, tries to force fellatio on fifteen-year-old Junior, heretofore well behaved, she balks: "While the Administrator's hands were busy unbelting, hers went to the back of his knees, upending him over the railing. He fell one story. Only one" (116–17). Publicly astonished by Junior's unexplained alteration in attitude, all the Administrators are privately afraid of falling even a single level and fearful of their rehabilitation results: their form of reform refines their inmates' insight.

Other than patrolling at all hours of the day to net black female flesh or baiting black men to become their financial fish, Morrison's "ambitious, under-occupied police" generally hang around to bring back, hold back, harass, or condescend to others, who in response hurt each other (15). Chief Buddy, with his big round hat and badge, gently returns runaway Christine to get to watch her disconcerted mother slap the child's face into her shoulder. The police seem to react more kindly than May when Christine tries to kill Dr. Rio's Cadillac, but their respect translates into prejudgment "as though her violence was not merely understandable but justified" (90). The police force more than quadruples after World War II. The youth Sandler describes as "shaped by fear of vigilantes" grows into a manhood degraded by dark-blue uniforms; a "one-sheriff, one-secretary department" consists currently of four squad cars and eight peacekeepers in what remains a one-horse town (15). Similar to a plague, however,

Police-heads serve a purpose. L believes "It's like being exposed to tuberculosis. After it fills the cemetery, it strengthens whoever survives; helps them know the difference between a strong mind and a healthy one; between the righteous and the right—which is, after all, progress" (139). For Sandler and other black men, Lacan's Law of the Father turns out to be, after all, otherwise as well as progressive.

Because, like birth, pain repeats itself, *Love*'s male figures can become stuck like a broken record. Their story ostensibly shows "how brazen women can take a good man down" (10). However, it actually reveals an unwise imbalance between Dark and his son (Light). Contrary to the father he brags on in public, Bill Cosey inherits his fortune from a "Courthouse informer. . . . Well paid, tipped off, and favored for fifty-five years, Daniel Robert Cosey kept his evil gray eye on everybody." DRC's motivation must be power because he takes no joy in his job, nor does "the money he got from being at the beck and call of white folks in general and police in particular" bring comfort to him or those close to him. Called Danny Boy by his benefactors, his own people reduce him to his initials, which add up to Dark. Dark dies a stooge to "114,000 resentful dollars." His son responds to the father's withholding and holding back by spending his share on the things Dark cursed: "good times, good clothes, good food, good music, dancing till the sun came up in a hotel made for it all. The father was dreaded; the son was a ray of light. The cops paid off the father; the son paid off the cops. What the father corrected, the son celebrated." And Bill's beloved first wife, caught between an extremely charming husband and her besieged farming father, "froze when she learned how blood-soaked her husband's money was" (68).

The second part of the story addresses the girl. Dark sends his young son to spy on the neighbors. Instructed each dawn to play in their yard, Bill finally reports a man slipping out the back door and that same afternoon witnesses the man "dragged through the street behind a four-horse wagon." Following the vehicle, and crying, runs a raggedy little girl who falls in horse manure. Onlookers laugh. Bill may or may not have joined in, but he does "nothing at all" (45). The ensuing impression, however, fused with his father's bleak image, haunts his behavior for the rest of his life.

Only the names change in this recurring tale, but like Lacan says, language is all. Known for her name games, Morrison makes *Love* no exception. As does Julia Kristeva, however, she maintains that the "symbolic order of which Lacan writes is in reality the patriarchal sexual and social order of modern class-society, structured around the 'transcendental signifier' of the phallus, dominated by the Law which the father embodies."

Instead of celebrating the symbolic order at the expense of the imaginary, Morrison attacks the oppressiveness of such a system and substitutes for the symbolic the semiotic, or the play of forces inherent within language. The semiotic represents the " 'other' of language which is nonetheless intimately entwined with it. Because it stems from the pre-Oedipal phase, it is bound up with the child's contact with the mother's body, whereas the symbolic . . . is associated with the Law of the Father" (Eagleton 187–88). Thus, although the semiotic is attached to the feminine, its language does not exclude men because it arises from a pre-Oedipal stage that recognizes no gender distinctions.

Asserting that truth manifests itself in the letter instead of the spirit—that is, in the way we actually express ourselves rather than in our intended meaning—Lacan's theories support writers and critics in their attempt to look for the letter (the style and form) of a text in addition to reading for content. Lacan believes that the phallus "can play its role only when veiled" and that it does so in the agency of the letter (288). The letter *s* is "probably the most important letter in Lacan." He uses it "to stand for the signifier, the signified, the symbolic, and the subject." An absent *s* becomes a "text of knowledge without cognizance" (Gallop 175–76).[6] Instead of a small symbolic *s*, however, Morrison's L capitalizes (on) the letter to comment about Bill Cosey's lack: "He didn't have an S stitched on his shirt and he didn't own a pitchfork" (200). Morrison also plays with the entwined double Cs on Christine's favorite silver spoon. While Bill's neglected granddaughter believes they stand for her name, they could as easily indicate Bill's dream of domesticating Celestial, his free-spirited sporting woman.

Christine and Heed share Bill's fascination with Celestial. Morrison introduces the childhood playmates to Bill's lover when they overhear a man call out, "Hey, Celestial," in a privately knowing, slyly humorous, poignantly envious way to a beautiful young woman in a red sundress. As she ignores the man and turns a thinly scarred, initially cold profile "etched against the seascape" to wink at them, they "clench and curl their toes with happiness." The shivery ecstasy that the woman in red evokes in the children causes them to name their playhouse Celestial Palace, where they invent a word world all their own. When they want to say " 'Amen,' or acknowledge a particularly bold, smart, risky thing, they [mimic] the male voice crying 'Hey, Celestial.' " The man's attitude implies his yearning to possess the woman; the female inversion means "you go, girl!" Their most private code, however, they call "idagay," a rhythmically upbeat rap saved especially "for intimacy, gossip, telling jokes on grown-ups." Only once do they use it "to draw friendly blood"

(188). Idagay leads her readers to understand the letter and the spirit of Morrison's law: language can be reinvented to resist rather than support a patriarchal status quo. In fact, this writer uses language to subvert expectations. By "stressing the self-referentiality of her names," Morrison not only "protects the integrity of her fiction," which "can only be explicated in its own terms, not on ours," but she also creates subversive voices that expose the void Lacan perceives at the center of identity (Rosenberg 195). In so doing, she encourages a self-awareness that can transform culture.

Even Morrison's place names take on agency in *Love*. Like *Sula*, also about beautiful black boys and childhood sweethearts, *Love*'s setting emphasizes the class clashes mocked by the upscale BBC comedy *Upstairs, Downstairs* as well as the village "nigger joke" describing Medallion's tops and Bottom. The white world of Silk remains an encroaching constant. Cosey's Hotel and Resort at Sooker Bay, juxtaposed against L's swampy Up Beach on a fictionally Floridian East Coast, give way to Oceanside, which it isn't, and an unsafe Harbor. The story repeats itself in what resembles a backwoods Georgia present, with its own scatty Settlement and conflicted Correctional. Out There contains Heed, who spends the last twenty years of her life in a single upstairs bedroom, after honeymooning one time in a hotel on Broad Street, possibly in the Big Easy.[7] It also unveils Christine at Maple Valley School for girls, after which she becomes attached overseas to the "biggest, totally male entity in the world" (i.e., the military), returns to Idlewild before it becomes JFK, resides for a spell with Fruit and on Rio, and survives her last years in the downstairs kitchen of her grandfather's house (92).[8] The two women live there together "in a spotlight separated—or connected—by the darkness between them" (25).

The address of Bill Cosey's Silk house, which, Sandler informs Junior, looms as large as a church—or a jail—used to be number 1. Reassigned now to 1410 or 1401, it shares space with shabbily built government houses like Sandler's in a town with streets named by white men for epic movie heroes and trees. One Monarch Street belonged to Bill Cosey. His ironic change in address suggests both his former position as Silk's blacktop king-of-the-road and the fact that he represented the one and the only: "It ain't been number one for a long time now, but you can't tell [Heed and Christine] that. Can't tell them nothing" (14). The house remains site of the formal dinner party during which Bill spanks his child bride, changing forever her relationship with her friend. For revenge, Heed sets Christine's bed on fire; her husband merely chuckles and, noting Dark's stormy gray eyes in those of Christine, sends his granddaughter away. Cosey's portrait still reigns over tiny Heed's big bed. As L says later: "The problem . . . is what to do about revenge—how to escape the sweetness of its rot. So you can see why families make the best enemies. They have time and convenience to honey-butter the wickedness they prefer. Short-sighted, though. What good does it do to keep a favorite hate going when the very person you've poisoned your life with is the one (maybe the only one) able or willing to carry you to the bathroom when you can't get there on your own?" (139).

L leaves the Silk house after Bill's funeral to reclaim her mother's shack on boggy Up Beach because, as she puts it, "mosquitoes don't like my blood" (105). L will not be prey, but she also declines dependency. Rather, she is "priestly" and, like the goddess Morrison names her for, a source of life and death (37). Having served all the Coseys since she was fourteen, she never really dies. Love, however, literally kills Bill. Sandler's wife, Vida, calls it murder; the doctor pronounces "heart attack." L says "heart ache," May says "school busing," Bill's enemies say "syphilis," and Sandler says "eighty-one years was enough. Bill Cosey was simply tired" (37). It turns out that Vida notes correctly the cloudy glass of water and Bill clutching his stomach, though not the right source. L confirms: "I had to stop him. Had to." Unless Love rids One Monarch Street of its prince, everything except "a boat he left to Sandler Gibbons" goes to "the one person who would have given it away rather than live in it or near it; would have blown it up rather than let it stand as a reminder of why she was not permitted to mount its steps but was the real sport of a fishing boat." Then May's old age would be spent in a straitjacket, Heed would have to "go back to a family who had not spoken to her since Truman," and "whatever [Christine] was into wasn't going to last" (200–201). Up Beach leaves L free afterward to be with her main man the sea. But Up Beach also contains the likes of Wilbur Johnson, who sells his child Heed-the-Night to Cosey for two hundred dollars and a pocketbook for his wife.

Intended as an escape for black insiders, becoming enough for outsiders to know it is there, Cosey's Hotel and Resort at Sooker Bay signifies in reality "a nightmare with lipstick" (201). Bill buys up property the Spanish call Sucre for its sugar-white sand from the owner of a "whites only club" who likes the smell of the deal more than that of shrimp and so will break his word that he wouldn't sell to "niggers" (102). Such local swindlers "tore [Sucre] up for all time" to name the place Sooker and have some fun with "nigger suckers" (8). Successfully fusing Cosey's charm and L's food, however, the resort's good times seem certain to roll. People continue to speculate about why it fails: cannery odors offensive to a new generation of guests, Hyatts and Hiltons, civil rights, shift in clientele, or

Cosey's loss of interest. Even before Hurricane Agnes, Sooker Bay drifts in danger of drowning. After she hits, the hotel part of the resort starts to lean backward yet still maintains the mirrored panels on its big double doors. So far nobody has smashed the glass because it reflects "your own face as well as the view behind your back. . . . No matter the outside loneliness, if you look inside, the hotel seems to promise you ecstasy and the company of all your best friends. And music. The shift of a shutter hinge sounds like the cough of a trumpet; piano keys waver a quarter note above the wind so you might miss the hurt jamming those halls and closed-up rooms" (7). From the perspective of Lacan's imaginary, the vision appears perfect. But unlike Love's natural resistance to parasites, along with her serene conviction that they are "life simply being itself" (9), Cosey must learn that "if you kill the predators, the weak will eat you alive" (42). He chooses to assume royalty while L opts for private service, so the rest "become court personnel fighting for the prince's smile" (37). When Daddy becomes too Big, he relegates his dream to a nightmare. Morrison continues to press home her point that utopian fantasies about safety provide ready food for suckers; nevertheless, people don't need to act stupid. She guarantees only that readiness is all.

Her black male characters, then, including Bill Cosey, are neither readily stupid nor totally responsible. She allows locals left out of the American Dream "a tick of entitlement, of longing turned to belonging in the vicinity of the fabulous, successful resort controlled by one of their own. A fairy tale that lived on even after the hotel was dependent for its life on the people it once excluded." Cosey's Resort, however, represents "more than a playground" (42, 35). Priding herself on her good sense as well as her heart, Vida views it as "a school and a haven where people debated death in the cities, murder in Mississippi, and what they planned to do about it other than grieve and stare at their children. Then the music started, convincing them they could manage it all and last" (35). In essence, his people call on Cosey to sell out to white law in a way merely different from that of his father. The weak pressure Bill to play not Dark but a black Big Daddy.

L swears that something else, in other words an old folks' tale, "made up to scare wicked females and correct unruly children," causes Bill's mishaps (10). She explains that "Bill Cosey was a smart man. He helped more colored people here than forty years of government programs. And he wasn't the one who boarded up the hotel and sold seventy-five acres to an Equal Opportunity developer for thirty-two houses built so cheap my shack puts them to shame" (9). Part of the problem, however, is that while Bill stands for the people, he is not of or even with the people.

Besides his odd relationship with Sandler, Cosey refuses to mix publicly with locals, "which is to say he employed them, joked with them, even rescued them from difficult situations, but other than at church picnics, none was truly welcome at the hotel's tables or on its dance floor" (41). Such distance makes for a princely image but also for misconceptions. If *Love* spills over with the messiness of its characters' fully lived lives, Bill Cosey exists as its void. Actually appearing nowhere in the novel, he nonetheless embodies the logos of the novel, never speaking directly but always talked about. Morrison titles her chapters after the roles others assign to him: Portrait, Friend, Stranger, Benefactor, Lover, Husband, Guardian, Father, Phantom. We agree with Sandler when he says that the more he learns about the man, the less he feels he knows. Always of "two minds about Cosey," watching Bill comes to be "not so much about changing his mind; it [is] more like an education" (45). Bill himself recalls Lacan's speculations about self-identity and its lack when he says about his son: "We had some good times. Good times. More like pals than father and son. . . . I was so caught up with him, I never took the trouble to know him. . . . Maybe he was somebody else and I made him my . . . shadow. And now I'm thinking *I* don't understand anybody. So why should anybody understand me?" (43).[9]

What we come to understand about this black father makes us of two minds. Like most people, his positive qualities turn out to be merely his negative ones upside down—and the other way around. Bill possesses the kind of passion that moves Love to tears at the sight of his wife and him in the sea. L is only five years old to Bill's twenty-four when she sees him holding Julia above the waves with such tenderness that "nine years later, when [she] heard he was looking for house help, [she] ran all the way to his door" (64). His gentleness, however, relates to his sorrow. Apart from Celestial, Cosey tells Sandler, he "never felt connected to a woman. His adored first wife thought his interests tiresome, his appetite abusive" (110). After Julia's blood freezes from the heat of Dark's money, Bill transfers "all of what he felt" over to twelve-year-old Billy. Even as a child, Billy Boy figures out his father. Upon Julia's death, Bill looks to him to make life interesting; on his own, he decides to be good. Father and son become inseparable. Billy finds Celestial for Bill. Her fingers dripping red as Bill's son gets to her on the beach, a nine- or ten-year-old girl has caught herself on her homemade fishhook. Coolheaded and deft, Billy removes the nail from her cheek. Celestial stands gratefully quiet under his hand, holding up "her face without a tear or a moan." Hoping "she was too strong for lockjaw," L treats her wound (101). The scarred girl will not be silenced, but the good boy smothers. While Bill defines Billy Boy's rambles on the road with father as "life's real education," L retorts: "It looked to me like truancy from his own father's school. A way to flunk the lessons Dark had taught him" (101). Bill tells Sandler that Billy drowned quickly: "Walking pneumonia they call it. No symptoms. A cough or two and the lights go out" (43). But Bill Cosey does not see the long-standing signals. Trapped constantly traveling by his father's side, the son cannot breathe.

On the other hand, the father opens wide his cozy home, welcoming Billy's wife indoors. May trusts in Big Daddy's generous resources and manufactured reputation to protect her from a world of disruptions; Cosey finds in May's hand-me-down dresses and over-mended coat a material ally. Bill is initially dismayed when Billy Boy brings a bride home. He relaxes, however, as he learns that a placid youngest daughter's experience with itinerant Christian humility teaches her not to take over but to pitch in and help. Capitalizing on the fact that, other than "disapproving white folk," nothing frightens May more than the live death of Negro poverty, Bill gains a helpmate instead of losing a son. May weans her daughter at three months of age, and when her husband dies, the wife, more insulted than sad, "put all her energy into the hotel's business" (137). Big Daddy also shelters an even younger girl who must wear a man's undershirt for a dress. Out of this deal he acquires an eleven-year-old wife to "educate to his taste" (110). (Mother) May (I?) goes from defense mode to outright militancy when a shiftless, skirt-raising Up Beach Johnson arrives on May's hard-won turf to remind her of her deprived past. Her heroic efforts to erase it are rewarded "by watching her father-in-law marry her twelve-year-old daughter's playmate and put that playmate ahead of everything, including herself, her daughter, and all she had worked for. Not only that. She was supposed to teach and train the playmate to take charge of [her and hers]" (138). Each household dependent describes a different Bill. Is he the grief-stricken husband-and-father looking to help a little girl—or the grown-up little boy still trying to make his own life interesting? Does he provide a home for vulnerable girls or buy orphans from their fathers, steal them from their friends, and then turn one out to protect another—or because he can't stand her sight?

L answers that "he liked her" (139). So is Cosey a milkman or a pedophile? Is he attracted to females, and they to him, or does he misuse them? L claims that "most people married young back then (the sooner a girl was taken over by a man, the better), but eleven?" (138). We don't know whether to be shocked or informed by Morrison's descriptions of fifty-year-old Bill introducing children to sex (77). She deliberately creates these scenes to be among the most disturbing in a disturbing novel, to the girls as well as to her readers. Heed's first sexual experience and exposure to shame occurs when she runs up to get jacks and bumps into Bill. Excited about a picnic with Christine "and the flavor of her bubble gum," she moves down the hall shaking her hips to the beat of bar music. Bill's casual touch to her chin drops down to her chest "or rather the place under her swimsuit where a nipple will be if the circled dot on her chest ever changes." Christine encounters separately the fallacy of "a time when innocence did not exist because no one had dreamed up hell." In the gazebo guarding their food, she goes to meet her friend. As she gazes up toward her bedroom "where Heed would be looking for the jacks," she sees in the frame of her window her grandfather masturbating. Her laughter converting to vomit, ashamed of him and of herself, she cannot face Heed, who thinks the blame is hers alone. Morrison is quick to point out that the arousals are not altogether unpleasant. It is the "other thing: The thing that made each believe, without knowing why, that this particular shame was different and could not tolerate speech—not even in the language they had invented for secrets." Even idagay cannot help them to comprehend the birth of sin or answer the crucial question: "Would the inside dirtiness leak?" (190–91).

The guilelessly dirty old man assures Sandler that he does not penetrate his child bride until "her period came." Then he waits a full year and "only then took her on a honeymoon for the initiation." Instead of acknowledging the touchy, artificial woman she turns into, as anyone who "had jumped from a log to a castle overnight" and "had envy plus May on her back" would have to become, Bill remembers Heed even twenty-five years later as "a long-legged angel with candle eyes and a smile he couldn't help but join." He never explains the attraction any other way except to tell Sandler he "wanted to raise her and couldn't wait to watch her grow" (147–48). Sixty-year-old Heed still looks forward to the feeling of water on her skin. Pleasure for her now involves her body's memory of nights like the one after her wedding, submerged in seawater in Cosey's arms: "Creeping away from the uncomfortable reception, out the back door into the dark, rushing in tuxedo and way-too-big bridal gown across sea grass to powdery sand. Undressing. No penetration. No blood. No eeks of pain or discomfort. Just this man stroking, nursing, bathing her." Her body arched, he stands at her back, "placed his hands behind her knees, and opened her legs to the surf" (77–78).

With scenes like these, Morrison evokes the dual sensations of pleasure and repulsion, preventing her readers from a singular response. Her attitude toward male sexuality would seem to support the Berkeley Men's Center Manifesto, published in 1970: "We want to love ourselves. We want to feel good about and experience our sensuality, emotions, intellect, and daily lives in an integrated way. . . . We want to enjoy masturbating without feeling guilty or that masturbation is a poor substitute for interpersonal sex" (Franklin 7). The shame appears to be not so much about sexuality but about age, race, gender, class, and education. Cosey stays ignorant about some of the consequences of giving to or taking from vulnerable children a grown-up pleasure. Whether he joined in or not, Bill cannot get out of his head the image of a little girl running after a wagon, raggedy "as Lazarus," laughed at by white folks for falling in shit (45).

There can be no question but that Bill has a big heart. While he is smart enough to understand that "where there is music there is money," he also knows that "if colored musicians were treated well, paid well, and coddled, they would tell each other about such a place where . . . their instruments were safe, their drinks unwatered, their talent honored so they didn't have to go to Copenhagen or Paris for praise." He uses his heart "like Santa Claus." Quietly underwriting funerals, bails, hospital bills, and college fees, he establishes during the Depression a sanctuary for people who "studied ways to contradict history" (102–3). His generosity succeeds in outweighing jealousy until both get to be, as Baby Suggs puts it, too much. Even so, he handles 1968 detractors with aplomb. He is repairing a fishing rod behind his hotel, having refused to sell land to locals who want to build a commune, when a protesting youngster throws offal onto his pants. Speaking courteously to the crowd, his tone communicating "neither stranger nor enemy," Bill is prevented by May or Heed from selling his own land yet manages to bridge the ensuing disruption simply with talk. Vida, on the other hand, remains thankful that the deal did not go through. She insists that "Housing was more important than pottery classes" and considers the choice not "whether to surrender to power or dislodge it. It was to do your duty to your family, and at the moment, that meant serious talk to a grandson" (150).

Bill provides Vida with her first, and only, seriously satisfying job. A high "leap out of the fish trough" where she works before, her position as hotel receptionist requires that she wear sheer hosiery and one of two really good dresses that Bill buys for her himself. She believes that the "powerful, generous friend" gazing out from the portrait hanging behind the reception desk surrenders to "feuding women, letting them ruin all he had built" (36–37, 45). Paid "good money," she values even more what she learns from her boss, things that she "never would have known about if [she'd] kept on living over a swamp in a stilt house" (18). Vida's husband, however, sees in addition to the man's "cracked glass eyes" the scarred women who stand in front of the eyes in the painting (46).

Convinced that, far from "pure," the past is "simply stifled," Sandler defends Bill's wife in spite of her touchiness but objects when his wife forgives a "commanding, beautiful man" for all his sins (147, 36).

Bill gives Sandler a job, too, waiting tables at the hotel like Billy Boy. He offers Sandler an unconventional education when he is about the age Bill last remembers his son, taking Sandler fishing and reminiscing about the past. Unlike others, however, Sandler pays attention yet keeps his distance. Claiming to know only his employer's habits but perceiving Cosey would be more comfortable with a plant foreman than an employee, he leaves the resort for a cannery supervisor's position. He senses Bill's connection to Celestial, though the older man never speaks of her by name. Cosey agrees with his protégé that a lion mates for life. Sandler grasps that his mentor met his match in the hooker who catches herself. "Naked as truth," Celestial will dive far out into the sea despite threats of Police-heads who have already done plenty of damage. L observes her actions: "This woman kept on wading out into black water and I could tell she wasn't afraid of them—or of anything—because she stretched, raised her arms, and dove" (106). Once Celestial walks away from the waves, her hair rises up to take on—upside down—the shape of dark Police-head clouds, and the noise she makes sounds somewhere between "a word, a tune, or a scream" (106). Having "changed—well, limited—her caseload" for her lover but absolutely refusing the silver spoons he orders specially made containing entwined double Cs, Celestial leaves town. Whether or not she is pregnant, "neither could break the spell. And the grave didn't change a thing" (106). The woman who scares off Police-heads with a word or a note continues to love her daddy but will in no way deliver up Big Daddy's sweet Cosey child.

Junior Viviane reminds L of Celestial. Bill's paternalism extends beyond the grave after the former spots a portrait in the Silk house of what she comes to call her Good Man. During her early days at Correctional, Junior experiences recurring nightmares about "upright snakes on tiny feet" whose green tongues tempt her to come down from the apple tree into which she has climbed. Standing slightly apart from the snakes, an unidentified male presence implies rescue. Morrison associates this princely image with Junior's longing for her father. The only information Vivian offers when her daughter begs relentlessly to see Ethan Payne Jr., other than "he weren't nothing, baby," is that the man who names her for himself, or after his longing for a son, probably left to join the army (55). Her refusal to give up a stolen G.I. Joe doll gets Junior sent to Correctional. Long-buried feelings surface as Bill Cosey's chiseled face and rugged jaw stare out at her from the portrait mounted over the bed of the new boss she heeds immediately for wearing a "warden's righteous shield" (29). In Junior Viviane's Eden, the snakes are female. Converting Lacan's Law of the Father into mother-rule, Morrison associates his theories of self-identity with a traditional awareness of sin. A faint scent of aftershave turns Junior's dreams about rigid female vipers that lay down the law into soft daytime fantasies. Her Good Man embodies "A handsome man with a G.I. Joe chin and a reassuring smile that pledged endless days of hot, tasty food; kind eyes that promised to hold a girl steady on his shoulder while she robbed apples from the highest branch" (30). However, the girl whose name derives from both father and mother must learn that a Good Man is not only hard to find; it may not always be good for a girl to find him.

Indisputably a Good Man, Bill Cosey tries to be a decent daddy, but the scar left by the white Law of the Father just cuts too deep. So he becomes a Big Daddy instead. Sociologist Elijah Anderson defines the inner-city decent daddy as embracing "certain responsibilities and privileges: to work, to support his family, to rule his household, to protect his daughters, and to raise his sons to be like him, as well as to encourage other young people to demonstrate these qualities, too." A complex figure coming from every walk of life, he "tends to carry the weight of the race on his shoulders and represents his community to outsiders. He is highly principled and moral" yet possesses the tangible connections that can provide young people with jobs. Politically conservative, typically low-key, he rejects excuses that blame discrimination or the lack of employment for the failures of fathers and husbands. Holding individuals to higher standards than the system, he nonetheless takes it upon himself to defeat racial apartheid. A decent daddy believes that being "good enough—that is, assimilating the values of the wider, dominant system—would . . . lead to acceptance in that system" (180–87).

Love supports radical change in the system along with being good. Anderson concedes that the role of the decent daddy is "problematic in today's economic and social circumstances" (204). Images of decency associated with leaders like Martin Luther King Jr. have been challenged; ethnic particularism has resurged; white culture continues to resist integration. The good part of Cosey got too Big, which leads to tension, repression, and resentment. Too closely tied to dreams of good times, Bill ultimately comes to despise the weak who depend on him to provide those good times. L states that "what looked like seven years of self-pity and remorse was really vengeance, and that his hatred of the women in his house had no level. First they disappointed him, then they defied him, then they turned his home into a barrel of quarreling she-crabs and his life's work into a cautionary lesson in black history" (201). Whether or not Bill's vendetta has merit, Love must stop him from doing more damage. And she does—temporarily. But not without acknowledging that "You could call him a good bad man, or a bad good man. Depends on what you hold dear—the what or the why. I tend to mix them. Whenever I see his righteous face correcting Heed, his extinguished eyes gazing at Christine, I think Dark won out. Then I hear the laugh, remember his tenderness cradling Julia in the sea; his wide wallet, his hand roughing his son's hair." In the final analysis, Bill Cosey is just "an ordinary man ripped, like the rest of us, by wrath and love" (200–201).

It is Cosey's Hotel that creates this ripple effect. *Love*'s other extremely ordinary men, spreading outward from the resort's environs, exist also in the eyes of its women. As with *Sula*'s Nel, the idea of a husband at home dominates Heed. Christine, like Sula, sails beyond Harbor to be disillusioned by various males, married and unmarried. At twenty-eight Heed becomes disabused of her apparent barrenness when she has a fling with Not Here Knox. Brother of a clarinet player drowned by Police-heads when his new wife perhaps plays around, Knox Sinclair arrives at the hotel to collect his brother's remains and stays for six days. Heed has never seen a sober man cry, and "suddenly aware of the difference between being needed and being obliged," she prepares a sandwich and beer to feed his "adorable paunch," fleeing from his room before she "kiss[es] his belly" (172). She fails to understand, however, that this (need), too, shall pass. Promising each other forever, the two plan to elope. Knox never shows. Seven telephone calls to his Indiana home cause his mother to say pleasantly but firmly that he never will. Learning she is pregnant, happier to be needed by a child than a father, Heed will not accept her miscarriage until L slaps her in the face: "Wake up, girl. Your oven's cold" (172–74).

Christine heats up more than one male "to secure her place" (174). Caught between impressions of a car driver who mocks what he interprets as a homeless woman and a bus driver who "either misunderstood or understood completely" her pressing need for shelter and directs her to Manila's, she wanders from man to man. She stops over at Manila's for the first time after she vows that her grandfather will never see her again. Fueled by visions of independence and privacy, she believes she would not have stayed, but she "will never know because, being a colored girl in the 1940s with an education that suited her for nothing but wifehood, it was easy as pie for Ernie Holder to claim her that very night." Pfc. Ernest Holder looks merely to "buy some fun" at Manila's. He finds instead a "beautiful girl in a navy suit and pearls reading *Life* magazine on a sofa." Capitalizing on "desire so instant it felt like fate," he marries her and takes her abroad but does not hold her (92–93). Found in the "arms of the staff sergeant's wife," Ernie motivates less Christine's jealous rage, mustered primarily for the other wives' morale in the newly desegregated unit, than her puzzlement over who this raggedy private first class thinks he is to prefer a sordid fling above her "gorgeous well-bred self" (162).

Her affair with Fruit concludes in despair. Returning to Idlewild, Christine gets a job waitressing in the Big Apple "on looks alone" until they discover she can cook. Fruit takes all her attention. While she looks for a husband and locates three other women's, he disrupts her unbridled aimlessness with his gift for "clarity," a "canvas satchel and a flawlessly ironed work shirt." Fruit is "fierce, uncorruptible, demanding" and because he likes dirt, though he could never make time to cultivate it, would never treat her as such. With "apology for her light skin . . . and hair threatening a lethal silkiness," she becomes his designated Jill-of-all-trades, mistress of none (162–63). Civil disobedience requires personal sacrifice and Chris's acceptance of the younger man's other women. The first bite into the Fruit n' Chris combo comes about as a result of a rapist comrade and the girl's Good Daddy Big Man. When a seventeen-year-old volunteer volunteers to Christine that a comrade has raped her but she refuses to inform her university dean father, Christine goes ballistic. She corners Fruit; he promises to expel the menace. However, the girl's "violation carried no weight against the sturdier violation of male friendship," especially since clearly "the raped one did not belong to [Fruit]" (166).

The closing of Christine's "disinterested eye" contributes to her disillusionment. She is accustomed to relying on abortions to prevent prospective children, who would stand in the way of her being "in" with Fruit. An "insignificant toilet flush" represents the arrival of the end, though "unrecognizable as such." Spotted in "a blur of congealed red," however, a "noncommittal eye" grabs her attention at the oddest times. This "quietly interested profile" remains, in fact, right "at home in the chaos of cops and tears" (166–67). Since revolutions need men but not fathers, Fruit fails to suggest that Christine stop before her seventh miscarriage or be as aware of children's rights as she is about abortion rights. Sensing her resistance to being held back giving way to despair after her grandfather's funeral, and her probable infertility, he comes to find his lover, along with children, clearly irrelevant, and "they parted as friends" (166–67).

If Eddie is not first class enough to hold her and Fruit's personal revolution clearly no longer requires her, Dr. Rio needs Christine as merely a light substitute. Sixty to her forty-one, this wealthy general practitioner makes a habit of displacing gold-toned women. Youthful, playful, passionate but "mightily undivorcable," he welcomes each new mistress with a gift of flowers and cologne. Had Christine spent more time at Manila's, she might have exposed Rio's particular pattern: "He fell head over heels, seduced, offered his expensive apartment on Trelaine Avenue, and sent dracaena and White Shoulders on the day the replacement moved in." Interpreting the dracaena accurately as an esoteric symbol of "legitimacy, permanence," Christine never quite acquires the common sense to understand the simple significance of the cologne. She does concede that Kenny Rio "could have sent a bottle of Clorox and a dead Christmas tree—she would have done whatever he wanted for what he made available. Complete freedom, total care, reliable sex, reckless gifts." Most important, he gives her a steady position "in the pecking order of a certain middle-class black society that understood itself to swing, if the professional credentials and money were right" (83–84).

The only thing Ken lacks is the white shoulders of the correct Barbie. Still searching, he has Christine forcibly ejected from his apartment after three years, forbidding her return and retaining for his next experiment Christine's expensive clothes and her diaphragm. She must forfeit the contents of four Samsonite suitcases with which she left Silk, only to come back carrying a Wal-Mart bag containing all that she owns. Before going home to Heed-the-Night for good, Christine finds out that many a classy man wants merely a temporarily kept woman. Considerable reflection allows her to convert "a return to Silk in shame and on borrowed money into an act of filial responsibility: taking care of her ailing mother, and a noble battle for justice—her lawful share of the Cosey estate" (86). However, she fails to realize the plain fact that Rio's "mimeographed copy of her bourgeois grandfather" rejects black women because they are not white (167).

Morrison's African American parable about looking for love starts over again in an inland Settlement and on Oceanside. Silk stays Silk. It takes growing up in the settlement and experience with Correctional to secure Junior Viviane a place at Cosey's renumbered Monarch Street address. The sprawling, huddled, mountain valley settlement resembles a mixed-up, black-and-white Bottom, or a rural Hood. Junior is as beautiful and as wild as a settlement dog: "Fifty strong, they swung between short chains and unfettered roaming. Between fights and meals they slept lashed to trees or curled near a door. Left to their own devices, hounds mated with shepherds, collies with Labradors. By 1975, when Junior was born, they were an odd, original, astonishingly handsome breed instantly recognizable to folks who knew as settlement dogs—adept at keeping outsiders out, but at their brilliant best when hunting" (55). Although Vivian does her best to prevent her daughter from becoming prey, throwing stones at uncles and brothers when the men wake up in a stalking mood, the mother is not always successful. Her male relations break even the Otis Rick mold. "Sudden fighters—relentless and vicious," familiar to Guidance Counselors by the code name "Rurals," boys like Otis go for blood on the school playground then ignore the "expelled notices stuck in [their] shirt pocket." Testing rather than acquiring his proffered education, Otis arrives back every day to sit silently in class, his "victim's dried blood still on his sleeve" (53–54). The principal who makes an official visit to his house to prevent him from returning to school has to "cover the whole length of the valley on foot," given that he is given neither time nor opportunity to make it back to his car. The DeSoto must be "towed back to town by State Troopers because nothing could make its owner go back to retrieve it" (53–54).

The first Rural to "make a stab at her homework," Junior finds a schoolmate in a fellow but different outsider by the name of Peter Paul Fortas. For Christmas she takes the Jewish boy a baby cottonmouth in a jar; a delighted Pee Pee returns the favor by giving her jumbo crayons. Junior's uncles, "idle teenagers whose brains had been insulted by the bleakness of their lives," object. Whether they get upset because something of the settlement is lost to a symbol of their failures or "it was too late for possum," they come alive the day after Christmas and set out loaded for Junior. Finding her asleep on a stained "Jesus Saves" pillow, they kick her in gear and kick back to enjoy the fun. Morrison's portrait of certain Rurals supports her continuing argument that a lack of self-awareness limits social change: the uncles "didn't know themselves . . . why a snake was important to them. They wanted the cottonmouth returned to its rightful home" (57). Peter Paul, on the other hand, educated by nickname and religion to remain indifferent to popular opinion, stays insatiably curious about other people. Uninterested in Junior's body, he wants to know "whether it was the calves or the smell of milk that attracted snakes." He asks whether or not Junior is "Colored" and, when she says she will find out, responds that it makes no difference: "He couldn't invite Gentiles to his house anyway. He didn't want her feelings hurt" (56–57).

Her desensitized uncles threaten her with Vosh if she refuses to return the snake. A reminder of *Sula*'s Shadrack, Vosh is the "old man in the valley who liked to walk around with his private parts in his hand singing hymns of praise," an inland inversion of ocean Police-heads. Junior, clutching her crayons, flees her howling uncles. Thinking she has escaped, hoping to find Peter Paul for help, she simply jumps the wrong way in the road, and the front fender of their truck knocks her sideways while the back tire crushes her toes. Vivian tells her barely conscious daughter she is lucky her rural relatives arrived before some "town bastard" could do more damage. The girl suffers chance, lies, humiliation, and excruciating pain in silence as her toes knit together but exchanges her broken crayons for a sharp knife "ready for Vosh or an uncle or anyone stopping her from committing the Settlement version of crime: leaving, getting out." Ripe for Correctional, in two years Junior is "fed, bathed, clothed, educable, and thriving. Behind bars" (59). At eighteen she comes out of this, too, a half-grown woman still slightly crippled and carrying a weapon but quite able to strut.

Oceanside exists as home to Romen's story. Just back of the ocean, adjacent to Silk and Café Ria, comprised of Cosey's house and Sandler's driveway, this community represents Morrison's expansive, complex, out-of-the-ordinary, un-ideal American substitute for Lacan's narrow site of self-awareness. His "Hotel Make Believe" imaginary stands as a disturbing, mirrored shell of itself (167). Having left it once for good to relocate Up Beach, L is persuaded by Maceo to cook side dishes and cinnamon bread for his Silk business. Morrison continues her semiotic revolution by comically omitting two central letters from the name of its sign, which seriously alters its sound and significance. A cross between an old-fashioned local diner and a contemporary cafeteria, Maceo's Café Ria combines Big Daddy's single-minded efficiency with L casually propped against the stove to entice people to come. L leaves Café Ria once, too, although this time not for good. Her feet start to swell, and she becomes unable to make the walk all the way from Up Beach to Silk. But, bothered by his empty space, Mah CEO offers to drive her back and forth, then fashions for her a queenly "high chair with wheels so [she] could scoot from stove to sink to cutting table." Although L's food service CEO maintains "a certain reputation for fried fish (sooty black and crisp on the outside; flaky tender inside)," he comprehends astutely that it takes two to combo. His "side orders let you down every time," so the restaurant "really belonged to [L]." Having died there years ago, after doing all she could for Cosey's women, she "glides there still" to oversee its patrons, among whom are Junior and Romen (64–65).

Sandler reveals as much creative forethought concerning his private driveway as Maceo exhibits in his public kitchen. The first in Silk to be impressed by Junior's good legs, he stands outside his house when she stops for directions, sprinkling ice salt on the frozen pavement in a place where they "never get snow. Never." Junior responds more smartly than she knows to Heed's declaration: "Since he already had [ice salt], he must have expected to use it" (24). With such obvious good sense, Sandler is "prepared for freezing weather in a neighborhood that had no history of it." He stores away seemingly useless stuff to ensure that the people he safeguards, namely Vida and Romen, would be "safe from falling" (14). However, Sandler makes it equally possible for his people to acquire their own protection via firsthand experience. Vida picks up a job as a hospital aide after the hotel closes along with the schooling its receptionist receives there. Sandler asks Heed to give Romen handyman's work at the Silk house, where, unbeknownst to him, Junior finds Romen quite handy indeed. Forced to take early retirement, Sandler maintains his "hilarious pension" wandering through malls at night as a security officer and spends his daytime hours keeping the house "just fine" (17).[10] Vida continues to cook and serve not always perfect family dinners. She represents Morrison's version of what Anderson calls the black grandmother, and Sandler is the decent daddy, struggling together to maintain their moral authority in a generation so modern it makes them nervous. Convinced, nonetheless, that if "Parents idle, children sidle," the two are "pleased" to rear their grandson when his parents enlist in land and sea enforcement (15).

His name suggesting a nature caught fluctuating between Daniel's Dark and Bill's Light, Sandler becomes a decent rather than Big daddy by reason of his father and the offbeat education offered him by Cosey. One of his last conversations with Bill about Heed prevents the listener from being "as repelled as he'd expected to be, since the picture that emerged from the telling called to his mind not a child but a fashion model." Such tolerantly critical empathy enables him to keep his own tongue from "tilting his wife's idol with a blow of insight" and to understand his precarious position with respect to his grandson: "Oh, well. This is what I'm for, he thought. The day Romen came to stay he knew he had to protect him. From bad cops, street slaughter, dope death, prison shivs, and friendly fire in white folks' wars. He never would have believed a female would be a serious threat and his first real danger" (148). Sandler accepts sooner than Cosey, however, the necessity of symbiotic predator-prey relationships (42). When his fellow fisherman expresses annoyance at the perniciousness of the weak, the younger man replies: "Everything has its place, Mr. Cosey" (42).

Thus, Sandler responds to the provocatively dressed young woman with the nose earring who asks the way to Bill's house by admiring her but declining to string her along. He scans her legs and thighs, reckoning they are "stinging from the cold her tiny skirt exposed them to" and "marveled at the height of her bootheels." However, the picture that emerges when he overcomes the distraction of the fluffy hair blowing in her face suggests "a sweet child, fine-boned, gently raised but lost" (14). On the other hand, he can imagine Bill's reaction. Despite the latter's complaint that women are "all over the damn place. . . . In the bed . . . the kitchen, the yard, at your table, under your feet, on your back," Bill would have bitten—invited her in out of the cold, offered to drive her to her destination "instead of barking at her, doubting her accuracy." He would have "done more"—and it would have worked (40). Sandler prefers to keep his distance but can connect with people perfectly well when the time is right. In addition, he can chuckle about committing his dirty-old-man adulteries of the heart. Smothering his laughter at the image of an "over-fifty grandfather faithful and devoted to his wife giggling into a boiler dial in the cellar, happy to be arousable by the unexpected sight of young thighs," he gives Vida her due. His wife is right to tease him about being "struck by the girl's legs." He realizes his gruffness with said girl "had been a reaction to the feelings she stirred and believed she knew it too" (38). Always of two minds, Sandler can perceive Bill's eyes radiating "pain like cracked glass" as well as the possessive eyes in the portrait (42).[11] He acknowledges both connotations of Heed's touchiness and remains convinced that "You can't blame her for what her daddy did" (146).

His similarity to his daddy, however, as well as his difference from Bill keeps Sandler standing in his own driveway. Bill is able to entice a twenty-year-old into fishing with an older man because Sandler misses his father. Still adroit at preparing bait, the old man now lives up north with his daughter because "Young girls easier to push around." Catching his faux pas and trying to "clean it up in case Cosey was offended," Sandler explains that he has been trying to convince his father to stay with him, since the house belongs to the elder Gibbons anyway, but the man refuses for some reason. Cosey replies simply, "Fathers can be hard." As their conversation becomes easier, Sandler confesses that his "old man did all right by [him]. . . . Not with money. Never had none, but I could always count on him, and he knows he can count on me no matter what" (111). Like his son, the father remains more concerned with family than finances, and he manages to keep his connections while he maintains his distance. Though drawn, then, Sandler does not feel compelled to give himself over to Bill.

Sandler relies on his father's example to establish a relationship with his grandson. While he does not try to coerce a friendship, he knows that "It ain't nothing if there's nothing you can control" (154). He also realizes that if he forbids Romen's affair with Junior, the whole thing would just become "hotter, more enticing. He wouldn't be telling him to choose one girl over another, but to give up the only one he had complete physical access to. Like telling a duck not to waddle. He would have to think up something else." Gramp would be satisfied with condoms, but Gran "expected more—an end to the relationship." Gramp can see things from Romen's perspective ("he wasn't doping, ganged up, courting arrest, and his house manners had definitely improved") as well as Gran's ("The neighborhood had changed and so had the times"). Morrison weaves Sandler's reminiscences about his childhood after-school education from Cosey in and through his thoughts about Romen and Junior. Concluding that, all things considered, Romen looks to be handling his first sex pretty well, Sandler decides simply to find a way to talk to the boy. To his surprise he learns that the boy is as eager for time alone together as he is (146).

Although today's parents seem "flummoxed" over what to do about their children, Sandler finds driving with his grandson to deliver Vida's meals on wheels fairly successful. As usual, Morrison suggests a balance between masculine and feminine approaches as well as between a time when children were sidelined and an era when they appear center stage. When Romen tries to enter a dinner-table discussion Sandler and Vida introduce about sex, work, murder, and paradise in the context of a Cosey conversation, he is torn between one and the other grandparent siding with him and both turning on him "as if his fly was open" (16). This exercise tells him to take nothing for granted and to assess each situation individually. Sandler's deliveries take place partly for but not too obviously about Romen, and as they benefit the housebound, they also teach the boy about some of the ways of certain women. The grandfather starts out struggling to think of a conversation opener, something "they could share before the interrogation or the lecture began." Then he tries to remember the approach of his own father and grandfather: "Short, biting commands. . . . No long sermons and no talking back." Romen, however, fails to respond well to this sort of tactic; he reacts merely by sulking. Opting to use the model of popular music, "Straight no chaser. Black no sugar. Direct as a bullet," Sandler turns to his grandson and inquires: "She pregnant?" (148–51).

Being as frank as his father "minus the threat" works. Romen is "startled but not angry or evasive." Sandler learns that the young couple breaks into Cosey's Hotel and that Junior likes her beautiful black boys "nice and mean," her attic sex "dark." "Moans of pleasure and pain" mix with crashing cartons and splitting floorboards "raking their nakedness and sharpening their play, lending it a high seriousness [Romen] could never have imagined." As the scene shifts from "black to red," a sweet boy finds himself standing "next to himself, cold, unsmiling, watching himself inflict and suffer pain above scream level where a fresh kind of joy lay" and then perceiving the girl's feet as cloven. Cleverly inserting the facts in between Romen's lies to his grandfather, Morrison suggests how insightful adults can piece together partial truths by reading between the lines. Because the real issue involves a fourteen-year-old boy's guilt about losing his innocence, the most effective line Sandler can call on to elicit honest conversation becomes "Romen, we men or not?" The older man's continuing reliance on questions instead of chuckles or reproach encourages Romen not to close down but to begin the difficult process of being responsible for himself. His creator is too savvy, though, to stop there. Sandler looks cheerful as the two complete their errands, thinking he has successfully concluded negotiations with his grandson, asleep now against the headrest. Eyes closed but body aroused, however, by the mere memory of his encounter with the girl, Romen swallows "the saliva gathering in his mouth in anticipation of Junior's" (151–57). Morrison knows that it takes far more than one occasion for the questions to sink in. Nevertheless, the answer to the gap between generations is "Talk, then, respectful but serious" (149).

On the other hand, conversation signifies nothing without a context. Romen must gain the experience that will give his grandfather's words meaning, and sometimes this means pain as well as pleasure. The name Romen sounds like roamin'. It calls to mind a small, agile deer along with the concept of fish eggs, especially those still massed in the ovarian membrane. It spells a variant of Roman. These connotations taken together outline the traits of teenage roe-men, a difficult stage for boys in any context. This boy certainly comes honestly by his propensity for contradiction. His father, Plaquemain, manages to finish two years of college before he is forced to join the service, his branch of choice being the Merchant Marines. From a mother who serves in the army and from her parents, Romen inherits a "natural tendency to care for people," though he seems "nowadays, not to know what to do with it" (150). Work at the Cosey house brings his profile into focus. It provides him with a special education, which teaches him that caring for others can rest just this side of causing them pain.

The Cosey job clarifies Romen's reactions to and feelings about a prior rape. Morrison fashions this incident to be the core of her novel. Despite the fact that, for her, a small gathering "can be likened to a rock star making a club appearance," she continues to elicit response from the people for whom she writes upon the release of a book. In this case she takes *Love* to tea in Brooklyn with thirteen members of the "Mocha Moms," a "nationwide support group for at-home parents of color" (Italie 9A). The scene that resonates most with her readers depicts the backroom gang rape of a young girl named Pretty-Fay ("or Faith"). Last in line to take his part, Romen stands "ready, too, in spite of the little hands and in spite of the mewing in her throat." Although he wells up with "girlish tears," possibly a "weakness the others recognized and pinpointed even before he punked out," he is "charged by Theo's brays and his head bobbing above the girl's face, which was turned to the wall and hidden beneath hair undone by writhing." Erect with illicit lust, he anticipates becoming the Rom[a]n "he'd always known he was: chiseled, dangerous, loose. Last of a group of seven" (46–47).

Morrison's crisp single page of prose puts *Love* into perspective. Romen does not yet understand why he "stepped forward to take Theo's place, then watched in wonder as his hands moved to the headboard." He unties the girl's folded, plum-polished, nail-bitten hands, wraps her limp body in the bedspread, picks up her high-heeled shoes, and carries her out accompanied by the cymbal clashes of catcalls and the trumpet sounds of sneered names. If either Romen or Fay "had been drunk earlier, they weren't anymore." Romen thinks to say something but suddenly cannot stand the sight of the girl much less her thanks. She says nothing. His cohorts, however, have plenty to say. For the next three days, he becomes the butt of a running joke. His new friendships lost, holding stares impossible, he is eliminated from talk at the link fence, ignored at Patty's Burgers, and refused passes on the basketball court. Responding in kind would be signaling the wrong kind of connection, like defending the girl again as though "he *and* her had been tied to a bed; his legs *and* hers forced open" (47–48).

The code of the street prohibits him companionship even with Lucas Breen, a white boy "whose hoop skill was envied," since the sneering "trumpet's repertoire" contains other ear-splitting insults. One former ally, Freddie, brings Romen the leather jacket he leaves at the party and advises that he not "get shook." But Freddie leaves quickly to join Theo and Jamal and the rest of the magnificent six when they beat Romen up, aiming blows carefully so as not to leave marks in case he turns out to be a sissy snitch as well as a punk. Romen fights back fine but remains "more fearful of being rescued than of passing out with vomit on his jeans." Wondering if he could "ever live his body down," he shares the disgust of his friends and cannot comprehend "what had made him melt at that moment—his heart bursting like a pump for a wounded creature who a few seconds earlier had been a feast he was eager to gnaw. . . . What was that thing that had moved him to untie her, cover her, Jesus! Cover her!" He can only answer at this point that the "fake Romen, preening over a stranger's bed, was tricked by the real Romen, who was still in charge here in his own bed, forcing him to hide under a pillow and shed girl tears. The trumpet stuttering in his head" (48–49).

Not until he overpowers his adversaries with his very own girl, and then gives that power away, is Romen able to distinguish between love and possession, resist the temptation to blame the victim, and understand the real possibility for good but out-of-control people to enjoy doing serious damage to others and themselves. Remembering Correctional guards manhandling black boys shooting baskets at Campus A, all aroused because female inmates watch, Junior initiates her affair with Romen by charging roughly: "Don't tell me you're fucking these old women too." Embarrassment struggling with pride, Romen recalls Theo: "She assumed he was capable of it. Of having scored so many times he could choose any woman—and in pairs, Theo, in pairs" (62). Junior shows her colors again connected to Romen as she picks out cafeteria food for them both and Maceo's son serves it up. The only boy to take seconds with Pretty-Fay, "no count" Theo displays his attraction to Junior by slopping food all over her plate. L looks incensed but says nothing. Junior, however, can handle herself. Never removing her eyes from the trays until Theo counts out her change, she finally gazes straight into his "hateful stare" and says levelly: "I can see why you need a posse. Your dick don't work one on one?" A shouted response by the CEO's son falls totally flat with no one there but L to hear his ugly sounds. Refusing to specify what names Theo hurls, Morrison illustrates the impotence of language devoid of meaning. Although Theo comforts himself by repeating his epithets, Junior has skillfully deflated him by deflecting his words' power to do harm. L comments tartly: "Typical. Young people can't waste words because they don't have too many." She also, however, gives the boy his due. Having exhausted his verbal armory, Theo turns to dribbling air balls "in his dream court behind the register. As if he'd just been signed by Orlando and the Wheaties people too. Not a bad way to work off shame. Quick, anyway. Takes some people a lifetime" (66–67).

Romen's overwhelming question is to be or not to be ashamed of enjoying rough sex with Junior. His grandfather's advice helps him discover his answer. When Sandler, undistracted like Theo's father by running a business, notices Romen's skulk replaced by a loose-limbed strut, he pays attention but declines to deflate him yet. Cherishing his own "maiden voyage (free of embarrassment now)," he worries that "introducing shame along with sound advice" would likely "pervert future encounters without stopping them" (109–10). He decides that allowing him to "preen awhile" might prevent the boy from doing like Bill Cosey—"dog-chasing women his whole life," forever "on the prowl for a repeat of that first first time" (109–10). Though he misreads both males' motivations, Sandler's conclusions remain sound. As Romen's body language becomes unmistakably loud, and the grandfather is certain the girl is Junior, he addresses the threat by talking to the boy whose shame might harden into annoyance. Sandler tells his grandson to pay attention to himself. If he has "hooked up" with someone who makes him uneasy, he should simply walk away: "That kind of feeling is more than instinct; it's information, information you can count on. You can't always pay attention to what other people say, but you should pay attention to that. Don't worry about whether backing off means you a wimp. It can save your life. You not helpless, Romen." In addition, the man tells the boy to find and stay with a "good good woman," to "make tracks" from any other kind (154).

Replying in the affirmative but reacting otherwise, Romen walks right back to Junior—until she says she left Heed-the-Night hurt in Cosey's Hotel. Her confession inspired after he kisses her misshapen foot and she feels something like love for the very first time, they lie post-coitus in Heed's bed, under Bill's portrait, when she tells him to turn off the light. Mentally connecting Heed's useless arthritic hands with the curved fingers of the raped girl, Romen stands outside himself once again. Instead of flipping the switch, he scoops up the keys. Running fast, released by his grandfather's whisper that he is never helpless, he understands now that Sandler was trying to "warn him, make him listen, tell him that the old Romen, the sniveling one who couldn't help untying shoelaces from an unwilling girl's wrist, was hipper than the one who couldn't help flinging a willing girl around an attic" (195). When he returns with Christine and Heed's body, after ignoring Junior's shouts and driving slowly under terrible conditions, he gives Christine back the keys to the car and locks a startled but not yet ashamed Junior in L's old rooms with the key Christine instructs him to remove from the bread box.

The recurring image of a little girl laughed at by white folks for falling in dirt brings shame down on Bill Cosey. Afraid he may have joined in, he allows his life to fragment into hours wasted "between the elbows of women whose names he couldn't remember and whose eyes he avoided. Except for one" (110). And that one remains socially beneath his reach. Romen recollects a girl's tiny, helplessly bound hands that he may have helped to tie. As a result, he runs to save the lives of two bad good women, one whose body he covers with a blanket before he drives her to the morgue while the bereft other weighs the possibility of doing some good. The gaze he holds "without a blink" belongs to a girl still to be redeemed. As he speeds along "trying not to disturb his passenger," Police-head profiles can be seen in the clouds "sailing over the roof of One Monarch Street" (197–98). They darken all but the single window where Christine sits illuminated by the light in L's kitchen, talking seriously with Heed the Night about whether they should stir up enough trouble to set Junior free.[12]

Obviously Toni Morrison, now herself an Ardelia who values "word work," would not deny the power of language beautifully crafted to tell stories like Romen's. However, she also acknowledges what has traditionally been a part of Chloe Anthony Wofford's village code: even well wrought, language which is devoid of meaning, where "all is known and nothing understood," creates desire destined for an urn. L laments the fact that "Nowadays silence is looked on as odd and most of my race has forgotten the beauty of meaning much by saying little." Instead of indulging Lacan's symbolic order and allowing "tongues [to] work all by themselves with no help from the mind," Morrison wants us to "figure out how precious the tongue is" (3–4, 201). Supported by restraint as well as sympathetic understanding, it "can save you from the attention of Police-heads hunting desperate women and hardheaded, misraised children." This writer wants her readers to stand "right under their wide hats, their dripping beards" and scare them off with a word or a note (201).

It takes two, though, to tangle with them. The smell of shaving soap has to yield sometimes to a waft of cinnamon. If so, Love, though long dead slumped over a stove while smothering pork chops, will prevail. A grandmother must stop Cosey, but a grandfather signals Romen to go get his keys. Morrison's L represents Lacan's Law of the Father turned on its head. Like his rendition of desire, she is "born in rough weather," marked by "going from womb water straight into rain" (64). Venus rose up out of the sea, which unlike the womb that gives birth to desire, *Love* associates with a man, specifically Bill Cosey. Unconnected, however, to the transforming faith in contradiction and transcendence that Morrison names love, the needle of desire gets stuck in a painful groove. L comments, "if your name is the subject of First Corinthians, chapter 13, it's natural to make [love] your business." Her subject claims that even if we have prophetic powers, if we "understand all mysteries and all knowledge, and . . . have all faith, so as to remove mountains, but do not have love," we are "nothing." The passage "bears watching, if you can stand to look at it" (199):

> Love is patient; love is kind; love is not envious or boastful or arrogant or rude. It does not insist on its own way; it is not irritable or resentful; it does not rejoice in wrongdoing, but rejoices in the truth. It bears all things, believes all things, hopes all things, endures all things.

> Love never ends. . . . And now faith, hope, and love abide, these three; and the greatest of these is love.

The lyricists of *Love*'s stuck record are made free, then, simply by virtue of love. Salvation becomes possible for Junior not through her glorified Good Man but by two old women's grace. Redemption looks even more likely for Romen via the then-ignored memory of his grandfather's whisper. One black man laughs white lies into life to stave off Dark; another black man sounds serious when he tells his grandson he is not helpless, not even in the dark. If the boy will simply ignore Big Daddy and listen to the voice of his decent daddy, he can save his own life and sometimes that of others. With the ongoing help of Others, Bill and Celestial can incorporate Ro[e]men and Junior women. In *Love*, Morrison's love affair with black men comes full circle. At the beginning of her books, she refuses to allow the white master narrative to exclude black masculinity from the Community square. Toward the conclusion of her career, she insists that black male magic can be made not above nor below but alongside the tales of black women. If the women open only their legs, the men grow irritated. If they want something back, something just for them, and if L hears and joins in, the hum they make together goes way beyond language. It's "Hey, Celestial."

Coda

Chatting animatedly beside me prior to the opening curtain of the *Margaret Garner Opera*, libretto by Toni Morrison, sat two women, clearly a couple. When I informed the closest partner that over 250 other members of the Toni Morrison Society from across the globe had accompanied me to this gala Cincinnati premier in July 2005, she perked up even more. "What in the world does a person in the Toni Morrison Society *do*?" she inquired. A medical doctor, she anticipated similarly innocent sentiments expressed by the Reverend Jean Frable of the predominantly white Richwood Presbyterian Church in Richwood, Kentucky, where slave Margaret Garner worshipped, when the society crossed the Ohio River two days later to visit that site of memory: "Do you read books other than Toni Morrison's? *Harry Potter*, perhaps?"

Citing time constraints, this female pastor refused society participants the opportunity to contradict naïve comments such as hers. Her willful ignorance about the political ramifications of literary study manifested itself in her decision to close group discussion about the Margaret Garner story in favor of nonreciprocal lectures. Here she obviously deferred to the wishes of her parishioner Ruth Wade Cox Brunings, descendant of Garner's white slaveholders and current occupant of the Gaines's lovely Maplewood Farm, inspiration for *Beloved*'s Sweet Home.[1] Only under society pressure were scholars Steven Weisenburger and Delores Walters granted permission to visit the farm.[2] Under the influence of Morrison's lyrics, however, my opera cohort eagerly elicited conversation, whispering questions well into the first aria. When I explained that most Morrison Society members, the majority of whom are women, read (not just Morrison's) books, write, teach, activate, counsel, reach out, and generally try to shake things up, she replied, "What fun." When I described the serious gist of my own current scholarship on masculinity and Morrison, maintaining that we need to pay more attention to American boys, she replied: "But aren't they already privileged enough?"

I answered her that most black boys aren't especially privileged and that many white ones miss the advantage of a culturally broad self-awareness. Like Morrison, I've come to believe that Americans still want black males dead or alive. My introduction to Richwood certainly supports this supposition. Northern Kentucky police cars greeted the Toni Morrison Society to control what officers claimed would be an inevitable traffic jam in the tiny hamlet, caused by the arrival of four average-sized tour buses and a minivan. Among our motley crew of threatening, disorderly academics politely lined up to enter the church stood a slender female society member who, like me, had dragged her husband and children along on the jaunt. Once inside we found our families forced to sit at opposite ends of the Amen pew since everybody else had claimed the back seats. Although my silver-bearded, ponytailed, fifty-something replica of Sean Connery looked pretty impressive sitting in his kilt with his wife and young daughter at front left in the church, the blue gaze from the pulpit and the multicolored eyes in the audience stared mostly at the tall, jet-black, forty-something father sitting quietly in slacks and open-necked shirt with his slim wife and two small children to the right.

The front-row families found much to laugh seriously about that night after witnessing an unusually intense exhibition of defensive white guilt. Given her opportunity to talk, Ms. Brunings haltingly proposed that the moral conflict driving the Garner slavewoman to terminate an "adulterous relationship" with Archibald Gaines "could have been a compelling motivation for Margaret to run away from Maplewood as well as reunification with her husband" (39). Brunings's own slaveholding ancestors, added the University of California at Berkeley graduate in social work, had not had an easy time of it either. Her minister prepared us for Brunings's *Slavery and the Tragic Story of Two Families: Gaines and Garner* by explaining that, progressive even in 1855, Richwood Presbyterian Church allowed the slave into baptized membership and that the Reverend Frable herself had worked for the Salvation Army as well as with chain gangs. The *coup de maître* consisted of a retired Berkeley economist, Dr. Jack Michaelsen, a personal friend of Ms. Brunings's, who took his convoluted turn in the pulpit to argue, we think, that slavery was profitable. Lacking a close look at *Beloved* or the opera based on it, our three speakers completely missed Morrison's imagined history of pride, possessiveness, idealized physical beauty, unrealistic romantic love, repressed sexuality, and other unspeakable things unspoken tearing men and women into pieces. Plenty of unacknowledged shame still abides to go around and get beyond. Weary of such seriously strange talk and fast tiring of standing in the Hilton hallway afterward, joking about literature and politics with our pew partners, my twelve-year-old daughter finally took to her bed. But the rest of us lingered on into the night to recapture from most of its circuitous angles a telling scene about the ramifications of not hearing.

As in the sanctuary, our eyes in the hall watched the beautiful face of the black father, who reported two reactions to the day's experience, one that echoed my husband's impulse to walk en masse out of the church. The other was to stand and speak out. However, the father realized that for a big black man to rise up in the midst of such silly white angst would create more stir than successful change and managed to silence himself until he could find friends with whom to laugh. An artist as well as a father, he'd learned long ago the hard way to pick his battles and to merge flight and humor with fight for converting hurt into affirmation. The respective wives expressed some typically feminine reactions. The white one wondered if she could somehow use her gender, race, age, and class to connect with other college-educated, middle-aged white women, helping them locate a little more insight and a lot more peace of mind; the black one simply said she was glad some white folks were there. Next morning I regaled Professor Morrison herself with the tale when she sailed unexpectedly into a society seminar to sit down beside me. Laughing out loud, she exclaimed, "So you got caught in hostile territory, huh?" Laughing right back, I looked her in the eye: "No. Not caught. And not hostile. Merely murky."

The Cincinnati/Richwood scenario clarified for me that race, class, gender, sexuality, and age continue to shape individual perspective, that self-awareness remains crucial for understanding others, that Americans still have a Thing about black masculinity, and that distortions together with positive change occur as everybody tries to get home. The writer who presents Sula's homecoming not as straightforward defeat but as the circular triumph of returning to, and thus recognizing, beginnings informed us during the after-seminar questions that supercilious Louvre directors had requested she guest curate an exhibit, which she tentatively planned to call "Home." Dryly attributing the administrators' selection of a black artist to the current unrest in Paris of former colonials, Morrison noted the transnational significance of her topic in the face of contemporary alienation. She also chuckled that one of her sons half-jokingly suggested she incorporate a sample pyramid into her show. Outfitted by Egyptian royalty right down to the slaves deemed necessary to ensure civilized life after death, live burial of others certainly confirms the extremes to which people will go to get home.[3]

Writing this book has meant, for me, going home. I started my career as a young white feminist writing about young white women. Now a middle-aged white feminist, I write about young black men. Classically trained as a specialist in Early Modern English literature, I began in graduate school what has become a lifelong romance with modern African American texts. Two powerful memories from my early years at the small university where I teach, as well as a sixteen-year-old son whom I missed before he left me, helped shape the focus for a book on the subject. The first arose from a series of Saturday-morning seminars I provided to the college community in 1988 during my stint as director of the Women's Studies program. Asking various faculty members to present a relatively unknown feminist text, I took as my contribution Hurston's *Their Eyes Were Watching God*. Having been introduced to the novel only a decade back myself by Professor R. Baxter Miller, when finding enough copies in print for teaching assistants to use in their classes was no easy task, I was delighted with my offering. I will never forget my disappointment when two female colleagues stood up to insist stridently that, because Janie locates her self through relationships with men, my selection did not serve as a feminist text; another detractor demanded to know why Janie has no children. I found myself at a humiliating loss for words until I read Mary Helen Washington's account of Alice Walker talking back to Yale scholar Robert Stepto at a 1979 MLA convention when Stepto argued that Janie never finds her voice, that Hurston undercuts Janie's power as speaker. While others on that memorable Sunday morning struggled to find their voices, Alice Walker "rose and claimed hers, insisting passionately that women did not have to speak when [others] thought they should, that they would choose when and where they wish to speak because while many women *had* found their own voices, they also knew when it was better not to use it." Henry Louis Gates Jr. now employs "its concern with the project of finding a voice" to define *Their Eyes* as "a bold feminist novel, the first to be explicitly so in the Afro-American tradition" (*Their Eyes Were Watching God* xi–xii, 187).

The second site of memory occurred when I became head of the English department at Alfred University in 1990. Sent to Phoenix, Arizona, by my dean to attend a National Institute for Leadership Development seminar promoting women in higher education administration, I knew immediately I was in the wrong place when its psychologist director required her participants to, literally, act like roses and bloom. Appearing awkwardly thorny like the outsider I felt, I observed a group of young black women, who also kept to themselves. During one of the workshop's impassioned feminist discussions, which inevitably led to male-bashing, one of these women finally spoke up. "We have some different concerns from the rest of you," she said quietly. "We're not as worried about our women as we are about our men."

I choose now to see my former silence as golden. Like Morrison's characters who refuse to be scapegoated, I learned from my experiences not to take it but to make it—and wrote my book, following my mentor's lead of writing books to answer questions. I wanted to understand men so I would really know what it means to be a woman. I have watched men that I love contending mightily with the alienation caused by rigid American masculinity. My father's membership in the Greatest Generation appears to bring him more pain than pride as younger generations take over and he closes out his life; my mother reports the same pattern with respect to her World War I–afflicted father. My male colleagues struggle to maintain their manhood as they retire. My teenage son seems to exhibit the most possibility, even in the midst or perhaps because of his conflictedness about what it means to be a man. Influenced by hip-hop and a mother who won't take it, he also benefits from a flexible father who refuses his own father's stiff masculinity. Perhaps the New Black Man sitting across the Amen pew from a New White Man will produce a New Man in American culture.

Who knows where such information will take us next? I do know that, for many of us who form the society whose members Morrison adamantly claims as colleagues, not groupies, she is a friend of our mind. Echoing her books and my state of mind, current events at the Cincinnati opera drew to an unsatisfyingly inconclusive end. In deference to all Morrison codas, so does *Can't I Love What I Criticize?* Final scenes in *The Bluest Eye* picture Cholly outdoors and his daughter crazily flapping her arms as she picks through garbage, victims both of distorted white Western male attitudes about physical beauty, ownership, sexuality, and romantic love. *Sula* shows Shadrack and Nel at cross-purposes, the Bottom having rejected a woman who acts like a man. *Song of Solomon* sees Milkman release Pilate's spirit and leap joyfully into the killing arms of his brother, promising androgynous griot possibility for black masculinity. *Tar Baby* depicts Son running lickety-split straight into myth, refusing to compromise black male magic. *Beloved* puts Paul D's story alongside Sethe's, paving the way for both their escapes from Beloved's blues tone. *Jazz* sends Joe Trace under closed yet wide-open covers, which he has washed along with his wife, hanging them in tandem out on the line. *Paradise* focuses on the elusory, complex, androgynous, imperfect haven provided by Piedade, and *Love* leaves us with Celestial perched cross-legged on Bill Cosey's tombstone, softly singing the raunchy, down-home songs that could save his life.

While the tales Toni Morrison tells on black men are too painful to pass *on*, they are equally too important to *pass* on. Unlike too many of their white counterparts, black men traditionally work hard to keep their balance connected to women, though Br'er Rabbit simultaneously continues to play in and through the American briar patch with his mates. The ancestors of Morrison's community still tell its males "what it is to be a woman so that [they] may know what it is to be a man" (*Nobel Lecture* 28). Early Modern tragedian John Webster beautifully captures the contrary plight of white Western manhood when the *Duchess of Malfi*'s Duke Ferdinand, attempting to eliminate his sister's husband for love and money, wants Antonio's head "in a business" (3.5.27).[4] Signifying a similarly equivocal relationship between the taking and the preserving of life but emphatically rejecting the language of commerce, Morrison's contemporary, tragicomic attitude toward American masculinity concludes that "everybody wants the life of a black man" (*Song of Solomon* 222).

Notes

Chapter One. Something Other Than a Family Quarrel

1. Defining a womanist as a black feminist, Alice Walker's theory encompasses the survival of a community, female and male. This African American writer claims that "Womanist is to feminist as purple to lavender" (xi–xii).

2. Walker re-creates black female conflictedness between race and gender into story. See "Advancing Luna and Ida B. Wells" in *You Can't Keep a Good Woman Down.*

Chapter Two. Black Boys, White Gaze

1. Morrison asserts during an interview: "I write without gender focus. . . . It happens that what provokes my imagination as a writer has to do with the culture of black people. I regard the whole world as my canvas and I write out of that sensibility of what I find provocative and the sensibility of being a woman. But I don't write women's literature as such. I think it would confine me. I am valuable as a writer because I am a woman, because women, it seems to me, have some special knowledge about certain things. [It comes from] the ways in which they view the world, and from women's imagination. Once it is unruly and let loose, it can bring things to the surface that men—trained to be men in a certain way—have difficulty getting access to" (qtd. in Awkward 136). The children described in Morrison's Nobel Prize lecture ask an androgynous griot to "tell [them] what it is to be a woman so that [they] may know what it is to be a man" (28). A growing number of contemporary critics on black masculinity, whom Guy Sheftall calls "black male feminists" (347)—a term Awkward argues is not an "oxymoronic formulation" (5)—employ feminist analytical frameworks and reject masculinist paradigms. What Neal calls the "New Black Man," in other words, incorporates varied practices of masculinity that struggle to be antisexist and antihomophobic, reflecting and embracing an African cultural history of androgyny and bisexuality.

2. Because these values have become so pervasive in American culture, their debilitating effects victimize people across real or imagined binaries of race, class, and gender. However, recent scholars distinguish African American masculinity from the larger field of masculinity studies; Hazel Carby argues compellingly that the pressure on black manhood entitles it to a racial representativeness of crisis not accorded black womanhood (9–41).

3. See my article "Symbols in the Sewer: A Symbolic Renunciation of Symbols in Richard Wright's *The Man Who Lived Underground*." I include such comparisons to other literary texts and figures not to validate Morrison's work but to expand the literary imaginations of my readers.

4. It is fruitful to note all the references to food in this scene. Mr. Henry, like Marie, receives some physical gratification by replacing touch with food. The churchwomen, on the other hand, remain concerned with clean plates. Mama declares to her girls that she would not let a bad woman like Marie eat off even one of hers.

5. Faulkner also introduces a child to life's underbelly in a section of *Sanctuary* that Malcolm Cowley calls "Uncle Bud and the Three Madams."

6. While Morrison's novels do not reject the possibility that some pedophiliac crimes remain irreducible traits in human nature irrespective of cultural particularity, she renders characters such as Mr. Henry, Cholly, Soaphead Church, and Bill Cosey to suggest, with Franklin, that many problems are "individually caused and culturally nurtured" (359).

7. Beavers maintains that a secular world no longer requiring "rituals whose sacred vessels include an uncommodified earth and sky" causes Morrison's characters to "fall victim to their appetites." Analyzing the influence of spatial politics on southern black males who move north, he confirms that desire in the new landscape becomes an end unto itself. Hence, Morrison's characters tie manhood to the world of capital and thus ally themselves with forces yoked to their demise (71).

8. Morrison's oeuvre implies alternatives apart from the accusatory critique of a dominant white male, Western worldview. It suggests that masculine anxiety is not necessarily race specific and that "African American identity constitutes a problem not for black people alone" (Harper xi). Approaching white patriarchal ideals of a "discrete, unified selfhood and the sovereignty of the will" as "dangerous fantasies," she apprehends black manhood as a "discursive construct shaped by words and by generational dialogues about cultural heritage." Affirming the viability of pluralistic masculinities, she believes men must "acknowledge that traumatic, shameful Otherness" lurking beyond rational control and beneath idealized self-images (Reed 538–39). Utterance of trauma begins the process of transforming the hollow shell of hegemonic masculine identity into a genuine expression of selfhood, which embraces diversity and accepts certain patriarchal practices as useful while rejecting others. The central challenge for Morrison's males involves reimagining themselves as men "whose subjectivity is not bound up in the context of work or the concatenations of the city scape." Wage labor

and overstimulation, because bound to hierarchy, lead to exploitation. Rejecting the phenomenology of the twentieth-century drive to become "a thing apart, the Other as power," Morrison defends the importance of collective talent; self-ownership occurs when "men give themselves up to those forces beyond their grasp" (Beavers 68–75). For her, the elusive masculine dream can best be reached by collaboration.

9. The cat's eyes are actually described as "bluish green," shining in reflected light like "blue ice." Morrison thus uses the trope of the cat to suggest Geraldine's conflicted self, unable to balance yearning for the order and material comfort that Morrison associates with green and desire for the absolute freedom she defines as blue.

10. The yin in Taoist philosophy suggests the passive, negative, feminine principle within the universe, contrasting with and complementary to the active, positive, masculine yang, source of light and heat. With her characterizations of Soaphead and Velma, then, Morrison once again engages in playfully telling inversion as she advocates androgyny.

11. Whitcomb seems fairly self-evident: a white comb for Elihue's soaphead?

Chapter Three. An Elegy on Black Masculinity

Parts of this chapter appear as an article in the *African American Review* 37.4 (2003): 517–33.

1. The four elements comprising the core of manhood are compassion, honor, responsibility, and enterprise. Gurian defines the ten "integrities" taught to children around the world as lineal (or ancestral) integrity, psychological integrity, social integrity, spiritual integrity, moral integrity, emotional integrity, sexual integrity, marital (or gender) integrity, physical integrity, and intellectual integrity.

2. Encouraging black men to adopt qualities of "the bottom fish," Byrd defines Hurston's use of the term *shad* to mean "deep," as in "values knowledge, truth and wisdom." Unlike the hegemonic top dog, the bottom fish appreciates "process and improvisation"; "collective work and solitude"; "dialogue, listening and harmony"; "tenderness"; "freedom and responsibility"; "justice"; and "peace" (2–6).

Chapter Four. Flying without Ever Leaving the Ground

1. For a discussion of the griot, oral historian and educator in African society, see Gross and Barnes, *Talk That Talk: An Anthology of African-American Storytelling*.

2. The term "feminine masculinity" or, in deference to Alice Walker, "womanist masculinity" recalls Jung's anima/animus duality as well as Judith Halberstam's related construction, "female masculinity." As Awkward points out, however, Morrison's descriptions of Hagar inhibit a radical feminist reading of *Song*

of Solomon (143–44) or the possibility of conceptualizing "masculinity without men" (Halberstam 2). For Morrison, the psychic health of gender and community requires the cooperative participation of the best of male and female. In "Rootedness," Morrison perceives more danger than fruit in developing a specifically black feminist model of inquiry because "any model of criticism or evaluation that excludes males from it is as hampered as any model of criticism of Black literature that excludes women from it" (344).

3. A number of black scholars, critics, and writers, including Zora Neale Hurston, Houston A. Baker Jr., and Henry Louis Gates Jr., have devoted much of their professional lives to recording and analyzing African and African American language games. In "Recitation to the Griot: Storytelling and Learning in Toni Morrison's *Song of Solomon*," Joseph Skerrett focuses on the forms of black vernacular that appear specifically in *Song of Solomon*, which function as a communal response to the hero's call.

4. Many outstanding black male vocal performers have obviously contributed to American musical traditions ranging from work and prison songs to spirituals, gospel, blues, rock and roll, Motown, and even country and western. Morrison's research into black men "almost as a species," however, concludes that they are at least as inclined to talk/sing or play as to sing while black women have traditionally been more confined to singing. The men are also more apt to harmonize with a group of brothers.

5. In "Mr. Brown and the Sweet Science," a tribute to one of the important men in his life, Randall Kenan describes the imperative that the African American boy "understand himself via his maleness, via his history, via his soul" as "the difference in some cases between life and death." If the young black male "does not come to terms with the myths that the world holds about him and the realities of what lies in wait outside the gates of his home, then his ignorance may well rise up in the middle of the night and slay him like a thief" (65).

6. The trope used here, referring to the condemned prisoner taking his final walk to the execution chamber, captures Morrison's irony. Macon Dead condemns himself to a life of psychological violence, terrorist tactics, and walking death. In addition, "dead man walking" reflects the signifying voice—an example of the African American litany of horror stories converted into humor.

7. In *Race-ing Justice, En-gendering Power: Essays on Anita Hill, Clarence Thomas, and the Construction of Social Reality*, Morrison refers to the specter of repressed race as "Freddy's back" (xxii).

8. Echoing Faulkner's subject matter and grotesque humor, Morrison's scene revises Miss Emily's necrophilia in "A Rose for Emily."

9. Morrison simply cannot resist a joke, especially when it rejects sentimentality. She elicits great sympathy for Macon as he recalls watching at twelve the body of the man he loves and admires twitching in the dirt. Feeling himself going numb, he marvels that "His father had sat for five nights on a split-rail fence cradling a shotgun and in the end died protecting his property" (51). With slam-bang humor, however, Morrison jerks us back to African American reality, cueing us in right

on time that the "Butler," Rhett or otherwise, did it and didn't even have to hide the evidence. He also ends up with the property.

10. Morrison's description of Hagar echoes current research supporting the importance of paternal involvement in child development: "Hagar does not have what Pilate had, which was a dozen years of a nurturing, good relationship with men. Pilate had a father, and she had a brother, who loved her very much, and she could use the knowledge of that love for her life. Her daughter Reba had less of that, but she certainly has at least a perfunctory adoration or love of men which she does not put to very good use. Hagar has even less because of the absence of any relationships with men in her life. She is weaker. Her grandmother senses it. That is why Pilate gives up the wandering life" (McKay 401).

11. The druggist bullied by Miss Emily into filling her request for arsenic, with which she will poison Homer Barron, writes on the prescription label simply: "For rats" (439).

12. Guitar takes his name not because he plays but "Because [he] wanted to. When [he] was real little. So they tell [him]" (45).

13. Various texts on social psychology reveal that males engage in overtly aggressive behavior more frequently than females, unilateral disarmament makes people vulnerable to attack, and those who adopt an unconditionally cooperative strategy are often exploited. See Feldman, *Social Psychology;* Myers, *Social Psychology;* and Sherif et al., *Intergroup Conflict and Cooperation: The Robbers Cave Experiment.*

14. Beavers attributes Guitar's adult life of "blasted aspiration and despair that assumes destructive forms" to his relocation from the rural South to the urban North with all of its ensuing changes in geography. This critic believes that "violence functions in Morrison's fiction as an essential element of self-definition in the North," where village values become perverted and men often "turn the vitriol of their inner struggles upon those whose circumstances most resemble their own." Because he embodies a fixed definition of masculinity, Guitar engages in "rituals of recovery that do not rejuvenate [him], but instead enable [his] spiritual defeat" (62). A model of self-discipline, his life has been rendered coherent by violence associated with selfhood and determined by reading signs of white oppression. Rejecting the idea that the self on display indicates physicality, geography, or manhood, however, Morrison argues for "finding a reflection of individual struggle in the struggle of the group" (72–75).

15. Leak concludes that Morrison clearly "appreciates the rich lives of black men" as she simultaneously reveals "two tenuous strands of black male heterosexual identity formation: virulent differentiation from women and homophobia," which constitute the "quandaries of black manhood." He argues that Milkman must come of age among men, "engaging in supposed masculine behavior." But Shalimar's black men, "gatekeepers to the available women in the community," remain deprived of economic and political power and thus "seek to control the two things with which they associate black masculinity: 'pussy' and 'dick'" (110–13).

16. Since "coon" is a well-known Southern epithet for a black person, the old men challenge Milkman with a means to comprehend the essence of his community and himself. Coon or snipe hunting occurs as a night game during which sophisticated players take the uninitiated into the woods on a wild-goose chase, supposedly to locate prey. The object involves a lesson in woodsman's skills or "street smarts."

17. Several of the essays in *Representing Black Men*, edited by Blount and Cunningham, explore the complex relations between violence and violation with respect to negotiating black masculinity.

18. The fourth of the core elements in Gurian's paradigm of manhood, enterprise joins compassion, honor, and responsibility (231).

19. Uncovering a record of sexism that belies the radical objectives of the black freedom struggle of the 1960s and 1970s, the writings of activist Angela Davis note the "widespread presence of an unfortunate syndrome among some black male activists—namely to confuse their political activity with an assertion of their maleness. They saw—and some continue to see—Black manhood as something separate from Black womanhood. These men view Black women as a threat to their attainment of manhood" (161).

20. Neal contends that comparatively little discussion exists about the forms of violence black men exhibit toward black women. Maintaining that "black men are under siege in white America," he concedes that they "also exhibit behaviors that do real damage to others" and that "[one] form of oppression cannot be used to justify another" (152–53). Leak connects Milkman's transformation to his reconciliation with the women in his life and, concurrently, the revelation of his family history (108).

21. Leak observes that Milkman will uncover "a way out of the Freudian trap of Oedipal antagonism with the father" by viewing his mother as a complex human being who needs to be needed (103).

22. Morrison substitutes another metaphorical beverage to signify on the folk idiom: "Why should [Milkman] buy the cow if he can get the milk for free?" Inverting Rosalind's comically practical advice to Phebe that she must "sell when [she] can" because she is "not for all markets," Morrison's version questions the association of male arousal with buying or working for and highlights Milkman's romantic callousness (*As You Like It* 3.5.60).

23. Gurian's description of the "third parent" or mentor essential to adolescent male development concludes: "One of his acts of benevolence towards his protégés is to test whether they really can handle his mentorial energy" (163). Morrison's androgynous griot employs male (direct) or female (indirect) modes of testing, depending on the personality and needs of her student.

24. Morrison deems it useful for her dicty Corinthians to scrub the floors of a rich white poetess. The novelist does not object to a black woman getting on her knees to clean house but to a house that refuses a black woman the confidence born of responsibility or the "genuine lift" of fair pay (190).

25. Unlike *Tar Baby*'s Therese, who escorts Son to the possibility of perpetual

fraternity, Pilate shows Milkman how to merge feminine with masculine. It is Guitar who now needs the support of his friend in order to fly.

26. By rescinding her name, Pilate associates herself with the biblical Yahweh who answers ambiguously Moses's question about his identity: "I am who [or what] I will be." With her death, Pilate becomes divine but accessible, a symbol of liberation yet the revelation that makes community possible.

27. Morrison concludes that "African Americans' sociopolitical problems can only be exacerbated by their own attempt to institute patriarchal forms of social organization." Black people must confront and work through their unresolved traumatic heritage "in ways incompatible with patriarchal forms of identity" if they are to escape the cycles of violence that plague their communities (Reed 539). Milkman's androgynous call does cause Guitar to lay down his gun before he jumps off a cliff—or lifts off to fly.

28. Leak concurs that Morrison does not suggest black men behave irresponsibly through "flight" but that they embrace their history and acknowledge the complex nature of human experience (130).

Chapter Five. The Nigger in the Woodpile

1. See "Paradise Lost and Found: Dualism and Edenic Myth in Toni Morrison's *Tar Baby*," *Contemporary Literature* 28.3 (1987): 363–77.

2. My reading of Morrison's decision to call Son's ship H.M.S. *Stor Konigsgaarten* resembles the process by which Macon Dead Senior names his beloved daughter Pilate for the sheltering way the large, majestic figure in the group of letters bends protectively over the smaller ones. Deconstructing print because I could not read the words, I relied directly on my senses to locate the accuracy. I spotted "H.M.S.," "store," "nigs," and "garden" to make my own meaning before I acquiesced to a more "knowledgeable" (i.e., powerful) reader who translated the ship's title as "Big Garden of the King." Since Morrison knows that most of her English readers will not be able to decode other languages, I am convinced that she does this deliberately here and elsewhere in *Tar Baby*.

3. A number of reviewers object to what they consider the overdone anthropomorphism of the novel. Other scholars accept the ubiquitous presence of the island's plant and animal life by associating it with the magical realism of contemporary South American writers. Grewal compares the airs and sprites of Isle des Chevaliers to those on Prospero's island. Morrison prefers to define these figures as expressions of black people's imaginative fusion of shrewd practicality and supernatural visitations (Davis 414). The self-assured swamp women and kissing maiden aunt fog act as chorus or bear witness to human actions and epiphanies.

4. Morrison strives for gender balance on the island by naming it for the horsemen but showcasing her female figures.

5. Morrison laughingly confesses to perceiving trees as female.

6. Valerian mocks Margaret's halting French as a way to remind her of her working-class origins. As his protégé, Jadine studies at French schools, takes

French lovers, and becomes a Parisian haute couture model. It takes Son to remind her "whatever you learned in those colleges that didn't include me ain't shit" (264). Trying to think in English stops the flow of island conjure woman Therese's imagination until she spits it out of her mouth altogether and lets "the story shimmer through the clear cascade of the French of Dominique" (108). Like *Song of Solomon*, *Tar Baby* acknowledges the power that print cultures assume by controlling the names of things and people. It also recognizes that oral cultures must locate ways to defuse this power and ignite their own.

7. Charles Fishman reports that Morrison names Valerian after Valeranius, who came to Roman power "during an epoch of near national bankruptcy and, after his defeat, at the hands of the Goths . . . was taken prisoner, and disappeared from history" (40). Valerian is also an herbal with sedative or antispasmodic properties. Used to calm horses or produce a soothing tea, it acts as a kind of herbal valium appropriate to Morrison's character.

8. The intensely controlled passion that Valerian attempts to breed into his offshoots parodies the rational approach to lovemaking prescribed in such sex manuals as the *Kama Sutra*, with its exhausting permutations of sexual positions. Valerian's precisely planned ideas about raising plants can be compared to the fanatic theories about child rearing and education tried as experiments on Elihue Micah Whitcomb, a.k.a. Soaphead Church, by his schoolmaster father in *The Bluest Eye*, to the measurements and calculations schoolteacher carries out on Sethe in *Beloved*, and to the experiments performed on Jews in Nazi Germany. Such fanaticism ultimately brings not generation but distortion and death back onto the fanatic.

9. Comparisons can certainly be drawn here to the thousand-year-old practice of foot binding. The prospect of splayed feet horrified upper-class Chinese women of the T'ang (618–906) and Sung (960–1279) dynasties more than the painful, straitjacket confinement it took to avoid them. During the Ming period (1368–1644) and the Ch'ing Dynasty (1644–1911), the custom permeated all social and economic classes of Chinese society.

10. Morrison takes note of the American history of homophobia. She also outlines what critics like Awkward, Byrd, Guy-Sheftall, and Neal call "black male feminism" or "New Black Man," which eschews homophobia.

11. The increasing "terror of growing up vacuum-pressured in this country" alarms Morrison. She remains concerned about the " 'successfully' educated male, alien in his own company, stunned and hampered by the inadequacy of his fine education." Lacking the skill of sustained reading that she calls the dancing mind and describes in her 1997 speech of the same name, he never moves outside the "surfeit and bounty of excess" to experience the peace of one open mind engaging another (12–13).

12. Morrison has her usual fun with names here. Robert Michelin is a blimp like the Michelin (not Goodyear) tire symbol. He is built to bear up under the machinery above him and to flatten whatever lies in his way.

13. Morrison contrasts Ryk's attitude toward women with that of various black

male characters to defend the emotional quotient of her free male concept. Unlike conventional Jude, who is too ashamed of sex with Sula to go apologize to his wife, Ryk avoids emotional entanglements entirely because he lacks depth of feeling. Ajax and a transformed Milkman, like the insightfully free horsemen, desire androgynous women who do not want to own them.

14. Neal's flexibly free "New [World] Black Man" encourages gender equality and embraces androgynous gender roles.

15. The lead prisoner in *Beloved*'s chain gang, responsible for maintaining its slave-working rhythm, is known as "Hi Man." Pilate mocks Guitar and Milkman's use of the greeting, informing them that "You say 'Hi' to pigs and sheep when you want 'em to move. When you tell a human being 'Hi,' he ought to get up and knock you down" (37).

16. Associated like William Green with the color of grass, Jade reflects nature transformed into art while Son tries to remain the real thing.

17. The image of the small, dark, fleet-footed yet leashed dogs contains the energy of Jadine's primal instincts, so difficult for her to repress. Morrison uses tar to represent the sacred, slow but steady, life-giving and life-sustaining properties of black women. The tar baby, then, is the "black woman who can hold things together" (LeClair 372). Refined, Jadine's tar becomes the oil that refuses to mix with Son's water.

18. Yellow is Morrison's color for sensual, natural vitality. She associates it with Cholly, Rochelle, and Sula and connects it to African American authenticity in *Tar Baby*. Ironically, it also references Jadine's "whiteness."

19. Acknowledging his sexual aggressiveness, Trudier Harris nonetheless claims that "Son certainly does not rape anyone" (120) while John Duvall maintains that Son attempts to rape Jadine into a " 'correct' subject position" (341).

20. Morrison expresses reservations about the term "black magic" and about references to her own writing as magical realism. She claims that these labels imply a lack of intelligence on the part of the artist and become a "convenient way to skip again what was the truth in the art of certain writers" (Davis 414–15).

21. A female nigger in the woodpile of Son and Jadine's fiery relationship, Nommo takes her name from an androgynous African deity, mysteriously multiplying god twins. In Greek, *nomo* means "law" or "custom."

Chapter Six. Circles of Sorrow, Sites of Memory, Forms of Flooding

1. See Valerie Smith, " 'Circling the Subject': History and Narrative in *Beloved*."

2. As she explains to Denver that she has trouble believing in time, Sethe states: "Places, places are still there. If a house burns down, it's gone, but the place—the picture of it—stays, and not just in my rememory, but out there, in the world. What I remember is a picture floating around out there outside my head. I mean, even if I don't think it, even if I die, the picture of what I did, or knew, or saw is still out there. Right in the place where it happened." Thus, for Sethe "nothing ever dies" (36).

3. I have chosen to de-emphasize the cottage industry of scholarship that *Beloved* has inspired in order to let chronological critiques of her male characters lead me more directly to Morrison's conclusions about the profound effects of slavery on American masculinity. The unremittingly emasculative pain of enslavement certainly turns African American males into traumatized blues men who obsessively finger the jagged grain. However, it also affords them the humility and ensuing potential for self-knowledge, which promote compassion and embrace difference. If my readers follow me following Morrison's men around, they will see Morrison connect the circular process by which black men resolve the trauma of American slavery with the possibility of a pluralistic African American masculinity expressed in Neal's "New Black Man." Thus, process in this chapter becomes as important as product.

4. Morrison most certainly compares Beloved's rebirth to myths about other spirit women springing fully formed out of some preconsciousness, such as Zeus's Athena or Satan's Sin.

5. Embodying both her mother and her father, "Seth—thuh" becomes an androgynous spokesperson for Morrison's rewriting of the typically masculine slave narrative (30).

6. A successful graduate of Suggs's school of African American survival, Baby blames herself for allowing pride to blunt her training. She stands innocently in her garden before The Misery, "smelling disapproval, feeling a dark and coming thing, and seeing high-topped shoes that she didn't like the look of at all" (147). Overwhelmed by the sight of Sethe and Halle's children, however, she ignores the signs and fails to act. Baby's option to take Suggs's surname illustrates another difference between black and white feminists. If taking a name separate from that of their husbands stands as a sign of independence for many white women, assuming their husband's name can imply a form of freedom for black women.

7. See Philip Page's *Dangerous Freedom: Fusion and Fragmentation in Toni Morrison's Novels* (1995).

8. In his 1964 play *Dutchman*, LeRoi Jones warns white males about the dangers of passing on this intellectual legacy of Western rationalism: "With no more blues, except the very old ones, and not a watermelon in sight, the great missionary heart will have triumphed, and all of those ex-coons will be stand-up Western men, with eyes for clean hard useful lives, sober, pious and sane, and they'll murder you. They'll murder you, and have very rational explanations. Very much like your own" (36).

9. In devising the manner of schoolteacher's experimental rape, Morrison alludes to the use of black slavewomen as wet nurses for white children. Sethe understands firsthand what it means to get "what was left. Or none," to be "without the milk that belongs to you" (200). While she is proud of having milk enough for all, she remains determined to hold her supply in reserve for her own children.

10. Freddie the janitor names Milkman in *Song of Solomon* for his connection to women (13–15).

11. Beavers outlines the destructiveness that occurs when characters fall victim to their appetites so that desire becomes an end in itself. While he focuses primarily on southern black males who move north after Reconstruction, the effects of overstimulation operate negatively on *Beloved*'s characters as well.

12. When Milkman declares to Guitar, "I got a right to be what I want to be, and I want to be a [soft-fried] egg," Guitar retorts: "Then somebody got to bust your shell." Explaining that "a nigger can't be a egg," Milkman's streetwise male mentor is well aware that African Americans cannot afford to remain innocent (*Song of Solomon* 115–16).

13. Interestingly, Halle is a shortened and feminized revision of the male name Harold, the given name of Morrison's former husband, a Jamaican architect. Morrison, like the iron-eyed Sethe called by the feminine form of her father's name, certainly never looks away.

14. In Sixo, Morrison creates a comic African American inversion of secretively unpredictable and dashingly masculine British superagent 007, James Bond. Associated like Guitar with music and time, Sixo's sixth note is the submediant and the superdominant tone, the tone five degrees below or above any given tone in an ascending diatonic scale. In addition, it produces a minor key and becomes the chord formed by a triad in which the fundamental tone is raised an octave, creating a new interval of a sixth. In other words, Sixo stays irrepressibly hypertonic. His number name also reminds us of the heightened awareness that we call the sixth sense, the social and political unrest of the American 1860s and 1960s, the "Sixty Million and more" to whom Morrison dedicates *Beloved*, and the fact that Sixo simply creeps to the beat of a different drum.

15. Morrison shares her recipe for successful male child rearing when Pilate shows Milkman and Guitar how to create a perfect soft-boiled egg. Her method calls not for roasting or frying but for a gentle simmering during which the temperature of the water does not get the upper hand over that of the egg. Because the griot and the child "have to meet each other on a kind of equal standing," the "temperature has to be the same for both." It does, however, take two. Sixo may be the sixth tone, but he must bring himself up alone (*Song of Solomon* 39–40; see also chapter 4 in this book).

16. Embracing postmodern pluralism requires resisting schoolteacher's Enlightenment rationality, the "straight lines" that Morrison reveals to be fatal to black manhood. The poststructuralist blues/jazz process, in contrast to this linear rationality, engages with the fluidity of signifiers and makes meaning without stable referents. If schoolteacher's power rests on the implicit claim that "definitions belong to the definers," Sixo models a way of undermining this assumption, at least provisionally—for example, his exploitation of the sliding signification of "stealing." Sixo essentially riffs on "take and feed," making any single definition impossible and thereby undercutting "the definers' " claim to ownership. The "riff," then, becomes his African American rejection of the white scholar's control of language.

17. In the game of craps, an appropriate metaphor for the hazardous waste

that constitutes slave life, Sixo sounds his victory. The number seven becomes significant in play because a first throw of seven wins while any other first throw besides two, three, or twelve must be repeated to win before another player throws a seven. Any way you cut it, Sixo wins at craps, hands tied.

18. Since Georgia was settled originally by exiled inmates, Morrison's irony appears as the offspring of abused white prisoners assimilate the proper manner of mistreating black prisoners. His effort to kill Brandywine predicts Paul D's need to stun pain with alcohol, foreshadowing his method of coping with counting Sethe's feet.

19. In her version of Homer's story about a "weaver-lady," Morrison comically inverts the intent of Penelope's winding-sheet.

20. Morrison reiterates during a 1981 interview with Thomas LeClair that "[her] people are being devoured" (371).

21. Flagging *Beloved*'s blues players to start their engines with "1—2—4" instead of "1—2—3—4" allows them to break immediately with a linear time signature. Naming her house 124 instead of 123 allows Morrison to sing her blues about something gone missing, in this case Beloved and everything she signifies. It also explains why an abused blues house would be spiteful. Because it resists linear progression and tells multiple stories simultaneously, the jazz that blues evolves into embodies inherent poststructuralist pluralism. Blues musicians trying to get out of the groove would approve of Morrison's signal to play.

22. Morrison explains Marie Cardinal's definition of "the Thing" in the preface to *Playing in the Dark* (vi).

23. Morrison's application of the medicinal plant to the lovers' bittersweet but ultimately restorative meeting becomes particularly appropriate. When Sethe tells him she has removed her shoes and stockings to wash sap off her legs, Paul D makes a wry face and says: "I don't want to even hear 'bout it. Always did hate that stuff" (7).

24. The reference to raw passion incorporated into a red heart appears in *The Bluest Eye* as the heart of a watermelon and in *Song of Solomon* as the heart of a bobcat.

Chapter Seven. Classically Re-training Blues Boys

1. In *Blues, Ideology, and Afro-American Literature*, Houston A. Baker defines African American culture as a "complex, reflexive enterprise which finds its proper figuration in blues conceived as a matrix." The blues represent the "multiplex, enabling *script* in which Afro-American cultural discourse is inscribed" (3–4). Jazz scholar Paul Berliner links jazz with narrative and illustrates how musicians adopt metaphors of storytelling to convey the meaning of jazz oratory (*Thinking in Jazz* 202, 208, 252, 255). Morrison inverts this process to view narrative as music, constructing her own work like a Duke Ellington composition. She claims that a jazzlike structure became especially deliberate in *Jazz;* it was, in fact, the "raison d'être of the book" ("The Art of Fiction" 110). Identifying music

as the art form that until recently "was healing for Black people," she believes that if the music can no longer keep them alive, the novel can ("Rootedness: The Ancestor as Foundation" 340).

2. Morrison confesses her commitment to openings in medias res because she is less interested in crime and punishment and more in how things happen, who did what to whom and why, and who survives. She entices her readers to join her in such musings by putting significant details up front. See Morrison, "Unspeakable Things Unspoken," and Schappell and Lacour, "Toni Morrison: The Art of Fiction."

3. Alluding to evening prayer and the evening star, Vesper, the sixth of the seven canonical hours, reminds us of Sixo. It also admonishes us to listen carefully, as jazz players do, before talking back. In fact, "one of the worst accusations that can be flung at a [jazz] musician is that 'he doesn't listen' " (Collier 52).

4. Derrida defines the "trace" as the mark of an individual's relationship with the transcendent "other," indicating the absence of presence and the beginning of binary thinking. In historical terms the trace becomes a track, a historical moment of rupture such as slavery. The track can be followed toward reconnection, but it will never allow a return to the original. Tracking results in a mixture that contains elements of the original along with those created from cultural contact (*Of Grammatology* 47). As people, tied to the traces, pursue the track, they grow vulnerable to cracks and crevices. Derrida views these "breaches" as disruptive but also as contributing to the process of identity formation. They encourage understanding of the entities being separated and thus provide opportunity for discovery, self-development, and peace (Page 164–65).

5. The name Dorcas means deer. Morrison also compares Wild to a frightened deer (152–53).

6. Caroline Brown observes that the Golden Gray segment would appear to rest outside the boundaries of the jazz ethos. It actually represents, however, the "voice of the non-hermeneutic, the textual negotiation of freedom." The nonhermeneutic in *Jazz* "is deployed to destabilize the text, rejecting strict aesthetic order, interpretive certainty, or linear progression" (630, 639). The story of Golden Gray attempts through narrative what Jelly Roll Morton calls a musical surprise or "the break." This jazz pianist affirms the importance of breaks and the beautiful ideas they inspire (Gioia 75). Like Golden Gray, Joe must learn to "take the break" and play the self. Derrida uses the term *breach* to indicate possibilities for disruption and discovery. The deepest breach or "the unnameable bottomless well" is "the abyss" as well as the center. In *Jazz*, Rose Dear's well becomes both "the absence of play and difference, another name for death" and a wide-open opportunity for self-development (*Writing and Difference* 296–98).

7. *Jazz* suggests that Vera Louise has an affair with Henry LesTroy / Hunters Hunter, perhaps the offspring of Wordsworth Gray and True Belle and thus Vera's biracial half-brother, the by-product of which would be Golden Gray. True Belle realizes with the rest of the slaves that "a Negro boy from out Vienna way was called on to ride with Miss Vera"; she even knows "what part

of the woods [Vera] preferred to ride in" (140). Morrison's reference to Vienna recalls Freud's connections of sexuality with incest in Greek tragedy. The frequent allusions to Charles Bon in *Jazz*'s Golden Gray break also intimate that "it's the miscegenation, not the incest, which [the Wordsworth Grays] cant bear" (*Absalom, Absalom!* 356). Because she is called to "tend to whatever Miss Vera Louise wanted or needed, including doing her laundry, some of which had to be soaked overnight in vinegar once a month," and Vera Louise "knew [True Belle] knew" about the absence of menstrual blood, True Belle can either laugh or cry: "There was never any need to speak of it. The only people who didn't know were the fathers," including the father-to-be (140). She chooses to laugh and transform her tears into reforming her grandson.

8. Claudia and Frieda admit in *The Bluest Eye* that "Maureen Peal was not the Enemy and not worthy of such intense hatred. The *Thing* to fear was the *Thing* that made *her* beautiful, and not us" (74). The enemy is racial self-hatred resulting from white Western ideals about physical beauty and romantic love.

9. Slang for skin or flesh, Morrison's terms indicate that Honor thinks Golden stalks dark meat (i.e., sex with a black person).

10. Golden Gray's long, curly, blonde locks recall those of Chaucer's squire as well as the Goldilocks story.

11. Whether, and whenever, Wild bites his cheek or taps him on the shoulder with her fingertips, Hunter revisits his relationship with the renegade Vera Louise.

12. As *Tar Baby*'s woman in yellow indicates, yellow is Morrison's vital sign, and blue is the color of freedom. See chapter 2, note 9.

13. Beavers suggests that Morrison uses her southern men who move north "as cautionary devices, meant to warn the reader of the inherent dangers of overstimulation." Because life in the South offers so little in the way of material satisfaction, urban living appears attractive because desire becomes an end in itself. In the North, Morrison's black men tie manhood to capital, fall victim to appetite, and "maintain an allegiance to forces yoked to the engine of their demise" (71). Instead of inculcating resistance, this process leads them to violence. *Fay* is pig Latin for "ofay" or "foe," a disparaging term for white folks.

14. Jazz-era aficionados use the term *bird* to signal their affection for a free black male, as in the street name of saxophonist Charlie "Bird" Parker. My mother still calls me a "bird" when she thinks I've done something delightful.

15. See chapter 2.

16. Morrison perceives the city as a "secular world that no longer has the need for rituals whose sacred vessels include an uncommodified earth and sky," a place where men "fall victim to their appetites" (Beavers 71).

17. Gates describes how the Talking Book, "the ur-trope of the Anglo-African tradition," came to represent for former American slaves the possibility of self-expression. Early black texts published in English explain the conviction of the African American community that "black people could become speaking subjects only by inscribing their voices in the written word" (*Signifying Monkey* 127–69). The classical counterpart to this trope could be called the "Talking Sonnet." Im-

ported from Renaissance Italy, the subject/object of the English or Shakespearean sonnet resists annihilation by striving for immortality through literary art.

18. Like Shakespeare, Morrison employs the sexual innuendo associated with "lifting" or "turning" the pages of a book. Shakespeare's Othello kills his wife because "she can turn, and turn, and yet go on / And turn again" (4.1.248–49). Alice Manfred recalls her dead husband, now with "no fingers to lift her hips as he had lifted others" (85).

Chapter Eight. Putting down Parking Lots out There

The chapter title alludes to a line from songwriter Joni Mitchell's "Big Yellow Taxi" (1970): "They paved paradise and put up a parking lot."

1. Katrine Dalsgard and Jill Jones address *Paradise* as Morrison's re-vision of the American Puritans' "city upon a hill." The novel frames a question that Morrison claims has continually intrigued her and that served as the seed for her book: "Why paradise necessitates exclusion" (Murline 71).

2. Leslie Fiedler's *Love and Death in the American Novel* (1960) introduces this identity plot, developed more recently by the scholarly work of Gail Bederman, David Leverenz, and Lee Clark Mitchell.

3. Morrison theorizes in *Playing in the Dark* that attitudes toward an abiding Africanist presence in America arose from the need to establish difference among European males who came with nothing to find a New World. Identifying a Greek shipbuilder's primary connection with an Irish farmer or a Puritan preacher to be the color of his skin, she recognizes blackness as a readily available and subjectively inscribed "Other." The "new white male can now persuade himself" that darkness, desire, savagery, and alarm are " 'out there' " (45).

4. Kristin Hunt connects the strain of double consciousness and the Ruby founders' disassociation from the natural world, represented in *Paradise* by African communal space and Arapaho values, with the New Fathers' sense of restlessness and lack of freedom. I would argue that this contributes to their stiff-necked hubris as well.

5. This marvelous name also comes from *Love*. I am grateful to Tessa Roynon and the Morrison Society's bicentennial conference on "The Politics of Learning" for a discussion of Morrison and tragedy. Numerous American writers from Hawthorne to Le Guin to Morrison herself in *Sula* have acknowledged that an earthly paradise must embrace evil as well as good, that a desire for perfection can lead only to the creation of a scapegoat. My 1982 dissertation, "The Adulterous Wife in Renaissance Drama," indicates that women have been employed as scapegoats for a very long time.

6. Jones views *Paradise* as a self-conscious riff on Faulkner's *Absalom, Absalom!* Unlike the latter, however, Morrison's novel holds out both warning and hope, rendering it an American version of the jeremiad. Sacvan Bercovitch finds that the American jeremiad represents "profound disquiet" as well as faith in the ideal "errand" or "mission" of this country (xiv, 11).

7. Andrew Reed states that *Paradise* "combines an innovative intervention in the debates over the representation of black men with a critique of traditional Western notions of masculinity." As she engages current controversies over cultural depictions of African American men, including the stereotypes regarding criminality, misogyny, and violence central to this controversy, Morrison "departs radically from the explanations for these problems that structure dominant racial discourse." In particular, she rejects the association of black male violence with a dysfunctional African American matriarchal society outlined in the 1965 Moynihan Report. Also refuting the accusation that recent African American women's fictions present black men as "control freaks," *Paradise* defines black masculinity not as fixed but rather as a "discursive construct, continually shaped and reshaped by the influence of hegemonic American ideologies of manhood, the cultural heritage of African American history, and the traumatic psychical consequences of race oppression" (527–28).

8. These terms suggest titles of popular films, starring John Travolta and Robert Redford, respectively. While the urban cowboy takes a top-down attitude toward life, the horse whisperer, a more mystical figure, literally gentles his charges by approaching them holistically and with respect.

9. Gwendolyn Brooks, "Kitchenette Building."

10. Morrison names her character with the term used in radiotelephony to indicate reception of a message. Roger knows best about signaling, "Right!"

11. In her essay "High John De Conquer," Hurston defines a black man as "deep" when he knows himself and the fluctuating structures of the worlds he moves and moves through. This masculine knowledge, which combines potentialities with the actualities necessary for resistance and survival, views life as improvisation and process. It also denies sexism and homophobia. The veins running through the ore of Morrison's 8-rocks can be mined to "honor the deep masculine that is not macho, but human" as her blackbloods walk through the whirlwind in the tradition of John De Conquer (Byrd 6–22).

12. Toontown is the Hollywood-spoofed setting for Steven Spielberg's *Who Framed Roger Rabbit?*, a gangster-style film western in which human actors interact with cartoon characters.

13. Norma Keene Fox suggests shades of *Tar Baby*'s Margaret Street.

14. *The Good, the Bad and the Ugly* refers to the most successful of Clint Eastwood's spaghetti westerns, directed in 1966 by Sergio Leone.

15. Known as "Paladin," Richard Boone starred in the popular 1960s television western *Have Gun, Will Travel.*

16. See also Wendell Berry, *The Unsettling of America: Culture and Agriculture.*

17. By locating Ruby's men in a patriarchal ordered community, Morrison contests the notion that black male violence stems from the failure of fathers to fulfill conventional patriarchal roles. She defines black masculinity as a discursive construct, influenced by hegemonic American ideologies of manhood. Slavery and subsequent racism have stripped African American men of the paternal author-

ity transmitted from fathers to sons so central to Western concepts of masculinity. Instead, the men of Ruby pass on the unresolved trauma of a dehumanizing shame. They repress the shame and self-hatred, most damaging to people who aspire to conventional manhood, and project them onto a humiliated and excluded Other. Morrison identifies the town that manifests this maleness as merely repressed trauma, an African American riff on Hamlet's "rub." She implies that patriarchy aggravates the dysfunctions which render violence an indication of male willpower and "critiques any ideology that prescribes particular, fixed, and ahistorical forms of masculine identity as the solution to the problems of African American men or as a singular 'true' expression of black manhood." Morrison suggests that black men may acquire alternative masculinities through connections with women, who discover the self as a fluid construct transcending "all ideologically constructed binary oppositions." Since attempts to institute patriarchy exacerbate African American sociopolitical problems, an "unresolved traumatic African American heritage must be confronted and worked through, in ways incompatible with patriarchal forms of identity," if black people are to escape the cycles of violence (Reed 527–39).

18. Ralph Ellison uses this term to explain the emergence of jazz from blues in *Shadow and Act* (78–79). See chapter 7, "Classically Re-training Blues Boys."

19. Scout is the name of Tonto's horse in the *Lone Ranger*, the 1940s radio show with Brace Beamer as the voice of the Lone Ranger and a 1950s television program costarring Jay Silverheels as the stalwart Indian compatriot, Tonto. Morrison's concept of an Other (frequently Africanist) presence as crucial to American consciousness appears here in Native American form.

20. Hoss Cartwright is the gigantic, good-natured middle son from the long-lived 1960s television western, *Bonanza*, revived briefly in the 1990s and currently rerunning. He was played originally by Dan Blocker.

21. Reed explains Steward's "losses" as the "gradual erosion of all of the positive traits that had enabled the original success of this community." The possessions and status so crucial to the formation of modern masculine identity make the townspeople distrust one another and deny the communal bonds responsible for their ancestors' achievements (533).

22. For that matter, another potentially fatal scene can be found in "The Girls in Their Summer Dresses" (Irwin Shaw, 1939).

23. Here Morrison offers a comically grotesque parallel with transubstantiation.

24. Although Dovey's Friend bears the surname of Arnold Friend from Joyce Carol Oates's "Where Are You Going, Where Have You Been?" (a 1970 short story that opens "Her name was Connie"), Connie's cowboy wears Arnold's mirrored sunglasses. Morrison creates dual alternative replications of the character in her midlife inversion of Oates's teenage female coming-of-age narrative.

25. Morrison uses nonverbal language to invoke Connie's memories of home and to describe her lovemaking with the "living man." While her "Sha sha sha" suggests the androgyny embraced by Morrison's griots, the dismissive "Sh,"

spoken by Consolata's mother superior, leaves out "a[ll]." This permits the binary opposition of she/he and prohibits the healing that comes with articulating trauma.

26. Morrison names Misner as the character in *Paradise* with whom she most identifies (Jaffrey 4).

27. As Captain Kirk, William Shatner intones "Space, the final frontier" to initiate each episode of the popular 1960s television space western, *Star Trek*, echoed by Patrick Stewart as Captain Picard in the 1990s *Star Trek: The Next Generation*. Like the earlier visions analyst Gene Roddenberry, Morrison identifies the physical space in her *Paradise*—the fictional story on the actual pages between the opening account of the shootings from the men's point of view and the final account from the women's perspectives—with the human space of "insight, of new knowledge, the potential for a work of art to change the way we see" (Krumholz 22). Morrison calls this final frontier, in a chapter named for it, "Grace."

Chapter Nine. Laying down the Law of the Father

Because *New York* magazine refers to Toni Morrison as the D. H. Lawrence of the black psyche, this chapter subtitle alludes to Lawrence's *Women in Love*.

1. *Love* remains complicatedly "For and with Ardelia." Published biographical information on Morrison concurs that her full name is Chloe Anthony Wofford. She states candidly to Christopher Bigsby in 1992: "I am really Chloe Anthony Wofford. That's who I am. . . . I regret having called myself Toni Morrison when I published my first novel" (28). Anthony appears to be the name given to her at her Christian confirmation, shortened to Toni in college because "the people at Howard seemed to have difficulty pronouncing" Chloe (Dowling 50). Wofford becomes Morrison when she marries Jamaican architect Harold Morrison in 1958. George and Ramah Wofford, however, originally named their daughter, now a grandmother herself, Chloe Ardelia Wofford after Ramah's mother, Ardelia Willis. The title page of Morrison's 1955 Cornell University M.A. thesis on alienation employs "Ardellia" [*sic*] as her middle name; the Department of Health in Lorain, Ohio, contains her birth certificate (Duvall 330). Thus, the narrative voice of *Love*'s author not only answers to Ardelia in the same fashion that Eleanor Traylor suggests *Tar Baby*'s narrator is accountable to its dedicatees (149). *Love*'s L *is* the black grandmother Ardelia (R?), both Willis and Morrison.

2. Both black and white southerners frequently refer to a family's male elder as "Big Daddy" (see Tennessee Williams's *Cat on a Hot Tin Roof*). "The Man" also signifies mostly white authority (see James Baldwin's *Going to Meet the Man*).

3. *Ria* is a playful feminization of the Spanish word for *river* (as opposed to Rio Grande), an allusion to the Spanish for laughter (*risa*), and a spoof on Rio de Janeiro, a contemporary ocean playground popular with rich and famous Westerners.

4. Evelyn Schreiber argues that texts which articulate the nothingness of

Lacan's real "through the unsettling gaze of the Other" create self-awareness that can lead to social change (20–21).

5. When Bill Moyers asks Morrison to articulate a metaphor that captures the current state of being African American, she replies "love": "We need to love ourselves." She also comments that love is something you do not for anybody else but for yourself.

6. Cognizance makes all the difference between a Freudian slip and a Morrison joke.

7. Broad Street defines a mostly black New Orleans neighborhood. Cheryl Gerber captures the essence of contemporary, pre–Hurricane Katrina Broad Street life in a marvelous photo-essay.

8. New York City's Idlewild Airport was renamed for President John F. Kennedy on December 24, 1963.

9. Arguing that self-awareness constitutes a community project, Morrison associates Bill's insufficient understanding of himself with his inadequate understanding of others. His name suggests an interesting merger between entertainer Bill Cosby and President Bill Clinton, acknowledging the vulnerability of public figures to domestic dramas. The recently published autobiography by William Jefferson Clinton renders self-awareness as significant as its analysis of contemporary United States history.

10. In her exposé on American families caught in a "nostalgia trap," Stephanie Coontz argues that black men, "in spite of 'macho' images and language, are *more* likely to share housework than are their white counterparts" (242).

11. Morrison expresses this double consciousness in *Jazz* as Joe's sad, clear, two-color eyes.

12. The comical paradox of "L's kitchen" echoing Hell's Kitchen is classic Morrison.

Coda

1. A contemporary newspaper account describing Margaret Garner's killing of her two-year-old daughter, Mary, subsequent to the family's escape from Maplewood Farm and recapture by slave catchers in Cincinnati, provided Morrison with her site of memory for *Beloved* and for the *Margaret Garner Opera*. See M. A. Harris, *The Black Book*.

2. Ms. Brunings calls Weisenburger's *Modern Medea: A Family Story of Slavery and Child-Murder from the Old South* "factually flawed," presenting "the author's personal speculations and biases as historical fact. His book has been discredited by historians" (Brunings e-mail). A comment from Delores M. Walters, however, community research specialist at the National Underground Railroad Freedom Center and assistant professor of social sciences at Northern Kentucky University, clarifies the Gaines daughter's resistance: Weisenburger "theorizes that sexual violation may explain Margaret's motivation for running away and infanticide, noting that Margaret's pregnancies occurred after Archibald Gaines

arrived in Richwood and were concurrent with his wife's pregnancies. As Weisenburger further notes, Gaines's extreme reaction to seeing the murdered toddler was also telling" (86).

3. Morrison ultimately named her exhibit, which was on display at the Louvre November 6–29, 2006, *The Foreigner's Home*. Acknowledging her signature multiple meanings and crossings, the Toni Morrison Society bridged the Atlantic to host an accompanying scholars' roundtable discussion in Paris on November 18, 2006, titled "International Perspectives on Toni Morrison."

4. Duke Ferdinand's message to his sister, the Duchess of Malfi, reads in full: "Send Antonio to me; I want his head in a business" (3.5.27–28). The duchess notes immediately her brother's covertly condescending threat to the steward that, in Ferdinand's eyes, "only smelled of ink and counters, / And ne'er in's life looked like a gentleman / But in the audit time," and responds wryly to her husband, Antonio: "A politic equivocation: / He doth not want your counsel but your head: / That is, he cannot sleep till you be dead" (3.3.70–72; 3.5.29–31). Like Macbeth's witches, the duke employs ambiguity to supposedly implore Antonio's presence as Ferdinand, incestuously taken with his twin sister, implies that he will actually have his brother-in-law's head struck off. While Webster's white royal seeks, like Morrison's men, to know his feminine side, his language, unlike that of the free black male, destructively reduces life and death to a business transaction.

Selected Bibliography

Anderson, Elijah. *Code of the Street: Decency, Violence, and the Moral Life of the Inner City*. New York: Norton, 1999.

Andrews, William L. "The Black Male in American Literature." In *The American Black Male: His Present Status and His Future*. Ed. Richard G. Majors and Jacob U. Gordon. Chicago: Nelson-Hall, 1994. 59–68.

Awkward, Michael. *Negotiating Difference: Race, Gender, and the Politics of Positionality*. Chicago: University of Chicago Press, 1995.

Baker, Houston A., Jr. *Blues, Ideology, and Afro-American Literature: A Vernacular Theory*. Chicago: University of Chicago Press, 1984.

Bastien, David T., and Todd J. Hostager. "Jazz as Social Structure, Process, and Outcome." In *Jazz in Mind: Essays on the History and Meanings of Jazz*. Ed. Reginald T. Backner and Steven Weiland. Detroit: Wayne State University Press, 1991. 149–65.

Beavers, Herman. "The Politics of Space: Southernness and Manhood in the Fictions of Toni Morrison." *Studies in the Literary Imagination* 31.2 (Fall 1998): 61–77.

Benston, Kimberly. "Re-weaving the 'Ulysses Scene': Enchantment, Post-Oedipal Identity, and the Buried Text of Blackness in Toni Morrison's *Song of Solomon*." In *Comparative American Identities: Race, Sex, and Nationality in the Modern Text*. Ed. Hortense J. Spillers. New York: Routledge, 1991. 87–109.

Bent, Geoffrey. "Less Than Divine: Toni Morrison's *Paradise*." *Southern Review* 35.1 (Winter 1999): 145–49.

Bercovitch, Sacvan. *The American Jeremiad*. Madison: University of Wisconsin Press, 1980.

Berendt, Joachim. *The Jazz Book: From Ragtime to Fusion and Beyond*. Rev. by Gunther Huesmann. Trans. H. and B. Bredigkeit et al. Brooklyn: Lawrence Hill, 1992.

Berliner, Paul F. *Thinking in Jazz: The Infinite Art of Improvisation*. Chicago: University of Chicago Press, 1994.

Berry, Wendell. *The Unsettling of America: Culture and Agriculture*. New York: Avon, 1977.

Bigsby, Christopher. "Jazz Queen." *Independent* (London) 26 Apr. 1992, Sunday review sec., 28.

Bjork, Patrick Bryce. *The Novels of Toni Morrison: The Search for Self and Place within the Community*. New York: Peter Lang, 1992.

Blount, Marcellus, and George P. Cunningham, eds. *Representing Black Men*. New York: Routledge, 1996.

Boykin, Keith. *One More River to Cross: Black and Gay in America*. New York: Anchor, 1996.

Brannon, Robert. "A Scale for Measuring Attitudes about Masculinity." In *Beyond Sex Roles*. Ed. A. Sargent. St. Paul, Minn.: West, 1985.

Brown, Caroline. "Golden Gray and the Talking Book: Identity as a Site of Artful Construction in Toni Morrison's *Jazz*." *African American Review* 36.4 (Winter 2002): 629–42.

Brunings, Ruth Wade Cox. "Slavery and the Tragic Story of Two Families: Gaines and Garner." *Northern Kentucky Heritage* (Fall–Winter 2004): 37–46.

———. "Re: Thanks and Three Questions." E-mail to the author. 11 Aug. 2005.

Bryant, Cedric Gael. "The Orderliness of Disorder: Madness and Evil in Toni Morrison's *Sula*." *Black American Literature Forum* 24.4 (1990): 731–45.

Butler, Robert, and Yoshinobu Hakutani, eds. *The City in African American Literature*. Madison: University of Wisconsin Press, 1995.

Byerman, Keith E. *Fingering the Jagged Grain: Tradition and Form in Recent Black Fiction*. Athens: University of Georgia Press, 1993.

Byrd, Rudolph P., and Beverly Guy-Sheftall, eds. *Traps: African American Men on Gender and Sexuality*. Bloomington: Indiana University Press, 2001.

Campbell, James. "Dark and Light in the Territory." *Times Literary Supplement* 14 Nov. 2003: 21–22.

Campbell, Joseph. *The Hero with a Thousand Faces*. 1949. Bollingen Series XVII. Princeton: Princeton University Press, 1969.

Carabi, Angels. "Interview with Toni Morrison." *Belles Lettres* 10.2 (1995): 40–43.

———. "Toni Morrison." *Belles Lettres* 9.3 (Spring 1994): 38–39, 86–90.

Carby, Hazel V. *Race Men*. Cambridge: Harvard University Press, 1998.

Carmean, Karen. *Toni Morrison's World of Fiction*. Troy, N.Y.: Whitston, 1993.

Christian, Barbara T. *Black Feminist Criticism: Perspectives on Black Women Writers*. New York: Pergamon, 1985.

———. "Layered Rhythms: Virginia Woolf and Toni Morrison." Third Annual Conference on Virginia Woolf. Lincoln University, Jefferson City, Mo. 10–13 Jun. 1993. Rpt. in *Toni Morrison: Critical and Theoretical Approaches*. Ed. Nancy J. Peterson. Baltimore: Johns Hopkins University Press, 1997. 19–36.

———. "The Race for Theory." *Cultural Critique* 6 (1987): 51–63.
Collier, James Lincoln. *Jazz: The American Theme Song*. New York: Oxford University Press, 1993.
Collins, Patricia Hill. *Black Feminist Thought: Knowledge, Consciousness, and the Politics of Empowerment*. London: Routledge, 1991.
Coontz, Stephanie. *The Way We Never Were: American Families and the Nostalgia Trap*. New York: Basic, 1992.
Dalsgard, Katrine. "The One All-Black Town Worth the Pain: (African) American Exceptionalism, Historical Narration, and the Critique of Nationhood in Toni Morrison's *Paradise*." *African American Review* 35.2 (Summer 2001): 233–48.
David, Deborah, and Robert Brannon. *The Forty-nine Percent Majority*. Reading, Mass.: Addison-Wesley, 1976.
Davidson, Rob. "Racial Stock and 8-Rocks: Communal Historiography in Toni Morrison's *Paradise*." *Twentieth-Century Literature* 47.3 (Fall 2001): 355–73.
Davis, Angela. *An Autobiography*. New York: Random House, 1974.
Davis, Christina. "Interview with Toni Morrison." *Présence Africaine: Revue Culturelle du Monde Noir*. 1st Quarterly (1988). Rpt. in *Toni Morrison: Critical Perspectives Past and Present*. Ed. Henry Louis Gates Jr. and K. A. Appiah. New York: Amistad, 1983. 412–20.
Derrida, Jacques. *Of Grammatology*. Trans. Gayatri Chakravorty Spivak. Baltimore: Johns Hopkins University Press, 1974.
———. *Writing and Difference*. Trans. Alan Bass. Chicago: University of Chicago Press, 1978.
Dickinson, Emily. "A narrow fellow in the grass." In *Selected Poems and Letters of Emily Dickinson*. Ed. Robert N. Linscott. Garden City, N.Y.: Doubleday Anchor, 1959. 170–71.
Dickinson, Vanessa D. "The Naked Father in Toni Morrison's *The Bluest Eye*." In *Refiguring the Father: New Feminist Readings of Patriarchy*. Ed. Patricia Yaeger and Beth Kowaleski-Wallace. Carbondale: Southern Illinois University Press, 1989. 108–27.
Douglass, Frederick. *Narrative of the Life of Frederick Douglass, an American Slave*. New York: Penguin, 1982.
Dowling, Collette. "The Song of Toni Morrison." *New York Times Magazine* 20 May 1979: 40+. Rpt. in *Conversations with Toni Morrison*. Jackson: University Press of Mississippi, 1994. 481–95.
Dreifus, Claudia. "Chloe Wofford Talks about Toni Morrison." *New York Times Magazine* 11 Sept. 1994, sec. 6: 72–75.
Du Bois, W. E. B. *The Philadelphia Negro*. New York: Schocken, 1899.
Duvall, John N. "Descent in the 'House of Chloe': Race, Rape, and Identity in Toni Morrison's *Tar Baby*." *Contemporary Literature* 38.2 (1997): 325–49.
Eagleton, Terry. *Literary Theory: An Introduction*. Minneapolis: University of Minnesota Press, 1983.
Ellison, Ralph. *Invisible Man*. New York: Vintage, 1947.

———. *Shadow and Act*. New York: Random House, 1964.

Evans, Mari, ed. *Black Women Writers (1950–1980): A Critical Evaluation.* New York: Anchor-Doubleday, 1984.

Faulkner, William. *Absalom, Absalom*! 1936. New York: Vintage, 1972.

Feldman, R. S. *Social Psychology*. 2nd ed. New York: Prentice-Hall, 1998.

Fishman, Charles. "Naming Names: Three Recent Novels by Women Writers." *Names: Journal of the American Name Society* 32 (March 1984): 33–44.

Foucault, Michel. *Madness and Civilization: A History of Insanity in the Age of Reason*. Trans. Richard Howard. New York: Vintage, 1965.

Franklin, Clyde W., II. "Ain't I a Man? The Efficacy of Black Masculinity for Men's Studies in the 1990s." In *The American Black Male: His Present Status and His Future*. Ed. Richard G. Majors and Jacob U. Gordon. Chicago: Nelson-Hall, 1994. 271–83.

———. "Black Male–Black Female Conflict: Individually Caused and Culturally Nurtured." In *Men's Lives*. Ed. Michael S. Kimmel and Michael A. Messner. 5th ed. Boston: Allyn and Bacon, 2001. 359–66.

———. "Men's Studies, the Men's Movement, and the Study of Black Masculinities: Further Demystification of Masculinities in America." In *The American Black Male: His Present Status and His Future*. Ed. Richard G. Majors and Jacob U. Gordon. Chicago: Nelson-Hall, 1994. 3–19.

Frye, Northrop. *Anatomy of Criticism: Four Essays*. Princeton: Princeton University Press, 1957.

Furman, Jan. *Toni Morrison's Fiction*. Columbia: University of South Carolina Press, 1996.

Gallop, Jane. *Reading Lacan*. Ithaca: Cornell University Press, 1985.

Gates, Henry Louis, Jr. *The Signifying Monkey: A Theory of African-American Literary Criticism*. New York: Oxford University Press, 1988.

Gerber, Cheryl. "Broad St. People: A Photo-Essay about Life in the Broad St. Neighborhood of New Orleans." Mark McGrain, 1999–2007. www.plunge.com/broadstreet.htm.

Gibbs, Jewelle Taylor. "Anger in Young Black Males: Victims or Victimizers?" In *The American Black Male: His Present Status and His Future*. Ed. Richard G. Majors and Jacob U. Gordon. Chicago: Nelson-Hall, 1994. 127–43.

Gioia, Ted. *The Imperfect Art: Reflections on Jazz and Modern Culture*. New York: Oxford University Press, 1988.

Giroux, Henry. *Border Crossings: Cultural Workers and the Politics of Education*. New York: Routledge, 1992.

Grewal, Gurleen. *Circles of Sorrow, Lines of Struggle: The Novels of Toni Morrison*. Baton Rouge: Louisiana State University Press, 1998.

Gross, Linda, and Marian E. Barnes, eds. *Talk That Talk: An Anthology of African-American Storytelling*. New York: Touchstone, 1989.

Grossman, Lev. "Love and the Laureate." *Time* 3 Nov. 2003: 75.

Gurian, Michael. *A Fine Young Man*. New York: Tarcher/Putnam, 1998.
Halberstam, Judith. *Female Masculinity*. Durham, N.C.: Duke University Press, 1998.
Hanchard, Michael C. "On 'Good' Black Fathers." In *Men's Lives*. Ed. Michael S. Kimmel and Michael A. Messner. 5th ed. Boston: Allyn and Bacon, 2001. 467–73.
Harper, Phillip Brian. *Are We Not Men? Masculine Anxiety and the Problem of African-American Identity*. New York: Oxford University Press, 1996.
Harris, M. A., ed. *The Black Book*. New York: Random House, 1974.
Harris, Trudier. *Fiction and Folklore: The Novels of Toni Morrison*. Knoxville: University of Tennessee Press, 1991.
Hirsch, Marianne. "Knowing Their Names: Toni Morrison's *Song of Solomon*." In *The American Novel: New Essays on Song of Solomon*. Ed. Valerie Smith. New York: Cambridge University Press, 1995.
Holloway, Karla F. C., and Stephanie Demetrakopoulos. *New Dimensions of Spirituality: A Biracial and Bicultural Reading of the Novels of Toni Morrison*. New York: Greenwood, 1987.
hooks, bell. "Men: Comrades in Struggle." In *Men's Lives*. Ed. Michael S. Kimmel and Michael A. Messner. 5th ed. Boston: Allyn and Bacon, 2001. 527–35.
———. *Sisters of the Yam: Black Women and Self-recovery*. Boston: South End, 1993.
———. *Talking Back*. Boston: South End, 1989.
Hovet, Grace Ann, and Barbara Lounsberry. "Flying as Symbol and Legend in Toni Morrison's *The Bluest Eye*, *Sula*, and *Song of Solomon*." *College Language Association Journal* 27.2 (Dec. 1983): 119–40.
Hunt, Kristin. "The Destructive Forces of Double Consciousness and Boundaries in Toni Morrison's *Paradise*." In *Reading under the Sign of Nature: New Essays in Eco-Criticism*. Ed. John Tallmadge and Henry Harrington. Salt Lake City: University of Utah Press, 2000. 117–27.
Hurston, Zora Neale. "High John De Conquer." In *The Sanctified Church: The Folklore Writings of Zora Neale Hurston*. Berkeley: Turtle Island Foundation, 1981.
———. *Their Eyes Were Watching God*. New York: J. B. Lippincott, 1937.
Italie, Hillel. "Toni Morrison Gets Personal with Parent Support Group." *Hornell (N.Y.) Evening Tribune* 27 Oct. 2003: 9A.
Jaffrey, Zia. "The *Salon* Interview: Toni Morrison." *Salon* Feb. 1998. www.salonmagazine.com/books/int/1998/02/cov_si_02int.html.
Johnson, Michael K. *Black Masculinity and the Frontier Myth in American Literature*. Norman: University of Oklahoma Press, 2002.
Jones, Carolyn M. "Traces and Cracks: Identity and Narrative in Toni Morrison's *Jazz*." *African American Review* 31.3 (1997): 481–96.

Jones, Jill. "The Eye of a Needle: Morrison's *Paradise*, Faulkner's *Absalom, Absalom!*, and the American Jeremiad." *Faulkner Journal* 17.2 (Spring 2002): 3–24.

Jones, Le Roi. *Dutchman*. New York: William Morrow, 1964.

Jung, C. G. *The Portable Jung*. Ed. Joseph Campbell. New York: Viking, 1971.

Kakutani, Michiko. "Family Secrets, Feuding Women." *New York Times* 31 Oct. 2003: 35+.

Katz, William Loren. *Black People Who Made the Old West*. New York: Thomas Y. Crowell, 1977.

Kearly, Peter R. "Toni Morrison's *Paradise* and the Politics of Community." *Journal of American and Comparative Cultures* 23.2 (Summer 2000): 9–16.

Keller, Evelyn Fox, and Christine Grontkowski. "The Mind's Eye." In *Discovering Reality: Feminist Perspectives on Epistemology, Metaphysics, Methodology, and Philosophy of Science*. Ed. Sandra Harding and Merrill B. Hintikka. Boston: D. Reidel, 1983.

Kelley, Robin. "Confessions of a Nice Negro, or Why I Shaved My Head." In *Men's Lives*. Ed. Michael S. Kimmel and Michael A. Messner. 5th ed. Boston: Allyn and Bacon, 2001. 299–305.

Kenan, Randall. "Mr. Brown and the Sweet Science." *Speak My Name: Black Men on Masculinity and the American Dream*. Ed. Don Belton. Boston: Beacon, 1995. 61–72.

Kimmel, Michael S. "Clarence, William, Iron Mike, Tailhook, Senator Packwood, Spur Posse, Magic . . . and Us." In *Men's Lives*. Ed. Michael S. Kimmel and Michael A. Messner. 5th ed. Boston: Allyn and Bacon, 2001. 540–51.

Kimmel, Michael S., and Michael A. Messner, eds. *Men's Lives*. 5th ed. Boston: Allyn and Bacon, 2001.

Kolmerten, Carol A., and Stephen M. Ross, eds. *Unflinching Gaze: Morrison and Faulkner Re-envisioned*. Jackson: University Press of Mississippi, 1997.

Kristeva, Julia. *Desire in Language: A Semiotic Approach to Literature and Art*. Ed. Leon S. Roudiez. New York: Columbia University Press, 1980.

Krumholz, Linda J. "Reading and Insight in Toni Morrison's *Paradise*." *African American Review* 36.1 (Spring 2002): 21–34.

Kubitschek, Missy Dehn. *Toni Morrison: A Critical Companion*. Westport, Conn.: Greenwood, 1998.

Lacan, Jacques. *Écrits: A Selection*. Trans. Alan Sheridan. New York: Norton, 1977.

Leak, Jeffrey B. *Racial Myths and Masculinity in African American Literature*. Knoxville: University of Tennessee Press, 2005.

Le Clair, Thomas. " 'The Language Must Not Sweat': A Conversation with Toni Morrison." *New Republic* 21 March 1981: 22–29. Rpt. in *Toni Morrison: Critical Perspectives Past and Present*. Ed. Henry Louis Gates Jr. and K. A. Appiah. New York: Amistad, 1993. 369–77.

Lepow, Lauren. "Paradise Lost and Found: Dualism and Edenic Myth in Toni Morrison's *Tar Baby.*" *Contemporary Literature* 28.3 (1987): 363–77.

Limerick, Patricia Nelson. "Common Cause? Asian American History and Western American History." In *Privileging Positions: The Sites of Asian American Studies.* Ed. Gary Y. Okihiro et al. Pullman: Washington State University Press, 1995. 83–99.

Majors, Richard G., and Janet Mancini Billson. *Cool Pose: The Dilemmas of Black Manhood in America.* New York: Lexington Books, 1992.

Majors, Richard G., and Jacob U. Gordon, eds. *The American Black Male: His Present Status and His Future.* Chicago: Nelson-Hall, 1994.

Majors, Richard G., et al. "Cool Pose: A Symbolic Mechanism for Masculine Race Enactment and Coping by Black Males." In *The American Black Male: His Present Status and His Future.* Ed. Richard G. Majors and Jacob U. Gordon. Chicago: Nelson-Hall, 1994. 245–59.

Marable, Manning. "The Black Male: Searching Beyond Stereotypes." In *Men's Lives.* Ed. Michael S. Kimmel and Michael A. Messner. 5th ed. Boston: Allyn and Bacon, 2001. 17–23.

Mayberry, Susan Neal. "Something Other Than a Family Quarrel: The Beautiful Boys in Morrison's *Sula.*" *African American Review* 37.4 (Winter 2003): 517–33.

———. "Symbols in the Sewer: A Symbolic Renunciation of Symbols in Richard Wright's *The Man Who Lived Underground.*" *South Atlantic Review* 54 (1989): 71–83.

McAdoo, John Lewis and Julia B. "The African-American Father's Roles within the Family." In *The American Black Male: His Present Status and His Future.* Ed. Richard G. Majors and Jacob U. Gordon. Chicago: Nelson-Hall, 1994. 285–97.

McDowell, Deborah. "Harlem Nocturne." *Women's Review of Books* 9.9 (1992): 1–5.

McKay, Nellie. "An Interview with Toni Morrison." *Contemporary Literature* 24 (Winter 1983): 413–29. Rpt. in *Toni Morrison: Critical Perspectives Past and Present.* Ed. Henry Louis Gates Jr. and K. A. Appiah. New York: Amistad, 1993. 396–411.

———, ed. *Critical Essays on Toni Morrison.* Boston: G. K. Hall, 1988.

Miles, Margaret R. *Image as Insight: Visual Understanding in Western Christianity and Secular Culture.* Boston: Beacon, 1985.

Miller, Laura. "The Last Resort." *New York Times Book Review* 2 Nov. 2003: 10.

Minzesheimer, Bob. "Leafing through the Serious Season." *USA Today* 4 Sept. 2003: 1–2D.

Mobley, Marilyn Sanders. "Call and Response: Voice, Community, and Dialogic Structures in Toni Morrison's *Song of Solomon.*" In *The American Novel: New Essays on Song of Solomon.* Ed. Valerie Smith. New York: Cambridge University Press, 1995.

Morrison, Toni. *Beloved*. New York: Knopf, 1987.
———. *The Bluest Eye*. 1970. New York: Knopf, 1994.
———. *The Dancing Mind*. New York: Knopf, 1997.
———. *Jazz*. New York: Knopf, 1992.
———. *Love*. New York: Knopf, 2003.
———. *The Nobel Lecture in Literature*. New York: Knopf, 1993.
———. *Paradise*. New York: Knopf, 1997.
———. *Playing in the Dark: Whiteness and the Literary Imagination*. New York: Vintage, 1992.
———. "Rootedness: The Ancestor as Foundation." In *Black Women Writers (1950–1980): A Critical Evaluation*. Ed. Mari Evans. New York: Anchor Books, 1984. 339–45.
———. "The Site of Memory." In *Inventing the Truth: The Art and Craft of Memoir*. Ed. William Zinsser. Boston: Houghton Mifflin, 1987.
———. *Song of Solomon*. New York: Knopf, 1977.
———. *Sula*. New York: Knopf, 1973.
———. *Tar Baby*. New York: Knopf, 1981.
———. "Unspeakable Things Unspoken: The Afro-American Presence in American Literature." *Michigan Quarterly Review* 28.1 (1989): 1–34.
———. "What the Black Woman Thinks about Women's Lib." *New York Times Magazine* 22 Aug. 1971: 14+.
———, ed. *Race-ing Justice, En-Gendering Power: Essays on Anita Hill, Clarence Thomas, and the Construction of Social Reality*. New York: Pantheon, 1992.
Morrison, Toni, and Claudia Brodsky Lacour, eds. *Birth of a Nation'hood: Gaze, Script, and Spectacle in the O. J. Simpson Case*. New York: Pantheon, 1997.
Morrison, Toni, and Slade Morrison. *Who's Got Game? The Ant or the Grasshopper?* New York: Scribner, 2003.
Moyers, Bill. "Toni Morrison: A Writer's Work." In *The Moyers Collection: A World of Ideas*. Princeton: Films for the Humanities and Sciences, 1994.
Murline, Anna. "This Side of 'Paradise.'" *U.S. News & World Report* 19 Jan. 1998: 71.
Myers, D. G. *Social Psychology*. 4th ed. New York: McGraw-Hill, 1993.
Naylor, Gloria, and Toni Morrison. "A Conversation." *Southern Review* 21.3 (July 1985): 567–93.
Neal, Mark Anthony. *New Black Man*. New York: Routledge, 2005.
O'Reilly, Andrea. "In Search of My Mother's Garden, I Found My Own: Mother-Love, Healing, and Identity in Toni Morrison's *Jazz*." *African American Review* 30.3 (Fall 1996): 367–79.
———. *Toni Morrison and Motherhood: A Politics of the Heart*. Albany: State University of New York Press, 2004.
Otten, Terry. *The Crime of Innocence in the Fiction of Toni Morrison*. Columbia: University of Missouri Press, 1989.

Page, Philip. *Dangerous Freedom: Fusion and Fragmentation in Toni Morrison's Novels.* Jackson: University Press of Mississippi, 1995.

Paquet-Deyris, Anne-Marie. "Toni Morrison's *Jazz* and the City." *African American Review* 35.2 (Summer 2001): 219–31.

Paster, Vera S. "The Psychosocial Development and Coping of Black Male Adolescents: Clinical Implications." In *The American Black Male: His Present Status and His Future.* Ed. Richard G. Majors and Jacob U. Gordon. Chicago: Nelson-Hall, 1994. 215–29.

Peterson, Nancy J. *Toni Morrison: Critical and Theoretical Approaches.* Baltimore: Johns Hopkins University Press, 1997.

Pipher, Mary. *Reviving Ophelia: Saving the Selves of Adolescent Girls.* New York: Ballantine, 1994.

Pleck, Joseph. *The Myth of Masculinity.* Cambridge: Massachusetts Institute of Technology Press, 1981.

Powell, Timothy B. "Toni Morrison: The Struggle to Depict the Black Figure on the White Page." *Black American Literature Forum* 24 (Winter 1990): 747–60.

Ravage, John. *Black Pioneers: Images of the Experience on the North American Frontier.* Salt Lake City: University of Utah Press, 1998.

Reed, Andrew. "'As if word magic had anything to do with the courage it took to be a man': Black Masculinity in Toni Morrison's *Paradise.*" *African American Review* 39.4 (2005): 527–40.

Rose, Charlie. "Interview with Toni Morrison." 20 Jan. 1998. Charlie Rose Communications, USA Networks.

Rosenberg, Ruth. "And the Children May Know Their Names: Toni Morrison's *Song of Solomon.*" *Literary Onomastics Studies* 8 (1981): 195–217.

Ross, Marlon B. *Manning the Race: Reforming Black Men in the Jim Crow Era.* New York: New York University Press, 2004.

Saint-Aubin, Arthur Flannigan. "Testeria: The Dis-ease of Black Men in White Supremacist, Patriarchal Culture." *Callaloo* 17.4 (1994): 1054–73.

Schappell, Elissa, and Claudia Brodsky Lacour. "Toni Morrison: The Art of Fiction CXXXIV." *Paris Review* 128 (Fall 1993): 85–125. Rpt. in *Women Writers at Work.* Ed. George Plimpton. New York: Random House, 1998. 338–75.

Schreiber, Evelyn Jaffe. *Subversive Voices: Eroticizing the Other in William Faulkner and Toni Morrison.* Knoxville: University of Tennessee Press, 2001.

Scruggs, Charles. *Sweet Home: Invisible Cities in the Afro-American Novel.* Baltimore: Johns Hopkins University Press, 1993.

Shakespeare, William. *Othello: Authoritative Text, Sources and Contexts, Criticism.* Ed. Edward Pechter. New York: Norton, 2004.

Shange, Ntozake. *For Colored Girls Who Have Considered Suicide When the Rainbow Is Enuf.* New York: Bantam Books, 1975.

Sherif, Muzafer, et al. *Intergroup Conflict and Cooperation: The Robbers Cave Experiment.* Norman: University of Oklahoma Press, 1961.

Skerrett, Joseph T. "Recitation to the Griot: Storytelling and Learning in Toni Morrison's *Song of Solomon*." In *Conjuring: Black Women, Fiction, and Literary Tradition*. Ed. Marjorie Pryse and Hortense J. Spillers. Bloomington: Indiana University Press, 1985. 192–202.

Smith, Valerie. " 'Circling the Subject': History and Narrative in *Beloved*." In *Toni Morrison: Critical Perspectives Past and Present*. Ed. Henry Louis Gates Jr. and K. A. Appiah. New York: Amistad, 1993. 342–55.

Smith, Valerie, ed. *New Essays on Song of Solomon*. New York: Cambridge University Press, 1995.

Spillers, Hortense J. "Mama's Baby, Papa's Maybe: An American Grammar Book." *Diacritics* 17.2 (Summer 1987): 65–81.

Staples, Brent. "Stereotypes of Black Male Sexuality: The Facts Behind the Myths." In *Men's Lives*. Ed. Michael S. Kimmel and Michael A. Messner. 5th ed. Boston: Allyn and Bacon, 2001. 410–14.

Staples, Robert. *Black Masculinity: The Black Male's Role in American Society*. San Francisco: Black Scholar Press, 1982.

———. "The Myth of Black Macho: A Response to Angry Black Feminists." *Black Scholar* 10.6–7 (March/April 1979): 24–33.

Stepto, Robert. *From Behind the Veil: A Study of Afro-American Narrative*. Urbana: University of Illinois Press, 1979.

———. " 'Intimate Things in Place': A Conversation with Toni Morrison." In *Chant of Saints: A Gathering of Afro-American Literature, Art, and Scholarship*." Ed. Michael S. Harper and Robert Stepto. Urbana: University of Illinois Press, 1979. 213–29. Rpt. in *Toni Morrison: Critical Perspectives Past and Present*. Ed. Henry Louis Gates Jr. and K. A. Appiah. New York: Amistad, 1993. 378–95.

Tate, Claudia. "Toni Morrison." In *Black Women Writers at Work*. Ed. Claudia Tate. New York: Continuum, 1983. 117–31.

Traylor, Eleanor W. "The Fabulous World of Toni Morrison: *Tar Baby*." In *Critical Essays on Toni Morrison*. Ed. Nellie Y. McKay. Critical Essays on American Literature. Boston: G. K. Hall, 1988. 135–50.

Twain, Mark. *Adventures of Huckleberry Finn*. 1876. Berkeley: University of California Press, 1985.

Walker, Alice. *In Search of Our Mothers' Gardens*. New York: Harcourt Brace Jovanovich, 1967.

Wallace, Maurice O. *Constructing the Black Masculine: Identity and Ideality in African American Men's Literature and Culture, 1775–1995*. Durham, N.C.: Duke University Press, 2002.

Wallace, Michelle. *Black Macho and the Myth of the Superwoman*. New York: Dial Press, 1979.

Walters, Delores M. "Margaret's Desperate Solution." In *Cincinnati Opera: 2005 Summer Festival* (program notes), 23, 86–87.

Watkins, Mel. "Talk with Toni Morrison." *New York Times* 11 Sept. 1977, sec. 7: 48–50.

Webster, John. *The Duchess of Malfi*. Ed. Brian Gibbons. 4th ed. New York: Norton, 2001.

Weisenburger, Steven. *Modern Medea: A Family Story of Slavery and Child-Murder from the Old South*. New York: Hill and Wang, 1998.

White, E. Frances. "Africa on My Mind: Gender, Counterdiscourse, and African American Nationalism." In *Words of Fire: An Anthology of African American Feminist Thought*. Ed. Beverly Guy-Sheftall. New York: New Press, 1995. 504–24.

Widdowson, Peter. "The American Dream Refashioned: History, Politics and Gender in Toni Morrison's *Paradise*." *Journal of American Studies* 35.2 (2001): 313–35.

Wright, Richard. *The Man Who Lived Underground*. In *Eight Men*. Cleveland: World, 1940. 27–92.

Index

www.ingramcontent.com/pod-product-compliance
Lightning Source LLC
LaVergne TN
LVHW050912220826
846195LV00026B/148